DICTIONARY

OF BLACK CULTURE

DICTIONARY
OF BLACK CULTURE

by
WADE BASKIN, Ed.D.
and
RICHARD N. RUNES, J.D.

PHILOSOPHICAL LIBRARY
New York

E
185. 96
.B33

The problem of the twentieth century is the problem of the color line—the relation of the darker to the lighter races of men in Asia and Africa, in America and the islands of the sea.

—W. E. B. Du Bois, *The Souls of Black Folk*

ACKNOWLEDGEMENT

While it is not possible for us to acknowledge our indebtedness to all those who through their encouragement, support, and counsel have helped us to complete this compendium of information about black Americans and their culture, we would like to express our appreciation to Dr. Donald N. Brown. Professor Brown, whose doctoral dissertation covers negro politics in the Bourbon era, has supplied us with many useful publications and bibliographical materials. We would like also to thank Mr. Lucius R. Wyatt, a graduate student at the Eastman School of Music in Rochester, and Mr. Henry E. Sam, Senior Vice President of Progressive Black Associates, for identifying or supplying valuable information. For the shortcomings that persist despite their help, we alone must accept responsibility.

DICTIONARY

OF BLACK CULTURE

A

AARON, HANK

Athlete. After joining the Milwaukee (later Atlanta) Braves in 1954, the quietly efficient superstar led his team to two pennants; won the National League's most valuable player award in 1957 with a .322 batting average and 44 home runs; and in 1971 joined Babe Ruth and Willie Mays in hitting 600 home runs. In 1972 at the age of 38, he hit his 648th homer, then went on to take second place on the all-time list and aim at Babe Ruth's record of 714.

ABBOTT, ROBERT S.

Editor and publisher (1870-1940). He founded the Chicago *Defender* in 1905 and made it the nation's third largest and most influential black newspaper. By 1956, when his nephew, John H. Sengstacke, converted it from a semi-weekly to a daily, it had reached a circulation of more than 200,000. See Roi Ottley, *The Lonely Warrior: The Life and Times of Robert S. Abbott* (1955).

ABDUL, RAOUL

Critic. He has served for years as drama and music critic for the Associated Negro Press.

ABERNATHY, RALPH DAVID

Civil rights leader (b. 1926). Born in Linden, Alabama, he was ordained as a Baptist minister in 1948, earned a degree in mathematics from Alabama State College in 1950, and pastored the First Baptist Church in Montgomery from

11

1951 to 1961. With the Reverend Martin Luther King, Jr., he organized the Montgomery Improvement Association, forerunner of the Southern Christian Leadership Conference (SCLC). With the death of King, Abernathy took over leadership of SCLC, promoted the Poor People's Campaign, presented Congress with demands for jobs and guaranteed incomes for those unable to work, coined the name 'Resurrection City,' and began to transform SCLC into a more militant organization.

ABOLITIONISM

A program reflecting the antislavery tendencies of all Americans, developed mainly 1830-60, and advocating the compulsory freeing of slaves. Its failure to take root in the South was offset somewhat by the common ground shared by civil rights and antislavery sentiment in the North. See Black Abolitionists.

ABOLITIONISTS

The American Revolution spurred the formation of a number of state and local abolitionist societies, beginning with the Pennsylvania Society (1775) and the New York Society (1776), headed by John Jay. The first national convention at Philadelphia (1794) attracted representatives from ten state organizations, all dedicated to a persuasive approach to the abolition of the slave trade and the gradual termination of slavery. In the 1820s religious groups joined in the attack on slavery, and in the 1830s white abolitionists of the stature of William Lloyd Garrison, John Greenleaf Whittier, and Wendell Phillips intensified the crusade. Stringent slave laws in 1850, the underground railroad, and John Brown's raid on Harpers Ferry, together with the antislavery pronouncements of abolitionists espousing direct political action as well as moral suasion, set the stage for the Civil War and the Emancipation Proclamation. Women and young people were also active in the abolitionist movement. Lucretia Mott was the guiding spirit of the Female Anti-Slavery Society of Philadelphia (1833), whose charter was signed by Sarah Douglass, Harriet Purvis, Sarah Forten, and Margaretta Forten. A Boston

12

society had as one of its 5 counselors young Susan Paul. The First Anti-Slavery Convention of American Women (New York, 1833) drew more than 200 delegates from 10 states. Among the delegates were Sarah Douglass and Sarah Forten. The second national convention chose Sarah Douglass as treasurer and Susan Paul as a vice president. The first true negro abolitionist society for young people was formed as early as 1838. In that year four juvenile societies emerged at Carlisle, Pittsburgh, Providence, and Troy. The first of these was the 40-member Pittsburgh Juvenile Anti-Slavery Society, formed July 7, 1838, with David Peck as president and George Vashon as secretary.

ABOLITIONISTS, BLACK
See Black Abolitionists.

ABRAHAM, NEGRO
Diplomat. Born in Florida in the early 1800s, he escaped from slavery and was adopted by the Seminoles. The persuasive and gifted speaker represented Chief Micanopy when the United States tried to relocate the Seminoles in Oklahoma and Kansas.

ADAMS, JOHN
Teacher. In 1824 he became the first black teacher in Washington, D.C.

ADAMS, NUMA P. G.
Physician and educator (1885-1940). Named the first black dean of Howard Medical School in 1929, he stressed excellence throughout his tenure, raised faculty salaries, recruited promising black students and instructors, and encouraged graduate young men working toward the M.D. to acquire a Ph.D. in addition.

ADDISON, ADELE
Musician. A leading soprano, she is an accomplished interpreter of German Lieder.

AFRAM
Shortened form of Afro-American.

AFRICAN BENEVOLENT SOCIETY
Group organized in 1808 to provide a school for black children living in Newport, Rhode Island. The school operated until public education for blacks was provided by the city in 1842.

AFRICAN BLOOD BROTHERHOOD
Headed in the early 1920s by Cyril V. Briggs. the association claimed 150 branches throughout the country and a membership of 50,000. Its purpose was to encourage blacks to hit back when struck and not be branded cowards.

AFRICAN FREE SCHOOL
Opened in 1787 by the Manumission Society in New York City, it began with 40 students. Opposition subsided after 1810, when masters were required to teach all slave children the Scriptures. By 1820 the school enrolled more than 500 negro children. In 1824 New York City began to support the society's African Free Schools, taking them over altogether in 1834. In 1854 all the negro schools in New York City, taught entirely by blacks, were taken over by the newly organized board of education. Their many distinguished graduates included Patrick Reason, Henry Highland Garnet, and Ira Aldridge. The African Free Schools were the precursor of the New York public school system.

AFRICAN METHODIST EPISCOPAL CHURCH
First important black denomination in the United States. It traces its origin to the U.S. constitutional convention of 1787, when Philadelphia churchmen protested segregation. The AME church was founded as a separate denomination by Richard Allen in 1816. Allen had been ordained a deacon and later was consecrated bishop. Membership in the AME church totaled 1,166,301 in 1951. See Daniel A. Payne, *History of the African Methodist Episcopal Church* (1891).

AFRICAN METHODIST EPISCOPAL ZION CHURCH

Beginning as an offshoot of the John Street Methodist Church of New York City in 1787, the AMEZ church by 1970 had reached a membership of 940,000.

AFRICAN ORTHODOX CHURCH

Separatist church established by Marcus Garvey. It had a black God and Christ.

AFRICAN REPUBLIC

Established by participants in a mammoth international convention of blacks meeting in New York in 1920, the African Republic was headed by Provisional President Marcus Garvey.

AFRICAN UNION SOCIETY

Meeting in Newport, Rhode Island, on November 10, 1780, a group of 14 men formed the society to deal with the moral, social, and economic problems of black citizens.

AFRICANISMS

Cultural elements retained by negroes who had been transplanted from Africa to the New World. One factor governing the preservation of cultural elements from the African heritage was the numerical ratio of negroes to whites. See Melville J. Herskovits, *The Myth of the Negro Past* (1941).

AFRO-AMERICAN NATIONAL LEAGUE

Founded January 15-17, 1890, for the purpose of combating all forms of discrimination and promoting the advancement of blacks, it was the forerunner of the NAACP. It was founded in Chicago by T. Thomas Fortune. Its grandiose plans outstripping its resources, the movement died out in 1893.

AFRO-AMERICAN STUDIO FOR ACTING AND SPEECH

Directed by Ernie McClintock, the Harlem-based studio provides training for blacks and helps to shape their course closer to a reflection of the black experience.

AGENTS

Black speakers who toured the United States and England working for the antislavery cause. Well known agents were Frederick Douglass, Henry Highland Garnet, William Wells Brown, Frances E. W. Harper, Theodore S. Wright, Lunsford Lane, Charles Lenox Remond, Sarah Remond, Abraham Shadd, William Craft, Samuel Ringgold Ward, Nathaniel Paul, Alexander Crummell, and James W. C. Pennington.

AILEY, ALVIN

Choreographer. In 1958 he founded the Alvin Ailey American Dance Theater, which has appeared on every continent and in every European country including the Soviet Union (1970). He created *Cry* for Judith Jamison, the choreography for Samuel Barber's *Antony and Cleopatra*, which opened the Metropolitan Opera House; for Leonard Bernstein's *Mass*, which opened the John F. Kennedy Center for the Performing Arts; and for the world premiere of Virgil Thompson's *Lord Byron*. Over the past 8 years he has choreographed 8 works for his own theater. In 1971 he established the American Dance Center. In 1972 he was selected to be the choreographer for the Metropolitan Opera's opening production, *Carmen*.

AKINS, VIRGIL

Athlete. In 1955 he defeated Vince Martinez to win the middleweight boxing championship of the world.

ALBANY MOVEMENT

An unstable alliance formed by local clergymen, the SNCC, the SCLC, and the Albany, Mississippi, chapter of the NAACP. Founded in 1961 as a local protest movement, it set a precedent for citywide confrontations and perfected a new technique of nonviolent protest. Civil rights workers organized workshops on the tactics of nonviolent resistance. These workshops, which became a standard technique for civil rights organizations, had as one major feature a staged enactment of confrontations between law enforcement officials and nonviolent demonstrators. Dr. Wil-

liam Anderson was named president of the alliance and Slater
King, a businessman, vice president.

ALBRITTON, DAVID DONALD

Athlete (b. 1913). An Olympic high jump star, he set a new
world record and was elected to the Helms Foundation Hall of
Fame. He later was appointed a teacher and coach at Dunbar high
school in Dayton. In 1960 he was elected to the Ohio state general
assembly.

ALCINDOR, LEW

Athlete (b. 1947). Probably the most publicized high school
basketball player of all time, the 7-foot, 1-inch superstar scored
2,067 points during his four years at Power Memorial High School
in New York City, then moved to the University of California at
Los Angeles and led his team to repeated victories. He joined the
Milwaukee Bucks in 1969 and was a sensation as a professional.
In 1971 he averaged 31.7 points per game, won the most valuable
player award, and led his team to the National Basketball Association championship. After his conversion from Catholicism to
Islam while a student at UCLA, he changed his name to Kareem
Abdul Jabbar.

ALDRIDGE, AMANDA

Voice teacher (1866-1956). The daughter of Ira F. Aldridge,
she taught some of the best singers of the 20th century. Among
those who traveled to England to study with her were Marian
Anderson, Roland Hayes, and Paul Robeson.

ALDRIDGE, IRA F.

Actor (1807-1867). He studied at the African Free School in
New York City but had to go to England to achieve fame. He was
acclaimed throughout Europe for more than 30 years and honored
by kings and czars. His brilliant portrayals of Othello brought
invitations for command performances in Austria, Prussia, Russia,
and Sweden. He died in Poland while arrangements were being

17

made for him to tour his native land, where he had never been seen on stage. His children, Luranah, Ira, and Amanda, achieved recognition as singers and actors. See Mary Malone, *Actor in Exile, The Life of Ira Aldrige.*

ALEXANDER, ARCHIE A.
Engineer and public official (1888-1958). A successful businessman with his own civil engineering firm for more than forty years, he became governor of the Virgin Islands in 1954. Competing with white companies in the building of bridges, sewer systems, and power plants, he extended his business beyond the blacks ghettoes and into several states.

ALEXANDER, RAYMOND PACE
Jurist (b. 1898). In 1959 he became judge of the Philadelphia Court of Common Pleas. He was co-founder and editor of the *National Bar Journal.*

ALEXANDER, SADIE TANNER MOSSELL
Lawyer and economist (b. 1898). She was the first negro woman admitted to the bar in Pennsylvania. She holds a Ph. D. in economics.

ALI, MUHAMMAD
See Muhammad Ali.

ALI, NOBLE DREW
See Drew, Timothy.

ALL GOD'S CHILLUN GOT WINGS
Play by Eugene O'Neill, inspired by the Harlem Renaissance of the 1920s. In 1924 Paul Robeson had the lead role and made history by becoming the first black man to play opposite a white woman on the American stage.

ALLEN, HENRY
Musician (1907-1967). In the late 1920s he played the trumpet

with Louis Russell's band and made some classic blues recordings. He played with the Louis Armstrong band from 1937 until he formed his own group in 1940.

ALLEN, MACON B.

Lawyer. He holds the distinction of being the first negro formally admitted to the bar (in 1845).

ALLEN, RICHARDS

Clergyman (1760-1831). The founder of the African Methodist Episcopal church (AME) was born a slave in Philadelphia. He was a leader of the Free African Society (1787), founder of the Bethel African Methodist Episcopal Church (1794), and president of the first national convention of negro delegates (1830). With Absalom Jones, he walked out of St. George's Methodist Episcopal Church in Philadelphia one Sunday morning in 1787, angered because they had been asked to interrupt their prayers and move to the rear of the gallery. With the help of influential whites, they raised money for a new church for negroes. Allen was made a bishop of the AME branch of Methodism in 1816. See Charles H. Wesley, *Richard Allen, Apostle of Freedom* (1935, rev. 1969).

ALLEN, RICHIE

Athlete. In 1964 he was named rookie of the year. Since that time he has become one of the National League's superstars, displaying his ability at the bat in game after game with the Philadelphia Phillies.

ALLEN, WILLIAM G.

Abolitionist and teacher. Persecuted because he had decided to marry one of his white college students at Central College in McGrawville, New York, he fled to England with her. His autobiography is titled *The American Prejudice Against Color: An Authentic Narrative, Showing How Easily the Nation Got into an Uproar, by William G. Allen, a Refugee from American Despotism* (1853).

ALSTON, CHARLES

Artist (b. 1907). Internationally recognized for his achievements as a painter and muralist, he executed a mural under a WPA grant from the Harlem Hospital presenting the history of medicine.

AMBASSADORS

See Diplomatic Corps.

AME CHURCH

See African Methodist Episcopal Church.

AMERICAN AND FOREIGN ANTI-SLAVERY SOCIETY

Led by white abolitionist Lewis Tappan, the society maintained a firm antislavery policy after it separated from the American Anti-Slavery Society in 1840.

AMERICAN ANTI-SLAVERY SOCIETY

Organized in Philadelphia by negro and white abolitionists on December 4, 1833, the society eventually had chapters in other major cities. The spirit of abolitionism found expression in the twin objectives of the society: 'the entire abolition of slavery in the United States' and the moral elevation of 'the people of color.' The organizational meeting was attended by three blacks: James G. Barbadoes, Robert Purvis, and James McCrummell. Six blacks were named to the 12-man board of managers created by the convention: the three delegates plus John B. Vashon, Peter Williams, and Abraham D. Shadd. Blacks also took part in the organization of affiliates of the national society in Massachusetts, New York, and Pennsylvania. See Massachusetts Anti-Slavery Society, New York Anti-Slavery Society, and Pennsylvania Anti-Slavery Society.

AMERICAN CIVIL LIBERTIES UNION

An outgrowth of the Civil Liberties Bureau, established in 1917 as an adjunct to the American Union against Militarism founded in 1915. To some extent it has promoted civil rights causes: its

1961 program stressed equality before the law, due process, and free speech; and its 1969 survey showed that law enforcement agencies were waging a campaign against the Black Panthers, 'resulting in serious civil liberties violations.' See Lucille Milner, *Education of an American Liberal* (1954).

AMERICAN COLLEGE OF SURGEONS

In 1945, the ACS had only one black member, Dr. Louis T. Wright, who had been elected in 1934. Dr. George D. Thorne was refused an application in 1945, and his case became a matter of public concern. Mounting pressures forced the admission of Dr. F. D. Stubbs. Soon 4 other black surgeons were admitted, and by 1960 black members numbered more than 100.

AMERICAN COLONIZATION SOCIETY

Formed in 1816 by prominent men with the presumed aim of advancing the antislavery cause, the ACS persuaded Congress to appropriate $100,000 to establish Liberia as a bastion of freedom for ex-slaves. Because the stress was on sending free blacks out of the country rather than freeing blacks in the country, most blacks withheld their support. Liberia came into existence in 1822, and other societies, churches, and state legislatures supported the enterprise. Between 1817 and 1860, however, not more than 12,000 blacks chose to return to Africa. The experiment failed because of opposition from blacks and the rise of a vigorous abolitionist movement that caused the ACS to decline in significance in the early 1830s.

AMERICAN DILEMMA, THE

Classic sociological and political study documenting the nature and extent of racial inequality in the United States, published by Swedish scholar Gunnar Myrdal in 1944. Myrdal recently announced his intention of writing a new book, The American Dilemma Revisited.

AMERICAN MAJORITIES AND MINORITIES

Syllabus for teaching U.S. history in secondary schools, published by the NAACP in 1970. Written by Warren Halliburton and William Loren Katz, the 220-page volume places in perspective 'the many and varied contributions of racial and ethnic minorities.'

AMERICAN MISSIONARY ASSOCIATION

Formed in 1846 by several antislavery groups (Committee for the West Indian Missions, Western Evangelical Missionary Society, and the group formed to help the defendants in the Amistad case, among others), the AMA sent out missionaries to promote antislavery evangelical efforts. After the Civil War ended, the AMA founded Berea College, Fisk University, and Hampton Institute.

AMERICAN NEGRO ACADEMY

An association formed in 1897 by black scholars to refute the notion of black intellectual inferiority. Each year its members published studies on various aspects of Negro life. Several important papers on sociology, history, and education were contributed by W. E. B. Du Bois, Theophylus G. Steward, Alexander Crummell, and other distinguished scholars between 1897 and 1924. These papers have been republished in one volume by Arno Press.

AMERICAN NEGRO LABOR CONGRESS

Organized by the Communist Party in 1925 to win Negro converts, the ANLC tried various tactics—unionization of workers, social equality, creation of a forty-ninth state for Negroes—but failed to add many names to its list. The legal arm of the ANLC was called the International Labor Defense. See Scottsboro Case.

AMERICAN REVOLUTION

Fearing that recruitment of Negroes might lead to mass emancipation, General George Washington directed recruiting officers in 1775 not to enlist 'any stroller, Negro, or vagabond.' Within two months after the British announced their willingness to have negroes join their forces, Washington agreed to enlist free negroes. In the North, negro participation helped to liberalize the institution of slavery. The northern colonies provided most of the 5,000 Negro soldiers who took part in the Revolution. Black soldiers from every one of the original thirteen colonies fought in the Revolutionary army. Among the black participants in the major battles of the war were Crispus Attucks, Peter Salem, Cato Howe, Titus Coburn, Seymour Burr, Prince Hall, Pomp Fiske, and Alexander Ames. See *Black Heroes of the American Revolution 1775- 1783* (1965, NAACP).

AMERICAN SLAVERY AS IT IS

Title of white abolitionist Theodore Dwight Weld's carefully documented collection of evidence focusing attention on the brutality of slavery. Published in 1839, it is perhaps the greatest anti-slavery pamphlet ever written. Compiled from scores of southern newspapers with the help of the Grimke sisters, it was the most widely read of the many pamphlets published by Weld.

AMERICAN SOCIETY OF AFRICAN CULTURE

Group founded in 1957 by intellectuals and artists, including Duke Ellington and Langston Huges. President John A. Davis stated that the aim of the society was to present 'black African sculpture, dance, music, art and literature—the high culture of the African Negro as it has existed in Africa, in the United States and in Latin America.'

AMERICAN VETERAN COMMITTEE

Organized in 1945 to act as a lobby for veterans' interests, AVC refused to charter segregated local units. It gave its Americanism award to the nine black students who integrated Little Rock Central High School in 1957.

AMERSON, LUCIUS D.

Public official. Following passage of the Voting Rights Act of 1965, he became the first black sheriff of Macon County, Alabama, since Reconstruction.

AMEZ (AME ZION)

See African Methodist Episcopal Zion Church.

AMISTAD

Slave ship captured in 1839 by 53 Africans on board. In trying to return to Africa the slaves sailed to Long Island, where they were interned. Their defense before the U.S. supreme court, conducted voluntarily by ex-President John Quincy Adams, is a landmark in the legal history of the anti-slavery movement. They won their freedom in a historic decision delivered in 1841. See Mary Cable, *Black Odyssey; the Case of the Slave Ship Amistad* (1971).

AMISTAD SOCIETY

A committee on the history and culture of Americans of African descent, headed by Sterling Stuckey.

ANDERSON, AARON

Civil War hero. A landsman aboard the *Wyandank,* he won the navy's Medal of Honor for 'carrying out his duties courageously in the face of devastating fire' on March 17, 1865.

ANDERSON, CAROLINE VIRGINIA

Physician (b. 1848). The daughter of abolitionist William Still, she studied at Oberlin, Howard, and the Philadelphia Women's Medical College, where she received her medical degree (1878). A pioneer in her profession, she practiced in Philadelphia, where she also participated in many civic and educational activities.

ANDERSON, CHARLES W.

Public official (b. 1907). He was elected to the Kentucky legislature in 1935, the first black representative since Reconstruction. President Dwight D. Eisenhower later appointed him a delegate to the United Nations.

ANDERSON, EDDIE

Entertainer (b. 1905). Known to millions throughout the world as Rochester, he was a featured entertainer long before he teamed with Jack Benny. He made his debut as a singer in the chorus of *Struttin' Along*, joined a trio, the Three Black Aces, toured theatrical circuits in variety and vaudeville shows, was a featured performer at the Los Angeles Cotton Club, and was featured in *Broadway Rhythm* and *Cabin in the Sky*.

ANDERSON, ELIJAH

Underground railroad conductor (d. 1757). Known as the general superintendent of the railroad in northwestern Ohio, he worked from 1750 until his death, transporting more than 1,000 slaves to freedom. He died in a Kentucky state prison.

ANDERSON, GERTRUDE E. FISHER

Business executive (b. 1894). Left with three children to support after her husband's death, she began making and selling candy. She originated and now owns and manages Nanette Home-Made Candies in Birmingham, Alabama.

ANDERSON, JO

Inventor. A slave, he helped Cyrus McCormick to perfect the reaping machine, patented in 1834.

ANDERSON, JOSEPH G.

Musician (d. 1874). He conducted the Frank Johnson band, 1846-74.

ANDERSON, MARIAN

Singer (b. 1902). Her great contralto voice and calm dignity opened the doors of concert halls previously closed to blacks. With the help of Rosenwald fellowships she toured Europe to build a reputation (1933-35). Toscanini's praise brought her world fame but did not prevent the Daughters of the American Revolution from denying her the use of Constitution Hall in Washington, D.C. She sang instead at the Lincoln Memorial on

Easter Sunday, 1939. Her memorable performance was attended by a crowd of 75,000. In 1955, she became the first black singer to appear at the Metropolitan Opera in New York City, in the role of Ulrica in *The Masked Ball*. She also served as a delegate to the United Nations. Her autobiography is titled *My Lord, What a Morning* (1956).

ANDERSON, OSBORNE P.

Militant. He participated in the attack on Harpers Ferry on October 16, 1859. Later he served with distinction in the Civil War.

ANDERSON, WEBSTER

Hero. Sgt. Anderson lost both legs while protecting his artillery battery in Vietnam on October 15, 1967. He propped himself up, picked up a grenade that had landed next to a wounded crewman, lost his hand as a result of its explosion, and continued to fire his gun with the other hand and to encourage his men. He received the congressional Medal of Honor for his heroism.

ANDERSON, WILLIAM C.

Civil rights leader. A doctor practicing in Albany, Mississippi, he was named president of the Albany Movement when it was formed in 1961.

ANDREWS, LUDIE

Nurse. A member of the National Association of Colored Graduate Nurses, she instituted legal proceedings forcing the Georgia state board of nurses examiners to eliminate certain discriminatory practices.

ANDREWS, WILLIAM

Hospital administrator. With a master's degree in hospital administration, he directs the activities of Cleveland Metropolitan General Hospital's 42 departments and 1900 employees. He is the first black to have held such a position.

ANGELOU, MAYA

Actress and dancer. In 1961 she played in Jean Genet's *The Blacks*. Once a coordinator for the SCLC, she excels as a writer, scenarist, and film director. Her autobiographical *I Know Why the Caged Bird Sings* (1969) evoked images of a black girl's childhood in the South and was nominated for a National Book Award. In 1971 she became Hollywood's first female director when she contracted to direct the filming of her book. She also wrote the script and the music for *Georgia, Georgia*.

ANDREWS, BENNY

Artist (b. 1930). He has had many exhibitions and was the recipient of a John Hay Whitney fellowship. He illustrated the book *I Am the Darker Brother* (1968).

ANGLO-AFRICAN MAGAZINE, THE

Negro magazine which began publication in New York in 1959. The first volume, containing the 'Confessions of Nat Turner,' stories of slavery resistance, and a report of John Brown's death, has been reprinted by Arno Press.

ANTOINE, C. C.

Public official. Following in the footsteps of his father, who had fought under Andrew Jackson at New Orleans in 1814, he served as captain of a black company in a Louisiana Union regiment. He later served in the Louisiana state senate and as lieutenant governor.

APOLLO

Called the Mecca of black show business, Harlem's most famous theater has fostered the careers of a host of artists, such as Duke Ellington, Count Basie, Lionel Hampton, Dusty Fletcher, 'Pigmeat' Markham, Jackie (Moms) Mabley, Ella Fitzgerald, Sarah Vaughan, Nancy Wilson, Leslie Uggams, Nat King Cole, and Dinah Washington.

APPEAL TO THE COLORED PEOPLE OF THE WORLD

Radical antislavery pamphlet published in Boston by David Walker on September 28, 1829.

ARMED FORCES (DESEGREGATION)

The experience of blacks during World War I pointed up the fact that even those who were fighting for democracy in the world at large were doing so under segregated conditions. At the beginning of World War II segregation and discrimination still persisted. It was not until President Truman issued Executive Order 9981 that black servicemen received 'equality of treatment.' See Richard M. Dalfiume, *Desegregation of the U.S. Armed Forces; Fighting on Two Fronts, 1939-1953* (1969).

ARMISTEAD, JAMES

Double agent during the American Revolution. His daring role—he supplied misinformation to the enemy and vital factual intelligence to his superiors—enabled General Lafayette to trap General Cornwallis. Returning to New Kent County, Virginia, after the war, he took the name of James Lafayette. In 1824 he had the honor of meeting the famous Frenchman whose name he had selected.

ARMSTRONG, HENRY

Athlete (b. 1912) In 1937-38, over a 10-month period, he held the featherweight, welterweight, and lightweight boxing championships. He was elected to boxing's Hall of Fame in 1954.

ARMSTRONG, LOUIS 'SATCHMO'

King of jazz (1900-1971). The world's greatest trumpet player was born on Independence Day in New Orleans, the cradle of jazz. He played Storyville honkytonks, on Mississippi steamboats, and in the Tuxedo Brass Band before joining King Oliver's band in Chicago (1922), playing a year with a New York orchestra, and forming his own band (1924) and cutting a historic series of records in which he anticipated most of the innovations in modern jazz. He invented scat singing, toured many countries, and played in many movies. His recordings include 'Blueberry Hill' and 'Hello, Dolly.' He also acted as the State Department's goodwill ambassador. 'Jazz is spiritual music,' he said during one interview, 'it's suffering that gives jazz its spiritual dimension.' His trumpet style had a lasting influence on other jazz performers. His early experiences are recorded in *Satchmo: My Life in New Orleans* (1955). See also Albert J. McCarthy, *Louis Armstrong* (1961).

ART

Black artists appeared in America at the handicraft stage, embellishing the façades of public buildings and the interiors and exteriors of their masters' homes. In painting and sculpture, several names stand out: Scipio Moorehead, Joshua Johnson, Robert S. Duncanson, Edward M. Bannister, Henry O. Tanner and, later, men of the stature of William A. Harper, Archibald Motley, and Edward Harleston. Other black artists have won wide acceptance in the 20th century: Charles Alston, Hale Woodruff, Norman Lewis, and Jacob Lawrence, to cite only a few. See James A. Porter, *Modern Negro Art* (1943), and J. Edward Atkinson, *Black Dimensions in Contemporary American Art* (1971).

ARTERBERY, JOHN WESLEY

Artist. Born in Texas and educated in Oklahoma, he now teaches at Fisk University. He has exhibited his work widely in the United States.

ARTICLES OF CONFEDERATION

Ratified in March 1781, the Articles of Confederation represented a victory for the slave states inasmuch as Congress was empowered to fix quotas for the armed forces in proportion to the number of white inhabitants of each state. The articles provided, however, that a free inhabitant of one state could enjoy the same privileges as a free inhabitant in a sister state.

ASBURY, JOHN CORNELIUS

Businessman and civic leader (1862-1932). With a master's degree from Howard, he returned to Pennsylvania, established a law office in Philadelphia, and entered politics. He organized the Keystone Aid Society (1902), became editor-in-chief of *The Odd Fellows' Journal,* helped to organize the Mercy Hospital for Negroes, and founded the Farm and Vocational School for Boys at Pomeroy, Pennsylvania.

ASHE, ARTHUR, JR.

Athlete (b. 1943). He was the first black man named to the American Davis Cup Squad (1964). In 1968 and 1969 he led the U. S. team to Davis Cup international tennis championships. In 1968 he won both the U. S. amateur championship and the first U. S. Open. His experiences are recorded in *Advantage Ashe* (1967).

ASHFORD, EMMETT

Baseball umpire. In 1966 he made his debut in major league baseball, umpiring a game between the Cleveland Indians and the Washington Senators.

ASHMUM INSTITUTE

See Lincoln University.

ASNLH

See Association for the Study of Negro Life and History.

ASSOCIATION FOR THE STUDY
OF NEGRO LIFE AND HISTORY

It was founded in 1915 by Dr. Carter G. Woodson.

ATHENS, ALABAMA

Scene of a race riot touched off in 1946 by a fistfight between two white veterans and a black man.

ATLANTA

Scene of race rioting in 1906. Ten negroes were killed in Atlanta, Georgia, September 22-24, and martial law was proclaimed.

ATLANTA COMPROMISE

Doctrine set forth by Booker T. Washington in a speech delivered at the Cotton States Exposition in Atlanta in September 1895. Believing that whites really wanted blacks to improve their lot, Washington reiterated his doctrine that negroes should stop agitating for political and social rights and be provided with economic opportunities commensurate with their abilities so that they could earn these rights. His views were welcomed by whites and given national attention. Though black intellectuals opposed him, he had the support of many influential newspapers and magazines which he secretly controlled. The Tuskegee Institute News Bureau supplied supporting press releases. Washington's views prevailed for a generation.

ATLANTA MOVEMENT

A citywide attempt to abolish discrimination in all Atlanta public facilities was initiated in 1962. The movement was supported by SCLC, NAACP, and CORE.

ATLANTA UNIVERSITY PUBLICATIONS

In 1896 Atlanta University initiated a series of annual conferences on urban Negro problems. Out of these conferences, directed by W. E. B. Du Bois, grew a series of eighteen monographs containing evaluations of self-help efforts, schooling, craftsmanship, and economic cooperation among the Negroes, and several important bibliographies. Publications issued between 1898 and 1916 have been reissued in one volume by Arno Press.

ATTAWAY, WILLIAM

Writer (b. 1912). His novels include *Let Me Breathe Thunder* (1939) and *Blood on the Forge* (1941).

ATTUCKS, CRISPUS

Patriot (1723-1770). The first martyr of the American Revolution, he was killed in the Boston Massacre on March 5, 1770. Today he is honored by a statue in Boston Common. Born a slave, he escaped from his master, William Brown of Framingham, Massachusetts, in 1750. He disappeared without trace for 20 years. On March 5, 1770, he urged a crowd gathered on the Boston Square Dock to protest the clubbing of a barber's apprentice to attack the British soldiers responsible for the incident. He led the attack on the small British contingent and died a hero's death, along with three white colonists.

AUDUBON, JOHN JAMES

Artist and ornothologist (1785-1851). Of uncertain origin, he probably was born in Aux Cayes, Haiti. He taught drawing in New Orleans but changed occupations frequently. In 1826 he published his famous *Birds of America*. The National Association of Audubon Societies publishes *Audubon Magazine*.

AUGUSTA, ALEXANDER T.

Physician (b. 1825). A free-born Virginian, he served his medical apprenticeship in Philadelphia, graduated from Trinity Medical College in Toronto, Canada (1856), joined the Union forces (1863) with the rank of major, and became the first black to head any hospital in the United States (the Freedmen's Hospital in Washington).

AVERY COLLEGE

School for blacks established in Allegheny City in 1849. White philanthropist Charles Avery provided $300,000 for the Pennsylvania school.

AZIMPI

See Dorman, Isaiah.

B

BAILEY, CALVIN

Artist. He first gained recognition during the World's Fair in New York (1939-40), when his work was compared with that of Daumier in its social awareness. A staff caricaturist for NBC-TV in Hollywood, he has created and starred in his own award-winning show, 'Musical Sketch Book.'

BAILEY, PEARL

Musician (b. 1918). She starred in *St. Louis Woman, House of Flowers* (1954), and the black version of *Hello, Dolly!* In 1968 the singer-comedienne was elected Entertainer for the Year by *Cue* magazine.

BAKER, GEORGE

See Divine, Father.

BAKER, JOSEPHINE

Musician (b. 1906). A famous international star, she has sung in several languages and in all the great cities. Her appearance in the *Revue Nègre* in Paris (1926) was a climactic moment in the history of entertainment. During World War II she entertained troops in North Africa, served on the Belgian front as an ambulance driver, and earned the Legion of Honor medal for service with the Free French Resistance. With her French husband she bought an estate in Perigord where children of different racial origins are members of the same family.

BALBOA'S EXPLORATION
When Balboa made his journey to the Pacific, he took with him 30 negroes.

BALDWIN, JAMES
Writer (b. 1924). Born in Harlem of Southern migrant parents, he became a Pentecostal preacher in his early teens. As his interest in literature grew, he moved to Greenwich Village (1943), received encouragement from Richard Wright, and took up residence in prejudice-free Paris (1948), where he remained for ten years, completing his partly autobiographical novel *Go Tell It on the Mountain* (1953), *Notes of a Native Son* (1955), and *Giovanni's Room* (1956). He returned to America to become an interpreter of the race problem: *Nobody Knows My Name* (1961), *The Fire Next Time* (1964), and *A Rap on Ice* (1971). He has also written plays and short stories.

BALDWIN, MARIA LOUISE
Poet, educator, and lecturer (b. 1856).

BANJO
The only true American instrument, the banjo was invented before Emancipation. James Bland created a more versatile instrument by adding to it a fifth string.

BANKS, ERNIE
Athlete (b. 1931). He became the hardest-hitting shortstop in major league history and the first National Leaguer to be named most valuable player two years in succession (1958 and 1959).

BANNEKER, BENJAMIN
Scientist (1731-1806). Born free on a farm near Baltimore, he attended an integrated Quaker school and became a mathematician, astronomer, clock-maker, and surveyor. In his almanac for 1793 he outlined a remarkable peace plan proposing free schools, a Secretary of Peace, and a ban on military dress, titles, and capital punishment. He became the first black Presidential

appointee when, in 1791, Washington asked him to help with the survey of Washington. When the French surveyor Pierre-Charles L'Enfant quit following a dispute, Banneker helped to reproduce L'Enfant's plan from memory. Liberals throughout the world hailed him as living proof of what blacks could accomplish when freed from discrimination and oppression. A good account of his activities was printed in the *Journal of Negro History* in 1918: Henry E. Baker, 'Benjamin Banneker, the Negro Mathematician and Astronomer.' See also Silvio A. Bedini, *The Life of Benjamin Banneker* (1972).

BANNER, WILLIAM A.

Philosopher. Educated at Pennsylvania State, Yale, and Harvard, he has taught at Smith College, the University of Colorado, the University of Rhode Island, and Howard University. During a year as visiting professor at Yale, he wrote *Ethics: An Introduction to Moral Philosophy* (1968), in which he tried to relate social and metaphysical issues.

BANNISTER, EDWARD M.

Painter (1828-1901). The most renowned black artist of the nineteenth century, he specialized in landscapes. He won a first prize in the Philadelphia Centennial Exhibition (1876) and was a founder of the Providence Art Club (1880). Born in Canada, he moved to Boston at the age of 18, then to Providence (1871). Besides his prize-winning 'Under the Oaks,' he is acclaimed for 'Sabin Point, Narragansett Bay' (Brown University collection) and 'After the Storm' (Museum of the Rhode Island School of Design).

BAPTISM

At first a freedom-bestowing act, baptism was later administered to slaves without altering their status. The first slaves to arrive in the English colonies (1619) had received baptismal rites. They were treated not as slaves but as indentured servants. In 1667 the Virginia legislature declared that baptism did not 'alter the condition of the person as to his bondage or freedome.'

35

BAQUET, GEORGE
Musician. He played the clarinet with the New Orleans Original Creole Band in the early 1900s.

BARAKA, IMAMU AMIRI
See Jones, LeRoi.

BARBOSA, JOSE CELSO
Puerto Rican leader (1857-1921). He founded a political party advocating statehood and served on Puerto Rico's executive council five times.

BARES, BASILE
Musician (b. 1846). After studying in France, he returned to New Orleans and published a number of his dance compositions.

BARKSDALE, DON
Athlete. The All-American forward (UCLA, 1947) and Olympic team member (1948) was named to the Helms Amateur Basketball Hall of Fame.

BARNES, PIKE
Jockey. In 1888 he won the first running of the Futurity at Sheepshead and earned $50,000. He went on to win the Champagne Stakes (1889) and the Belmont and Alabama Stakes (1890).

BARNES, WILLIAM H.
Otolaryngologist (1887-1945). Famous for his bloodless operative techniques, he devised surgical instruments that are now used in otolaryngology. Born in Philadelphia, he received his M.D. from the University of Pennsylvania (1912), studied in France, became chief otolaryngologist at Frederick Douglass Hospital, and was elected a diplomat of the American Board of Otolaryngology (1927).

BARNETTE, CLAUDE A.

Journalist (b. 1889). He is the founder and director of the Associated Negro Press. Like his wife, Etta Moten Barnett, he is an authority on African art. He headed a delegation that met with war department officials the day after Pearl Harbor to urge the creation of a volunteer division open to blacks and whites alike. His proposal was finally rejected, late in 1943.

BARNETT, ETTA MOTEN

A concert singer and an authority on African art, she is the wife of Claude A. Barnett.

BARNETT, FERDINAND L.

Journalist. A Chicago attorney, he founded the *Conservator* (1878), the first black newspaper in Illinois. The Alabama-born crusader married Ida B. Wells in 1895. The Barnetts were leading opponents of the Atlanta Compromise policies of Booker T. Washington. He was the first black assistant state's attorney in Illinois.

BARNETT, IDA BAKER WELLS

See Wells, Ida B.

BARTHE, RICHMOND

Sculptor (b. 1901). America's preeminent black sculptor, he is noted for his sensitive small bronzes and monumental statues. Born in Bay St. Louis, Mississippi, he grew up in New Orleans, studied at the Chicago Art Institute (1924-28), and settled in Jamaica. Among his finest pieces are 'Shoe Shine Boy' (small bronze, Oberlin College Museum of Art), 'The Boxer' (small bronze, Metropolitan Museum of Art), a large frieze inspired by 'The Green Pastures' on a Harlem housing project, and statues of Toussaint L'Overture and Jacques Dessalines in Haiti.

BASEBALL

Although baseball is America's oldest team sport, black players were denied meaningful participation until recently. An amateur association ban on interracial teams (1867) established a practice interrupted only briefly prior to October 23, 1945, when Jackie Robinson signed with the Brooklyn Dodgers, and four other players signed contracts in time for competition in 1946 (Roy Campanella, Don Newcombe, Roy Partlow, and John Wright). In 1884 Moses Fleetwood Walker and his brother Welday played with Toledo in the old American Association, but most blacks played in obscurity on all-negro teams until Jackie Robinson broke the racial barrier. See the names of individual players, such as Frank Thompson, Andrew Foster, Dan Bankhead, Elston Howard, Richie Allen, John O'Neil, and Willie Mays.

BASIE, COUNT

Musician (b. 1904). He has gained an international reputation as a band leader and pianist by making excellent recordings and remaining loyal to blues as a basis form for over 30 years. In 1939 he won the Most Popular Band award. In 1957 his band became the first American band ever to play at a command performance before the Queen of England. See Raymond Horricks, *Count Basie and His Orchestra: Its Music and Its Musicians* (1957).

BASKETBALL

Blacks were playing basketball as early as 1904 and had teams of their own as early as 1910, when Robert J. Douglas formed the Spartan team in New York, later renamed the New York Renaissance Big Five or just The Rens. Soon other teams sprang up, and unofficial games with white teams were common. Outstanding college players found their way barred to most professional teams until the early 1950s, when Ed Cooper, Nat Clifton, and Don Barksdale joined the professional ranks. See the names of individual players: Lew Alcindor, Walt Bellamy, Wilt Chamberlain, Bill Russell, Elgin Baylor, Elvin Hayes, Maurice Stokes, etc.

BASS, CHARLOTTA

Political figure. In 1952 she was the Progressive Party candidate for the vice presidency.

BASSETT, EBENEZER DON CARLOS

Diplomat (1833-1908). The first of his race to be appointed to the diplomatic corps, he served as minister-resident to Haiti, 1868-77. After completing his assignment, he served for ten years as a general consul from Haiti to the United States.

BATES, DAISY

Civil rights leader (b. 1922). As president of the local chapter of the NAACP, she had a leading role in the integration of the Little Rock, Arkansas, Central High School (September 25, 1957). See Little Rock Central High School.

BATSON, FLORA

Musician (1870-1906). She had a remarkable soprano voice of great range and traveled throughout the world as a ballad singer.

BATTLE OF BUNKER HILL

See Bunker Hill, Battle of.

BAYLOR, ELGIN

Athlete. The Los Angeles Lakers superstar recovered from two injuries that threatened to end his basketball career (1965 and 1966) and went on to become their top scorer and best rebounder.

BEASLEY, MOTHER MATILDA

Nun (1834-1903). She gave her inheritance to the Sacred Heart Church for the founding of an orphanage for black children (the St. Francis Home for Colored Orphans) and spent her life ministering to the poor of Savannah, Georgia.

BEAUMONT RIOT

In June 1943 a riot was incited by a white woman in Beaumont, Texas, who claimed that she had been raped by a black man. Before Texas Rangers restored order, 75 blacks had been killed or injured.

BEAVERS, LOUISE

She achieved fame as a screen actress but was criticized by many negroes for playing the stereotyped role of a colored maid.

BECHET, SIDNEY

Musician (1897-1959). One European critic described the clarinetist and soprano saxophonist as an "artist of genius" as early as 1919. Probably the greatest reed man after Louis Armstrong, he recorded his experiences in a perceptive book published after his death, *Treat It Gentle* (1960).

BECKWOURTH, JAMES P.

Western pioneer (1798-1867). In the early 1850s, he discovered the Pacific Coast named in his honor. Born in Fredericksburg, Virginia, he moved with his mulatto mother and white father to St. Louis. Beckwourth (also spelled Beckwith) traveled throughout the West with fur trappers (1823-26) before settling down and living with the Crow Indians (1826-37), who took him for a long-lost member and made him a chief. Afterwards he worked as a guide, trapper, fur-company agent, Army scout, and hunter. Beckwourth Pass on the Pacific Coast is named after him. See T. D. Bonner, *The Life and Adventures of James P. Beckworth, Mountaineer, Scout, and Pioneer, and Chief of the Crow Nation of Indians* (1856).

BEGUINE

A dance resulting from a fusion of African and European elements. It originated in Martinique.

BELAFONTE, HARRY

Entertainer (b. 1927). He excels as a folk ballad singer, a nightclub entertainer, an actor, and a recording artist. His television specials have been memorable presentations. Born in New York City of West Indian parents, he spent months researching folk music before he began singing at the Village Vanguard in 1951. His calypso songs soon made him the most popular folk singer in America. He has also starred in movies (*Carmen Jones,*

Odds Against Tomorrow) and in Broadway shows (*Almanac, Three for Tonight*).

BELL V. MARYLAND

U.S. supreme court decision (1964) remanding a case involving 'the basic issue of the right of public accommodation' to a lower court for reconsideration.

BELL, AL

Businessman. He is executive vice president of Stax Records.

BELL, JAMES MADISON

Poet and lecturer (1826-1902). He left Ohio in 1854 and relocated in Canada, where he recruited men for John Brown. He migrated to California at the outbreak of the Civil War and became active in the struggle for civil rights. In 1865 he moved back to Ohio and continued the struggle. His collected poems were not published until 1901. Some of his best poems are 'Emancipation,' 'The Dawn of Freedom,' and 'The Triumph of the Free.'

BELLAMY, WALT

Athlete. In 1960 he played on the U.S. Olympic basketball team. In his first professional season, he set a new record with a field-goal percentage of .530 (Chicago Packers, 1961).

BENEFICIAL SOCIETIES

Many beneficial societies organized throughout the nation were connected with churches. They existed from the foundation of denominational churches and flourished after the Civil War. They were often the forerunners of secular insurance companies.

BENJAMIN, ROBERT C. O.

Lawyer (b. 1855). The first black attorney to be admitted to practice in California (1880), he was also the only black member of a prominent Los Angeles law firm. He was city editor of the Los Angeles *Daily Sun*.

BENNETT, LERONE, JR.

Historian, editor, and lecturer (b. 1928). A senior editor of *Ebony*, he authored *Before the Mayflower: A History of the Negro in America* (1962). He also had a major role in the publication of *Ebony's* monumental 3-volume *Pictorial History of Black America* (1971).

BENT, MICHAEL J.

Physician. In 1941 he became dean of Meharry. He studied at Columbia and Harvard before accepting an appointment as professor of bacteriology.

BETHEL AFRICAN METHODIST CHURCH

First Methodist church for negroes. Established by Richard Allen with the aid of Benjamin Rush and other influential whites in 1794, the Bethel African Methodist Church of Philadelphia later joined with other groups to form a separate branch of Methodism.

BETHEL CHARITY SCHOOL

Baltimore school for negroes, founded in 1816.

BETHUNE, MARY MCLEOD

Educator and humanitarian (1875-1955), She rose from the status of a laborer in the cotton fields of South Carolina to become a consultant to four U.S. presidents. She founded Daytona Normal and Industrial Institute for Negro Girls (now Bethune-Cookman College) in 1904 and served as its president until 1942. A vice-president of the NAACP, she received many awards for her service and accomplishments, including the Spingarn Medal (1935). See Catherine O. Peare, *Mary McLeod Bethune* (1951).

BETHUNE, THOMAS GREEN

Pianist (1849-1908). Born a slave, near Columbus, Georgia, he achieved fame as a pianist under the name of Blind Tom.

BIBB, HENRY

The book titled *Life and Adventures of Henry Bibb, an American Slave* (1849) paints a revolting portrait of the slave system.

BIGARD, BARNEY

Jazz clarinetist. In the 1920s he played with Duke Ellington's orchestra.

BIGGERS, JOHN T.

Contemporary artist (b. 1924). His drawings, sculpture, and paintings speak for the anonymous blacks of the rural South. After traveling to Africa, he wrote *Ananse: The Web of Life in Africa.*

BILLINGSLY, ANDREW

Sociologist. He wrote *Black Families in White America.*

BING, DAVE

Athlete. The NBA's 1966-67 Rookie-of-the-Year ended his second year with the Detroit Pistons as one of the All-NBA five.

BINGA, JESSE

Businessman (1865-1950). After moving from Detroit to Chicago (1893), he worked as a neighborhood vendor on the south side of the city, married Eudora Johnson, who inherited her uncle's estate, and used his wife's inheritance as the nucleus of his financial empire. He invested in real estate, controlled many rental properties, and established the Binga State Bank (1908). He had to close his bank during the economic depression (1932) and was never able to rebuild his empire.

BIRD, WILLIAM

In the early 1850s he went to England as a trainer of famous mounts. He had an enviable reputation as a trainer for well over a quarter of a century.

BIRMINGHAM DISORDERS

Nonviolent demonstrations to promote desegregation of public facilities in Birmingham, Ala., April, 1963, resulted in disorders that focused the attention of the nation on the plight of negroes in the South. Television cameras followed developments as police dogs, fire hoses, and rough handling by police became the order of the day. On June 11 President Kennedy declared that the black struggle for civil rights was a moral issue, and he appealed for understanding and calm. Subsequently he submitted to the U.S. congress the most far-reaching civil rights legislation since Reconstruction. See Project C.

BIRMINGHAM MANIFESTO

A statement of the demands of civil rights leaders, drafted by Martin Luther King Jr. and his aides in 1963. See Project C.

BIRTH OF A NATION

Racist film, released in 1915. Based on Thomas Dixon's *The Clansman* (1905), the film glorified the Ku Klux Klan.

BISHOP GRACE

See Grace, Bishop Charles Emmanuel.

BISHOP, JOSIAH

Clergyman. Toward the end of the eighteenth century, he pastored a mixed congregation in Northampton, Virginia. The famous preacher went on to Baltimore and later to New York, where he pastored the Abyssinian Baptist Church.

BISHOP ST. JOHN THE VINE

See Hickerson, John.

BLACK ABOLITIONISTS

'I am opposed to slavery, not because it enslaves the black man, but because it enslaves *man.*' Those words were written by Daniel A. Payne in 1839. Many black men and women with first-hand knowledge of the effect of slavery on human beings

44

took their stand besides white orators and agitators in the struggle to end slavery. Though often obscured by their white collaborators, many prominent Negroes worked to free slaves. The ranks of the outstanding black abolitionists included Frederick Douglass, Robert Purvis, Frances Ellen Watkins, James Forten, Jr., Martin Delany, Charles Remond, William C. Neil, William Wells Brown, and Henry H. Garnet. More militant than the whites, many of them rejected schemes for colonization and resettlement, reliance on moral persuasion and pacificism, and hopes of establishing utopian communities. Walker and Garnet finally converted Frederick Douglass to the activist position. See William and Jane Pease, *The Antislavery Argument* (1965); Martin Duberman (ed.), *The Antislavery Vanguard* (1965); and Benjamin Quarles, *Black Abolitionists* (1969).

BLACK AND TANS

The union of carpet baggers, scalawags, and blacks constituting the ruling caste in the South during Reconstruction. Black and Tan conventions revised state constitutions and their alliances dominated state legislatures.

BLACK ARTS THEATRE

Short-lived but important cultural center founded in 1965 by LeRoi Jones, who moved his cultural center to Newark the following year. Also called the Black Arts Repertory Theatre, it attracted such playwrights as Ben Caldwell and Ed Bullins.

BLACK BOURGEOISIE

Controversial book by E. Franklin Frazier, subtitled 'The Rise of a New Middle Class in the United States.' Published in 1962, the book analyzed the values and attitudes of those who, rejected by the white world and cut off from their own cultural traditions, had created a mythical world. Frazier maintained that the negro press represented essentially the interests of the black bourgeoisie, creating and perpetuating for them a world of make-believe.

He created a sensation by portraying the frustrations and insecurities of middle-class negroes nurtured on Booker T. Washington's doctrines and charging Washington with creating a collective inferiority complex. He received the coveted MacIver Award for his book.

BLACK CONGRESSMEN

See Congressmen, Black.

BLACK CAUCUS

A Congressional group composed of twelve negro representatives, all Democrats representing mainly Northern big-city districts. Permanently headquartered on Capitol Hill, the group has a full-time director and staff, including researchers and publicists. It maintains political liaison with other negro organizations. Its projects include preparation of a 'black agenda' to influence party platforms, electing as many as fifty representatives in the 1972 elections, developing a program for providing a political education for Negroes, and encouraging voters to register.

The members of the caucus include Charles C. Diggs, Robert N. C. Nix, Sr., Augustus Hawkins, John Conyers, William Clay, Louis Stokes, Shirley Chisholm, George Collins, Ronald Dellums, Ralph Metcalfe, Parren Mitchell, and Charles Rangel. See Congressmen, Black.

BLACK CODE, THE

State laws intended to control blacks and keep them inferior in status to white people. The Black Code originated in Louisiana under the French, was retained by the Spanish, and set an example of laws regulating relations between negroes and whites. Although such laws are popularly identified with the post-Civil War South, they flourished throughout the nation before the Civil War. After the war they defined the new status of freedmen. Intended to control the negro, they were the work of legislatures functioning under the Reconstruction policies of President Abraham Lincoln and his successor, President Andrew Johnson. Replacing defunct slaves codes, they stipulated that in making contracts negroes were to be known as servants, whites as masters (South Carolina), that negroes could be fined if they had

46

no lawful employment (Mississippi), that every negro had to be in the service of another person accountable for his conduct (Louisiana), that a negro could be employed only as a farm worker or a domestic servant (South Carolina), etc. They did give negroes the right to own property, to testify in court cases involving other negroes, to marry, and to sue and be sued. Such harsh measures caused even sympathetic Northerners to question the good faith of Southern legislators and put a powerful weapon in the hands of Republicans seeking to delay the readmission of the Confederate states until they could enfranchise southern negroes.

BLACK COMMUNITY DEVELOPMENT
Project recently organized by LeRoi Jones and headquartered in Newark, New Jersey.

BLACK ENGLISH
Term used to describe the regional speech forms familiar to black children. Perhaps through confusion of short-range necessities and long-range goals, the NAACP at its 62nd annual convention (1971) censured the 'insidious conspiracy to cripple our children permanently' by encouraging them to use freely in school the language already familiar to them.

BLACK ENTERPRISE
Monthly magazine for 'black men who want to get ahead.' Started in August 1970 by Earl G. Graves, it ended its first year 'in the black,' according to a newspaper account.

BLACK EXPO, INC.
A highly successful black trade fair held annually in Chicago. The brainchild of Jesse L. Jackson, the first fair (1969) drew national attention and resulted in an upsurge of interest in black capitalism. Jackson resigned as director of SCLC's Operation Breadbasket in December 1971, following a dispute over an investigation of Expo's affairs by the parent organization.

BLACK HARRY

Famous negro preacher who traveled with white Bishop Francis Asbury, establishing Methodist churches. Dr. Benjamin Rush declared him to be the greatest orator in America.

BLACK HISTORY

Blacks first examined their history in the New World more than a century ago. In 1841 James W. C. Pennnigton published his *Text Book of the Origin and History of the Colored People.* Before the Civil War his efforts had been supplemented by works by William C. Nell, and Martin R. Delany. After the war William Wells Brown, Joseph T. Wilson, and George Washington Williams made significant contributions to the study of black history. Then came W. E. B. Du Bois, W. H. Crogman, and G. F. Richings, whose works refuted the notion that black Americans had no history worthy of attention. Carter G. Woodson began the modern black history movement. A. A. Taylor, Horace Mann Bond, Charles H. Wesley, Luther J. Jackson, Sr.. Lorenzo Greene, and Rayford W. Logan worked in the fields of labor, political, and social history. By the middle of the 20th century black history had gained respectability and was forcing a reappraisal of accepted interpretations of issues and events, such as the Channing school's studies of Reconstruction. Vernon Wharton, Kenneth M. Stampp, and Leon P. Litwack are cases in point. Recently Rayford W. Logan, Benamin Quarles, and Lerone Bennett, Jr., have added their names to the growing list of historians whose scholarship is impeccable and who have produced general histories. Herbert Aptheker, Leslie Fishel, James McPherson have produced documentary histories. Atheneum, Arno, and Beacon are among the publishers who have shown an interest in reprinting source materials and older works that are out of print. In 1971 the NAACP published *American Majorities and Minorities; A Syllabus of United States History for Secondary Schools* by Warren Halliburton and William Loren Katz.

BLACK JEWS

See Church of God.

BLACK MAN

Magazine published by Marcus Garvey (1933-38) after he ceased publication of his failing newspaper, *Negro World*.

BLACK MANHATTAN

James Weldon Johnson's classic study of the role of the Negro in New York, from the days of the earliest Dutch settlements. It was published in 1930.

BLACK MANIFESTO

Demands presented on Sunday, May 4, 1969, at Riverside Church in New York City by James Forman. Based on the principle of reparations for past wrongs, the manifesto became a focal issue in churches throughout the land. It had originally been adopted by 187 delegates to the first National Black Economic Development Conference, held in Detroit late in April 1969 under the auspices of the Interreligious Foundation for Community Organization. The manifesto asked for 500 million dollars to be used for loans for black enterprises.

BLACK MOSES

Title given to Harriet Tubman, the most famous underground railroad conductor.

BLACK MUSLIMS

Members of a religious movement initiated in 1930 by a Mullah calling himself W. D. Farad Muhammad and claiming to be from the holy city of Mecca. His mission was to awaken the 'Dead Nation in the West' and prepare blacks for Armageddon, the confrontation between blacks and whites. He founded the first of the Temples of Islam in Detroit. In his new interpretation of history, Islam was the original religion of blacks, whose civilizations flourished 'long before the white man stood up on his hind legs and crept out of the caves of Europe.' The movement grew under Elijah Poole, who recruited most of his followers from the black ghetto. Poole, later renamed Muhammad, became Farad's most dedicated apostle, accepting the doctrine that the white man was a devil, created on the Isle of Patmos by the mad scientist Yakub and destined to rule for a limited time only. Muhammad became First Minister of Islam and head of the Fruit of Islam (FOI, the elite corps to be trained 'for the coming Armageddon'). He founded a second temple in Chicago, the present headquarters of the movement, and as the new Messenger of Islam began to establish temples or missions in major cities throughout the country. Farad made fewer and fewer public appearances as Elijah Muhammad rose to eminence. Farad made his last public appearance in 1934. The Muslims' ultimate aim is complete separatism. While they accept the Puritan ethic of capitalism (discipline, hard work, thrift, honesty, respect for authority), they stress rehabilitation of victims of alcohol and drugs, and they substitute black supremacy for black inferiority, an idealized Afro-Asian past for a heritage of slavery, brotherhood with darker-skinned peoples for racial pluralism, and a religion based on Islam for Christianity.

By 1970 Muhammad and his Black Muslims laid claim to a multi-million-dollar business and farming enterprise. They operated poultry, and dairy, lumbering, agricultural, and publishing facilities in Michigan, Georgia, Illinois, and Alabama, and they supported self-help businesses in operation from coast to coast. Members of the Nation of Islam do not refer to themselves as Black Muslims, a term popularized by C. Eric Lincoln, but they do not object to the use of the term by others. See C. Eric Lincoln, *The Black Muslims in America* (1961).

BLACK PANTHER PARTY

Formed in California in 1966 by Bobby Seale and Huey Newton, with the help of Stokely Carmichael, it was an outgrowth of the Lowndes County Freedom Organization and the Community Alert Patrol established in Los Angeles after the Watts riot. The radical group soon expanded to more than 40 chapters with 2,000 members and considered itself the vanguard of a Black Revolution. It spelled out the meaning of black power: free breakfasts for ghetto children, free health clinics, community control of police, black liberation schools. An unsuccessful merger with SNCC made Stokely Carmichael prime minister, H. Rap

50

Brown minister of justice, and James Forman minister of foreign affairs. Its announced aims included the promotion of full employment, adequate housing, and black studies; an end to the exploitation and murder of blacks; and protection from police brutality. Its angry young blacks soon were engaged in open conflict with authorities, and many of them were killed, jailed, or forced into exile. While many of the charges against Black Panthers have been dismissed or dropped, FBI director J. Edgar Hoover called them the most dangerous extremists in America. The party maintains an international coordinating section in Algiers.

Police and court action against Black Panthers attracted national attention in 1970, leading to charges that a systematic attempt was being made to destroy the movement. Yale president Kingman Brewster, Jr. opened his university to more than 13,000 peaceful demonstrators a week after he had stirred nationwide controversy by voicing skepticism over 'the ability of black revolutionaries to achieve a fair trial anywhere in the United States. Acquittals of most party members brought to trial in 1971, and of Angela Davis in 1972, helped to restore faith in the fairness of the American judicial system. See Black Power, Lowndes County Freedom Organization.

BLACK PATRIOTS

The participation of black patriots in the conflicts of the Revolutionary period, as well as in later national wars, was extensive. Among the most famous black patriots were Crispus Attucks, Peter Salem, Barzillai Lew, and Salem Poor.

BLACK PATTI

See Jones, Sisseretta.

BLACK POWER

Term popularized by Stokely Carmichael during the Meredith March through Mississippi in 1966. On August 5 the New York *Times* published excerpts from a position paper drafted earlier by dissident SNCC members, proposing that whites be excluded from

51

positions of leadership in SNCC, which should be 'black-staffed, black-controlled and black-financed.' In June the public had heard the words 'Black Power' and seen the clenched-fist salute symbolizing the movement as Carmichael and other civil rights leaders joined James Meredith's march from Memphis to Jackson to encourage voter registration.

Carmichael's theory of political activism to achieve full equality for blacks issued from the general feeling that social legislation had slowed following the 1966 congressional elections and that prospects for gains were minimal unless blacks could organize and 'speak from a position of power and strength rather than a position of weakness.' His street definitions of Black Power were incendiary, but his televisions interviews presented it as a way of encouraging negroes to rid themselves of their feelings of inferiority and dependence by becoming aware of their heritage, their potentialities, and their political and economic power. The slogan which he popularized soon engendered not only 'Red Power' but also 'Brown Power' 'Green Power,' and 'Gay Power.' Carmichael's views are set forth in a book which he co-authored with Charles V. Hamilton, *Black Power: The Politics of Liberation* (1968). See James Meredith, Freedom March.

BLACK POWER CONFERENCE

Held in Newark, New Jersey, in 1967, it lasted four days and was the largest meeting of its kind in American history. It was attended by over 400 blacks representing 45 civil rights groups from 36 cities. A similar conference had been convened in Washington, D. C., a year earlier. In 1968 a third Black Power Conference at Philadelphia explored the theme 'University through Diversity.'

BLACK RAGE

Title of a book by two black psychiatrists, William H. Grier and Price M. Cobbs. Published in 1968, the book was a best-seller. In it the authors examined the psychological foundations of the rage experienced by blacks who attempt to deal with an unsympathetic society.

BLACK REGULARS

Name applied to four negro units retained in the regular army after all others had been disbanded at the end of the Civil War: the 24th and 25th Infantry and the 9th and 10th Calvary. Some of these troops later saw action action against Indian tribes in the West, as a part of the expeditionary force landing in Cuba in 1898, and on the Mexican border in 1916. General John J. Pershing (called 'Black Jack' as a result of his involvement with black units) credited their role in the storming of San Juan Hill with forging a deeper feeling of unity among all troops, yet these four seasoned units were not allowed to see combat duty during World War II. See Buffalo Soldiers.

BLACK RENAISSANCE

See New Black Renaissance.

BLACK REPUBLICAN

Abusive epithet used by Democrats in the pre-Civil War period to indicate presumed Republican sympathy for blacks.

BLACK SCHOLAR, THE

Official publication of The Black World Foundation. The monthly (except July and August) journal of black studies and research, published by Nathan Hare and edited by Robert Chrisman, was started in November 1969.

BLACK STAR LINE

Stock company organized by Marcus Garvey in 1919 to acquire ships for commerce with Africa.

BLACK STUDIES

In recent years black studies, defined by Teachers College's Preston Wilcox as "that body of knowledge that blacks have had to summon in order to survive within a society that is stacked against them," have moved far beyond the recitations of black firsts in history typical of early ventures and now include courses in African history and religions, Swahili, and Afro-American literature, economics, and social and political thought. By 1972 more than 600 colleges were offering black-oriented courses.

Black studies, frequently one of the core grievances in campus incidents during the 1960s, have had an impact on education at all levels and provoked a mass black introspection without parallel. Moreover, as Roscoe C. Brown has noted, "tens of thousands of students have been introduced to the realities of racism in America and . . . to understand the universality of the human condition."

San Francisco State and Merritt Community College were among the first schools to develop black studies programs. By 1970 some 150 colleges had announced plans to develop programs. The movement toward black universities free of white domination produced Malcolm X Liberation University in Durham and Greensboro, North Carolina, and the Center for Black Education in Washington, D. C. The movement also led to the establishment of Nairobi College in California and the renaming of one of the city colleges of Chicago, now known as Malcom X College.

BLACK SWAN
See Greenfield, Elizabeth Taylor.

BLACK JOHNSON
See Johnson Publishing Company.

BLACK WORLD FOUNDATION, THE
Organization founded in 1969 'to begin the shaping of a revolutionary black culture.' Its 'instrument for the enhancement of black culture' is *The Black Scholar,* subtitled 'Journal of Black Studies and Research.'

BLACK WRITERS CONFERENCES
In the 1960s John O. Killens conducted conferences for young writers at Fisk, where he was writer-in-residence.

BLACKMAN, POMP

Colonial militiaman. He took part in the first military engagement of the American Revolution, at Lexington and Concord, and later served in the Continental Army.

BLACKPLATE

Term designating certain soul food items: backbone and dumplings, baked grits, pork brains, chitlins and cornbread, fried catfish, fried tripe, and the like.

BLACKWELL, GEORGE LINCOLN

Clergyman (b. 1861). Born of slave parents and largely self-taught, he held pastorates in Cambridge and Boston before he earned a degree from Boston University (1892). He taught at Livingston, managed the AMEZ publishing House (1896), and was elected bishop of his church (1908).

BLAIR, JOSEPH

Scientist (b. 1904). He had an important part in developing rockets.

BLAKE

Novel by Martin R. Delany dealing with the black underground in the 1850s.

BLAKE, ROBERT

Civil War hero. He won the navy's Medal of Honor for his service as a powder boy aboard the U.S.S. *Marblehead* during a victorious battle off Legareville, South Carolina, on December 25, 1863.

BLAND, ALDEN

Writer (b. 1911). His works include *Behold a Cry* (1945).

BLAND, JAMES

Musician (1854-1911). Better known as Jim Bland, the Virginia-born entertainer started his career in a minstrel show.

He wrote a number of popular songs and ditties, the most famous of them being the official state song of Virginia, 'Carry Me Back to Ole Virginny' (1855). He also added a fifth string to the banjo, creating the 'Bland Banjo.' See John Jay Daly, *A Song in His Heart* (1951).

BLAYTON, JESSE B.
Businessman (b. 1900). He was the first black certified public accountant of America and is still president of the Federal Savings and Loan Association of Atlanta.

BLEDSOE, JULES C.
Musician (1898-1934). An accomplished baritone, he sang *The Creation* with the Boston Orchestra under the direction of Serge Koussevitzky (1931) and appeared in the European premier of Gruenberg's *Emperor Jones* (1934).

BLIND PHILIP
In 1822 he conspired with Denmark Vesey to stage a revolt in Charleston. He was reputed to have the ability to see ghosts and other invisible phenomena.

BLIND TOM
See Bethune, Thomas Green.

BLUE, VIDA
Athlete (b. 1949). Star pitcher of the Oakland Athletics, he won the Cy Young award in 1971, his first full year in the major leagues. He won 24 games, led his team to the Western Division championship, and was named the American League's most valuable player.

BLUES
A form of musical expression originated by blacks, the blues feature syncopated rhythms and always consist of 12 bars. Among the pioneers were Clarence Williams, Tony Jackson, Jelly Roll Morton, W. C. Handy, Louis Chauvin, and the five

Smiths—Mamie, Bessie, Laura, Clara, and Trixie. Because the composers had no musical education, blues were not written before the 1890s. Looked upon as low-class music in the early 1900s, they became popular among whites in the 1920s. They have inspired or influenced more modern popular and classical music than any other musical art form. According to Charles Reich (*The Greening of America*, 1970), it is in the blues that the American Negro gives expression to his unique experience. The blues are typical of the new music of the rock culture in that they provide a means of expressing 'thoughts and feelings that most people conceal' from themselves and others. The blues express, particularly for the black man in the South, 'an identity, an identity oppressed, forbidden, and denied in other ways.' See Paul Oliver, *The Story of the Blues* (1971).

BLUES PEOPLE

Book by LeRoi Jones. *Blues People: Negro Music in White America* (1963) represented the first attempt of a black writer to re-evaluate the cultural context in which black music was created.

BLYDEN, EDWARD WILMOT

Scholar and diplomat (b. 1832). Born in the Virgin Islands, he came to the United States as a youth. In 1851 he accompanied his brother to Liberia, where he mastered several languages, traveled extensively, and undertook diplomatic assignments. He taught at Liberia College and later became president of the college (1881). His published works include *Our Origin, Dangers and Duties* (1865), *From West Africa to Palestine* (1866), *The Negro in Ancient History* (1869), *Africa and the Africans* (1903),*African Life and Customs* (1908), and 'The Koran in Africa,' in *The Journal of the Royal African Society*.

BOARD, ANDREW J.

Inventor. A railroad worker, he invented the coupling device known as the 'Jenny Coupler.' In 1897 a New York railroad paid him $50,000 for his invention.

BOLDEN, BUDDY
Musician (1868-1931). The New Orleans barber played the coronet and led a jazz band that played in honky-tonks, parties, and dance halls. His players included William Warner and Frank Lewis, clarinetists; Willy Cornish, trombonist; Brock Mumford, guitarist; James Johnson, bass player; and Cornelius Tillman, drummer. Singing, dancing, and acting as master of ceremonies Lincoln Park, he was the leading jazz celebrity for a dozen years (1895-1907), until he went berserk and was permanently committed to a hospital.

BOLES, ROBERT
Writer. *The People One Knows* draws a portrait of a sensitive young black struggling against racism. Associated with the New Harlem Renaissance, even though he was brought up in the capitals of Europe, he has also written *Curling*.

BOLEY
All-black town founded in Oklahoma in 1904.

BOLIN, JANE M.
Jurist (b. 1908). She was the first black woman judge in the United States (in New York City).

BOLLING V. SHARPE
One of the cases involved in the Brown v. Board of Education of Topeka ruling of the U. S. Supreme Court. In a unanimous decision handed down the same day as the Brown decision (May 17, 1956), the Court held school segregation in the District of Columbia invalid under the due process clause of the Fifth Amendment.

BOLLING, EDWARD A.
Educator (b. 1860). In 1915 the West Virginia state board of education took the unusual step of granting him a lifetime teaching certificate.

BOND, HORACE MANN

Educator (b. 1904). He was president of Lincoln University (Pennsylvania) and dean of the Atlanta University School of Education. He has written many articles and books on history and education.

BOND, JULIAN

Public official (b. 1940). A stubborn fighter for civil liberties and an outspoken opponent of American involvement in Vietnam, he is well known throughout the nation. Born in Nashville, Tennessee, he received his early education in Lincoln, Pennsylvania, then majored in English at Morehouse College in Atlanta. He left college during his senior year to become communications director of the SNCC. Moving on into politics after six years, he became one of 8 black men elected to the Georgia house of representatives in 1965. Successfully challenging the Georgia delegation at the Democratic convention in Chicago three years later, he became the floor leader of the remaining delegates and the first black to be nominated from the floor for the office of Vice President of the United States. See John Neary, *Julian Bond: Black Rebel* (1971).

BONDS, MARGARET

Musician. A noted composer whose compositions have won many awards, she is best known for her 'Ballad of the Brown King.'

BONGA, GEORGE

A prosperous trader of Duluth, on Lake Superior, he served as interpreter when the Chippewa treaty of 1837 was signed.

BONTEMPS, ARNA W.

Writer (b. 1902). Associated with both the Harlem Renaissance, and the New Harlem Renaissance, he has written novels, plays, and essays. His works include *Story of the Negro, Golden Slippers, Black Thunder* (1946), and *Negro American Heritage* (1965).

59

BOOTH, EDWARD

Pioneer (1810-1900). A freeborn black, he left Maryland for the West Indies in the early 1840s, amassed a fortune in trading, and returned to Baltimore. Learning of the discovery of gold in California, he made his way to the Coast (1849), staked claims near Sacramento, and returned to Baltimore for his family. He settled his family in California and made a fortune. He died in Alaska, where he had gone in search of more gold.

BOSTON MASSACRE

A pre-Revolutionary incident (1770) that took the lives of five members of a rioting crowd. A Negro, Crispus Attucks, was one of those killed by the British soldiers sent to Boston to enforce the Townshend Acts.

BOSTON, RALPH

Athlete. One of history's greatest broad jumpers, he started in 1954, at the age of 15, to improve his record by a foot a year. In 1961, in Moscow, he set a new world record by jumping 27 feet-1 3/4 inches.

BOUCHET, EDWARD A.

Physicist. In 1876 he earned a Ph. D. in physics from Yale, becoming the first American black to achieve such a distinction.

BOURNE, GEORGE

Militant white abolitionist. He wrote one of the most famous of all abolitionist works, *The Book and Slavery Irreconcilable* (1816). The Presbyterian minister became a founder of the American Anti-Slavery Society.

BOULWARE, JAMES H.

Physician (b. 1818). He financed his medical studies by working as a farm laborer. After receiving his degree in 1911, he became a member of the West Virginia State Medical

Association and medical examiner for the Supreme Life and Casualty Company.

BOURBON POLITICS

Term describing the politics of the former Confederate states during the period between 1877 and 1890, when effective leadership was in the hands of the heirs of the old aristocracy, who preserved a paternalistic feeling toward blacks.

BOUSFIELD, M. O.

Physician. During World Was II, the Chicago physician, assisted by 35 other black officers, organized a large, well-equipped hospital in the Arizona desert for the all-colored 93rd Division at Fort Huachuca, Arizona.

BOWEN, JOHN WESLEY E.

Clergyman and scholar (1855-1933). In addition to pastoring several Methodist Episcopal churches, he taught for 40 years at Gammon Theological Seminary in Atlanta and served as its vice-president and president.

BOWEN, ANTHONY

In 1853, he organized the first Negro YMCA, in Washington, D. C.

BOWERS, DAVID BUSTILL

Artist (b. 1820). A Philadelphia sign painter, he produced emblems and banners for organizations, did portraits, and painted landscapes. He painted a number of portraits of Abraham Lincoln.

BOWERS, THOMAS

Musician (b. 1836). Described as the 'American Mario' by critics of his day, the Philadelphia tenor wrote that he decided to become a concert singer 'to show to the world that colored men and women could sing classical music as well as the other race by whom they have been so terribly vilified.'

BOXING

From the beginning blacks have had an opportunity to excel in boxing, long regarded as a bestial and brutal activity. Blacks have entered the prize ring since plantation days and have generally dominated the sport. See the names of individual boxers, such as Tom Molineaux, Joe Walcott, George Dixon, Joe Gans, Jack Johnson, Joe Louis, Henry Armstrong, and Muhammad Ali.

BOYD, RICHARD HENRY

Clergyman and publisher (1843-1922). Founder of the National Baptist Publishing Board, the largely self-taught ex-slave wrote 14 volumes of Baptist literature for negroes, founded schools and churches in the United States and other countries, and was active in commercial ventures. He owned a Cincinnati bedstead factory employing 20.

BOYD, ROBERT F.

Physician (1858-1912). A prominent practitioner in Nashville, Tennessee, he was one of the wealthiest black physicians in the nation when he died at the age of 54. After graduating from Fisk University, he completed his training at Meharry Medical School (1882), did postgraduate work at Ann Arbor and Chicago, and became the first president of the National Medical Association (1895).

BRADLEY, ISAAC T.

Lawyer (b. 1862). After graduating from Kansas State University (1887) and being admitted to the bar, he was elected justice of the peace (1889). He also served as assistant prose-cuting attorney of Wyandotte County, Kansas.

BRADY, WILLIAM

Musician (d. 1854). His compositions include 'Anthem for Christmas' (1851).

BRAITHWAITE, WILLIAM S. B.

Scholar (1878-1962). He achieved recognition as a historian, critic, and writer. He also edited a poetry magazine, the *Anthology of Magazine Verse*, 1913-29.

BRANTON, WILEY A.

Lawyer and civil rights leader (b. 1923). In 1957 he was chief counsel for the black plaintiffs in the Little Rock school cases. He was later director of the Voter Education Project of the Southern Regional Council, 1962-65. Following the shooting of Freedom Rider Jimmy Travis during a voter education project, he asked all registration workers in all sections of the state to move into Greenwood, Mississippi, where the shooting had occurred. Violence mounted until Medgar Evers was murdered on June 12, 1963, creating controversy around the world.

BRAWLEY, BENJAMIN G.

Writer and educator (1882-1939). His works include *A Social History of the American Negro* (1921), *The Negro Genius,* (1937), and *Early Negro American Writers.*

BREEDLOVE, SARAH

See Walker, Madame C. J.

BRER RABBIT

Hero symbol appearing as the central figure in folktales incorporating the main ingredients of African fables. The helpless, frightened rabbit became by turn a braggart, wit, practical joker, trickster, and lady's man. Always, however, his essential characteristic was the ability to triumph over bigger and stronger creatures.

BRICE, EDWARD WARNER

Public official (b. 1916). He earned a Ph. D. at the University of Pennsylvania, taught at South Carolina State College and was dean of education extension, became president of Clinton Junior College in Rock Hill, South Carolina, and held a number of federal positions: chief of U. S. educational missions in Liberia and Nepal (1952-58), director of adult education and specialist in basic education (1958-66), and assistant secretary of education for DHEW. The third-ranking official in DHEW, he was also one of the most decorated of all U. S. civil servants (18 honorary degrees and awards). He has authored several books and had the key role in UNESCO's world literacy program.

BRIGGS V. ELLIOTT
See Brown v. Board of Education.

BRIGGS, CYRIL V.
Militant. He headed the African Blood Brotherhood in the early 1920s.

BRIGHT, JOHN
Presiding Bishop of the AME Church.

BRIMMER, ANDREW F.
Economist and educator (b. 1926). In February 1966, he became the first black member of the governing board of the Federal Reserve System. After receiving his M. A. (University of Washington, 1951) and Ph. D. (Harvard, 1957), he taught at Michigan State University, wrote many articles and *Life Insurance Companies in the Capital Markets* (1962), joined the Commerce department (1962), and became assistant secretary for economic affairs (1963). Concerned with pollution control, he advocates devoting a large share of new investment to 'repairing the environmental damages suffered in the past.'

BRITISH EMANCIPATION
Though slavery was ended in the British Isles in the 1770s and slave trade with other nations in 1807, emancipation was not achieved in the British West Indies until 1833. The planters of Jamaica, Barbados, Trinidad, and other Caribbean possessions received 20 million pounds for their slaves. British emancipation was an inspiration to American abolitionists, who extolled it in

their pamphlets, celebrated emancipation annually, and appealed to the British for aid in their own work.

BRITT, ARTHUR L., SR.

Artist (b. 1934). Currently chariman of the art department of Savannah State College, he has exhibited his works mainly at other schools. His paintings are represented in the collections of Atlanta, Lincoln, and New Mexico universities, and at Mississippi State, West Virginia State, and Stillman colleges.

BROADSIDE PRESS

Detroit enterprise specializing in short, inexpensive books of poetry. See Randall, Dudley.

BROOKE, EDWARD W.

Senator (b. 1919). He was the first black U. S. senator ever elected by popular vote and the first to fill the office since Reconstruction. Born of a Virginia family claiming descent from Thomas Jefferson, he practiced law before entering politics. He lost his bid for the Massachusetts legislature in 1950 and again in 1952, and for secretary of state in 1960, when he became the first black ever nominated for statewide office. He was elected attorney general in 1964 and again in 1966, the only black American ever to hold such an office. His election as a Republican senator on November 8, 1966, climaxed a career of public service to an electorate of which only two percent were blacks.

BROOKS, GWENDOLYN

Poet and novelist (b. 1917). A sensitive interpreter of Northern ghetto life, she is the only black recipient of the Pulitzer Prize, awarded to her for her book of poems, *Annie Allen*, in 1950. Reared in an artistic atmosphere in Chicago, she began writing poetry at seven. Her first poems were published in the Chicago *Defender*. Besides *Annie Allen* (1949), she has published the widely acclaimed *A Street in Bronzeville* (1945), *The Bean Eaters* (1956), *Selected Poems* (1963), the novel

Maud Martha (1953), and the children's book *Bronzeville Boys and Girls* (1956). Shy and unassuming, she now promotes the idea that blacks must develop their own culture.

BROOKS, ROBERT
Soldier in World War II. Son of a Kentucky sharecropper, he became the first American soldier of the armed forces killed in the Pacific. The main parade ground of the armored forces at Fort Knox, Kentucky, was named Brooks Field in his honor.

BROOKS, SHELTON
Popular composer. He wrote both words and music for 'Some of These Days,' 'Darktown Strutters' Ball,' and 'Walkin' the Dog.'

BROWN V. BOARD OF EDUCATION
Landmark segregation decision handed down by the U. S. Supreme Court on May 17, 1954. In a unanimous opinion the nine Justices held that segregation of public school children solely on the basis of race is unconstitutional under the equal protection clause of the Fourteenth Amendment. Their decision climaxed more than two centuries of litigation involving the legal status of negroes. It reversed the Plessy decision (1896) and held that separate facilities are inherently unequal. Though the ruling applied directly to public school education only, its implications for other institutions and publicly operated facilities made it the most significant document in the history of the civil rights movement.

The decision was the culmination of five separate legal actions: Gebhart v. Belton, Briggs v. Elliott, Davis v. County School Board of Prince Edward County, and Bolling v. Sharpe. Brown was the first name, alphabetically, in the first case on the docket for the 1953 October term. Oliver Brown's suit against the Board of Education of Topeka was the least important of the five. The 1954 ruling set forth the principle that state-imposed segregation was unconstitutional but said nothing about enforcement. A second decision in Brown v. Board of Education was handed down the following year, ordering school segregation

66

'with all deliberate speed' and requiring 'good faith compliance at the earliest practicable date.'

BROWN, ANNE
Entertainer. The original Bess in *Porgy and Bess,* she is also a concert singer.

BROWN, CECIL
Writer. Associated with the New Harlem Renaissance, he wrote the highly successful novel, *The Life and Times of Mr. Jiveass Nigger.*

BROWN, CHARLOTTE HAWKINS
Educator (1882-1960). In 1901 she graduated from the state normal school in Salem, Massachusetts, and began to raise money for a 'farm-life' school. She found a dilapidated shack near Sedalia, North Carolina, and opened a school for local children. Palmer Memorial Institute, supported by friends and benefactors, continues as a junior college.

BROWN, CLAUDE
Writer (b. 1937). Born in Harlem, he described his fight to survive in New York City in his national bestseller, *Manchild in the Promised Land* (1965).

BROWN, EARL
Journalist. As a staff member of *Life* magazine, he reported favorably on the role of negroes in the conduct of World War II.

BROWN, FRANK LONDON
Writer (1927-1962). A many-sided man who introduced the practice of reading short stories to jazz accompaniment, he was associate editor of *Ebony.* He published many articles, short stories, and the novel *Trumbull Park* (1959).

BROWN, HALLIE QUINN
Educator (1849-1949). She studied and taught at Wilberforce

University, used her dramatic and oratorical talents to make her school famous throughout the nation, was active in many national and international movements, and wrote several books. She campaigned for Warren G. Harding in 1920 and was a speaker at the Republican national convention in 1924.

BROWN, HENRY

Slave who escaped to freedom by shipping himself in a specially designed box. He traveled from Richmond, Virginia, to Philadelphia via Adams Express. He told his life story in *Narrative of the Life of Henry Box Brown: Written by Himself* (1851).

BROWN, HILLIARD A.

Educator (b. 1911). After completing his studies at Ohio State University, Dr. Brown taught and held administrative positions at four colleges before becoming superintendent of the public schools of Atlanta, Georgia.

BROWN, H. RAP

Black Power leader (b. 1943). Born Hubert Geroid Brown in Baton Rouge, Louisiana, he succeeded Stokely Carmichael as chairman of SNCC on May 12, 1967. Gunfire and arson became the expected sequel to his vitriolic speeches. He called the summer riots of 1967 'dress rehearsals' for a Black Revolution. He resigned his chairmanship of SNCC in the spring of 1968 only to be renamed to the post when the group agreed to change the organization's name from Student Nonviolent to Student National Coordinating Committee. Charged with abetting three youths to set fire to a school in Cambridge, Maryland, in the summer of 1967, he disappeared before the date set for his trial in March 1970 and was placed on the FBI's Ten Most Wanted List for flight to avoid prosecution on charges of inciting to commit arson. On October 16, 1971, he was wounded in a gun battle in New York City following a bar holdup. His views were set forth in a book, *Die Nigger Die!*

BROWN, JAMES

Singer (born c. 1936). He was hailed as 'Soul Brother No. 1' in the late 1960s and popularized the slogan 'Say it loud. I'm black and I'm proud.'

BROWN, JESSE L.

Military aviator. He was the first black American aviator killed in the Korean War. In 1971 the U. S. navy announced that its newest destroyer would be named for the ensign from Hattiesburg, Mississippi.

BROWN, JIM

Athlete (b. 1936). The greatest runner, and perhaps the greatest player, in the history of football, he deserted athletics at the peak of his career to become an actor. Born on St. Simon Island, Georgia, he moved to Manhasset, Long Island, where he later starred in basketball, football, baseball, and lacrosse. He won ten varsity letters at Syracuse University and made the All-American team in 1956. As fullback for the Cleveland Browns (1957-1966), he led the league in rushing every season except 1962. He was the National Football League's top attraction and highest-paid player, winning the Player-of-the-Year award in 1958, 1963, and 1965.

BROWN, JOE

Athlete (b. 1924). In 1956 he defeated Bud Smith to win the lightweight boxing title.

BROWN, JOHN

Civil War soldier. Serving with the South Carolina Volunteers in 1862, he was killed on St. Simon's Island off the coast of Georgia. He was leading a contingent assigned to flush out a band of rebel Conferedate guerrillas. He was probably the first black man to die in an armed encounter with the Confederates.

BROWN, LAURA A.

Civic leader (1874-1924). She helped to organize the Women's

69

Christian Temperance Union in Pennsylvania, sell savings bonds during World War I, and raise thousands of dollars for the relief of soldiers.

BROWN, LAWRENCE
Jazz trombonist. In the 1920s he played with Duke Ellington's Kentucky Club orchestra.

BROWN, MORRIS
Clergyman. He became bishop of the African Methodist Church in 1831.

BROWN, NELLIE E.
Musician. In 1865 she began her career as a church singer. In 1874 she sang in Steinway Hall in New York City. She appeared in concerts from Washington, D. C., to Canada.

BROWN, ROBERT J.
President Richard M. Nixon's White House assistant.

BROWN, ROOSEVELT
Athlete. He joined the New York Giants in 1953 and developed into one of football's most respected offensive tackles before he retired at the end of the 1961 season. He became the team's first black captain. After he retired as a player, he joined the coaching staff.

BROWN, STERLING A.
Writer and scholar (b. 1901). A poet, critic, and authority on black literature, he has authored *The Negro in American Fiction* (1937), *Negro Poetry and Drama* (1937), and *The Negro Caravan* (1941).

BROWN, WESLEY
First black man to graduate from the U. S. Naval Academy at Annapolis, Maryland (1949).

BROWN, WILLIAM G.

Educator. During the Reconstruction period, he served with distinction as superintendent of education in Louisiana.

BROWN, WILLIAM WELLS

Scholar, lecturer, and writer (1816-1884). The son of a slave mother and a plantation owner in Lexington, Kentucky, he escaped to freedom, became an antislavery crusader, spent five years in Europe advocating emancipation, and turned out the first fictional and dramatic works by a black American. His writings also brought him fame as a historian. He wrote *Narrative of William W. Brown, Fugitive Slave* (1847), *Three Years in Europe* (1852), *Clotel; Or, The President's Daughter* (1852), *The American Fugitive in Europe* (1855), *Experience; Or, How to Give a Northern Man a Backbone* (1856), *The Escape; Or, A Leap for Freedom: A Drama in Five Acts* (1858), *The Black Man, His Antecedents, His Genius and His Achievements* (1863), *The Negro in the American Rebellion: His Heroism and His Fidelity* (1867), *The Rising Son; Or, the Antecedents and Advancement of the Colored Race* (1874), *and My Southern Home; Or, the South and Its People* (1880).

BROWNE, WASHINGTON

Clergyman (b. 1849). He succeeded in uniting fraternal groups and establishing a newspaper, *The Reformer,* to serve a mutual benefit society. See Grand United Order of True Reformers.

BROWNHELM TOWNSHIP

In 1855 John Mercer Langston became the first black to win elective office in the United States by being elected clerk of Brownhelm Township in Lorain County, Ohio.

BROWNSVILLE RIOT

On the night of August 13-14, 1906, according to residents of the city of Brownsville, Texas, three companies of negro infantrymen stationed in nearby Fort Brown destroyed property and committed murder. Though the evidence was inconclusive, President Theodore Roosevelt dishonorably discharged every negro infantryman in the three companies. A Senatorial investigation began the next year, and some of the men were eventually reinstated.

BRUCE, BLANCHE KELSO

Public official (1841-1898). Born a slave, he became the only negro to serve a full term as United States senator from Mississippi (1875-1881). He was taught by plantation tutors, learned the printer's trade, opened schools for negroes in Lawrence, Kansas, and Hannibal, Missouri, became a wealthy planter, entered politics, and held such posts as assessor of Boliver County in Mississippi, sheriff and tax collector, and county superintendent of schools. After his senate term ended, he was appointed Register of the Treasury (1881-85 and 1897-98) and Recorder of Deeds in the District of Columbia (1891-93). His signature appeared upon the nation's currency when he was Register. See Philip Sterling and Rayford Logan, *Four Took Freedom* (1967).

BRUCE, JOHN EDWARD

Early black power advocate. Known widely by his pen name of 'Bruce Grit,' he exalted blackness and flayed white hypocrisy. See Peter Gilbert (ed.), *The Selected Writings of John Edward Bruce: Militant Black Journalist* (1971).

BRYAN, ANDREW

Clergyman (d. 1812). Born a slave in South Carolina, he was brought by his master to Savannah, where he was allowed to preach to mixed congregations. Opposition developed because some whites feared that his preaching would result in slave uprisings. His master allowed him to conduct services in a barn and eventually to build a church. At the time of his death, he was the acknowledged leader of black worshipers in Georgia.

BRYANT, WILLIAM B.

Jurist (b. 1911). He was appointed to the U. S. District Court for the District of Columbia in 1965.

BUCHANAN V. WARLEY

Supreme Court decision (1917) declaring unconstitutional a city zoning ordinance prohibiting negroes from living on predominately white blocks.

BUCKLEY, WILLIAM LEWIS

Scholar (b. 1861). Fluent in Greek, Latin, French, German, and Spanish, he received his Ph. D. in Latin languages and literature from Syracuse University in 1893. He started his teaching career at Clafin University in South Carolina in 1882.

BUFFALO SOLDIERS

Name given to the Tenth Cavalry Regiment and later to the Ninth Cavalry Regiment, both composed of black soldiers under the command of white officers. They had a major role in maintaining law and order on the Great Plains and on the Texas Border, 1867-91. Their combat record, their morale, and their diverse accomplishments on the untamed frontier, notwithstanding the ever-present obstacle created by racial prejudice, qualified them as first-rate units. They had a key role in promoting peace and advancing civilization along the last continental frontier. See William H. Leckie, *Buffalo Soldiers* (1967).

BULLINS, ED

Playwright. One of the young militants associated with LeRoi Jones, he maintains that there are no new ideas in the culture of the white man, who cannot 'perceive what is really happening, i. e. *Black.*' In 1968 he joined the New Lafayette Theater, following a stint with the Black House in San Francisco, as writer-in-residence. That same year he won the Vernon Rice Award for his trilogy of plays presented at the American Place Theater: *Clara's Old Man, The Electronic Nigger,* and *A Son Come Home.*

BUNCHE, RALPH

Statesman (1904-1971). Called the foremost negro of his generation, he symbolized the heights to which a black man could rise in the Establishment. As undersecretary for special political affairs, he was the highest ranking American in the United Nations and Secretary-General U Thant's most trusted adviser. He was also the first black to win the Nobel Peace Prize. The son of a Detroit barber and grandson of a slave, he worked his way through the University of California with the help of an athletic scholarship (1927), received a master's degree from Harvard (1928), founded and headed a department of political science at Howard University, became the first black to receive a doctorate in political science (Harvard, 1934), and helped Swedish sociologist Gunnar Myrdal complete research for *An American Dilemma* (1944). He worked for the Office of Strategic Services in World War II. With the State Department (1944-46), he wrote the trusteeship sections of the U. N. Charter, headed the U. N. Trusteeship Division (1946), became secretary of the Palestine Commission (1948), and mediated an end to the Arab-Israeli war in 1949. He also served as Dag Hammarskjold's special representative in the Congo in 1960. Though not in the forefront of the civil rights movement, he participated in the marches on Selma (1963) and Montgomery (1965).

BUNKER HILL, BATTLE OF

Black patriots who fought during the Battle of Bunker Hill included Peter Salem, Barzillai Lew, and Salem Poor.

BURGESS, JOHN M.

Clergyman (b. 1909). He was the first black to supervise white and black parishes of the Protestant Episcopal Church in America and the first to preside over a diocese. Bishop Burgess heads the diocese of Massachusetts.

BURNHAM, LINDON FORBES SAMPSON

Prime minister of Guyana. He led his country to independence on May 22, 1966, as head of the People's National Congress. A

74

moderate, his goals were to promote racial harmony, maintain good relations with the United States and Britain, and advance the political and economic unity of the Caribbean countries. After Guyana became a 'cooperative republic' within the Commonwealth of nations on February 23, 1970, he pledged to rid the nation of its 'colonial mentality' and channel its energies into 'a national system of cooperative ventures.' Born on February 20, 1923, he studied law at London University. He returned to British Guyana to become the cofounder of the People's Progressive Party. In 1955 the PPP split and he headed the PNC.

BURLEIGH, HARRY T.
Musician (1866-1949). He sang, composed and arranged many negro spirituals. The most famous black musician in the first decades of the twentieth century, he studied with Antonin Dvorak and sang for him spirituals whose melodies the Czech composer incorporated into his Fifth Symphony. Burleigh taught voice at the National Conservatory of Music and was baritone soloist at St. George's Episcopal Church in New York City and at Temple Emanuel. He also sang in J. P. Morgan's home and at his funeral, performed before American and European audiences, and twice gave command performances for Edward VII.

BURNETT, CALVIN
Artist (b. 1921). He has taught and lectured thoughout the nation and has illustrated several books. His works are in the collections of the Boston Public Library, the Fogg Museum of Fine Arts, and several colleges.

BURNS, ANTHONY
Fugitive slave whose arrest in Boston in 1854 so aroused the people that no fugitive was ever again returned from Massachusetts. Two thousand troops were required to suppress the mobs that attacked the federal courthouse where he was held and return him to his master.

BURRELL, BERKELEY G.
Businessman, president of the National Business League, and

co-author (with white John Seder) of *Getting It Together* (1971), offering profiles of several black businessmen who have recently achieved prominence.

BURROUGHS, MARGARET GOSS

Artist (b. 1917). She is the founder and director of the Chicago Museum of Negro History and Art.

BURROUGHS, NANNIE H.

Educator and religious church worker (1883-1961). She founded the National Training School for Women in Washington, D. C., in 1909.

BURWELL, L. L.

Physician. A graduate of Leonard Medical School, he became a successful practitioner in Selma, Alabama, in the early part of the century.

BUSH, GEORGE

Pioneer (1791-1867). A servant for a French family living in the region now known as Missouri, he fought under Andrew Jackson at New Orleans in the War of 1812, reached the Pacific coast in the service of the Hudson's Bay Company (1820), returned to Missouri as a cattle rancher (1830-43), traveled with his family and others over the old Oregon Trail to the Columbia River valley, and settled on the shores of Puget Sound (1849). The colony which he organized and led gave the United States a basis for claiming the land south of the 49th parallel. His son, William Owen Bush, became an influential member of the first state legislature of Washington.

BUSH, WILLIAM H.

Musician (b. 1961). He was organist at large churches for many years. In 1904 he was chosen to represent his state (Connecticut) at the St. Louis exposition.

BUSING

One means used to promote desegregation of public schools. The legal power to require busing derives from Supreme Court decisions, beginning in 1954. See Desegregation. See Swann v. Charlotte-Mecklenburg County, N. C.

BUTLER, H. R.

Physician. A successful practitioner in Atlanta, he became chairman of the first executive board of the National Medical Association (1895).

C

CABLE, THEODORE

Athlete. He held the intercollegiate championship in the hammer throw (Harvard, 1912 and 1913).

CAESAR

Pilot in the Navy of Virginia. The slave of Carter Rarrant of Hampton, he was cited for gallantry aboard the schooner *Patriot* during the American Revolution.

CAILLOUX, ANDRE

Civil War officer. A prominent, bilingual Catholic layman who boasted that he was the 'blackest man in America,' Captain Cailloux was educated in Paris. Idolized by his men, he died in the Union assault on Port Hudson, Louisiana (1963), having continued to lead his company, the color company, even after his left arm had been shattered.

CAIN, RICHARD HARVEY

Public official, clergyman, and educator (1825-1887). He served two terms as South Carolina's Congressman (1873-75 and 1877-79), became a bishop of the AME Church in 1880, and later served as president of Paul Quinn College in Waco, Texas.

CALDWELL, BEN

Playwright. One of the young militants associated with LeRoi Jones, he has written *Militant Preacher, Riot Sale or Dollar Psyche Fake Out, The Job,* and *Mission Accomplished.*

CALHOUN V. LATIMER

U. S. supreme court decision (1964) ordering the trial court to consider whether the school desegregation program was proceeding fast enough in Atlanta.

CALIVER, AMBROSE

Public official (b. 1894). He was a member of President Franklin Roosevelt's 'Black Cabinet.' In 1938 he was appointed chief of adult education in the U. S. office of education.

CALLENDER, GEORGE

Musician (b. 1918). 'Red' Callender made his record debut with Louis Armstrong in 1937. He was a versatile musician, mastering the tuba and bass as well as the alto horn. He wrote the pop hit, 'Primrose Lane' (1959).

CALLENDER'S CONSOLIDATED MINSTRELS

Famous minstrel troupe that toured Europe in 1882. Billy Kersands and Sam Lucas, the greatest of the early comedians, were members of the troupe. See Hicks, George B.

CALLENDER'S ORIGINAL GEORGIA MINSTRELS

Famous minstrel troupe that toured Europe in 1876. See Hicks, George B.

CALLOWAY, CAB

Musician (b. 1907). He has performed in the Cotton Club, Connie's Inn, the Savoy, and elsewhere. He is famous for his rendition of 'Minnie the Moocher.'

CAMPANELLA, ROY

Athlete (b. 1920). At the crest of his career with the Brooklyn Dodgers, he had won three most valuable player awards in the National League. In 1953 he had a .312 batting average, 142 runs batted in, and 41 home runs.

CAMPBELL, E. SIMMS

Cartoonist (1906-1971). A prolific and eminent cartoonist and illustrator for Esquire magazine and King Features, he was the creator of 'Esky,' the popeyed character who appeared on the cover of Esquire. He was the first black commercial artist to publish in major magazines.

CAMPBELL, JAMES EDWIN

Educator and poet (1867-1895). He taught school in Ohio and West Virginia before moving to Chicago, where he worked as a newsman for the *Times-Herald* and wrote poems in the negro dialect. He was credited by Richard Linthicum, editor of the Sunday *Times-Herald*, with portraying 'the philosophy and the humor of the race' in his poetry. His works include *Driftings and Gleanings* (1887) and *Echoes from the Cabin and Elsewhere* (1895).

CAMPBELL, MILT

Athlete. Powerful, versatile, and precocious, he excelled in football, track, swimming, and wrestling. In 1952 the 18-year-old athlete qualified for the Olympic contests and finished second; in 1956 he won a gold medal in the decathlon.

CANTERBURY SCHOOL

A school for black females, started in 1833 by Prudence Crandall, a white Quaker teacher. It was closed for the protection of the students after it was attacked by villagers. Miss Crandall had successfully contested a state law against free establishment of schools for blacks.

CAP

See Community Alert Patrol.

CARDOZO, FRANCIS LOUIS

Public official (1837-1903). Born in Charleston of a Jewish father and a mother of mixed ancestry, he was educated abroad and held high positions in the state government of South

Carolina during Reconstruction. He pastored Temple Street Congregational Church in New Haven, Connecticut, headed Avery Institute, served as a delegate to the South Carolina constitutional convention of 1868, was elected secretary of state (1868-72) and treasurer (1872-77). Unjustly convicted by the Democrats who regained political control, he was pardoned by the governor, moved to Washington to serve in the U. S. treasury and post office, and became principal of the city's negro high schools (1884-96).

CAREY, ARCHIBALD J., JR.

Clergyman and public official (b. 1908). A lawyer and business executive, he was the first black man to head a committee on government employment policy. President Eisenhower appointed him vice chairman of the committee in 1957. He had served as alternate delegate to the United Nations, 1953-56.

CAREY, LOTT

Slave who became foreman of a tobacco factory in Richmond, Virginia, gained his freedom, and served as a Baptist missionary to Liberia.

CARLOS, JOHN

Athlete. In 1968 he joined Tommie Smith in raising a black-gloved fist (the Black Power salute) at an Olympic victory ceremony following the 200-meter race. Their gesture almost provoked an international incident.

CARMEN JONES

Black version of Georges Bizet's opera. It captivated New York audiences when it opened in 1943.

CARMICHAEL, STOKELY

Black Power militant (b. 1942). Symbolizing revolutionary black leadership, he opened a new chapter in the civil rights movement when he became chairman of the SNCC on May 15, 1966, embraced retaliatory violence, proclaimed that full freedom must come before integration, and reduced white policymakers to the role of subordinates. Born in Trinidad, he moved to Harlem at the age of eleven. During his senior year at Bronx High School of Science, he joined CORE's youth group in picketing Woolworth's. While majoring in philosophy at Howard University, he was active in civil rights causes, and he was frequently beaten and arrested. After he graduated in 1964, he worked full-time for SNCC, travelling throughout the nation and delivering vitriolic attacks against white society. Replacing John Lewis as SNCC chairman in May 1966, he publicized the concept of Black Power, particularly on the Meredith March that June, then stepped down in May 1967 in favor of H. Rap Brown. He traveled throughout the world, urging violence and destruction of the existing system of government in the U. S. He became Prime Minister of the Black Panther party early in 1968 and was expelled by SNCC in May. Then, all but relinquishing his leadership in the Black Movement, he embarked upon a course of study and travel in Africa and elsewhere in an effort to spread pan-Africanism and Black Power ideas throughout the world.

CARMOUCHE, PIERRE L.

Army officer. In 1898 he volunteered to serve in the Spanish-American War, recruited 250 men, and went to Cuba as a 1st lieutenant in the 9th U. S. Volunteer Infantry.

CARNEY, HARRY

Musician. In the 1920s he played the saxophone with Duke Ellington's Kentucky Club orchestra.

CARNEY, PHILLITA TOYIA

In 1971 she became the first black homecoming queen in the history of the University of Utah.

CARNEY, WILLIAM H.

Patriot (b. 1840). The hero of the 54th Massachusetts Regiment in the Civil War rescued the flag from a wounded color sergeant and passed through a volley of enemy bullets to deliver it to a squad of his own regiment, shouting 'The Old Flag never touched the ground!' That flag is enshrined in Boston's Memorial Hall. Sergeant Carney was awarded the Congressional Medal of Honor (1863).

CAROLINE, J. C.
Athlete. In 1953 he went beyond the yardage record set by Red Grange in 1923. Playing for the University of Illinois, he gained 1354 yards, vs. the 1260 record set by Grange.

CARR, HENRY
Athlete. One of the nation's great runners, he competed in the Tokyo Olympics, winning both the 220-yard and the 200-meter sprints and setting new world records.

CARRIE STEELE ORPHANAGE
Founded by Mrs. Steele in 1889, by 1904 the Fulton County, Georgia, home had cared for some 500 children.

CARROLL, DIAHANN
Entertainer (b. 1935). One of the most successful blacks in television, she is known by millions of viewers as 'Julia.' She played Myrt in the movie *Carmen Jones* (1954), Clara in *Porgy and Bess* (1959), and in a Broadway musical written especially for her by Richard Rodgers, *No Strings* (1962). She appeared in several clubs, movies, and television shows before beginning her own television comedy series, 'Julia,' in 1968.

CARROLLTON MASSACRE
Twenty negroes were killed at Carrollton, Mississippi, on March 17, 1886.

CARTER, BEN
Actor (1912-1946). He was a member of the popular team of Carter and Moreland. He received an award from the Inter-

84

national Film and Radio Guild for his performance in *Crash Dive*, a movie in which he played a serious role.

CARTER, BENNET L.
Musician (b. 1907). He gained national recognition as a composer when he wrote much of the original music and played backgrounds for *M Squad* on television. He has also been seen and heard in many films, including *The View from Pompey's Head* and *Snows of Kilimanjaro*.

CARTER, JIMMY
Athlete. He defeated Lauro Salas in 1953 to win the lightweight boxing title.

CARTER, JOHN
Modern composer. He wrote *Requiem Seditiosam* to honor the memory of Medgar Evers.

CARVER, GEORGE WASHINGTON
Agricultural chemist (1864-1943). After completing his undergraduate and graduate studies at Iowa State College, he became director of the department of agricultural research at Tuskegee Institute (1896) and began a series of creative experiments to improve the economy of the South. From peanuts he developed some 300 synthetic products, including milk, coffee, flour, dyes, and soap; from sweet potatoes another 118 products, including starch, vinegar, and molasses; and from pecan nuts still another 60 useful products. He taught soil improvement, crop diversity, and systematic botany. He wrote many scientific papers, lectured widely, and earned many distinctions. His birthplace, near Carthage, Missouri, is a national monument. See Margaret Van Vechten Holt (Rackham Holt, pseud.), *George Washington Carver, an American Biography* (2d ed., revised, 1963).

CARY, LOTT
Missionary. Born a slave, he bought his freedom, helped to

organize the Richmond African Baptist Missionary Society, and served as a missionary to Africa.

CARY, MARY A. S.
Anti-slavery crusader (1823-1893). In 1850 she moved to Canada and helped fugitives to reach freedom there. In 1854 she began publishing *The Provincial Freeman,* a weekly paper devoted to the interests of fugitives.

CASEY, BERNIE
Athlete and artist (b. 1939). Born in Wyco, West Virginia, where his father was a mine laborer, he has excelled as a professional football player (he starred six seasons for the San Francisco Forty-Niners) and as an artist. He has also published a book of poetry.

CASOR, JOHN
See Johnson, Anthony.
CASSELL, ALBERT J.
Architect (b. 1895). As professor and head of the department of architecture at Howard, he drafted plans and supervised the construction of many of the university buildings.

CATO
Leader of a slave revolt that started on a plantation at Stono, South Carolina, in 1739. Thirty slaves and many whites were killed. A few slaves escaped to freedom.

CATLETT, ELIZABETH
Contemporary artist (b. 1915). She is a sculptor, painter, and print-maker.

CAUCUS, BLACK
See Black Caucus.

CAYTON, HORACE R.
Sociologist (b. 1901). A grandson of Hiram Revels, he

co-authored *Black Metropolis: A Study of Negro Life in a Northern City* (1945).

CENTER FOR BLACK EDUCATION
See Black Studies.

CENTRAL COLLEGE IN MCGRAWVILLE
See McGrawville Central College.

CESAR
Nineteenth-century medical practitioner. He was given his freedom by the South Carolina general assembly for his discovery of a treatment for a rattlesnake bite (published in the *South Carolina Gazette,* February 25, 1851).

CHARLESTON CONSPIRACY
In 1822 Denmark Vesey was alleged to have organized a conspiracy to seize the city of Charleston, South Carolina, and kill most of the whites. See Vesey, Denmark.

CHAMBERLAIN, WILT
Athlete (b. 1936). The greatest basketball scorer and gate attraction in the history of the sport, he received a yearly salary of $250,000, the highest of any American athlete. Named 'Wilt the Stilt' because of his height (seven feet, one inch), he prefers to be called 'The Big Dipper.'

CHARLES, EZZARD
Athlete. In 1949 he became the only black boxer to win the heavyweight title in an elimination bout. He won over Jersey Joe Walcott at Chicago, then over Joe Louis at New York in 1950.

CHARLES, RAY
Musician (b. 1932). An outstanding 'soul' singer, he is also a pianist, bandleader, composer, and saxophonist. Born in Albany, Georgia, he attended a state school for the blind in St. Augustine,

Florida. He began recording for Atlantic Records in 1954 but scored his first smash hit five years later on an ABC-Paramount release, 'Georgia on My Mind.' His 1963 recording, 'I Can't Stop Loving You,' sold two and a half million copies. Born Ray Charles Robinson, he dropped his surname to avoid confusion with 'Sugar' Ray Robinson.

CHARLTON, CORNELIUS
Hero of the Korean War. Sergeant Charlton received the congressional Medal of Honor for his heroism.

CHARLTON, SAMUEL
Patriot (1760-1843). Serving in the Revolutionary War as a substitute for his master, he fought at the Battle of Monmouth, in New Jersey, on June 28, 1778, the last major engagement in the North. After he had been given his freedom and a lifetime pension through his master's will, he moved to New York City.

CHASE, BARBARA
Contemporary artist. Her sculpture, always very personal, is at times remininscent of Giacometti.

CHASE, HYMAN Y.
Scientist. A student of Ernest E. Jut's at Howard, he made important studies on the effect of radiation upon animal cells.

CHATANOOGA NATIONAL MEDICAL COLLEGE
An obscure college for black medical students. During its brief existence the Tennessee school is listed as having had nine students and one graduate at the end of the 1903-04 session.

CHAUVIN, LOUIS
Early blues pianist.

CHAVIS, JOHN
Educator (c. 1763-1838). He is supposed to have run the best college preparatory schools in North Carolina. His pupils

included future governors, diplomats, and congressmen. A licensed Presbyterian minister and a missionary among blacks in Maryland, North Carolina, and Virginia, he is supposed to have been a pawn in a wager between two North Carolina gentlemen involving the capacity of a negro to learn. He attended Princeton and Washington Academy (now Washington and Lee University).

CHEATHAM, HENRY P.
Public official. He served as congressman from North Carolina, 1889-93.

CHE-CHO-TER
Wife of Seminole chief Osceola. Her capture and enslavement triggered the Seminole War. Famed for her beauty, she chose as her name the Seminole expression meaning Morning Dew.

CHEROKEE BILL
Outlaw (1876-1896). One of the most notorious outlaws in Indian Territory, he was born Crawford Goldsby at Fort Concho, Texas. His father, George Goldsby, was one of the famous Buffalo Soldiers.

CHERRY, GWENDOLYN SAWYER
Lawyer. She taught school for 17 years before becoming the first black to enroll in the University of Miami law school. The only negro woman lawyer in the state of Florida, she heads the legal department of a Neighborhood Center of the Federal Economic Opportunity Program.

CHERRY, PROPHET F. S.
Cult leader. See Church of God.

CHESNUTT, CHARLES W.
Lawyer, educator, and writer (1858-1932). He taught in North Carolina, worked as a journalist in New York, then returned to Cleveland, his birthplace, and began a lifelong career

in law (1887-1932). He contributed short stories imbued with his knowledge of black culture to various magazines and was encouraged by the response to these stories to publish his first volume, *The Conjure Woman* (1899). He received the Spingarn Medal in 1928. His writings include *The House Behind the Cedars* (1900), *The Marrow of Tradition* (1901), and *The Colonel's Dream* (1905).

CHICAGO RACE RIOT

In 1919 there were 25 riots in the United States. The one that made the deepest impression was the Chicago riot that resulted in the deaths of 25 black and 13 white people.

CHISHOLM, SHIRLEY

Congresswoman (b. 1924). The first black woman to serve in the U. S. Congress, she won her seat in 1968 by defeating James Farmer, her nationally known Liberal Republican opponent. Born in Brooklyn, she majored in sociology and graduated from Brooklyn College cum laude, earned a master's degree in elementary education at Columbia University, directed a nursery in Brownsville, headed a child-care center in Manhattan (1953-59), served as educational consultant on day care for New York City children (1959-64), and was elected to the state legislature on the Democratic ticket in 1964. Publicly opposing House leadership after her election in 1968, she won an unprecedented committee reassignment to Veterans Affairs.

A Gallup Poll in 1971 placed her among the ten women most admired by Americans. In 1972 she sought the nomination for the presidency on the Democratic Party ticket.

CHRISTIANA RIOT

Incident that occurred in Christiana, Pennsylvania, in 1851. A black vigilance committee killed two men who had come to claim three runaways. The fugitives escaped to Toronto, Canada.

CHRISTOPHE, HENRI

Patriot (1767-1820). After serving as a sergeant in the black legion commanded by Viscount de Fontanges at the siege of Savannah, Georgia (1779), he returned to Haiti, wounded but with new concepts of freedom. A confidant and successor of Toussaint L'Ouverture, he tried to establish a monarchy of the pure blacks (rather than the mulattoes, who were in control during the republic of Pétion).

CHURCH MEMBERSHIP

More than 11 million blacks belong to black churches, and 1.6 million have joined predominantly white congregations. Since colonial times participation in the life of the church has responded to the spiritual needs of blacks and also provided them with an opportunity to develop leadership qualities. See Churches.

CHURCH OF GOD

The cult known as the Church of God or Black Jews was founded by a man from the Deep South called Prophet F. S. Cherry. Self-educated, he was knowledgeable in Yiddish and Hebrew, used the Talmud as the sacred text of the cult, and insisted that the Black People were the earth's original inhabitants. He predicted that Hitler would drive the Pope out of Rome and that the world would never be right until Black Jews occupied high places then occupied by whites.

CHURCHES

Not satisfied with the practice of occupying pews in the rear of a church or in the gallery, Negro worshipers readily joined independent churches after Richard Allen and Absalon Jones founded, respectively, the Bethel African Methodist Church and the St. Thomas Protestant Episcopal Church in 1794. Each church was accepted in the communion of its denomination, but the desire for complete independence later caused the Bethel group of Philadelphia to join in 1816 with other newly formed churches and form a new branch of Methodism, headed by Bishop Allen and popularly known as the A. M. E. Negroes in New York City, who had organized a Methodist congregation in 1796, refused to join the Allenites. In 1821 the New York congregation, now calling themselves the African Methodist Episcopal Zion Church, organized as an independent body, popularly known today as A. M. E. Z. Under their first bishop, James Varick, they extended their influence far beyond New York City. After 1800 Negro Baptists, who previously had worshiped with whites, became began to establish independent churches. Thomas Paul, who later (1823) went to Haiti as a missionary, was active in the movement to establish independent Negro churches. A many-sided institution, the independent Negro church provided educational opportunities for boys and girls and served as a training ground for leaders. It also launched the colored convention movement. See E. Franklin Frazier, *The Negro Church in America* (1964).

CINCINNATI

Site of a race riot (August 10, 1829) that caused more than one thousand negroes to leave the city for Canada.

CINQUE, JOSEPH

Leader of a slave revolt (1811-1852). He and his 38 companions escaped from the hold of the *Amistad* and murdered all of the crew except two Spaniards who had purchased the slaves in Havana. Sighted off Long Island, the ship was brought ashore and the multineers imprisoned. Strong public reaction and the efforts of John Quincy Adams brought them their freedom to return to Africa. See Amistad.

CIVIL RIGHTS ACTS OF 1866

The first Civil Rights Act of 1866, enacted March 13, over President Andrew Johnson's veto and titled 'An Act to protect all Persons in the United States in their Civil Rights, and furnish the Means of their Vindication,' overturned the *Dred Scott* decision by giving negroes 'full and equal benefit of all law . . . as is enjoyed by white citizens.'

The second Civil Rights Act of 1966, passed on May 21, made it a criminal offense to kidnap a person with the intent of selling him or enslaving him.

CIVIL RIGHTS ACT OF 1867

On March 2, 1867, Congress passed 'An Act to abolish and forever prohibit the System of Peonage in the Territory of New Mexico and other Parts of the United States.'

CIVIL RIGHTS ACT OF 1870

The Civil Rights Act of 1870, known as the Enforcement Act, was passed on May 31. It imposed criminal sanctions for interference with voting rights granted under the Fifteenth Amendment. Sections 3 and 4 were ruled unconstitutional in 1876 (United States v. Reese), Section 5 in 1903 (James v. Bowman), and Section 16 in 1906 (Hodges v. United States).

CIVIL RIGHTS ACT OF 1871

Adopted April 20, 1871, the statute was titled 'An Act to enforce the Provisions of the Fourteenth Amendment.' Section 2 of the Act imposed penalties for depriving 'any person or any class of persons of the equal protection of the laws.' This section was declared unconstitutional (United States v. Harris, 1883, and Baldwin v. Franks, 1887).

CIVIL RIGHTS ACT OF 1875

Passed on March 1, 1875, the statute provided 'That all persons within the jurisdiction of the United States shall be entitled to the full and equal enjoyment of the accommodations, advantages, facilities, and privileges of inns, public conveyances on land or water, theaters, and other places of public amusement.' The act was declared unconstitutional in 1883, when the U. S. supreme court heard five suits involving individuals who had refused to admit 'persons of color' to hotels and theaters.

CIVIL RIGHTS ACT OF 1957

Enacted on September 9, 1957, the first civil rights bill since 1875 established a nonpartisan civil rights commission, strengthened the civil rights provisions of the United States Code, prescribed nondiscriminatory qualifications for the selection of federal jurors, and authorized the Justice Department to eliminate irregularities in federal elections. The measure was officially titled 'An act to provide means of further securing and protecting the civil rights of persons within the jurisdiction of the United States.'

CIVIL RIGHTS ACT OF 1960

Passed on May 6, 1960, the measure empowered the Justice Department to act on behalf of an injured voter wherever a 'pattern or practice' of discrimination existed. It required officials to preserve records in federal elections and provided for the appointment of voting referees.

CIVIL RIGHTS ACT OF 1964

Hailed as the most far-reaching legislative enactment since the 1870s, the Civil Rights Act of 1964 undertook to guarantee to all citizens the right to vote in national elections; access to public accommodations, facilities, and education; and equal opportunity to secure employment and participate in federal assistance programs.

CIVIL RIGHTS ACT OF 1968

Passed in April, the act contained an open-housing clause covering sales of certain buildings. The U. S. supreme court went a step further in June and upheld an 1866 statute giving all citizens the right to sell, lease, and hold property equally.

CIVIL RIGHTS CASES OF 1883

Most of the Reconstruction legislation designed to give equality to negroes was struck down by the Supreme Court decision in the Civil Rights Cases of 1883. Five suits involving the denial of admission of 'person of color' to public places were founded on the first and second sections of the Civil Rights Act of 1875. The Court reasoned that denial of equal accommodations does not impose a 'badge of slavery' upon the person affected, and it held that the 1875 Act went beyond the authority granted to Congress under both the Thirteenth and Fourteenth Amendments. Justice John Marshall Harlan dissented.

CIVIL RIGHTS COMMISSION

Nonpartisan commission established by the Civil Rights Act of 1957. It was empowered to gather evidence on voting violations.

CIVIL RIGHTS MOVEMENT

Determined white resistance to desegregation in the South and strong determination of whites and blacks to overcome this resistance prompted thousands of white Americans to join forces with blacks to form a dynamic civil rights movement in the 1960s. Black college students organized SNCC, which coordinated activities aimed at desegregating public accommodations throughout the South. Lunch counter demonstrations, economic boycotts, wade-ins at public beaches, and kneel-ins in segregated churches provoked violent reaction. CORE introduced Freedom Rides and drew support from the SCLC and the NAACP. The Civil Rights Act of 1964 was the outgrowth of the movement.

CIVIL RIGHTS REVOLUTION

Term designating the changes that were brought about in the area of civil rights during the period initiated by the Montgomery bus boycott of 1956 and concluded by passage of the Civil Rights Act of 1964. Significant steps toward the attainment of the goals of the civil rights leaders were the introduction of techniques of passive resistance such as the sit-in (1960), the decision of CORE to send Freedom Riders through the South (1961), the Albany Movement (1961), and three developments in 1963. These were the voter registration drive in Mississippi, spearheaded by SCLC, the Birmingham marches in which Martin Luther King figured prominently, and the March on Washington, in which a quarter of a million Americans participated. See Arnold Rose, *Assuring Freedom to the Free* (1964); John P. Roche, *The Quest for the Dream: The Development of Civil Rights and Human Relations in Modern America* (1963); and Leonard Broom and Gleen Norval, *The Politics Transformation of the Negro American* (1967).

CIVIL WAR

To Abraham Lincoln, whose election to the presidency and the subsequent secession of the Southern states precipitated the Civil War, the system of slavery was one of the main causes of the conflict. The activities of Negroes on the battlefield and on the home front contributed significantly to the final victory of the Union forces, and the emancipation of almost four million slaves gave concrete expression to one of their major goals, the promotion of human liberty. After hostilities broke out, following a Confederate attack on Fort Sumter, on April 12, 1861, President Lincoln issued a call for 75,000 men. In city after city, negroes offered their services, only to be refused. Later, however, as both North and South girded for a long engagement, prejudices were suspended as both sides tried to manipulate Negroes for military purposes. On August 6, 1861, Congress authorized confiscation of property used to support the rebel cause and the freeing of slaves forming a part of such property. The measure was aimed at Confederate use of slaves as military laborers. An act of March 13, 1862, forbade military commanders to return fugitive slaves to their masters. A month later 3,000 Negroes living in the District of Columbia were given their freedom. Early in June Congress authorized the exchange of diplomats with Haiti and Liberia. Shortly thereafter, Congress abolished slavery in the territories, freed rebel-owned slaves in Union hands, and authorized Negroes to perform 'any labor of any war service.' The immediate relatives of volunteer slaves were to be given their freedom. A preliminary emancipation proclamation issued on September 22, 1862, had been preceded by unsuccessful attempts to bring about compensated emancipation and deportation of Negroes. On April 10, 1862, Congress urged that states adopting a plan for the gradual abolition of slavery should be given federal financial aid. The same month, Congress also provided funds to aid in colonizing Negroes of the District of Columbia and, later, the slaves of disloyal masters. Distant Liberia offered to receive colonists, but attempts to establish refuges in Chiriqui, Panama, and in Cow Island, Haiti, failed. Despite the failure to provide a haven for freed slaves, Lincoln issued his proclamation on

96

January 1, 1863, freeing all slaves in the rebellious states, 'as a fit and necessary war measure for suppressing said rebellion.' Designed to deplete the manpower reserve in the South and enhance the Union cause abroad, the Emancipation Proclamation was received enthusiastically by Negroes. Ellen Watkins Harper expressed the attitude of most Negroes when she wrote:

> It shall flash through all the ages;
> It shall light the distant years ;
> And eyes now dim with sorrow
> Shall be brighter through their tears.

Thus an edict that had been issued 'upon military necessity' and applied only to those states in rebellion was interpreted first by Negroes and later by the nation as a fresh restatement of the human quest for freedom. Soon after the outbreak of the war, Negroes began to seek refuge in Yankee camps, and the refusal of Union officers to return fugitives to their masters initiated a series of migrations, by individuals and by groups of freedom-minded slaves. After the Emancipation Proclamation was issued, Northern states competed with the federal government in tapping the new reservoir of manpower. In less than three months, Adjutant General Lorenzo Thomas raised twenty brigades of colored troops. By the end of the war, some 180,000 Negroes comprised almost 10 per cent of all Union enlistments. Negro soldiers distinguished themselves particularly at Port Hudson (May 27), Milliken's Bend (June 27), and Fort Wagner (July 18, 1863). Edwin M. Stanton, Secretary of War, writing to Lincoln on February 8, 1864, referred to their 'performing deeds of daring . . . with a heroism unsurpassed by soldiers of any other race.' Four Negroes serving in the Navy, which had never barred free Negroes from enlisting and began in September 1861 to sign up former slaves, won the Navy Medal of Honor. Among the Negro civilians who made noteworthy contributions to the war effort were the women who worked in hospitals and camps, gave help to former slaves, and taught in regions controlled by Union forces. By the time the Confederacy collapsed on April

9, 1865, the Negro had proven his worth on the battlefield and the home front, won his freedom, expressed his desire for the right to vote, and deepened his sense of identity with the nation he had served.

See Dudley Taylor Cornish, *The Sable Arm* (1956); Agnes McCarthy and Lawrence Reddick, *Worth Fighting For: A History of the Negro in the United States during the Civil War and Reconstruction* (1965); and Benjamin Quarles, *The Negro in the Civil War* (1953).

CLAFIN UNIVERSITY

Founded by the Methodist Episcopal Church at Orangesburg, South Carolina, in 1869, it was designed to train freedmen for leadership.

CLARK, HARVEY

Bus driver. In 1951 he caused an uproar in Cicero, Illinois, by moving into an apartment building occupied by white families. The NAACP later announced that the building had been bought for occupancy by white and black veterans.

CLARK, KENNETH B.

Psychologist (b. 1914). Active in projects involving black youths, Dr. Clark has published many scholarly works. After receiving his Ph. D. from Columbia (1940), he worked as a professor of psychology at City College of New York and as president of its Metropolitan Applied Research Center. He won the Spingarn Medal in 1961, served as director of Harlem Youth Opportunities Unlimited and the Social Dynamics Research Institute, and was elected president of the American Psychological Association. His writings include *Prejudice and Your Child* (1963) and *Dark Ghetto* (1965).

CLARK, PETER HUMPHRIES

Educator (1829-c. 1895). Active in the underground railroad before the Civil War, he became a labor leader and an outstanding leader in education. When he retired from the public school system of Cincinnati in 1886, he was the highest paid principal in the system.

CLARK, ROBERT

Public official. In the 1960s he became Mississippi's first black state legislator in 74 years.

CLARKE, JOHN HENRIK

Editor (b. 1915). Best known as a critic, anthologist, and editor, he has also published short stories and poetry. He was co-founder of *Harlem Quarterly,* book review editor of *Negro History Bulletin,* associate editor of *Freedomways; A Quarterly Review of the Negro Freedom Movement.*

CLAY, CASSIUS

See Muhammad Ali.

CLAY, WILLIAM L.

U. S. representative from Missouri. He has been active in the civil rights movement for many years. In 1955 he organized the St. Louis NAACP Youth Council and led demonstrations to force the city's restaurants to desegregate. He has co-sponsored all of the poverty legislation that has been passed by congress since his arrival in Washington.

CLAYTON, WILBUR

Musician (b. 1911). In 1945 he won the Esquire Gold Award as the best musician in the U. S. armed forces. His distinctive trumpet sound was first heard in the late 1930s, when he played with Count Basie. 'Buck' Clayton toured Europe with his own combo in 1959.

CLEAGE, ALBERT

Religious leader. He is an organizer and spokesman of the Black Messiah movement.

CLEAVER, ELDRIDGE

Writer and activist (b. 1935). Born in Wabbaseka, Arkansas, and largely self-educated during many years of imprisonment for offenses ranging from petty theft to rape, he has written several forceful essays on the Black Panther ideology and the social and economic forces that have generated it. 'The price of hating other human beings,' he wrote, 'is loving oneself less.' His autobiographical *Soul on Ice* (1968) reveals his determinism to end racism and his brilliant insights concerning its genesis. Drawn to the Black Muslims and then to the Black Panther party, he became minister of information to the revolutionary group before going into political exile in Algeria in 1968.

CLEF CLUB

A chartered jazz group organized by Jim Europe. In May 1912, a group of 125 performers associated with the club appeared on the stage of Carnegie Hall. Alain Locke called the 1912 concert of negro music 'the formal coming-out party.' The band helped to make Vernon and Irene Castle famous. Its members joined the 369th Regiment Band at the outbreak of World War I.

CLEMENT, RUFUS

Educator (b. 1900). President of Atlanta University, he was also named to the Atlanta Board of Education, in 1953.

CLEMENTS, EMMA CLARISSA

'American Mother's Mother.' In 1946 she became the first black woman to be honored with the title of 'American Mother's Mother.' The award was originated in 1935 by the Golden Rule Foundation. Mrs. Clements, now 71, lives in Kentucky and is the mother of 7.

CLINTON

Mississippi town torn by racial strife in 1875. Several negro leaders were killed on September 4, with estimates ranging between twenty and eighty.

CLOSE RANKS

Famed editorial written in July 1918 by W. E. B. Du Bois, in what he later called 'one of my periods of exhaltation. In his statement, published in *Crisis,* he said, in part: 'Let us . . . forget our special grievances and close our ranks shoulder to shoulder with our own white fellow citizens and the allied nations that are fighting for democracy.'

CLOTEL, OR THE PRESIDENT'S DAUGHTER

Novel marking the advent of the negro writer in America. William Wells Brown's classic work details the life of Clotel, the fictional daughter of Thomas Jefferson and his negro housekeeper.

CLOTHILDE

Last slave ship to land its cargo on American shores, at Mobile Bay, Alabama, in 1859.

COBB, JAMES A.

Jurist (d. 1958). He was appointed judge of the District of Columbia municipal court in 1926.

COBB, W. MONTAGUE

Physician (b. 1904). Active in the NAACP, he has taught at Howard since the 1930s. He became editor of the *Journal of the National Medical Association* in 1949 and introduced a section entitled 'The Integration Battle Front' as well as the inclusion of materials on black medical history, a field in which he is now recognized as the nation's principal authority. He created Imhotep to eliminate 'segregation in the fields of hospitalization and health.' He is the leading historian of blacks in medicine.

COBBS, PRICE M.

Psychiatrist (b. 1928). He has worked for a dozen years with black patients and has taught at the University of California. He co-authored, with William H. Grier, the best-selling book *Black Rage* (1968).

COFFEY, ALVIN A.

Pioneer. He traveled across the plains to California in 1849 as a slave, bought his freedom, settled down and became the founder of a long line of prosperous Californians.

COFFIN, LEVI

White abolitionist and reputed president of the Underground Railroad. See Reminiscences of Levi Coffin, the Reputed President of the Underground Railroad: Being a Brief History of the Labors of a Lifetime in Behalf of the Slave, with the Stories of Numerous Fugitives, Who Gained Their Freedom through His Instrumentality, and Many Other Incidents. Reprinted by Arno Press.

COKER, DANIER

Missionary. A slave, he escaped to New York and became one of the co-founders of the AME Church. In 1814 he went to Africa as a missionary.

COLE, BOB

Musician (1868-1911). In 1898 he wrote, produced, and directed the first musical comedy ever written by a negro for negro talent. *A Trip to Coontown,* with a plot and well-developed characters, was a complete departure from minstrelry and the first step in popularizing musical comedy.

COLE, NAT KING

Musician (1919-1965). Beginning as a jazz pianist, Cole became a popular singer with record sales of more than fifty million, including 'Nature Boy' and 'Mona Lisa.' He was the only black musician with his own network radio program in the early 1940s and the first with his own national television show (1956-57).

COLE, ROBERT

Musician. At the turn of the century, he teamed with J. Rosamond Johnson to produce Broadway musicals.

102

COLE, WILLIAM 'COZY'

Musician (b. 1909). He studied at Juilliard (1942-45) and won the Esquire Silver Award (1944). He is one of the few drummers familiar with every jazz style.

COLEMAN, JAMES D.

Educator (b. 1863). After graduating from Wayland Seminary in Washington, D. C. (1885), he taught there and at Blue Field State College in West Virginia.

COLEMAN, JOHN WESLEY

Public official (b. 1865). He helped the state of California to develop Venice and Santa Monica. He also served as deputy constable of Los Angeles county and township (1904-19) and operated a real estate and employment office.

COLEMAN, ORNETTE

Musician (b. 1930). He explored free jazz in the 1960s, developing a style of saxophone playing described by authorities as truly original even though derived from that of Charlie Parker. His singular ear enabled him to become the embodiment of both traditional jazz and bebop. See A. B. Spillman, *Black Music* (1966).

COLEMAN, ROBERT JR.

Mathematician (1915-1941). A Phi Beta Kappa graduate of Western Reserve University at the age of 17, he was able to complete the requirements for a Ph. D. (Columbia, 1941) with the help of a Rosenwald Fellowship. He did not live long enough to develop his genius.

COLERIDGE-TAYLOR, SAMUEL

Musician (1875-1912). Already recognized as one of England's foremost composers, teachers, and conductors, he heard the Fisk Jubilee Singers during their first tour of England (1899), made three trips to America, and used negro thematic materials in his compositions.

103

COLFAX MASSACRE
In Grant Parish, Louisiana, on April 13, 1873, more than sixty negroes were massacred.

COLLINS, GEORGE W.
U. S. Representative from Illinois.

COLLINS, JANET
Ballerina. She was the first black dancer to appear in a leading role at the Metropolitan Opera (1951, in *Aida*).

COLONIAL AND REVOLUTIONARY WARS
At first Negroes served in militia companies in both northern and southern colonies. Negroes enlisted for service in the French and Indian Wars with a view to procuring their freedom. Prominent among those serving as militiamen prior to and in the early days of the Revolution were Pomp Blackman, Prince Estabrook, Peter Salem, Barzillai Lew, Salem Poor, and William Flora. Determined that the federal army would not become a refuge for runaways, the high command of the Continental Army, meeting in Cambridge on October 8, 1775, agreed to exclude both slaves and free Negroes. Objections were raised by Negroes already in service, and General George Washington recommended to Congress that these men be allowed to reenlist. Assuming that the war would soon end, all states except Virginia passed similar regulations. As the war dragged on, however, the need for additional recruits brought about a policy reversal. Recruitment of Negroes increased after Congress fixed quotas for each state in 1777 and some states allowed white draftees to supply Negro substitutes. In March 1779 the Congress unsuccessfully urged Georgia and South Carolina to raise 3,000 Negroes, offering $1,000 per head to each owner and freedom to and $50 to each slave. Outside the South, enlistments increased until, according to an official statement dated August 24, 1778, a total of 755 Negroes were scattered throughout fourteen brigades, within the Continental Army. The New England states recruited sizable numbers and probably furnished more black soldiers

than any other section. Virginia probably recruited more than 500 for her land and sea forces.

A Negro soldier generally performed menial tasks, lacked identity, being carried on the rolls simply as 'A Negro Man,' and held the rank of private. Few Negroes served in the cavalry or artillery. The only battle in which a predominately Negro regiment was conspicuous as a racial group was the Battle of Rhode Island. There the First Rhode Island Regiment held its ground during four hours of hard fighting against British-Hessian forces and inflicted many casualties on the enemy.

The Continental Navy and the state navies freely recruited Negroes for service in the lowliest ranks. South Carolina, Maryland, and Virginia also used them as pilots. Among the Negro pilots who achieved recognition were Caesar, who steered the schooner *Patriot*, and Minny, a Virginia pilot who met his death while trying to board an enemy ship.

Some Negroes such as James Forten, joined as privateers. In addition, some were used as guides, messengers, spies, and military laborers.

The British, as early as November 1775, encouraged Negroes to seek freedom behind their lines. Lord Dunmore, Royal Governor of Virginia, persuaded some 700 slaves to join his forces. Tens of thousands of slaves served the British in a variety of war-related tasks, leaving not more than 1,000 to bear arms. After the war came to an end, the British evacuated the Negroes to whom they had promised freedom: 4,000 from Savannah, 4,000 from New York, and 6,000 from Charleston. See Lorenzo J. Greene, *The Negro in Colonial New England, 1620-1776* (1942); Benjamin Quarles, *The Negro in the American Revolution* (1961).

COLONIAL SLAVERY

Blacks were listed as servants in the census counts of 1623 and 1624. Statutory recognition of slavery in Virginia came in 1661, when a law directed at white servants mentioned negroes and in 1662, when the colony indicated that newborn children would be bond or free according to the mother's condition.

105

Dissatisfaction inspired plots to rebel as early as 1687 and required the elaboration of a slave code based on practices in the Caribbean. In Maryland a law enacted in 1663 attempted to reduce all blacks to slavery even though some were free. A 1671 law stipulated that their slave status would not be affected by conversion to Christianity. Incentives in the form of land grants to settlers who brought in slaves resulted in an influx of negroes into the Carolinas; by 1724 there were three times as many negroes as whites living in the colony. Recalcitrant slaves in Georgia could escape into Florida. The middle colonies recognized slavery as a legitimate institution in 1684 and refined the slave code to such an extent that New York was able to pass a law in 1706 stating that baptism did not provide grounds for a slave's claim to freedom. New England participated in the slave trade but did not subject negroes to harsh codes. Since restrictions against the education of slaves were not so great as in other regions, negroes in New England frequently learned to read and write with little difficulty. See Lorenzo J. Greene, *The Negro in Colonial New England: 1620-1776* (1942), and Lerone Bennett Jr., *Before the Mayflower* (1962).

COLONIZATION

All-negro assemblies called to discuss the American Colonization Society's plan to send freed negroes to Africa unanimously condemned the plan. The first such assembly met in Bethel Church in Philadelphia in January 1817. Present were James Forten, Russell Parrott, Absalom Jones, and Richard Allen, along with 3,000 other persons. This assembly, like three others called 1817-19, recognized the evil effects that African expatriation would have on all negroes, slave and free.

COLOR LINE

The invisible boundary separating the races. Segregation in education, employment, labor unions, etc. was described in a famous book by Ray Stannard, *Following the Color Line* (1908).

106

COLORED METHODIST EPISCOPAL CHURCH

An offshoot of the Methodist Episcopal Church South, it came into existence in Jackson, Tennessee, in 1870.

COLORED CUMBERLAND PRESBYTERIAN CHURCH

Formed in 1869, the church was formed by black members of the Cumberland Presbyterian Church.

COLORED OPERA COMPANY

The first opera company organized by blacks, it was established in 1873, in Washington, D. C. John Esputa was its musical director.

COLORED PRIMITIVE BAPTIST CHURCH OF AMERICA

Church formed in 1865 by black members of the Primitive Baptist Church.

COLORED WOMEN'S LEAGUE OF WASHINGTON

First national organization for negro women. It was founded by Hallie Q. Brown of Wilberforce University, Ohio. Miss Brown formed the league in order to qualify negroes for inclusion in the planning of the Columbian Exhibition of 1893, after being told that membership on the managing board was open only to the representatives of a national organization.

COLTRANE, JOHN

Musician (1926-1967). He had a strong influence on young jazz musicians. Described as an impassioned, compulsive player, he made his professional debut as a saxophonist in 1945.

COLUMBUS' VOYAGE

Accompanying Christopher Columbus on his fourth voyage to the New World was Diego el Negro. Diego was the first black man to see America.

COMER, JAMES P.

Psychiatrist. After graduating from the medical school of

Howard University (1960), he studied public health, then joined the psychiatric residency program at Yale. He has studied the emergence of black power attitudes and doctrines. In 1969 he became the first black man to serve as associate dean of the Yale medical school.

COMMANDMENTS FOR THE VOLUNTEERS

A statement clearly defining the nonviolent techniques to be used in the drive to force concessions from the public officials of Birmingham, Alabama, in 1963. See Project C.

COMMISSION ON CIVIL RIGHTS, U. S.

A bipartisan agency established by the U. S. congress in 1957 to investigate complaints concerning voting rights, collect and serve as a national clearinghouse for information relating to denials of equal protection of the laws, and submit reports and recommendations to congress.

COMMISSION ON INTERRACIAL COOPERATION

Interracional group working in the South after World War I 'to make life . . . richer and more efficient for all the people.' Founded in April, 1919, it was mainly an educational agency. Its Association of Southern Women for the Prevention of Lynching was active in the fight against lynching, and the parent group used its influence to fight the Ku Klux Klan.

COMMITTEE AGAINST JIM CROW IN MILITARY SERVICE AND TRAINING

A negro civilian group headed by former army chaplain Grant Reynolds. Formed on October 10, 1947, the Committee persuaded President Harry S. Truman to issue an order creating a Committee on Equality of Treatment and Opportunity in the Armed Services and establishing equality of opportunity for all servicemen.

COMITTEE ON EQUAL EMPLOYMENT OPPORTUNITY

Created in April 1961 by President John F. Kennedy, the new

Committee was to bring about equality of opportunity in the federal government and in government contracts. The Committee also encouraged states and cities to enact laws against discrimination and labor unions to abolish segregated locals. By the end of 1962 a total of 21 states had passed fair employment legislation and the federal government had employed 292,836 negroes, representing 13.2 per cent of its employes.

COMMITTEE FOR IMPROVING THE INDUSTRIAL CONDITIONS OF NEGROES
See National Urban League.

COMMITTEE ON EQUALITY OF TREATMENT AND OPPORTUNITY IN THE ARMED FORCES
Named by President Harry S. Truman in 1948 to advise him on providing equality of opportunity for all servicemen, the Committee recommended in May 1950 that the Army, Navy, and Air Force rid themselves of every vestige of segregation.

COMMITTEE ON URBAN CONDITIONS AMONG NEGROES
See National Urban League.

COMMONWEALTH V. JENNISON
Legal case heard in Massachusetts in 1783 involving the treatment of a recalcitrant slave, Quock Walker, by Nathaniel Jennison. Chief Justice William Cushing set precedent in his charge to the jury by applying a written constitution directly as law. He held that 'the idea of slavery is inconsistent with our own conduct . . .; and there can be no such thing as perpetual servitude of a rational creature, unless his liberty is forfeited by some criminal conduct or given up by personal consent or contract.' The jury found Jennison guilty of assault and battery against his slave.

COMMUNITY ALERT PATROL
Group organized by the black people of Los Angeles, California, with federal funding, to protect members of the black com-

munity from police harassment and brutality. Organized following the 1965 Watts uprising, the CAP came to the rescue of people stopped for investigation and interrogation by police. The Black Panthers went a step further and initiated armed patrols.

COMMUNITY CONTROL

The principle of allowing the black community to participate in setting up a curriculum and selecting personnel for schools enrolling black children was established in 1966 when Intermediate School 201 in East Harlem went into operation. The movement for community control of schools soon spread across the nation.

COMMUNITY COUNCIL ON HOUSING

New York City group led by Jesse Gray. In 1963 the council began rent strikes against slum landlords. The courts refused to issue eviction orders until landlords made repairs requested by tenants.

COMPENSATED EMANCIPATION

A plan for ending slavery without civil war by offering payments to the owners of slaves. Payments from the sale of the public domain was rejected by northern legislators. Abolitionists objected to such a policy on moral grounds (sinners should not be paid for giving up their sins). Abraham Lincoln entertained the notion of compensated emancipation but saw it practiced only briefly in the District of Columbia.

COMPROMISE OF 1850

Though hailed as a final solution to the question of slavery in new territories, the Compromise of 1850 marked only a brief respite in the North-South conflict. Separate bills provided for the admission of California as a free state, the organization of Utah and New Mexico without mention of slavery, a more stringent law governing fugitive slaves, and prohibition of slave trade in the District of Columbia.

COMPROMISE OF 1877

In the disputed presidential election of 1876, Rutherford B. Hayes was the Republican candidate and Samuel Tilden his Democratic opponent. In 1877 Congress declared Hayes the winner, signaling a return toward slavery as the remaining troops were withdrawn from the South, which was granted home rule.

CONDUCTORS

Name given to those who helped slaves to escape to freedom on the underground railroad. Black conductors included John Mason, Elijah Anderson, Josiah Henson, Jane Lewis, and Harriet Tubman.

CONE, JAMES H.

Theologian. Dr. Cone teaches at Union Theological Seminary and is a leading theoretician of the black theology movement.

CONFERENCE OF COLORED MEN

On December 14, 1895, an important civil rights conference was held in Detroit, Michigan. The purpose of the conference was to stop the practice of lynching.

CONFESSIONS OF NAT TURNER, THE

See Nat Turner, the Confessions of.

CONFISCATION ACT OF 1861

Passed on August 6, the act declared that all slaves used against the Union were to become the prize and capture of the Union forces. See Contraband.

CONGA

A dance resulting from the fusion of African and European elements. It originated among the Congo negroes of Cuba.

CONGRESS OF AFRICAN PEOPLE

Meeting held in Atlanta in September 1970 to unite blacks

and blueprint political, social, and economic institutions to liberate them from oppression. Chaired by Hayward Henry, the meeting attracted 2,700 delegates, including 350 from 35 foreign countries.

CONGRESS OF RACIAL EQUALITY (CORE)

CORE, the oldest of the nonviolent direct action protest groups, was founded as a local group to combat discrimination. In 1942 CORE staged its first sit-in demonstration in a restaurant in Chicago and succeeded in bringing about its desegregation. James Farmer resigned as program director of the NAACP in 1961 to lead the organization which he had helped to found in 1942. Under his leadership (1961-65) CORE perfected Gandhi techniques of passive resistance, trained many young leaders in techniques of nonviolent protest, initiated Freedom Rides, and increased membership ('open to anybody who opposes racial discrimination') to 70,000, grouped in 146 chapters. After Floyd B. McKissick replaced him in 1966, the organization adopted a more aggressive approach to the achievement of full equality and freedom. Roy Innis took over the leadership of CORE in 1968 and promptly unveiled a three-point program of black liberation: (1) passage of the Community Self-Determination Bill to provide federally chartered community development corporations; (2) applying the theory that black participation at the community level (schools, police, etc.) should be proportionate to their numbers; and (3) adoption of a new federal constitution based on separatism. See Freedom Rides; McKissick, Floyd B.; Sit-Ins.

CONGRESSIONAL MEDAL OF HONOR

Between 1863 and 1968, 40 black soldiers won the Medal of Honor: Sgt. William Harvey Carney, 1863; Sgt. Major Christian A. Fleetwood, Sgt. Alfred B. Hilton, Cpl. Charles Veal, Sgt. Milton M. Holland, 1st Sgt. James E. Bronson, 1st Sgt. Powhatan Beatty, 1st Sgt. Robert A. Pinn, Sgt. Major Thomas R. Hawkins, Sgt. Alexander Kelly, Cpl. Miles James, Pvt. James Gardiner, 1st. Sgt. Edward Ratcliffe, Sgt. James H. Harris, Pvt.

William H. Barnes, and Sgt. Decatur Dorsey, 1864; Sgt. Emanuel Stance, 1870; Cpl. Clinton Greaves, 1877; Sgt. Thomas Boyne, Sgt. John Denny, and Sgt. Henry Johnson, 1879; Sgt. George Jordan, 1880; Sgt. Thomas Shaw, Sgt. George Jordan, 1st Sgt. Moses Williams, Sgt. Brent Woods, and Pvt. Augustus Walley, 1881; Cpl. Clinton Greaves, 1887; Cpl. William O. Wilson and Sgt. William McBryar, 1890; Pvt. Dennis Bell, Pvt. William H. Thompkins, Pvt. Fitz Lee, Pvt. George H. Wanton, and Sgt. Edward L. Baker, 1898; P. F. C. William Thompson, 1951; Sgt. Cornelius H. Charlton, 1952; Pvt. Milton L. Olive, III, 1966, Sgt. Webster Anderson, 1967; and Lt. Col. Charles C. Rogers, 1968.

In the same period, eight black navy men received the medal for gallantry in action: Robert Blake, 1863; Joachim Pease, John H. Lawson, and Clement Does, 1864; Aaron Anderson, 1865; Joseph B. Noil, 1872; and Daniel Atkins and Robert Penn, 1898.

Specialist Lawrence Joel was the first medical corpsman to win the medal in Vietnam.

CONGRESSMEN, BLACK

Twenty-two negroes served in the U. S. congress between 1870 and the turn of the century. Almost three decades then passed before another black congressman was elected. The list includes two Republican senators and twenty Republican representatives: Senators Hiram R. Revels (Mississippi, 1870-1871) and B. K. Bruce (Mississippi, 1875-1881); and Representatives Jefferson F. Long (Georgia, 1870-1871), Joseph S. Rainey (South Carolina, 1870-79), Robert C. DeLarge (South Carolina, 1871-73), Robert B. Elliot (South Carolina, 1871-74), Benjamin S. Turner (Alabama, 1871-73), Josiah T. Walls (Florida, 1871-76), Richard H. Cain (South Carolina, 1873-75 and 1877-79), John R. Lynch (Mississippi, 1873-77 and 1882-83), Alonzo J. Ransier (South Carolina, 1873-75), James T. Rapier (Alabama, 1873-75), Jeremiah Haralson (Alabama, 1875-77), John A. Hyman (North Carolina, 1875-77), Charles Nash (Louisiana, 1875-77), Robert Smalls (South Carolina, 1875-79, 1882-83, and 1885-87), James E. O'Hara (North Carolina, 1883-87), Henry P. Cheatham (North Carolina, 1889-93), John M. Langston, (Virginia, 1890-91), Thomas E.

Miller (South Carolina, 1890-91), George W. Murray (South Carolina, 1893-97), and George H. White (North Carolina, 1897-1901). Until recently these black congressmen received scant mention in most history books. Twenty-nine years passed before another black congressman was elected.

Since 1929, when Oscar S. DePriest took his seat as U. S. Representative from Illinois, there has been a gradual increase in the number of black congressmen, with ten serving in the 91st Congress and thirteen in the 92nd. The only Republican serving in the 92nd Congress is Senator Edward Brooke. These are the representatives who have served since 1929: Oscar S. DePriest (Illinois, 1929-35), Arthur W. Mitchell (Illinois, 1935-43), William L. Dawson (Illinois, 1943-70), Adam Clayton Powell, Jr. (New York, 1945-70), Charles C. Diggs, Jr. (Michigan, 1955-), Robert N. C. Nix, Sr. (Pennsylvania, 1959-), Augustus Hawkins (California, 1961-), John Conyers, Jr. (Michigan, 1965-), William Clay (Missouri, 1967-), Louis Stokes (Ohio, 1968-), Shirley Chisholm (New York, 1968-), George Collins (Illinois, 1970-), Ronald Dellums (California, 1970-), Ralph Metcalfe (Illinois, 1970-), Parren Mitchell (Maryland, 1970-), Charles Rangel (New York, 1970-). In 1971 Walter Edward Fauntroy was elected a delegate to the House of Representatives by voters of the District of Columbia.

See Maurine Christopher, *America's Black Congressmen* (1971).

CONSTITUTION OF THE UNITED STATES

The Constitution avoids the use of the word slavery but provides that direct taxes 'shall be apportioned . . . by adding to the whole Number of free Persons . . . three-fifths of all other Persons (Art. 1, Sec. 2); that the 'Migration or Importation of such Persons . . . shall not be prohibited by the Congress prior to the Year one thousand eight hundred and eight (Art. 1, Sec. 9); and that 'No person held to Service or Labour in one State, under the Laws thereof, escaping into another shall . . . be discharged from such Service or Labour, but shall be delivered up on Claim of the Party to whom such Service or Labour may be due (Art. IV, Sec. 2).

CONSTITUTIONAL CONVENTIONS

Called to write new organic laws for the former Confederate states, they were responsible for giving the South the best constitutions it had ever had. Blacks were in the majority in only one state, South Carolina. They were outnumbered in Georgia, Alabama, and North Carolina. They were equal in number to white convention delegates in Louisiana. Only a few black delegates were named in Arkansas and Texas. By the summer of 1868 all states except Virginia, Texas, and Mississippi had qualified for readmision by modifying or rescinding their black codes, providing free common schools, and forbidding voting discrimination based on race.

CONTRABAND

Union General Benjamin F. Butler set a precedent on May 24, 1861, when he refused to return three runaway slaves to their Confederate master on the grounds that they were 'contraband' and therefore subject to confiscation. His refusal was the first official decision to liberate Confederate slaves. The practice was followed by other Union generals and became U. S. policy under the first Confiscation Act, passed on August 6, 1861.

CONVENTION MOVEMENT

Church-trained leaders were instrumental in establishing national conventions to protest the status of the Negro in America. The first national convention, held at Bethel Church in Philadelphia in September 1830, was organized and presided over by Richard Allen. Attended by forty delegates from eight states, the convention lasted four days and laid the foundation for a permanent organization. The convention held the following year endorsed a proposal to found an industrial school for Negro boys. William Lloyd Garrison, then initiating his career, addressed the convention. These two conventions marked the beginning of organized activities among Negroes. National, states, and local conventions played an important role in antebellum America. Conventions were called for every conceivable purpose, and blacks living in the northern states were active participants in the convention movement of the day. Abolition of slavery, education, and moral reform engaged the attention of blacks throughout the era. Also discussed were the right of trial by jury, the right of suffrage, and the principle of equality before the law. Participants engaged in debate, passed resolutions, heard public addresses, and drew up petitions. Northern black leaders started as early as 1830 to plan a campaign against discrimination. Pre-Civil War conventions stressed education, moral reform, and self-help. In attendance at the conventions were notables such as Bishop Richard Allen, James Forten, Frederick Douglass, James W. C. Pennington, Martin R. Delany, and Henry Bibb. Perhaps the most important convention was the one held in Rochester in 1853, attended by 140 delegates from eight states and presided over by J. W. C. Pennington. A statement prepared by the committee on declaration of sentiments, chaired by Frederick Douglass, included this sentence: 'We ask that in our native land we shall not be treated as strangers, and worse than strangers.' Some negroes boycotted the conventions, seeing in them a form of self-segregation, but most Negroes who attended them also supported general reform movements.

In October 1864 a national convention held in Syracuse, New York, was atended by 144 delegates from 18 states. The delegates drew up, after four days of deliberation, an 'Address to the people of the United States' giving expression to their desire for the franchise and claiming that negroes had earned the right to vote. The convention movement met the special needs of blacks as no other avenue of expression could, and it left its indelible mark on the social, political, and intellectual history of the antebellum period. See Howard Holman Bell, *A Survey of the Negro Convention Movement 1830-.1861* (1969).

CONVENTION OF FREE MEN OF COLOR

Held in Buffalo, New York, on August 22, 1943, the convention was an anti-slavery rally. A highlight was Henry Highland Garnet's revelation of his brilliant plan for a general slave strike.

CONYERS, JOHN, JR.

Public official (b. 1929). Elected U. S. congressman from the first district of Michigan in 1965, he won re-election to a second term by an overwhelming majority.

COOK, JOHN FRANCIS, SR.

Clergyman and educator (d. 1855). He helped to organize the AME church in the nation's capital and, as a minister in the Presbyterian church, the Fifteenth Street Presbyterian Church and its school. One of his sons, John Francis, Jr., continued as its pastor; the other, George F. T. Cook, became assistant superintendent of the Washington school system.

COOK, MERCER

Diplomat (b. 1903). He has served as ambassador to Nigeria and director of African affairs for the Congress of Cultural Freedom. A noted scholar in the field of black literature, he served as head of the Romance languages department at Howard University. He has also served as U. S. ambassador to Senegal.

COOK, WILL MARION

Musician (1869-1944). He studied with Anton Dvorak, trained Broadway choruses, and toured Europe with the American Syncopated Orchestra, which he formed in 1919. His compositions include 'Clorindy: The Origin of the Cakewalk' (1898), for which Paul Dunbar wrote the lyrics. 'Clorindy' introduced syncopated ragtime music to the New York stage. The composer's son, Mercer Cook, became a noted scholar and diplomat.

COOKE, PAUL P.

Educator (b. 1917). He has served on the commissioner's advisory council on higher education in the District of Columbia, as a lecturer for the U. S. information agency, and as president of the District of Columbia Teachers College.

COOL JAZZ

'Modern' or 'cool' jazz, with its complexities of rhythm,

harmony, and improvisation, has won audiences for such performers as Randy Weston, Cecil Taylor, Oscar Peterson, Chico Hamilton, John Coltrane, Horace Silver, Dizzy Gillespie, Art Blakey, Charles Davis, and Miles Davis, to name only a few.

COON SONGS
Ragtime songs taking their name from the title of Ernest Hogan's 1895 hit, 'All Coons Look Alike to Me.'

COOPER V. AARON
Supreme Court decision (1958) denying the petition of the Little Rock, Arkansas, school board for a delay in its desegregation program. The Court unanimously held that the principles announced in the 1954 Brown decision 'are indispensable for the protection of the freedoms guaranteed by our fundamental charter for all of us. Our constitutional ideal of equal justice under law is thus made a living truth.'

COOPER, ANNA J.
Educator (1858-1964). She graduated from Oberlin College (1885) and earned a doctorate from the Sorbonne (1995). For 50 years she was associated with the M Street School in Washington, D. C.

COOPER, ED
Athlete. In 1950 he began playing for the Boston Celtics, after becoming the first black basketball player to sign with a professional team.

COPELAND, JOHN A.
One of the band that attacked Harpers Ferry on October 16, 1859. He was hanged with John Brown.

COPPIN, FANNY M. JACKSON
Educator (1836-1913). After serving for many years as principal of the Institute for Colored Youth (renamed the Cheyney Training School for Teachers), she accompanied her husband,

Bishop Levi J. Coppin, to Africa (1900) and helped him in his missionary work. Her autobiography is titled *Reminiscences of School Life, and Hints on Teaching* (1913).

CORBIN, J. C.

Educator (b. 1833). He taught at Lincoln Institute, served as Arkansas state superintendent of public instruction, and founded the Branch Normal College at Pine Bluff, Arkansas.

CORE

See Congress of Racial Equality.

CORNISH, SAMUEL

Journalist and reformer (1790-1859). A participant in many reform movements, he was an active member of the American Anti-Slavery Society, co-founder (with John B. Russwurm) of the first black newspaper, *Freedom's Journal* (1827), and a relentless fighter for full equality for the negro.

CORPS D'AFRIQUE

Name given to 1st, 2nd and 3rd Native Guards mustered in New Orleans, in May and June, 1862, as black combat troops. They were the first officially recognized combat troops mustered for service in the Civil War.

CORROTHERS, JAMES D.

Writer. He wrote mainly in the 1920s. His autobiography is titled *In Spite of the Handicap* (1916).

CORTEZ' CONQUEST OF MEXICO

Hernando Cortez, the conquistador, used slaves to transport the artillery used against the Aztecs. One of the negroes accompanying him harvested the first wheat crop in America.

COSBY, BILL

Entertainer (b. 1938). He broke down color barriers in television, becoming the first black to star in a non-black role. His success in *I Spy* (1965-68) won him the Emmy award in 1966 and 1967 as the best male actor. In 1969 he began a new series, *The Bill Cosby Show.* He paved the way for Diahann Carroll in *Julia* and for the highly successful *Flip Wilson Show.*

COTRELLE, LOUIS 'OLD MAN'
Musician. In the early 1900s, he was a leading New Orleans drummer.

COUNCIL ON EQUAL OPPORTUNITY
On February 7, 1965, President Lyndon B. Johnson issued an order creating a cabinet-level council to coordinate the civil rights activities of all federal agencies.

COUNCIL, WILLIAM HOOPER
Educator (b. 1849). Born of slave parents at Fayetteville, North Carolina, he became a clergyman, politician, and lawyer. Active in Alabama politics in the 1870s, he became associate editor of The Negro Watchman and president of the Alabama State Agricultural and Mechanical Institute (1875).

COUSHATTA MASSACRE
On August 30, 1874, several negroes were slain in Coushatta, Louisiana. The governor declared martial law.

COUVENT, MME. BERNARD
Philanthropist (d. 1836). Born in Africa and brought to New Orleans as a slave, she made provisions in her will for the founding of a school for negro orphans. Several years after her death, the *Ecole des Orphelins de Couleur* was founded in New Orleans and became the best of its kind.

CRAFT, WILLIAM AND ELLEN
Escaped slaves who returned to Georgia to found a school for negro children. Their 1848 flight to freedom and subsequent adventures are recounted in their autobiographical *Running a*

Thousand Miles for Freedom; or, the Escape of William and Ellen Craft (1860).

CREAM, ARNOLD RAY

See Walcott, Jersey Joe.

CREOLE AFFAIR

In 1841 the *Creole,* carrying 17 slaves from Norfolk, Virginia, to New Orleans, was diverted from its course by the rebellious passengers and taken to Nassau. The British freed all of the slaves except those implicated in the murder of their white masters. The United States demanded the return of the slaves. Antislavery groups denounced the government's action and the British authorities refused to extradite the insurrectionists.

CRISIS

Official organ of the NAACP. The monthly journal was founded in 1910 by W. E. B. Du Bois.

CROGMAN, WILLIAM H.

Educator (1841-1931). Born on an island in the Danish West Indies and orphaned at 12, he received no formal education during the first 25 years of his life but traveled widely. He entered Pierce Academy (1868), taught school, completed a classics program at Atlanta University, and was appointed professor at Clark in 1880. He was the first black to serve as president of that university.

CROMWELL, JOHN W.

First secretary and historian of the American Negro Academy, founded in 1897.

CROMWELL, OLIVER

Patriot (1753-1853). He accompanied Washington on the memorable crossing of the Delaware (1776); saw action at the battles of Trenton, Princeton, Brandywine, Monmouth, and

Yorktown (1781); and settled on a New Jersey farm, rewarded with a pension of $96 a year, to raise a family of six.

CROQUERE, BASIL

Swordsman. Interested in mathematics and philosophy, he was considered the best swordsman in ante bellum New Orleans, where he directed a fencing academy.

CROSTHWAIT, DAVID N., JR.

Engineer (b. 1898). He received a master's degree in engineering from Purdue and worked as a heating specialist in the research laboratory of the C. A. Durham Company in Indiana. His inventions and patents include an automatic waterfeeder (1920), a thermostat-setting device (1928), and a vacuum pump (1930). He also helped to design the heating system for the Radio City Music Hall in New York City.

CRUMMEL, ALEXANDER

Clergyman (1819-1898). He worked in Africa as an Episcopal clergyman from 1852-73 and served as an agent of the American Colonization Society. In 1873 he was assigned to St. Mary's Mission in Washington, D. C., where he founded St. Luke's Protestant Episcopal Church.

CRUSE, HAROLD

Writer and teacher. Born in Virginia, he worked as a community organiser in Harlem, collaborating with LeRoi Jones in the Black Arts Theatre. Now director of the black studies program at the University of Michigan, he has written *The Crisis of the Negro Intellectual* and *Rebellion or Revolution*.

CRY

Sensational dance created for Judith Jamison by Alvin Ailey in 1971. One of the most demanding solos ever choreographed, the 15-minute dance traces the saga of the black woman from Africa through the agrarian South to the ghettoes of the North.

Ailey dedicated the dance to 'Black women everywhere, especially our mother.'

CUFFE, PAUL

Seaman and colonizer (1759-1817). The youngest son of a freedman and a Wampanoag Indian woman, he was born on Cuttyhunk Island, off New Bedford. At 25 he owned a fishing schooner, at 35 he owned whaling boats, and at 45 he was the captain of vessels crossing the Atlantic. In 1815 he took the first step toward African colonization by transporting 38 negroes, at his own expense, to Sierra Leone on the *Traveller*. His fellow Quakers placed over his grave behind the Westport Meeting House a brief inscription: 'In memory of Captain Paul Cuffe, a self-made man, patriot, navigator, educator, philanthropist, friend, a noble character.' See Henry N. Sherwood, *Paul Cuffe* (1923).

CULLEN, COUNTEE

Poet (1903-1946). After receiving his masters degree from Harvard and spending two years in Paris on a Guggenheim fellowship, he returned to New York and taught in the public schools until his death. His first book of poetry, *Color* (1925), established him as a luminary of the 'Negro Renaissance.' His other works include *Copper Sun, Caroling Dusk* (1927), *The Black Christ*, and *On These I Stand* (published posthumously, in 1947).

CUNEY, NORRIS WRITHT

Public official (b. 1846). Active in Republican politics in Texas after the Civil War, he fought for racial equality and human rights.

CURTIS, AUSTIN MAURICE

Surgeon (1868-1938). Invited in 1896 to serve on the surgical staff of the Cook County hospital in Chicago, he became the first black to receive such an appointment in a nonsegregated hospital. After obtaining his M. D. from Northwestern, he

123

interned with Dr. Daniel Hale Williams (1891), whom he later succeeded as head of Provident Freedmen's Hospital in Washington (1898-1901), and taught at Howard (1928-38).

D

DABNEY, FORD

Musician. In the early 1900s he formed and directed a jazz band that became a regular feature of Florenz Ziegfeld's roof garden shows.

DADDY GRACE

See Grace, Bishop Charles Emmanuel.

DAILEY, PHYLLIS M.

Nurse. In 1945 she became the first black woman to serve as a nurse in the U. S. navy.

DAILEY, ULYSSES GRANT

Physician (1885-1961). He studied and taught at Northwestern University Medical School. After studying abroad, he set up his own hospital (1926). He was associate editor and editor of the *Journal of the National Medical Association*. After his retirement, he was named honorary consul in Haiti.

DANCE

All native American dance forms may be ascribed a black origin. The Fox-Trot or two-step variation, the basic step underlying all popular steps, was introduced by James Reese Europe, the bandleader who taught the step to the white dancing team Vernon and Irene Castle and accompanied them on their 1912 tour that broke Puritanical restraints and encouraged bodily contact in dancing.

DANDRIDGE, DOROTHY

Actress and singer (1924-1965). Nominated for an Academy Award for her performance in *Carmen Jones* (1954), she also had an important role in *Porgy and Bess* (1959), *Island in the Sun*, and *Tamango*. She was born in Cleveland, Ohio, and died in West Hollywood, California.

DAVID WALKER'S APPEAL

A disquieting document with a lengthy title, David Walker's abolitionist tract led Georgia and North Carolina to enact laws against inflammatory pamphlets and provoked a general reaction against abolitionists in the South, where it was called 'the diabolical Boston Pamphlet.' 'Remember Americans,' Walker wrote, 'that we must and shall be free and enlightened as you are, will you wait until we shall, under God, obtain our liberty by the crushing arm of power?' See Walker, David.

DAVID, CHARLES V., JR.

World Was II hero. A mess attendant in the Coast Guard, he died while rescuing his executive officer from the waters of the Atlantic.

DAVIS v. COUNTY SCHOOL BOARD
OF PRINCE EDWARD COUNTY

See Brown v. Board of Education; Griffin v. Prince Edward School Board.

DAVIS,ALEXANDER K.

Public official. He served as lieutenant governor of Mississippi during Reconstruction.

DAVIS, ALONZO JOSEPH, JR.

Artist (b. 1942). He owns the Brockman Gallery in Los Angeles, where he exhibits his work and promotes the work of minority artists.

DAVIS, ANGELA YVONNE

Teacher and political activist (b. 1944). Before she was jailed on murder and kidnap charges stemming from a shoot-out at a California courthouse in August 1970, she had been a popular but controversial lecturer in philosophy at the University of California at Los Angeles. An avowed Communist and a cause célèbre even before the trial began, she remained in the limelight during three months of testimony culminating in a verdict of not guilty of murder, not guilty of kidnaping, and not guilty of conspiracy. Following her acquittal in June 1972, she embarked on an extended speaking tour. While in prison she published *If They Come in the Morning* (1972).

DAVIS, ARTHUR P.

Educator and writer (b. 1904). Co-editor of the famous anthology *The Negro Caravan,* he has taught English at Howard since 1944. Dr. Davis is the author of *Isaac Watts: His Life and Works* (1943) and of many scholarly articles and book reviews.

DAVIS, BENJAMIN J., JR.

Public official (1903-1964). A member of the national committee of the Communist party, he was elected to the New York City Council in 1943. In 1949 he received a five-year prison sentence for conspiring to advocate the violent overthrow of the U. S. government. His autobiography is titled *Communist Councilman from Harlem.*

DAVIS, BENJAMIN O., JR.

Air force general (b. 1912). He was the first black air force general and the first black man to command an airbase. Following his retirement in 1970, he headed the force of federal marshals formed to bring an end to airplane hijacking.

DAVIS, BENJAMIN O., SR.

Army general (1877-1970). He was the nation's first black general. He retired in 1948, having served in the U. S. armed forces for half a century. His son became the nation's highest ranking black officer.

DAVIS, CHARLES

Artist (b. 1912). Largely self-taught, the Chicago artist has exhibited at Hull House. His 'Tycoon Toys' is in the Harmon Foundation.

DAVIS, ELIZABETH BISHOP

Psychoanalyst. Dr. Davis is in charge of the Harlem hospital department of psychiatry.

DAVIS, ELLABELLE

Musician. Beginning as a church soloist, she made her operatic debut in 1941 and stunned Mexico City in 1946 by her performance in *Aïda*.

DAVIS, ERNIE

Athlete. In 1959 he was a sophomore and the No. 1 back on the nation's No. 1 college team (Syracuse). In his senior year he won the Heisman Trophy and signed with the Cleveland Browns. He died of leukemia at 23.

DAVIS, GUSSIE L.

Musician. In the late 19th century, he wrote many popular ballads, including 'Down in Poverty Row.'

DAVIS, HARRIET TUBMAN

See Tubman, Harriet.

DAVIS, JOHN

Hero. He died at sea aboard the schooner *General Tompkins* in 1812.

DAVIS, JOHN WARREN

Educator (b. 1888). He studied at Morehouse College and the University of Chicago, taught at his alma mater, and became president of West Virginia State College (1919-53), which he transformed into one of the leading land-grant institutions. He also served as special director of the NAACP legal defense and educational fund and, after his retirement from the presidency, as director of the U. S. technical assistance program in Liberia.

DAVIS, MILES

Jazz musician. In the late 1940s he was one of the initiators of 'cool' jazz. See Michael James, *Miles Davis* (1961).

DAVIS, OSSIE

Actor and playwright (b. 1917). His greatest success came in 1961 when he and his wife, Ruby Dee, played the leading roles in his *Purlie Victorious,* later filmed under the title *Gone Are the Days.* A civil rights activist, he promoted the creation of black plays for black audiences.

DAVIS, OTIS

Athlete. In the 1960 Olympics, he won a gold medal in the 400-meter race.

DAVIS, SAMMY, JR.

Entertainer (b. 1925). Active in show business since the age of six, he has played in movies, Broadway musicals, and on television. He has also recorded songs and imitations of other famous personalities. The musicals *Mr. Wonderful* and *Golden Boy* were built around him.

DAVIS, WILLIE

Athlete. The all-pro defensive end joined the Green Bay Packers in 1960 and performed admirably as their defensive captain.

DAVISON, FREDERIC

Army general. In 1968 he became the nation's third black general.

DAWSON, WILLIAM L.

Congressman (1886-1970). The first black to head a congressional committee, the representative from Illinois also served longer than any other black. Born in Albany, Georgia, he graduated from Fisk University (1909), studied law at Kent College and Northwestern University, and won election to the office that made him the third Northern black and second black Democrat in the U. S. Congress (1942). During his long period of service (1942-1970), he became chairman of the House Committee on Government Operations.

DAWSON, WILLIAM LEVI

Composer (b. 1899). A cousin of congressman William L. Dawson, he has achieved worldwide recognition as a conductor and composer. He played trombone with the Chicago Civic Orchestra before becoming director of the school of music and of the choir at Tuskeegee (1931). His works include the Negro Folk Symphony No. 1 (1934) and several choral pieces.

DAY, THOMAS

Artisan (d. 1861). A celebrated craftsman from North Carolina, he produced hand-tooled mahogany tables and divans of exquisite beauty.

DEADWOOD DICK

See Love, Nat.

DEAS, EDMUND H.

Politician (b. 1855). He began as a precinct chairman in 1874, earned a reputation as the most aggressive politician in South Carolina, and was elected chairman of the Republican state committee in 1901.

DECATUR, DORSEY

Hero. During the Civil War he won the Congressional Medal of Honor (1864).

130

DECLARATION OF INDEPENDENCE

In an early draft of the Declaration of Independence Thomas Jefferson denounced George III for promoting slavery: 'He has waged cruel war against human nature itself, violating its most sacred rights of life and liberty in the persons of a distant people who never offended him, captivating and carrying them into slavery in another hemisphere. . . .' The passage was not preserved in the final draft.

DECLARATION OF THE RIGHTS OF
THE NEGRO PEOPLES OF THE WORLD

Proclamation issued by an international convention of blacks meeting in New York in 1920 under the leadership of Marcus Garvey.

DEDE, EDMOND

Musician (1829-1903). A violinist and composer before the Civil War, he became director of a Bordeaux (France) orchestra.

DEE, RUBY

Actress. Wife of Ossie Davis.

DE FACTO SEGREGATION

Racial segregation brought about by forces other than law or official action. The Supreme Court has dealt only with *de jure* segregation. Neighborhood schools and residential housing patterns account for most *de facto* segregation.

DEGRASSE, JOHN V.

Nineteenth century physician. He completed his medical courses at Bowdoin College in 1847, continued his studies in Paris, and practiced medicine in New York City, then in Boston. His reputation grew, and on August 24, 1854, he became the first black member of the Massachusetts Medical Society.

DE JURE SEGREGATION

Racial segregation based on law or official action. Until 1954,

131

17 states (Alabama, Arkansas, Florida, Georgia, Louisiana, Mississipppi, North Carolina, South Carolina, Tennessee, Texas, Virginia, Delaware, Kentucky, Maryland, Missouri, Oklahoma, West Virginia) and the District of Columbia maintained segregated public schools *de jure* ('by law').

DELANEY, BEAUFORD

Artist. His struggle to survive as an artist in Greenwich Village is described by Henry Miller in *Remember to Remember* (1947).

DELANY, HUBERT T.

Jurist (b. 1902). He is judge of the New York City domestic relations court.

DELARGE, ROBERT CARLOS

Public official (1842-1874). Prominent in Reconstruction politics and a delegate to the South Carolina constitutional convention in 1867, he was elected U. S. congressman in 1870. He was a magistrate in Charleston at the time of his death.

DELLUMS, RONALD V.

U. S. representative from California. He was skeptical when first approached to run in the 1970 Democratic primary but decided to try to work within the two-party system and make the Democratic party relevant to the people. His aim is to form a coalition of minorities—Chicanos, exploited women, young people, blacks—capable of taking over the 'entire apparatus of the Democratic Party' and making it 'the people's party.'

DELTA MINISTRY, THE

A subsidiary of the National Council of Churches. Described by Newsweek as 'the most creative and controversial church-supported civil rights group in the South,' the organization is the subject of a study by Bruce Hilton, The Delta Ministry.

DENNIS, GEORGE WASHINGTON

Pioneer. He bought his freedom and became a prominent real estate investor in California. One of his sons, Edward, became the first negro San Francisco policeman; his daughter Margaret became a linguist and taught in a Chinese school.

DENNY, JOHN

Military hero. In 1879 he brought a wounded comrade to safety while under fire in Las Animas Canyon, New Mexico. He was serving with Troop B, 9th U. S. Cavalry. He received the congressional Medal of Honor.

DE PAUR, LEONARD

See De Paur Infantry Chorus.

DE PAUR INFANTRY CHORUS

Concert choir formed by members of the armed forces. Under the direction of its founder, Leonard De Paur, the group presented over 600 concerts and was acclaimed one of the finest units of the day. After leaving military service, the chorus made its Carnegie Hall debut on December 7, 1947.

DEPRIEST, OSCAR

Public official (1871-1951). The first black man to serve in the U. S. congress after 1900, he served three terms as the representative of the 21st congressional district of Illinois. Born in Florence, Alabama, and reared in Salina, Kansas, he moved to Chicago and became active in real estate before entering politics. A staunch foe of racial bias in any form, he stood alone in the U. S. congress from 1929 to 1933, but he blazed the trail for the return of other blacks to the legislative branch of government. Though he was defeated in his campaign for re-election in 1934, he was a delegate to the Republican national convention in 1936.

DERHAM, JAMES

Physician (b. 1762). Born a slave in Philadelphia, he is

133

generally credited with being the first negro physician in America. By working as a male nurse, medical assistant, and apothecary in New Orleans, he was able to earn money to buy his freedom in 1783. Six years later he became an outstanding physician. After he moved to Philadelphia, he won the esteem of many of his colleagues, including Benjamin Rush.

DELANY, MARTIN ROBINSON

Scholar and public official (1812-1885). The first black to hold the rank of field officer in the Civil War, Major Delany was a medical officer in the Union army. An early advocate of black leadership, he acquired an international reputation as a scholar, became a member of the International Statistical Congress and of the Social Science Congress (Glasgow, Scotland), became a leader of the national convention movement, negotiated treaties with Abeokuta chiefs for land for prospective settlers, joined a large colony of expatriates in Canada, wrote a minor classic in the history of and exploration of 19th-century Africa (his *Report*), and served as a justice of the peace in Charleston, South Carolina. Schooled at New York City's African Free School, Canaan Academy in New Hampshire, Oneida Institute, and Harvard, he became a fiery spokesman for Negro rights. He wrote *The Conditions, Elevation, Emigration and Destiny of the Colored People of the United States: Politically Considered* (1852). See Frank A. Rollin, *Life and Public Services of Martin R. Delany, Sub-Assistant Commissioner, Bureau Relief of Refugees, Freedmen, and Abandoned Lands, and Late Major 104th U. S. Colored Troops* (1883).

DE SABLE, JEAN

Pioneer (c. 1745-1818). He built a thriving post at the portage between the Chicago and Des Plaines rivers about 1775. The city of Chicago grew up around his post. Born in Haiti, he married a Potawatomi woman (1771), operated a farm in Peoria (1773), and managed trading posts at Michigan City (1779) and Port Huron (1880). See Shirley Graham, *Jean Baptiste Pointe du Sable* (1953).

DESEGREGATION

Attempts to eliminate racial segregation in states maintaining separate but equal schools *de jure* ('by law') began with the 1954 ruling of the Supreme Court that 'Separate educational facilities are inherently unequal.' Progress was slow at first. Some schools were closed temporarily, several states promoted the operation of private schools, and many school districts refused to accept even token integration until forced to do so. A decade after the Supreme Court ruling, less than 2 per cent of all Negro students in the South were attending desegregated schools. Passage of the 1964 Civil Rights Act speeded up public school desegregation by authorizing the Federal Government to bring suit against laggard school districts and directing the Department of Health, Education and Welfare to deny federal aid to districts practicing segregation. By 1971 the South could demonstrate that 86 per cent of all its black pupils were attending mixed schools. See De Jure Segregation, Zoning, Pairing Freedom of Choice, Separate But Equal.

DESLANDES, CHARLES

Militant. He led a slave revolt in 1811. The uprising, near New Orleans, was suppressed by U. S. troops.

DESSALINES, JEAN JACQUES

Haitian emperor (d. 1806). Hero of the movement to drive out the French and establish the republic of Haiti, he consolidated his power, became notorious for his tyranny, and died at the hands of mulattoes who had formed a secret conspiracy against him.

DETROIT RIOT

The racial turmoil which shook Detroit during the week of June 20, 1943, caused the deaths of 25 negroes and 9 whites, and property damage exceeding $2,000,000. It shocked millions of Americans, causing them to realize that significant changes in the status of negroes could no longer be ignored. Within two years 17 governors and 16 mayors had appointed commissions to work toward the improvement of race relations. The riot had occurred after rumors resulted in clashes between white sailors and black civilians. Another serious racial disturbance occurred in Chicago in 1967, following a police raid on a drinking spot. On July 23, police raided a 'blind pig' and subsequently arrested 73 persons. After five days of havoc, property damage went beyond $200,000,000, more than 5,000 persons had been arrested, and 43 persons had died.

DETT, NATHANIEL R.

Composer (1882-1943). Many of his works are based on spirituals. His choral setting of 'Listen to the Lambs' was the first attempt by a black composer to use black speech in an extended art form.

DICKERSON, EARL B.

Businessman (b. 1891). He was the first black graduate of the Chicago University law school. Active in civic affairs in Chicago, he served on President Franklin D. Roosevelt's FEPC before becoming president of the Supreme Life Insurance Company.

DICKINSON, JOSEPH H.

Organ builder (b. 1855). An expert in his field, he helped to construct a large combination organ for the Centennial Exposition of 1876. He was awarded a diploma and a medal for his creation. He built two organs for the royal family of Portugal.

DICKSON, MOSES

Clergyman (b. 1824). He organized the Knights of Liberty, a secret society active in the underground railroad, then disbanded it to form the first Temple and Tabernacle of the Knights and Daughters of Tabor (1871).

DIEGO EL NEGRO

Cabin boy. He accompanied Columbus on his fourth voyage

in 1502, thus becoming the first Negro to set foot on New World soil.

DIGGS, CHARLES C.
Public official (b. 1922). Congressman Diggs, of Michigan, is leader of the 'Black Caucus' and chairman of a Congressional subcommittee on Africa. He has set as an 'attainable goal' the election of 45 to 50 negroes to Congress. Born in Detroit, he has served in the U. S. house of representatives since 1955.

DILLARD, HARRISON
Athlete. In the 1948 Olympics he won the first gold medal for an American track-and-field competitor; four years later he won another gold medal in the high hurdles.

DIPLOMATIC CORPS
Blacks have recently held important posts in the diplomatic service. Those holding ambassadorial rank are Jerome H. Holland (Sweden), Hugh H. Smythe (Syria), Clifton Wharton (Norway), Samuel Z. Westerfield (Liberia), Clinton Knox (Norway), Clarence Clyde (Uganda), Terence A. Todman (Chad), Franklin H. William (former ambassador to Ghana), and Patricia Harris (former ambassador to Luxembourg).

DITON, CARL
Musician. (b. 1886). In 1919 he helped to organize the National Association of Musicians. He studied at Juilliard and won the Harmon award for a composition incorporating African rhythms (1929).

DIVINE, FATHER
Religious cult leader (c. 1874-1965). Probably born as George Baker on Hutchinson's Island, Georgia, he headed the Kingdom of Peace, a movement embracing millions of followers, black and white, who lived communally and worshiped him as their God. He moved to Baltimore by 1899, became Samuel 'Father Jehoviah' Morris' 'Messenger and Son,' then moved southward,

137

proclaiming his own divinity. He moved to New York City in 1915, was associated with John 'Bishop St. John The Vine' Hickerson's Church of the Living God, and founded his first 'Heaven,' or communal dwelling, at Sayville, Long Island, in 1919. Rapid expansion followed during the 1930s and 1940s as other 'Heavens' were established and cult-owned property increased to $10,000,000. As head of the Kingdom of Peace movement, he enforced rigid rules that prohibited his followers from using tobacco, liquor, or cosmetics.

DIXON, DEAN

Musician (b. 1915). He has achieved international recognition as a conductor of symphony orchestras. After graduating from Juilliard (1936), he made guest appearances with American orchestras before moving to Europe to become a permanent director. In August 1941, he became the first black guest conductor of the New York Philharmonic. He organized the American Youth Orchestra in 1944. He conducted orchestras all over Europe before becoming director of the Hessian Radio Symphony in Frankfurt, Germany, in 1960. He returned from exile to conduct the New York Philharmonic in 1970, his first U. S. appearance in 21 years.

DIXON, GEORGE

Athlete (1870-1909). He was the first black to win the bantamweight and featherweight championships (1890-1900). In 1956 he was elected to boxing's Hall of Fame.

DIXON, JAMES E.

Telegrapher. In 1889 he was appointed branch manager of the Western Union Telegraph Office in New Bedford, Massachusetts.

DIXON, WILL

Musician. The first dancing conductor, he led the Memphis Students in the United States and Europe. He was also a composer.

DOBBS, MATTIWILDA

Coloratura soprano (b. 1925). Born in Atlanta Georgia, she made her debut in Holland (1952) and performed mainly in Europe before joining the Metropolitan Opera association (1957).

DOBY, LARRY

Athlete (b. 1924). In 1947 he became the first black to play in the American League. The next year he led the Cleveland Indians to a World Series championship.

DOCTOR HUGUET

A book written by Ignatius Donnelly to dramatize the plight of the freed slave. Published in 1891, the fictional work recounts the life of a southern aristocrat whom God changes into a Negro.

DODSON, JACOB

Explorer. In 1846 he set out with John Charles Frémont on the historic ride from Los Angeles to Monterey. He also accompanied Frémont on the trip that led to the discovery of Klamath Lake.

DODSON, OWEN

Writer (b. 1914). *Boy at the Window* (1951), which deals with the adolescence of a Brooklyn negro untouched by fear of segregation, is one of his best works.

DONNELLY, IGNATIUS

See *Doctor Huguet.*

DORMAN, ISAIAH

Interpreter. He is said to have accompanied General Custer through Sioux territory in the hope of bringing about a reconciliation between him and Sitting Bull. He died at the battle of Little Big Horn. The Sioux called him Azimpi.

DORSETTE, CORNELIUS

Physician (d. 1897). One of Booker T. Washington's teachers

and the first licensed black practitioner in Montgomery, Alabama, he founded Hale Infirmary.

DORSEY, DECATUR

Civil War hero. In 1864 Sgt. Dorsey won the congressional Medal of Honor in recognition of his valor. His unit captured 200 Confederate soldiers in a battle near Petersburg, Virginia.

DORSEY, THOMAS A.

Musician and composer. In 1925 he played boogie-woogie in Chicago and was known as Georgia Tom. He had composed Ma Rainey's popular theme song, 'Rain on the ocean, Rain on the deep blue sea. . . .' A few years later he emerged as the leading composer of gospel songs whose mighty rhythms rocked the churches, such as 'Someday, Somewhere.' He also played with the Whispering Syncopaters and organized a band for Ma Rainey.

DOUGHERTY, CHARLES

Athlete (1879-1940). He achieved recognition as a pitcher with the Leland Giants, American Giants, and Chicago Giants, 1909-15.

DOUGLAS, AARON

Painter and educator (b. 1899). He is best known for his impressionistic Haitian landscapes.

DOUGLAS, JOHN T.

Musician (b. 1847). A violinist, he played several instruments and composed many pieces for piano and orchestra.

DOUGLAS, ROBERT J.

In 1923 he founded the New York Renaissance Big 5, believed by some to be the greatest basketball team of its time.

DOUGLAS, ROBERT M., JR.

Artist. In 1833 he made a lithographed likeness of William Lloyd Garrison. He earned his living as a sign painter.

DOUGLASS, FREDERICK

Abolitionist (c. 1817-1895). Taking his name from Scott's *The Lady of the Lake* following his escape in 1838, he established and edited the Rochester, N. Y., abolitionist *North Star* for 17 years. The man who had been born a slave and named Frederick Augustus Bailey showed such talent as an orator that he was employed as a lecturer by the Anti-Slavery Society. In 1845 he published his classic autobiography, later revised and enlarged under the title *The Life and Times of Frederick Douglass* (1882). His freedom was bought while he was making a successful lecture tour in England. From 1847 to 1895 he was leader of his race, inspiring blacks by his unceasing militancy to fight against slavery, segregation, discrimination, and exploitation. He urged his friend Lincoln to make the Civil War crusade against slavery, closed his paper to concentrate on recruiting black soldiers, and saw his sons serve in the 54th Massachusetts. During Reconstruction he demanded the franchise for blacks, moved to Washington, D. C., became a prominent Republican orator, published the *New National Era,* and became the first black to serve as Recorder of Deeds (1881) and U. S. minister to Haiti (1889). See Benjamin Quarles, *Frederick Douglass* (1948).

DOUGLASS HOSPITAL

Founded in Kansas City, Kansas in 1899, it was the first hospital west of the Mississippi to serve all ethnic groups. Its founders were Dr. Solomon H. Thompson and Dr. Thomas C. Unthank.

DOWNING, GEORGE T.

Businessman and civil rights leader (1819-1903). In 1845 he established the firm of George T. Downing, Confectioner and Caterer, at 690 Broadway, in New York City. It became a favorite meeting place for the elite. In 1854 he built the Sea Girt Hotel in Newport, Rhode Island. Always active in the struggle for equality of educational opportunity for negro youth, he succeeded in bringing about the integration of the Rhode Island school system in 1866. He then turned his energies toward other civil rights causes. He tried to abolish laws enacted to prevent inter-racial marriages.

DOZIER, JOHN
Clergyman and legislator (b. 1800). The slave of a Virginia college president, he was self-educated. He founded a Baptist church in Uniontown, Alabama, and pastored it for 20 years. He served two sessions in the Alabama house of representatives, beginning in 1872.

DRAFT RIOTS
In 1863 blacks and abolitionists in New York City were attacked and killed in rioting caused by the drafting of blacks.

DRAKE, ST. CLAIR
Sociologist (b. 1911). A professor of African studies, he co-authored *Black Metropolis: A Study of Negro Life in a Northern City* (1945).

DRED SCOTT
See Scott, Dred.

DREW, CHARLES R.
Father of blood plasma (1904-1950). Born in Washington, D. C., he graduated from Amherst (1926), coached and taught at Morgan State College, received his M. D. from McGill University (1933), and taught pathology at Howard (1935). His research at the Columbia Medical Center in New York City resulted in the discovery that blood plasma could replace whole blood in transfusions. He set up and directed the British blood bank (1940-41), then the American Red Cross project to collect and store blood. He was dropped from the ARC project because he disagreed with the policy of refusing the blood of black donors and insisted that there was no scientific difference between the blood of blacks and whites.

DREW, TIMOTHY

Early black nationalist. In 1913 he founded the Moorish Science Temple Movement in Newark, New Jersey. He was also known as Noble Drew Ali.

DRINKING GOURD

Another name for the Big Dipper. See 'Follow the Drinking Gourd.'

DRISKELL, DAVID

Artist (b. 1931). Now professor and chairman of the art department at Fisk, he has taught at Howard and exhibited his works in many galleries. He is best known for his allegorical paintings of Georgia pines.

DU BOIS, WILLIAM EDWARD BURGHARDT

Scholar of international reputation (1868-1963). Beginning as a moderate who believed that blacks must forge their own destiny through their own efforts, he lost hope of effecting reform from within the system, espoused the Communist Party, and moved to Ghana, where he is buried. Born in Great Barrington, Massachusetts, 'with a flood of Negro blood, a strain of French, a bit of Dutch, but, thank God! no Anglo-Saxon,' he never knew his father, whose ancestry was partly French Huguenot. He earned a B. A. from Fisk (1888), an M. A. (1891) and a Ph. D. (1895) from Harvard. The first black to achieve the distinction of graduating *cum laude* from Harvard, he was also the first scholar to have his dissertation published in the Harvard Historical Series. His work on the suppression of slave trade became the first of the series. He charged Booker T. Washington with tacit acceptance of the alleged inferiority of blacks and set about reversing blacks' assessment of themselves. At a 1905 meeting of the Talented Tenth at Niagara Falls, Canada, he oversaw the drawing up of a manifesto calling for full freedom and proclaiming that blacks would protest forever and 'assail the ears of America with the story of its shameful deeds toward us.' He taught at the universities of Wilberforce,

Pennsylvania, and Atlanta. He helped to found the NAACP in 1909 and edited its journal, the *Crisis,* until a disagreement over policy caused him to break with the association in 1932. Active in pan-Africanism, he initiated or contributed to conferences in Paris (1919), London (1921), (1921, 1923), New York (1927), and Manchester (1945). He was vice-chairman of the U. N. council on African affairs (1949-54). Becoming increasingly involved in leftist affairs in the 1950s, he traveled widely in Soviet-bloc countries and was awarded the Lenin peace prize in 1959. He joined the Communist party in 1961 and moved to Ghana, where he worked as director of the *Encyclopedia Africana.* Two years later he became a citizen of Ghana. His works include *The Suppression of the African Slave-Trade to the United States of America* (1896), *Atlanta University Studies of the Negro Problem,* (1896-1914), *The Philadelphia Negro* (1899), *The Souls of Black Folk* (1903), *John Brown* (1909), *Quest of the Silver Fleece,* (1911), *The Negro* (1915), *Darkwater: Voices from within the Veil* (1920), *The Gift of Black Folk: The Negro in the Making of America* (1924), *Dark Princess* (1928), *Encyclopedia of the Negro* (editor in chief, 1933-1945), *Black Reconstruction in America, 1860 1880* (1935), *Black Folk: Then and Now* (1939), *Dusk of Dawn: An Autobiography of a Race Concept* (1940), *Color and Democracy: Colonies and Peace* (1945), *The World and Africa* (1946), *In Battle for Peace: The Story of My 83rd Birthday* (1952), *The Black Flame, a Trilogy* (*Ordeal of Mansart,* 1957, *Mansart Builds a School,* 1959, *Worlds of Color,* 1961), and *An ABC of Color* (1964). He died in Accra, Ghana, on August 27, 1963. The best biographies are F. L. Broderick's *W. E. B. Du Bois: A Negro Leader in a Time of Crisis* (1959) and E. M. Rudwick's *W. E. B. Du Bois: A Study in Minority Group Leadership* (1961). See also Julius Lester (ed.), *The Seventh Son: The Thought and Writings of W. E. B. Du Bois* (2 vols., 1971).

DUDLEY, EDWARD R.

Jurist and diplomat (b. 1911). Born in Boston, Virginia, he earned his law degree at St. John's in Brooklyn (1941), was elected assistant state assistant attorney general (1942), and served on the NAACP's legal staff (1943-45), before being appointed ambassador to Liberia (1948-53). In 1965 he became associate justice of the state supreme court in New York.

DUNBAR, PAUL LAURENCE

Poet (1872-1906). Best known for his poems in dialect, he wrote beautiful poems, novels, and stories in standard English, and he towers above all other black writers prior to the Harlem Renaissance of the 1920s. He succeeded in spite of many hardships and tragic illness in achieving recognition on both sides of the Atlantic. After publishing *Oak and Ivy* (1892) and *Majors and Minors* (1896) privately, he succeeded in having the best works from both collections republished, with an introduction by William Dean Howells, in *Lyrics of Lowly Life* (1896), which was an instant success. He toured England the following year, reading his verse, married Alice Ruth Moore (1898), almost died of pneumonia (1899), but continued writing verse: *Lyrics of the Hearthside* (1899), *Lyrics of Love and Laughter* (1903). His prose writings include *The Sport of the Gods* (1902) and *The Heart of the Happy Hollow* (1904).

DUNCAN, TODD

Musician (b. 1904). A concert singer, he had the male lead in *Porgy and Bess,* 1935-43. He appeared in White House concerts (1935), as a soloist with major symphonies throughout the world, in the movie *Syncopation* (1940), and in the Broadway musicals *Cabin in the Sky* (1940) and *Lost in the Stars* (1950), for which he won the Critics Award for the best male performance. He taught at Howard University until 1945.

DUNCANSON, ROBERT

Artist (1817-1872). Born in New York of a black mother and a white Canadian father, he was schooled in Canada and Scotland. He painted many portraits for prominent families in Cincinnati and Detroit, exhibited his works during a European tour (1862), and spent his last years in Detroit, where many of his works are on exhibit. His masterpiece was the landscape 'Blue Hole, Flood Waters, Little Miami River' (1851), now in the Cincinnati Art Museum.

DUNHAM, KATHERINE

Dancer and choreographer (b. 1910). Born in Chicago, she still serves as president of the Katherine Dunham School of Cultural Arts, which she founded in New York City in 1945. She staged and starred in *Bal Nègre,* performed in motion pictures, and was acclaimed in the United States and abroad for her revues. Her choreography reflects studies of primitive rituals conducted in the West Indies on a Rosenwald Fellowship (1936-37) and described in her book, *Journey to Accompong* (1946). In 1963 she became the first black choreographer at the Metropolitan Opera, using her artistry in a new production of *Aïda.* Her autobiography is titled *A Touch of Innocence* (1959).

DUNJEE, ROSCOE

Newspaper publisher. In 1955 he was publicly commended for his accomplishments during 40 years as a newspaper publisher. Founder and publisher of the Oklahoma *Black Dispatch,* he used his newspaper to promote his views and arouse people to action. His editorials have been called 'a preview of the cavalcade of civil rights movements during the first fifty years of this century.'

DUNMORE PROCLAMATION

Issued on November 7, 1775, aboard the *William* in Norfolk harbor, by John Murray, Earl of Dunmore, the proclamation promised freedom to all slaves 'able and willing to bear arms' if they would join 'His Majesty's Troops.' The deposed royal governor of Virginia prompted thousands of blacks to join the forces of the Crown.

DUNN, OSCAR JAMES

Public official (1826-1871). Born a slave in New Orleans, he became lieutenant governor of Louisiana in 1868. Incorruptible, he died in office after serving only 3 years of his term.

DURHAM, JOHN STEPHENS
Journalist and diplomat. In 1886 he received a bachelor's degree from the University of Pennsylvania, where he edited the *University Journal*. Later he edited worked for the Philadelphia *Times* and the *Evening Bulletin*. After 1891 he performed brilliantly as U. S. minister to Haiti.

DU SABLE, JEAN BAPTISTE POINTE
See De Sable, Jean.

DUTCHMAN, THE
Play by LeRoi Jones. A shocking encounter between a white prostitute and a black intellectual, the play won the Obie Award as the best Off-Broadway production in 1964.

DYKE, HENRY VAN
Writer. He wrote two novels during the 1960s *(Ladies of the Rachmaninoff Eyes* and *Blood of Strawberries)*.

E

EBONY

Most successful black publication in history. The magazine's success opened the door to lucrative advertisements for all black publications. By 1970 it had reached a paid circulation of one and a quarter million. Publisher John H. Johnson observed on its twentieth anniversary that *Ebony* came into being as a medium for 'projecting the image of the Negro in America—an image that had long been shattered and distorted in media oriented primarily to whites.' In 1971 the editors published a three-volume *Ebony Pictorial History of Black America,* described as 'the most extensive attempt to date to present a total visual image of the black experience.'

ECONOMIC STATUS OF NEGROES

See Social and Economic Status of Negroes in the United States, 1970.

EDUCATION

Religious institutions and groups took the lead in fostering literacy among negroes. As early as 1720 some English clergymen had expressed their interest in extending religious training to those 'in bondage beyond the seas' and had made some progress toward accomplishing their goal. A century later the Presbyterians were in the forefront in making education directly available to blacks. In 1740 a negro school was opened in Charleston by a pious Presbyterian (Hugh Bryan). By 1755 other schools had been opened in Virginia. Quakers soon were providing the rudiments of a viable educational system under slavery and by

1808 had begun a familial system of instruction for household servants and free negroes, fostering the emergence of articulate black leadership (Denmark Vasey, David Walker, Nat Turner, William Wells Brown, Thomas H. Jones, Lunceford Lane, Frederick Douglass, etc.).

During the Civil War the concentration of black refugees within Union lines brought into bold relief the depth of misery of the deprived masses and generated a philanthropic concern that resulted in the upsurge of a complex of benevolent freedmen associations which provided a foundation for a freedmen's school system. By 1865 14 southern states had established 575 schools attended by 71,779 negro and white children. The American Missionary Association took the first step toward establishing a system of higher education for negroes by opening Fisk University and Talladega College (1865). In 1867 Atlanta University was chartered to provide 'opportunities of the highest advantages' to all. The following year Hampton Institute opened, introducing the idea of vocational education for negroes. The American Baptist Home Mission Society helped to establish Wayland Seminary in 1864, Richmond Theological Seminary in 1865, and later Morehouse College, Shaw University, and other religiously oriented institutions. The Methodist Episcopal Church established colleges for freedmen in other areas of the South: Chaflin University at Orangesburg, South Carolina, and Walden College at Nashville (1865). The First Congregational Church took the lead in setting up Howard University (1867). During Reconstruction each state legislature passed some type of law establishing a free public school system, but most southerners opposed a mixed school policy. The result was the formation of a system aimed at perpetuating the segregated order. The Southern Education Board (1901), invested with the power to mold public opinion in matters of education and to handle private funds for promoting public education, consolidated efforts to achieve a unified system of segregated education at all levels. Philanthropic agencies like the Slater and Rosenwald foundations put secondary and higher education in reach of most negroes. Training in the manual arts predominated, for a while, as some of the institutions that had been founded to promote liberal arts programs imitated Hampton and Tuskegee, and as some of the older normal schools embraced the manual arts and were converted into a system of negro land-grant colleges. By the turn of the century, however, negro education had become a duplication of education for white chlidren as colleges inclined their programs toward literary and professional fields. The separate but equal doctrine was the law of the land until reversed by the Brown decision of 1954. See Henry Allen Bullock, *A History of Education in the South* (1967).

EDWARDS, EDWIN B.

Musician (1893-1963). Born in New Orleans, he was a founder and trombonist of the 'Original Dixieland Jazz Band' (1916).

EDWARDS, HARRY

Advocate of Black Power in sports. Born in East St. Louis, Illinois, November 22, 1942. He became an outstanding athlete at Fresno City College in California and San Jose State, where he later taught sociology and anthropology. He drew nation-wide attention during much of 1968 by advocating a Negro boycott of the Olympic Games. Declaring that black athletes should not be used 'as performing animals for a little extra dog food.'

EDWARDS, SAM

One of the conspirators in the Southampton County, Virginia, insurrection of 1831. See Turner, Nat.

ELAINE, ARKANSAS

Scene of a race riot in 1919. See Red Summer.

ELDER MICHAUX

See Michaux, Elder Lightfoot Solomon.

ELFE, WILCIE

Nineteenth century pharmacist. He managed a Charleston,

South Carolina, drug store and became so knowledgeable that he was able to concoct a number of patent drugs that were sold throughout the state.

ELLINGTON, DUKE

Musician (b. 1899). An outstanding composer, he has led the most enduring of all jazz orchestras since the 1920s. Born Edward Kennedy Ellington, in Washington, D. C., he composed his first piece ('Soda Fountain Rag') and played in local bands while still in high school. He went to New York in 1922 and by 1927 had made successful recordings, achieved a reputation for his Washingtonians, and begun broadcasting on the CBS radio network. He made movies, played in theaters, hotels, nightclubs, and concert halls throughout the world. Working with him were such great performers as drummer Sonny Greer, trombonist Charlie Irvis, trumpeter Bubber Miley, saxophonist Harry Carney, trombonist Joe 'Tricky Sam' Nanton, trumpeter Cootie Williams, saxophonist Johnny Hodges, trombonist Lawrence Brown, bass player Jimmy Blanton, and clarinetist Barney Bigard. His son, Mercer, is now his manager. His granddaughter is one of the June Taylor Dancers. Among his hundreds of compositions are the tone poem 'Black, Brown and Beige,' the dance 'Black and Tan Fantasy,' 'Mood Indigo,' and 'Creole Rhapsody,' for which he won the New York School of Music award for 1933. He has performed his own compositions at Carnegie Hall, the Metropolitan Opera House, and the White House.

ELLIOTT, ROBERT BROWN

Public official (1842-1884). A brilliant lawyer, born in Boston of West Indian parents and educated in England, he was elected to the South Carolina legislature (1868) and as U. S. congressman from South Carolina in 1871 and 1874. Each time he resigned his congressional seat after a few months of service to devote his time to his law practice and state politics.

ELLIS, JIMMY

Athlete (b. 1940). In 1968 he beat Jerry Quarry for the World Boxing Association title. He was defeated by Joe Frazier in 1970.

ELLISON, RALPH

Writer (b. 1914). Born in Oklahoma, he studied at Tuskegee Institute before going to New York in 1936. His first novel, *Invisible Man* (1952), received the National Book Award and the Russwurm Award. His best writings are collected in *Shadow and Act.*

EMANCIPATION PROCLAMATION

Though he recognized slavery as a primary issue in the Civil War, President Abraham Lincoln, to avoid alienating the border states, refrained from issuing an edict at the beginning of his term of office. On July 22, 1862, he read to his cabinet a draft of the Emancipation Proclamation formally issued on January 1, 1863. The proclamation freed only slaves in rebellious states and was intended as a measure 'for suppressing said rebellion.' Negroes interpreted it as an expression of a desire to advance the freedom of all mankind and received it with joy and thanksgiving. See Civil War.

EMPEROR JONES

Play by Eugene O'Neill in which Brutus Jones, an ex-convict and Pullman porter, makes himself emperor of a West Indian island. The demanding role established Charles Gilpin as one of America's great dramatic actors. He appeared alone in six of the eight scenes and was a sensation during the four-year run of the play (1920-24).

ENCORE

Monthly publication launched in 1972. See Lewis, Ida.

ENFORCEMENT ACT

See Civil Rights Act of 1870.

EQUAL RIGHTS PARTY

In 1872 Frederick Douglass was nominated for vice-president of the United States by a group called the Equal Rights Party.

ESPUTA, JOHN

Musician. He was musical director of the nation's first black operatic group, the Colored Opera Company, organized in Washington, D. C., in 1873.

ESSENCE

Magazine for black women, launched in May 1970.

ESTABROOK, PRINCE

Colonial militiaman. He was wounded in the first engagement of the Revolution, at the Battle of Lexington and Concord.

ESTAVANICO

Explorer (c. 1500-1539). A Moroccan scout, guide, and ambassador for Pánfilo de Narváez and Cabeza de Vaca, 'Little Stephen' was one of four surviving members of the daring party that set out in 1527 to explore the Florida coast and the region bordering the Gulf of Mexico. In 1539 he served Fray Marcos as guide and interpreter. He was the first non-Indian to see the regions of the present state of New Mexico. He was reported to have seen the Seven Cities of Cibola before his death at the hands of Indians.

ETHIOPIAN MANIFESTO

Published in 1829 by Robert A. Young, the *Ethiopian Manifesto, Issued in Defence of the Blackman's Rights, in the Scale of Universal Freedom* promised blacks that a messiah would arise and free his people.

EUROPE, JAMES REESE

Jazz bandleader. As conductor of the 'Clef Club,' the first black jazz orchestra, he taught the white dancing team Vernon and Irene Castle the revolutionary Fox-Trot. He demonstrated jazz in Carnegie Hall for the first time in 1912 and is credited by many with being the first original musician to orchestrate ragtime, jazz, and the blues. He was killed by a fellow musician about 1920.

EVANS, HENRY
Religious leader. The pioneer of Methodism in Fayetteville, North Carolina, he began preaching there about 1800 and soon drew both white and black auditors.

EVANTI, LILLIAN
Musician. The first black singer to appear with an organized European opera company, she appeared in *Lakmé*, with the Nice Opera Company, after World War I.

EVERS, CHARLES
Civil rights leader (b. 1923). The mayor of Fayette, Mississippi, attended Alcorn College, operated funeral and hotel enterprises in Philadelphia, then moved in 1957 to Chicago, to teach and engage in business ventures. He succeeded his murdered brother, Medgar, as field secretary of the NAACP in 1963, conducted a campaign based on the theme of love and nonviolence, and won election in 1969 to the office of mayor. He vowed to make Fayette a 'clean and righteous town' without showing favoritism to either race. His campaign and victory influenced politics throughout the state, putting other black candidates into political offices. In 1971 he became the first black politician to run for governor of Mississippi.

EVERS, MEDGAR WILEY
Civil rights leader (1926-1963). As Mississippi field secretary of the National Association for the Advancement of Colored People, he worked effectively to promote integration. He was shot from ambush in Jackson, Mississippi, on June 12, 1963. He was awarded the Spingarn Medal posthumously for his dedication to the fight for freedom.

EXECUTIVE ORDER 8802

Issued on June 25, 1941. President Franklin D. Roosevelt's executive order brought about better conditions for negro workers. As a result of the decree, three years later some 100,000 negroes were working in aircraft plants and 323,000 had an opportunity to learn industrial skills.

EXECUTIVE ORDER 9981

Issued by President Harry S. Truman in 1948, it called for 'equality of treatment and opportunity' in the armed forces.

EXECUTIVE ORDER 10730

Issued on September 24, 1957, after the command contained in Proclamation No. 3204 and issued the previous day had not been obeyed, President Dwight D. Eisenhower's order authorized the use of federal troops to insure the admission and protection of negro children seeking to enter Central High School in Little Rock, Arkansas. See Little Rock Crisis.

F

FAIR EMPLOYMENT PRACTICES COMMITTEE

Established by Executive Order 8802 following A. Philip Randolph's proposed march on Washington, the FEPC processed complaints and conducted public hearings. It stated that vocational training should be nondiscriminatory and that defense contracts should include nondiscrimination clauses. Issued on June 25, 1941, it reaffirmed the policy established in the National Defense Training Act and gave official sanction to the recomendations of he National Defense Advisory Commission.

In 1943 a new executive order set up a new committee in the Office of Emergency Management and emphasized the need for equal employment opportunities, particularly under government contracts. In 1947 Congress refused to grant funds for the work of the committee, but some states enacted FEPC legislation. Finally, the Civil Rights Act of 1964 undertook to guarantee to all Americans equal opportunity to secure employment and participate in federal assistance programs.

FAIR HAVEN INFIRMARY

Black-controlled medical center established in Atlanta, Georgia, by Dr. Henry R. Butler.

FAIR, RONALD

Writer. In *Many Thousands Gone* (1965) he used fantasy to make telling points about human behavior.

FANON, FRANTZ

Philosopher (1925-1961). Born in Martinique, he had become the acknowledged architect and philosopher of the revolutionary movements in the so-called Third World before his death in the cause of the Algerian Liberation Movement. His brilliant work, *The Wretched of the Earth* (1965), outlined the revolutionary's task and provided many insights into the social and psychological effects of racism. See Peter Geisman, *Fanon* (1971).

FARAD, WALI

Cult leader (born c. 1877). Also known as Farad W. D. Muhammad, he is thought to have been an orthodox Muslim born in Mecca. He appeared in Detroit on July 4, 1930, and identified himself as the prophet or messiah who was to lead blacks into the millenium that was to follow the Battle of Armageddon. He established his first mosque in Detroit in 1931 and a second one shortly thereafter in Chicago. He promised his followers that he would help them to overcome their enslavement to their white masters and be restored to a position of dignity among the peoples of the world. Following his disappearance sometime after June 30, 1934, he was succeeded by Elijah Muhammad. Farad was the founder of the Nation of Islam, the Black Muslim movement.

FARLEY, J. C.

Photographer (b. 1854). He began his work in photography in Richmond, Virginia, in 1872. In 1895 he opened the Jefferson Fine Art Gallery. Prominent Americans and Europeans sought his services.

FARMER, JAMES LEONARD

Civil rights leader (b. 1920). Born in Marshall, Texas, he earned a divinity degree at Howard but refused ordination in the Methodist ministry because of his antisegregation views. In 1942 he helped to found CORE, which gained attention in 1947 when freedom rides first tested the implementation of the 1946 U. S. supreme court decision forbidding discrimination in interstate travel. He established CORE as a powerful force in the civil rights movement of the 1960s by promoting sit-ins, freedom rides, picketing, and other forms of nonviolent protest. He served as national director of CORE until 1965, wrote *Freedom—*

158

When?, ran unsuccessfully against Shirley Chisholm for U. S. congressman from New York's 12th district, and became assistant secretary of DHEW. Until he resigned in December 1970, he was the highest ranking black in government service.

FATHER DIVINE

See Divine, Father.

FAUNTROY, WALTER

Public official (b. 1933). He is a nonvoting delegate from the District of Columbia to the U. S. congress. He is a member of the Black Caucus. He calls the ballot 'the most effective nonviolent tool ever invented.' Long associated with Martin Luther King, Jr., he was a coordinator for the 1963 civil rights march on Washington and the Poor People's Campaign of 1968. A graduate of the Yale Divinity School (1958), he continued to pastor the New Bethel Baptist Church in Washington after his election to the House of Representatives in 1971.

FAUSET, CRYSTAL BIRD

First negro woman elected to a state legislature. She was elected to serve in the Pennsylvania House of Representatives in 1938.

FAUSET, JESSIE REMOND

Writer (b. 1884). One of the most successful female novelists of the 1920s, she dealt with the problem of color in *There Was Confusion* (1924) and *Plum Bun* (1929).

FAX, ELTON C.

Contemporary artist, writer, and lecturer. He has toured Africa and South America under the auspices of the U. S. state department.

FAYETTE COUNTY

Tennessee county which in 1960 became a symbol of the conflict in the South between blacks determined to vote and white southerners determined to keep them from becoming a political force. Blacks in the county were subjected to evictions and boycotts by the white minority. Outside Somerville some 150 blacks set up Freedom Village (also called Tent City) and solicited aid from abroad. The 13 tents focused the attention of the world on Fayette County. Aid came from the NAACP, CORE, and people all over the nation. By the end of the year 1,000 blacks in the area had registered to vote.

FEDERATION OF SOUTHERN COOPERATIVES
Association formed in 1967 to provide technical assistance to some 90 member cooperatives throughout the South.

FERGUSON, ANGELA
Pediatrician (b. 1925). She heads the research section of pediatrics at Howard University.

15TH AMENDMENT
Proposed to the states by Congress February 26, 1869, and proclaimed in force March 30, 1870, the Fifteenth Amendment to the U. S. Constitution declared that the right to vote should not be denied 'on account of race, color, or previous condition of servitude.'

54TH MASSACHUSETTS REGIMENT
Unit comprised of blacks from free states, slave states, and Canada. Famous black leaders helped to recruit volunteers for the regiment.

FILMS
Black audiences started flocking to see black films in the 1970s. The trail had been blazed by Sidney Poitier, who won an Academy Award for his performance in *Lilies of the Field,* and by Harry Belafonte, who produced and starred in John O. Killens' *Odds Against Tomorrow.* In 1970 the Ossie Davis production of Chester Himes' *Cotton Comes to Harlem* started the boom. Melvin Van Peebles' *Watermelon Man, Sweet Sweetback's Baadasssss Song,*

and *Shaft*, directed by Gordon Parks, kept the audiences coming. *Soul to Soul*, featuring Wilson Pickett and Ike and Tina Turner on a tour of Ghana, and *Black Jesus*, a fictionalized biography of Patrice Lumumba, were released before the year ended.

FIRE NEXT TIME, THE

Though not James' James Baldwin's first work, it is a landmark in black writing. It established Baldwin as a social prophet, for in it he predicted the violence of a Black Revolution that had not yet surfaced.

1ST KANSAS REGIMENT

On January 28, 1862, the 1st Kansas Regiment, made up of black troops, forced the Confederates to withdraw at Island Mounds in Missouri. This was the first battle waged by black troops in the Civil War.

1ST RECONSTRUCTION ACT

Passed in 1867, the act inaugurated an era of democracy and equal rights which lasted for almost a decade.

1ST REGIMENT OF SOUTH CAROLINA VOLUNTEERS

The first black regiment mustered into Union service, it performed creditably under the command of its white colonel, T. W. Higginson.

FISHER, MILES MARK

Clergyman. Active in the ministry for many years, he provided a completely new approach to spirituals in his *Negro Slave Songs in the United States* (1953), the revised and updated version of his doctoral dissertation. Published by the American Historical Society, the important study interprets spirituals as a means of conveying veiled messages between blacks and concludes that they provide blacks with 'uncommon strength' in their suffering and troubled lives.

161

FISHER, RUDOLPH

Physician and writer (1897-1934). Practicing medicine to support his career as a writer, he turned out superb works like *The Walls of Jerico* (1928), a satire on Harlem society, and *The Conjure Man Dies* (1932). He also arranged songs for Paul Robeson.

FISK JUBILEE SINGERS

Nine black youths who traveled under the direction of George L. White throughout the United States and Europe, 1871-78. They raised money for Fisk University and introduced negro spirituals to the white world.

FISK UNIVERSITY

Founded in 1865 by the American Missionary Association, in Nashville, Tennessee, the liberal arts school today draws 80 percent of its black students from other states.

FITZBUTLER, HENRY

Physician and educator (1842-1901). Born in Ontario, he graduated from the medical school of the University of Michigan and moved to Louisville, Kentucky, where he became the first black physician to practice in the state. He founded the Louisville National Medical College in 1888 and served as its first dean. His wife, Dr. Sarah H. Fitzbutler, served as superintendent of the school's auxiliary hospital.

FITZGERALD, ELLA

Entertainer (b. 1918). An incomparable vocalist, widely acclaimed as 'The First Lady of Song,' she ranks with the all-time favorite singers of blues, ballads, swing numbers, calypso, or pop songs. She is unique as a scat singer. Born in Newport News, Virginia, she was schooled in an orphanage in Yonkers. 'A-Tisket A-Tasket,' based on a nursery rhyme and written in collaboration with Chick Webb, brought her nationwide fame in 1938. Her other compositions include 'You Showed Me the Way' and 'Oh! But I Do.' She has appeared at the Hollywood Bowl and Carnegie

162

Hall. For 18 years, until 1972, she was judged the No. 1 female vocalist in *Downbeat's* reader poll.

FIVE BLACK LIVES

Subtitled *The Autobiographies of Venture Smith, James Mars, William Grimes, the Reverend G. W. Offley, and James L. Smith,* the recently published book (Wesleyan, 1971) is a good example of black heroic literature.

FLACK, ROBERTA

Singer. In 1972 she won *Downbeat's* reader poll and replaced Ella Fitzgerald as the nation's No. 1 female vocalist. She first studied operatic vocal technique, then earned a following as a nightclub performer. She went on to gain national prominence with her gold record hit, 'The First Time Ever I Saw Your Face.'

FLETCHER, ARTHUR

Assistant Secretary of the U. S. department of labor. He graduated from Washburn College in Topeka, Kansas, where he was the first black to work on the athletic staff. Before becoming assistant secretary, he headed the office of contract compliance. He now serves as executive director of the United Negro College Fund.

FLEXNER REPORT

Formally titled Medical Education in the United States and Canada, the report prepared by Abraham Flexner in 1909 for

the Carnegie Foundation strongly influenced medical college standards and led to the closing of all black medical schools except Meharry and Howard.

FLINT MEDICAL COLLEGE

Established in New Orleans in 1889, it graduated 120 medical students during its 22-year existence. Its graduates included J. H. Lowery.

FLIPPER, HENRY OSSIAN

Army officer (1856-1940). He was the first black graduate of the U. S. military academy at West Point. He joined the 10th Cavalry in 1878. Four years later Lt. Flipper, the only black officer in the U. S. army, was cleared on a charge of embezzlement but convicted of 'conduct unbecoming' and discharged. He maintained that he had been the victim of a plot hatched by resentful white officers (he had found a pretty riding companion after his A Company moved to Fort Concho on the Great Plains). His West Point experiences are recorded in *The Colored Cadet at West Point* (1878). See also Theodore D. Harris (ed.), *Negro Frontiersman: The Western Memoirs of Henry O. Flipper* (1963).

FLORA, WILLIAM

Virginia militiaman (d. 1820). A free Negro serving with the local militia in the Battle of Great Bridge in December 1775, he was the last sentinel to leave his post under enemy fire.

FLOWERS, TIGER

Athlete. In 1926 he defeated Harry Greb to become the first black middleweight boxing champion of the world.

FOLK STORY

A part of the African heritage of the American negro is the folk story. Slaves brought with them legends, myths, proverbs, and animal stories that had survived for centuries in outline form in their Africa. The best known adaptation of this oral treasury are the Uncle Remus stories. Shulo the Hare is the African equivalent of Uncle Remus.

FOLLOW THE DRINKING GOURD

The words of the song 'Follow the Drinking Gourd' were supposed to constitute a musical map for slaves on their way to freedom over the underground railroad. Drinking gourd was another word for the Big Dipper, pointing northward to freedom.

164

FONTAGES LEGION

A Haitian unit aiding the American cause during the Revolutionary war. The black fighters served with gallantry at the siege of Savannah, Georgia, where they prevented the collapse of the American lines.

FOOTBALL

The first college game between black football teams was played on Thanksgiving Day, 1892, in North Carolina. Biddle University (now Johnson C. Smith) beat Livingston College, 4 to 0. The first black to play in organized pro football was Fritz Pollard of the Akron Indians, 1919. The first black college all-American team was selected for the Washington *Star* (1911) by Edwin Bancroft Henderson. The first black college football bowl game was the Prairie View Bowl contest, when Prairie View met Wiley College (1929) in the now famed State Fair of Texas Classic. Blacks were prominent in professional football 1919-33 but disappeared from the game thereafter until 1946, when Kenny Washington, Woody Strode, Bill Willis, and Marion Motley signed contracts. For other firsts in football, see the names of individuals: William H. Lewis, Fritz Pollard, Homer Harris, Sandy Stephens, Duke Slater, Kenny Washington, Joe Perry, Levi Jackson, Ben Kelley, and J. C. Caroline. Consult A. S. 'Doc' Young, *Negro Firsts in Sports* (1963).

FORD, BARNEY

Businessman (d. 1902). A fugitive who came to Colorado in 1860, he became a successful businessman, took an active role in territorial politics. In Denver he built the Inter-Ocean Hotel, which later became a showplace for millionaires and presidents.

FORMAN, JAMES

Civil rights leader (b. 1929). When he took over the leadership of SNCC at the age of 33, he resolved to end segregation in all areas of American life. A graduate of Roosevelt University, where he had earned a degree in political science and public administration, he completed additional studies at the Institute of African

Affairs at Boston University before returning to the Deep South to help the sharecroppers in the region where he had visited with his grandparents as a child. He joined the SNCC and served as its executive secretary, 1961-66. He resigned his position when Stokely Carmichael came into the picture, and was dropped from membership as a result of his involvement with the Black Manifesto. Turning to international politics, he delivered a paper in Zambia on racism and appeared before a United Nations committee to discuss colonialsm in the United States and in South Africa. He has published a book, *Sammy Younge, Jr.*, and served as the Black Panthers' minister of foreign affairs.

FORT BROWN
See Brownsville Riot.

FORT DES MOINES
Iowa camp where about one-half (639) of the negro officers commissioned during World War I were trained.

FORT PILLOW, TENNESSEE
Site of one of the bloodiest encounters of the Civil War. On April 12, 1864, as they sought to surrender to Confederates, 300 soldiers of the 6th U. S. Colored Heavy Artillery and the 2nd Colored Light Artillery were murdered. The massacre rallied blacks everywhere to fight with redoubled determination.

FORTEN, CHARLOTTE L.
Writer (1837-1914). She was the granddaughter of James Forten. *The Journal of Charlotte L. Forten,* edited by Ray Allen Billington (1953), provides revealing insights into the life of blacks in nineteenth century America.

FORTEN, JAMES
Businessman, philanthropist, and abolitionist (1766-1842). Born free in Philadelphia, he became a powder boy on the privateer *Royal Louis* (1781), was captured by the British, imprisoned on the *Jersey,* and released after seven months. He spent a year in

England after the Revolution ended, apprenticed himself to Philadelphia sailmaker Robert Bridges, took control of the business
(1798), invented a device to handle sails, and amassed a fortune.
He opposed the American Colonization Society, was active as
an abolitionist and in the Negro Convention movement, supported
and influenced William Lloyd Garrison, and served on the board
of managers of the American Anti-Slavery Society. He recruited
2,500 blacks to defend Philadelphia against the British in 1814,
received a citation from the Humane Society in 1821 for rescuing
drowning persons, and entertained many prominent abolitionists,
including Garrison, in his home. His son-in-law, Robert Purvis,
was a prominent abolitionist. Charlotte L. Forten was his granddaughter.

FORTUNE, TIMOTHY THOMAS

Journalist (1856-1928). Born in Florida of slave parents, he
studied at Howard, returned to Florida to teach, then moved
to New York and started the *Rumor,* a newspaper later named
the *Globe.* When the *Globe* died in 1884 as a result of a dispute
between Fortune and his partner, he founded the *Freeman,*
which became one of the most militant black newspapers and
was renamed the *New York Age.* He published three books,
including *Black and White: Land, Labor and Politics in the
South* (1884).

FORT WAGNER

Confederate fortress on Morris Island, South Carolina. It was
assaulted by the Massachusetts Fifty-Fourth, the first Negro regiment organized in the North. Although the assault was repulsed
with heavy casualties, the regiment won praise throughout the
North for its bravery under fire.

FOSTER, ANDREW

Athlete (1879-1930). The founding father of black baseball,
'Rube' Foster organized and pitched for one of the great negro
teams, the Leland Giants, later called the Chicago American

Giants. In 1920 he helped to form a negro professional league, the National Negro Baseball League.

14TH AMENDMENT

Designed to help former slaves to gain full status as citizens and prevent state action discriminating against them, the Fourteenth Amendment has become the basis for a broad national system of civil rights. Frequently invoked in civil rights cases in federal courts is the clause forbidding any state to enact any 'law which shall abridge the privileges or immunities of citizens of the United States.' Adopted June 13, 1866, by a 'rump Congress' that had excluded representatives from ten Southern states, the amendment was rejected by these ten states, Delaware, Kentucky, and Maryland. The Republicans turned this very rejection to their advantage, claiming that the South had rejected a reasonable proposal and passing the Reconstruction Act of 1867. Governments set up under the act ratified the amendment, which was proclaimed in force July 28, 1868.

FOWLER, BUD

Athlete. In 1872 he became the first known black to play with a predominantly white team, in Newcastle, Pennsylvania.

FOXX, REDD

Entertainer. In 1972 the veteran comic, famed for his blue nightclub material, starred in a novel television situation comedy series, *Sanford and Son*. The comedian's real name is John Sanford.

FRANCIS, JOHN R.

Refused admission to the Medical Society of the District of Columbia in 1894, he became the first black to establish a sanitorium in the nation's capital. He was a graduate of the University of Michigan and a member of the board of trustees of Howard.

168

FRANKLIN, ARETHA

Musician (b. 1942). The epitome of soul, she was the first female vocalist to be awarded 5 gold records. Her first record with sales in excess of 5 million copies came out in 1960. She has performed in concerts in the United States and Europe.

FRANKLIN, GEORGE W.

Businessman (b. 1865). After building his own hearse and establishing his first mortuary in Rome, Georgia, he moved to Chatanooga, Tennessee. There he established a similar business (1903) which was also a profitable enterprise.

FRANKLIN, JOHN HOPE

Historian (b. 1915). After receiving his doctorate from Harvard in 1941, he taught at Fisk, Howard, and Cambridge, among other universities; authored *The Free Negro in North Carolina, 1790-1860* (1943), *From Slavery to Freedom: A History of American Negroes* (1947), *The Militant South* (1956), *Reconstruction after the Civil War* (1961), *Emancipation Proclamation* (1963), and *Color and Race* (1968); and rendered services to UNESCO and many other organizations, including the American Council on Human Rights. In 1972 he was named to the Oklahoma Hall of Fame.

FRANKLIN, MARTHA

Founder of the National Association of Colored Graduate Nurses (1908).

FRANKLIN, W. H.

Educator (b. 1852). Ordained a Presbyterian minister in 1883, he later established Swift Memorial Institute and served as director of Maryville College, both in Tennessee.

FRAZIER, E. FRANKLIN

Sociologist (1894-1962). After receiving his doctorate from Chicago University in 1931, he published seven books and many articles on the sociology of the negro race. He became professor and chairman of the sociology department at Howard University, president of the American Sociological Association, and a founding member of the International Institute for the Study of Afro-Americans. His works include *Negro Youth at the Crossways* (1940), *The Negro in the United States* (1949), and *Black Bourgeoisie: The Rise of a New Middle Class* (1957).

FRAZIER, JOE

Athlete. In 1970 he defeated Jimmy Ellis to become world heavyweight boxing champion. He successfully defended his title against Muhammad Ali in 1971.

FREDERICK DOUGLASS MEMORIAL HOSPITAL

Founded by Dr. Nathan Francis Mossell, Philadelphia's Frederick Douglass Memorial Hospital and Training School for Nurses opened its doors to people of all races on October 31, 1895. Dissident young physicians led by Dr. Edward C. Howard broke away in 1907 and founded Mercy Hospital. The two were united in 1948 as the Mercy-Douglass Hospital.

FREE AFRICAN SOCIETY

Organization founded in Philadelphia in 1787 by men and women pledged to lead sober and orderly lives. Led by former slaves Richard Allen and Absalom Jones, the society helped many whites during the great plague of 1793.

FREE NEGROES

Free negroes, constituting approximately one-eight of the total black population of the United States in 1850, were treated with contempt in the South and lived under the constant threat of re-enslavement. Most of the free negroes were in the North, where they were also held under rigid restraints, with little opportunity to exercise their competence in the art of freedom and much to remind them of their inferior status. By 1790 some 59,000 free negroes were living in the United States. By 1830 the number had increased to 319,000, and by 1860 to 488,000, almost equally

170

divided between the South and the North. A child's status was generally determined by that of his mother. Slave codes made the free black's existence precarious. The citizenship rights of free blacks were steadily eroded in the 19th century. Despite their handicaps, some free blacks survived and prospered. Thomy Lafon, James Forten and John Russwurm are cases in point. Free negroes took the lead in the antislavery movement. Prominent among the abolitionists were Frederick Douglass, Charles Remond, and Henry Highland Garnet. Active in journalism and public speaking, they also published books, organized conventions, and established churches and fraternal associations. Some slaves were freed by their masters, others gained their freedom through service in the colonial wars and the American Revolution, and still others ran away from their owners. Abolitionist societies and religious groups helped to pass legislation bringing freedom to additional numbers. Slaves with special skills could hire themselves out and buy their freedom. Among those who took this course were Lunsford Lane, Lott Carey, George Moses Horton, Newport Gardner, Denmark Vesey, and James Derham. A free negro had to carry a 'free paper' giving his name, height, complexion, and an account of the manner in which he had obtained his freedom. Throughout the South, the burden of proof was on the negro: he had to prove that he was not a slave. He could not hold public office, vote (except in Tennessee after 1834 and in North Carolina after 1835), testify against a white person, use firearms, travel freely between states, or join the militia.

FREE SOIL PARTY

A political party formed in 1847-48 by opponents to the extension of slavery into territories acquired from Mexico. Its ticket made possible the election of Zachary Taylor as President. Its radical antislavery element continued until the new Republican party absorbed it in 1854. Frederick Douglass was present at the founding of the Free Soil Party and later endorsed its candidates in his newspaper.

FREE SOUTHERN THEATER

Touring group founded in New Orleans in 1964. Featuring plays dealing with issues affecting negroes, the group encouraged discussion between actors and audience at the end of each performance.

FREEDMEN

Southern states sought to adjust to the new conditions created by the existence of some 4 million freedmen by resorting to Black Codes and holding freedmen under conditions differing but slightly from slavery. Reconstruction measures, which enforced freedmen's civil rights at gunpoint and with the help of the Freedmen's Bureau, were vitiated by political ambitions. Philanthropic individuals and agencies could not provide adequate schools for them, and the *Nation* soon ceased to fulfill its mission of serving as a medium for discusing their problems. Reconstruction ended with the legal transformation of the master-slave relationship into an owner-tenant modus vivendi.

FREEDMEN'S BUREAU

U. S. government agency established by an act of March 3, 1865, to help newly freed negroes in the South. Offering a variety of services to the impoverished, whether white or black, it established 40 hospitals, acted as legal guardian to freedmen, took control of confiscated and abandoned lands, enforced contracts, and operated schools at all levels. In spite of its successes in specific areas, it failed to promote mutual confidence between the races or to dispel the myth of negro inferiority. See Paul S. Pierce. *The Freedmen's Bureau* (1904).

FREEDMEN'S BUREAU SCHOOLS

Before the Civil War had ended, the U. S. congress had passed a law establishing the Freedmen's Bureau 'to aid these helpless, ignorant, unprotected people . . . until they can provide for and take care of themselves.' Operating as an agency of the War Department, the bureau helped in the foundation of a system of schools for negroes, giving 'central organization, encourage-

172

ment, protection, and financial support to the efforts of philanthropists, freedmen, and states.' Between 1865-67 many schools
were burned, but at its peak the bureau operated some 4,000
primary schools, 74 normal schools, and 61 industrial schools
for negroes. The educational activities of the bureau continued
for three years after its main work ended in 1869. Its better
features were the establishment of free public schools in the
South, Hampton Institute, and Fisk, Howard, and Atlantic
universities. Termination of the bureau placed education back
in the hands of the states. See George R. Bentley, *A History
of the Freedmen's Bureau* (1955).

FREEDMEN'S HOSPITAL

Major Alexander T. Augusta supervised the treatment of
freedmen at Camp Barker in 1863. In 1865 the newly created
Freedmen's Bureau was put in charge of the hospital facilities.
By order of General O. O. Howard, buildings were erected on
the grounds of Howard University and the Freedmen's Hospital
was established on a permanent basis, with a bed capacity of
300. Dr. Charles B. Purvis, appointed surgeon-in-chief in 1881,
became the first black civilian to head such an institution.

FREEDMEN'S SAVINGS AND TRUST COMPANY

Bank created in 1865 by the federal government. It opened
its doors in New York on April 4, 1865, and soon had branches
throughout the South. Its business was confined to blacks, but
not its management. A few blacks were eventually hired, and
Frederick Douglass became its president in 1874. Not even
Douglass could save the bank from disaster, however, following
the Panic of 1873, and thousands of depositers suffered losses
when it closed its doors on June 28, 1874.

FREEDOM ASSOCIATION

Group formed by New England negroes to help fugitive slaves.

FREEDOM MARCH

See James Meredith Freedom March.

FREEDOM NATIONAL BANK

With assets of more than 35 million dollars in 1971, the New York bank was the leading black financial institution. Jackie Robinson is its board chairman and William R. Hudgins is its president.

FREEDOM OF CHOICE

The practice of allowing each pupil to attend the school of his choice. In 1968 the Supreme Court held that such a plan, while not unconstitutional of itself, is not sufficiently effective 'as a tool of segregation.' See Green v. New Kent County, Virginia.

FREEDOM RIDERS

Group organized by the Congress of Racial Equality to protest segregation on buses. CORE choose 13 persons, including James Farmer and 6 whites, to travel from Washington to New Orleans. Departing on May 4, they traveled without incident through Virginia, the Carolinas, and Georgia. They encountered violence in Alabama, however, and had to travel from Birmingham to New Orleans by plane. The Freedom Riders were joined by three other groups—SCLC, SNCC, and the Nashville Student Movement —as well as hundreds of other persons, black and white. On November 1, 1961, an order by the Interstate Commerce Commission banned segregation in interstate terminal facilities.

FREEDOM SUITS

Attempts of slaves to gain their freedom through legal means. Some slaves, like Jenny Slew, were successful in winning their freedom through the courts in colonial days.

FREEDOM TO SERVE

Report prepared by a committee appointed by President Truman in 1948 to study the problem of integration in the armed services. It blueprinted the steps by which integration was to be achieved.

FREEDOM VILLAGE
See Fayette County.

FREEDOM'S JOURNAL
First negro newspaper, published in New York City, beginning on March 16, 1827. Published by Samuel E. Cornish and John B. Russwurm, the first edition was devoted to the issues of slavery and discrimination.

FREEMAN, HENRY LAWRENCE
Composer (1869-1954). He taught at Wilberforce university in Chicago and at his own Freeman School of Music. His fifteen operas, all based on negro, Oriental, or Indian themes, include *African Kraal* (1903), *The Octoroon* (1904), *Voodoo* (1928), and a tetralogy titled *Zululand* (1932-37).

FREEMAN, PAUL
Musician. In 1968 he became associate conductor of the Dallas Symphony.

FREEMAN, RALPH
Clergyman. In the early 1800s he was ordained and became an able Baptist preacher. A slave, he baptized and administered communion in Anson County, North Carolina, until the law forbade him to preach.

FRIENDS OF NEGRO FREEDOM
Association formed by radicals in New York in 1920 for the purpose of unionizing migrant workers and curing numerous others social ills. The organization was largely ineffective and was in existence for only three years.

FRONTIER HISTORY
Blacks played an important role in frontier history. They frequently intermarried with the Indians and, because of the preferential treatment shown them by the Indians, were mediators between the two civilizations. As trappers, traders, scouts, and

175

interpreters, they have left their imprint on frontier history. George Bush, Beofge Bonga, Jean de Sable, James Beckwourth, York, Robert Love, and Isaiah Dorman are prime examples. See Kenneth Wiggins Porter, *The Negro on the American Frontier* (1971).

FRUIT OF ISLAM

A protective, militaristic group formed by Wali Farrad. See Muhammad, Elijah.

FUGITIVE SLAVE ACT OF 1793

Legislation giving the master of an escaped slave the right to regain possession of his property. Passed by Congress on February 12, 1793, it set up the machinery for the return of fugitives slaves. The Supreme Court upheld its constitutionality in Prigg v. Pennsylvania.

FUGITIVE SLAVE ACT OF 1850

Approved on September 18, 1850, the stringent act to control fugitive slaves was one of the key elements in the Compromise of 1850. It strengthened the provisions of the Act of 1793 and placed enforcement under federal jurisdiction. Its passage was a signal victory for the South, only partially offset by an act to end slavery in the District of Columbia.

FUGITIVE SLAVE LAWS

Federal acts of 1793 and 1850 which provided for the return between states of escaped slaves. The 1793 law was relaxed as Northern states abolished slavery and passed personal liberty measures allowing fugitives to have a jury trial. The second act, incorporated in the Compromise of 1850, assumed that the runaway slave was guilty until proven innocent, denied his testimony, and applied even to fugitives who had enjoyed their freedom for years. Abolitionists converted the measure into a powerful propaganda weapon. They referred to it as 'the Bloodhound Bill' and 'the Man-Stealing Law.'

176

FUGITIVE SLAVES

Blacks who escaped from bondage were a key factor in abolitionism since their flight contradicted the proslavery argument that they were happy creatures in need of their masters' protection. Moreover, they created legal problems as well as social problems. The Fugitive Slave Acts of 1783 and 1850 were landmarks. The first was readily accepted in the North as well as in the South, whereas the second was treated with scorn in the North. It was a fugitive who inspired *Uncle Tom's Cabin*. Such fugitives as Harriet Tubman were able to function boldly and effectively in the North.

FULLER, HOWARD

Educator. He spearheaded the recent founding of Malcolm X Liberation University in Durham, North Carolina.

FULLER, META WARRICH

Sculptor (b. 1877). She is famous for her sculptures symbolizing the sufferings and aspirations of the negro. 'Water Boy' is one of her best works.

FULLER, S. B.

Businessman (b. 1905). He is publisher of the *Pittsburgh Courier*.

FULLER, SOLOMON C.

Psychiatrist and neuropathologist. He came to the United States from Liberia in 1889, received his M. D. from Boston University in 1897, and taught neurology, pathology, and psychiatry at the Boston University Medical School for more than 30 years. He studied in Germany under Emil Kraepelin, edited the Westborough State Hospital Papers (1913), and wrote many technical papers. He is best known for his work on dementias and on Alzheimer's disease.

G

GABRIEL

Leader of an abortive slave uprising in Virginia. Inspired by the deeds of Toussaint L'Ouverture, he armed some 1,000 slaves for a march on Richmond in the summer of 1800. A rainstorm and informers wrecked his plan. He was hanged, along with about thirty of his followers.

GAG RULE

A measure passed in 1836 by the Congress to rule out the presentation of anti-slavery petitions. The eight-year fight to remove the 'Gag Rule' was led by ex-President John Quincy Adams.

GAIDI, BROTHER

See Henry, Milton R.

GAINES V. MISSOURI

U. S. Supreme Court decision handed down in 1938. The Court ordered the University of Missouri to admit a negro applicant who had no other way to receive legal training within the state.

GAINES, ERNEST

Writer. His novels reflect his early life on a Louisiana plantation. *The Spook Who Sat by the Door* (1969), published after several earlier rejections, received critical praise and was called 'the first revolutionary black novel' by *Negro Digest*.

GAITHER, ALONZO SMITH

Football coach (b. 1903). As athletic director, head football coach, and director of the physical education department at Florida A. and M., he has compiled an impressive record: winner of the league title every year except two during a 17-year period, beginning in 1945, with a total of 139 wins, 21 losses, and 4 ties. In 1961 he was elected to the Helms Foundation Hall of Fame.

GANS, JOE

Athlete (1874-1910). Pound for pound, he was reputed to be the best fighter of all time. He reigned as king of the lightweights, 1901-08. He was elected to boxing's Hall of Fame in 1954.

GARDNER, ELIZA ANN

Anti-slavery leader (1831-1922). Her Boston home was an underground railroad station. She was also active in the AMEZ church.

GARLAND, C. N.

Physician. In 1908 he founded Plymouth Hospital in Boston. He earned his M. D. at the Leonard Medical School and completed postgraduate work in England.

GARDNER, NEWPORT

Slave who won money in a lottery and used it to purchase his freedom from his North Carolina master.

GARNER V. LOUISIANA

Supreme Court decision (1961) reversing sit-in convictions based on breach of the peace laws.

GARNER, ERROLL

Musician (b. 1921). The world's greatest jazz pianist, sales of his records exceed those of any other jazz instrumentalist. The youngest of six children in a Pittsburgh musical family, he picked out on the piano tunes he heard at the age of three, yet he never learned to read music. He began playing in New York nightclubs in 1943, recorded his first big hit, 'Laura,' in 1946, became the first modern jazz instrumentalist to give a solo recital (Cleveland, 1950), and composed scores for ballet, movies, and Broadway musicals. His works include 'Misty' and the popular album *Concert by the Sea.*

GARNET, HENRY HIGHLAND

Clergyman (1815-1882). In New York he pastored the Negro Presbyterian Church, conducted a school for negro children, and preached a social gospel. On February 12, 1865, he became the first black man to preach in the Capitol. He delivered a sermon on the abolition of slavery. In 1843, at the Convention of Free Men in Buffalo, New York, he had outlined a brilliant plan for a general slave strike.

GARVEY, MARCUS MOZIAH

Black nationalist (1887-1940). A forerunner of today's black separatists, he united millions after World War I in a movement stressing black pride, racial separation, and the resurrection of a great black nation in Africa. A descendant of Maroons who resisted enslavement, he was born in Jamaica, traveled to England (1912), returned to Jamaica (1914) to found the Universal Negro Improvement Association and urge blacks to unite under the motto 'One God! One Aim! One Destiny!,' came to America (1916), founded a Harlem branch of UNIA (1917), founded the weekly newspaper *Negro World* (1918) to spread its gospel, staged street parades, conferred titles of nobility, and attracted more than a million followers. He focused attention on pride in race, founded the African Orthodox Church, castigated light-skinned negro intellectuals, called for the establishment of an independent nation in the ancestral homeland, styled himself its provisional leader, and created the African Legion. He began selling stock in his Black Star Line in 1919, founded the Negro Factories Corporation (1919), was jailed for mail fraud (1923), pardoned and deported as an alien (1927), and forced to close his newspaper (1933). He began publishing the magazine *Black*

Man (1933) but in 1935 moved his headquarters to London. See E. David Cronon, *Black Moses: The Story of Marcus Garvey* (1955), and Theodore G. Vincent, *Black Power and the Garvey Movement* (1971).

GARY PLAN

Scheme proposed by racist M. W. Gary for maintaining white supremacy in the South in the 1870s. His plan of intimidation called for each Democrat to 'control the vote of at least one Negro, by intimidation, purchase, keeping him away. . . .' His master plan for South Carolina, based on methods tested in Mississippi, was adopted also in Florida and Louisiana.

GASTON, ARTHUR G.

Businessman (b. 1892). A self-made millionaire, he has been active in banking, insurance, real estate, and funeral homes.

GAUNT, WHEELING

Philanthropist (1812-1894). After purchasing his freedom and his wife's, he moved from Kentucky to Ohio, bought property, farmed, and invested his profits in real estate in Yellow Springs and Xenia. After his death his estate went to Wilberforce University as an endowment for deserving students. Other bequests were made to churches and to unfortunate widows. The land was once rented as farm and is now the Wheeling Gaunt Recreation Park.

GAYLE V. BROWDER

U. S. supreme court decision (1956) declaring state statutes requiring racial segregation on the buses of Montgomery, Alabama, to be unconstitutional. The case overruled the separate-but-equal doctrine laid down in Plessy v. Ferguson (1896).

GEBHART V. BELTON

One of the legal actions making up the School Segregation Cases. See Brown v. Board of Education.

182

GEEK

Derogatory word used by blacks to refer to white people.

GENTRY, HERBERT

Artist. He calls himself a Direct Expressionist and urges black artists to paint what they feel. He has lived and exhibited his works in the U. S., Sweden, France, and Switzerland.

GEORGE, ZELMA WATSON

Musician. In 1949 she created the role of Mme. Flora in the Cleveland, Ohio, presentation of Menotti's The Medium. In 1960 she was named an alternate delegate to the United Nations general assembly.

GEORGIA MINSTRELS

The first all-negro minstrel troupe, organized by George B. Hicks in 1865.

GIBBS, JONATHAN C.

Educator. The first state superintendent of instruction in Florida, he was a graduate of Dartmouth. He established a successful system during the Reconstruction and continued in his post until his death in 1874.

GIBBS, MIFFLIN WISTER

Publisher and magistrate (1823-1918). He rose from bootblack to become publisher of the California's first negro newspaper, *Mirror of the Times*. In 1873 he was elected to a judgeship in Arkansas. His autobiography is titled *Shadow and Light* (1902).

GIBSON, ALTHEA

Athlete (b. 1927). After breaking the color bar in lawn tennis in 1950, she went on to win the Wimbledon and Forest Hills championships seven years later. In 1958 she retired to become a professional golfer.

GIBSON, BOB

Athlete and public figure. Born in Omaha, Nebraska, on November 9, 1935, he suffered as a child from rickets, asthma, and a rheumatic heart condition. He became an all-state basketball player in high school, turned to baseball at Creighton University in Omaha, and after graduation joined the Harlem Globetrotters. The iron-armed pitcher achieved national prominence in 1967 by hurling the Cardinals to a World Series victory over the Boston Red Sox. Gibson also conducted a radio-TV show in Omaha and was a member of the city's Human Relations Board.

GIBSON, JOSH

Athlete (d. 1947). The great all-star catcher of the Homestead Grays was one of the major baseball attractions of his era.

GIBSON, KENNETH A.

Public official. With the help of LeRoi Jones' Black Community Development, he was elected mayor of Newark, New Jersey, in 1970.

GIBSON, TRUMAN K., SR.

Businessman (b. 1882). A prominent civic leader, he established the Chicago Supreme Life Insurance Company.

GILBERT, JOHN WESLEY

Scholar (b. 1864). He participated in excavations in Eretria undertaken by the American School at Athens, Greece, 1890-91. He received the scholarship for excellence in Greek awarded by the school.

GILLEM REPORT

Prepared by a board of generals appointed by the War Department in 1945, the Gillem Report called for the grouping together of white and negro units and the expansion of opportunities for negroes to serve as officers.

184

GILLESPIE, DIZZY

Musician (b. 1917). Born John Birks Gillespie in Cheraw, South Carolina, he formed a band when he was only fourteen, studied harmony and theory at Laurinburg Institute in North Carolina, played in a Philadelphia band (1937), then moved to New York to play with Teddy Hill, Cab Calloway (1939-41), and other band leaders. He formed a bebop quintet in 1945 but did not achieve national prominence until 1946-50, when bebop became the rage. He toured Europe and Asia under the sponsorship of the U. S. State Department in 1956. See Michael James, *Dizzy Gillespie* (1959).

GILMORE, 'BUDDY'

Musician. A drummer who played with the Memphis Students in the early 1900s, he introduced trick trap-drumming. He performed juggling and acrobatic stunts while manipulating several noise-making devices besides the drums.

GILPIN, CHARLES S.

Actor (1872-1930). The first famous black dramatic actor in America, he created the role of Emperor Jones in Eugene O'Neill's play. Born in Richmond, Virginia, he became a variety performer, touring and perfecting song and dance routines at fairs, restaurants, and theaters when not working as an elevator operator, printer, porter, or in some other non-theatrical job. He appeared in the Lincoln Theater in Harlem (1910-17), helped to organize and manage the Lafayette Players (1916), and finally appeared in Broadway (1919) in John Drinkwater's play *Abraham Lincoln*.

GIOVANNI, NIKKI

Poet, author and lecturer. One of the most celebrated young black poets of America, she is editorial consultant for *Encore*.

Early in 1972 the 28-year-old poet was aclaimed for her autobiographical *Gemini*. An honor graduate of Fisk, she is a major figure in the black oral poetry movement.

185

GLEASON, RALPH J.

Jazz critic. He has written and edited many books on jazz, including *Jam Session: An Anthology of Jazz* (1958).

GLOUCESTER, JOHN

Pioneer clergyman and abolitionist. In 1817 he was named to a committee of 12 that met with white abolitionist Robert Finley, a key figure in the American Colonization Society, to discuss plans for expatriating negroes. Gloucester was a leader in the African Presbyterian Church in Philadelphia.

GO DOWN, MOSES

The song 'Go Down, Moses' is supposed to refer to one of the most celebrated conductors of the underground railroad, Harriet Tubman.

GODFREY, GEORGE

Athlete (b. 1853). The first boxer to win the negro American heavyweight title, he was born on Prince Edward Island and made his home in Boston. John L. Sullivan refused to fight him.

GOLDSBY, GEORGE

See Cherokee Bill.

GOLF

Though at least seven cities had black-owned golf clubs as early as 1928, few blacks have been able to compete successfully in this predominantly white sport. Notable exceptions: Charles Sifford, Lee Elder, Ted Rhodes, and Pete Brown.

GOOD NEIGHBOR LEAGUE

Religious league formed in Washington by Elder Michaux. The organization was said to have fed 250,000 poor people in its Happy News Cafe in 1933. The league helped to organize the black vote for Franklin D. Roosevelt.

186

GOODE, MELVIN R.

News correspondent. In 1962 he became the first black news commentator on network television. On August 29 he joined ABC-TV as a United Nations correspondent. He covered events during the Cuban missile crisis.

GOODLE, JOSEPH

President of North Carolina Mutual Life Insurance Company.

GORDONE, CHARLES

Dramatist. He was the first black dramatist to win the Pulitzer Prize (*No Place to Be Somebody,* 1970).

GORDY, BERRY, JR.

Musician and businessman (b. 1930). The composer of some hit tunes, he has been even more successful as head of the Motown Recording Company. See Motown.

GRACE, BISHOP CHARLES EMMANUEL

Cult leader (d. 1960). Better known as Daddy Grace, he came to the United States around 1920. A man of mixed parentage, Negro and Portuguese, he worked as a cook before he started to preach (1925) and founded the United House of Prayer for All People. Erotic dancing was a main feature of the ritual. At his death, he had amassed a fortune by investing in all kinds of businesses.

GRAHAM, SHIRLEY

Writer (b. 1907). The first editor of *Freedomways,* she is the author of *Dr. George Washington Carver* (1944), *The Story of Phillis Wheatley* (1959), and *Jean Baptiste du Sable* (1953). In 1950 she won the Anisfeld Wolf award for her biography of Benjamin Banneker, *Your Most Humble Servant.*

GRAMBLING COLLEGE

Founded by Dr. Ralph Waldo Emerson Jones in 1936, the Louisiana college has a unique record in turning out scholar-

187

athletes who have gone on to stardom in professional sports. Since 1948 more than 60 Grambling men have become professional football players in the United States and Canada.

GRAND UNITED ORDER OF TRUE REFORMERS

Fraternal association founded by Washington Browne. In 1876 the religious leader succeeded in bringing together 27 Alabama Fountains known as the Grand Fountain of True Reformers, with 2,000 members and a newspaper, *The Reformer*. He became Grand Worthy Master of an association of True Reformers in Virginia. The Grand United Order of True Reformers which he headed organized a weekly newspaper, a bank, some real estate enterprises, and a building and loan association. Though its venture into mutual insurance failed, blacks acquired valuable experience preparing them for more successful ventures, for other fraternal organizations established successful insurance programs.

GRANDFATHER CLAUSES

State constitutional provisions restricting voting rights. Added to some southern state constitutions after 1890, they exempted descendants of men who voted before Reconstruction days from literacy and property restrictions. Alabama, Georgia, Louisiana, North Carolina, South Carolina, and Oklahoma had such provisions in their constitutions. The Supreme Court ruled that the Oklahoma voting restriction violated the Fifteenth Amendment (Guinn and Beal v. United States, 1915).

GRANGER, LESTER BLACKWELL

Civil rights leader (b. 1896). After graduating from Dartmouth, he served as an officer in World War I, taught at St. Augustine's, completed graduate work at New York University and the New York School of Social Work, and became a special adviser to the Secretary of the Navy in World War II. The committee on which he served was instrumental in bringing about the armed services desegregation program of 1950. In 1934 he began working with the National Urban League, assuming the directorship in 1941 and continuing in that capacity until demands for a more militant policy forced his retirement in the early 1960s, when he accepted a teaching position at New York University.

GRANT, EARL

Musician (d. 1970). Killed in a car crash at the age of 39, he had won national acclaim as an organist. He began his career as a 4-year-old soloist in his father's Baptist church in Idabel, Oklahoma. He performed throughout North America, in Europe, and in the Orient. His recording of 'Ebbtide' sold in the millions. He also appeared in such movies as *Tender Is the Night* and *Imitation of Life*.

GRANT, THOMAS L.

Politician. In 1908 he was a delegate to the Republican national convention in Chicago. The South Carolina Republican served on the committee to notify the presidential nominee of the convention's decision.

GRAVELY, SAMUEL L., JR.

Admiral. One of the first two black officers selected to attend the U. S. Naval War College (1963), he was the first black man to command a U. S. warship, the destroyer escort *Falgout* (1962). He now commands the U. S. 2,250 ton *Taussig*. In 1971 he was made the first black admiral in the U. S. navy. See Thompson, George.

GRAVES, LEMUEL E., JR.

Journalist (b. 1915). A 1934 graduate of St. Augustine's College, he worked with the *North Carolina Times* in Raleigh, then with the *Norfolk Journal and Guide*. He achieved recognition as a war correspondent during World War II.

GREAT WHITE HOPE, THE

Play produced during the 1968-69 season. Starring James Earl

Jones, it was based on the life of Jack Johnson. The following year Jones starred in the film version of *The Great White Hope.*

GREAVES, CLIFTON

Army hero. He was awarded the congressional Medal of Honor for his heroism under fire. In 1877 he broke through the circle of Apaches threatening to kill him and his 9 companions in the Florida Mountains, allowing the troopers to escape with minor wounds. See Buffalo Soldiers.

GREEN V. NEW KENT COUNTY, VIRGINIA

Generally known as the Green decision, the ruling handed down by the Supreme Court in 1968 held that freedom of choice plans did not represent a 'sufficient step' to comply with the 1954 decision outlawing segregation. Noting that schools are 'clearly charged with the affirmative duty to take whatever steps might be necessary to convert to a unitary system in which racial discrimination would be eliminated root and branch,' the Court suggested zoning and pairing as possible means of accomplishing desegregation.

GREEN, RICHARD THEODORE

Educator and public official (1844-1923). The first black student to graduate from Harvard, he taught in secondary schools and at the University of South Carolina and Howard, practiced law, and served as U. S. consul at Bombay and Vladivostok.

GREEN, SAMUEL

Methodist preacher. In 1858 he was jailed in Maryland because he had been found reading Uncle Tom's Cabin.

GREEN, SHIELDS

One of John Brown's raiders. See Harpers Ferry.

GREENE, LORENZO JOHNSTON

Scholar (b. 1899). After completing his early educational training at Howard and Columbia, he helped Carter G. Woodson to collect the materials for The Negro Wage Earner (1930), taught at Lincoln University in Missouri, and unearthed a vast array of neglected facts about the role of the negro in colonial history. His doctoral dissertation, *The Negro in Colonial New England* (Columbia, 1941), is the definitive work in this field of American history. He has published many scholarly articles and has served as president of the ASNLH.

GREENER, RICHARD T.

Educator (1844-1922). The first negro graduate of Harvard, he began teaching metaphysics at the University of South Carolina in 1873. He also served as dean of Howard law school. An advocate of negro migration from the South, he argued that a reduction in the labor supply would benefit those who remained.

GREENFIELD, ELIZABETH TAYLOR

Musician (1809-1876). Born a slave, the Mississippi singer was the first black musician to achieve renown both here and abroad. Better known as the 'Black Swan,' she sang for Queen Victoria in 1854 With a sensational range of three and a quarter octaves, she sang for audiences in the free states before moving to London.

GREENWOOD

Mississippi town in which Stokeley Carmichael proclaimed the doctrine of Black Power in June, 1966. Ironically, the town was named for one of his slave-holding ancestors, Greenwood Leflore, who was also a Choctaw chief.

GREER, HAL

Athlete. At Marshall University he became the first black in West Virginia to play on a varsity team in a major college. In 1968 he played his eighth consecutive all-star game and was named the NBA's most valuable player.

GREGORY, DICK

Comedian and civil rights leader (b. 1932). Born Richard Claxton Gregory, a welfare case in St. Louis, he became one of

191

America's best known night club and television entertainers, using his singular talent for racial humor to dissipate myths and call attention to the rich heritage of his race. By participating in demostrations and rallies, exerting a calming influence at crucial moments, and conducting political campaigns (against Mayor Richard Daley of Chicago and as a presidential candidate on the Freedom Party ticket), he has helped his people to achieve a better life.

GREGORY GEORGE

Athlete. Named to a variety of All-American football teams in 1930 and 1931, he went on to become the director of the Harlem Children's Center of the Children's Aid Society.

GRIER, WILLIAM H.

Psychiatrist (b. 1926). He has worked extensively with black patients and has taught at Wayne State University and the University of California. He co-authored, with Price M. Cobbs, the best-selling book, *Black Rage* (1968).

GRIFFIN V. PRINCE EDWARD SCHOOL BOARD

One of the original cases making up Brown v. Board of Education of Topeka. To avoid compliance with the judicial mandate, officials had closed the Prince Edward County (Virginia) public schools. Only white children attended 'private' schools supported by public funds from 1959 to 1963. In 1964 the Court ordered Prince Edward County to reopen the public schools on a desegregated basis.

GRIGGS, SUTTON

Clergyman and writer. A Baptist minister and lecturer on race problems, he spoke for other black writers painfully aware of the attitudes of a white audience in saying that 'The bird that would live must thrill the hunter with its song.' His writings include five novels: *Imperium in Imperio* (1899), *Overshadowed* (1901), *Unfettered* (1902), *The Hindered Hand* (1905), and *Pointing the Way* (1908).

GRIMKE, ARCHIBALD

Lawyer and diplomat (1894-1930). The son of a black slave and a white plantation owner, he was for a while the slave of his half-brother. His white aunts, the abolitionist Grimkes, encouraged him to study law at Harward. He later served as consul to Santo Domingo and held other high posts. See Janet Stevenson, *Spokesman for Freedom: the Life of Archibald Grimke.*

GRIMKE, CHARLOTTE L. FORTEN

See Forten, Charlotte L.

GRIMKE, FRANCIS J.

Clergyman. He was one of four negro signers of the proclamation that led to the formation of the NAACP.

GRIST, RERI

Musician (b. 1934). An accomplished coloratura soprano, she has sung in the main opera houses of Europe. She was acclaimed for her performance at the Salzburg Festival in Austria in July 1964.

GUINN AND BEAL V. UNITED STATES

See Grandfather Clauses.

GULLAH

Dialect spoken by the descendants of slaves inhabiting the sea islands and coast districts of Georgia, South Carolina, and northeastern Florida. See Lorenzo Turner, *Africanisms in the Gullah Dialect* (1949).

GULLAH JACK

Angolese witch doctor involved in the conspiracy led by Denmark Vesey. He was supposed to have the ability to make the Charleston conspirators invulnerable.

H

HABANERA
Named for the city of Havana, the habanera is a dance of Afro-Spanish origin.

HALE INFIRMARY
Black-controlled medical center established in Montgomery, Alabama, by Dr. Cornelius N. Dorsette.

HALL, AMOS T.
Jurist and civil rights leader (1896-1971). A leader of the fight against discrimination, he became Oklahoma's first black elected judge in 1970.

HALL, GEORGE CLEVELAND
Physician (1864-1933). A leading Chicago surgeon and diagnostician, he devoted most of his life to his patients in Provident Hospital but managed to find time to conduct surgical clinics before medical associations in Alabama, Georgia, Kentucky, Missouri, Tennessee, and Virginia, and to establish infirmaries throughout the South. He brought NUL to Chicago, was active in NAACP, and was one of the founders of ASNLH. A public library in Chicago is named after him.

HALL, JUANITA
Entertainer. A singer and actress, in 1949 she became nationally famous for her portrayal of 'Bloody Mary' in *South Pacific,* winning the Tony, Donaldson, Box Office, and Bojangles awards.

HALL, LLOYD

Chemist (b. 1894). He has published many monographs and holds numerous patents. His discoveries of curing salts revolutionized the meat-packing industry. He has registered more than a score of patents relating to processing and packing food products and has served as president of the Chemical Products Corporation of Chicago.

HALL, PRINCE

Founder of black Masonry (1748-1807). Born in Barbados of an English father and free black mother of French extraction, he made his way to Boston in 1765. He earned his living as a leather worker, studied at night to overcome his lack of schooling, became the minister of a Methodist church in Cambridge, petitioned the state legislature in 1777 to end slavery, and served in the Revolution. Initiated into the Masonic order by a military lodge garrisoned in Boston three months before the outbreak of the war, he secured a charter from the Grand Lodge in England and, in 1787, was named grand master of African Lodge No. 459. In 1797, he granted warrants to establish other lodges in Philadelphia and Providence. See George W. Crawford, *Prince Hall and His Followers* (1914).

HALLELUJAH

First movie with an all-black cast, produced by King Vidor in 1929.

HAMLET, JAMES F.

U. S. army general. In 1972, at the age of 50, he became the second black in U. S. history (after Benjamin O. Davis, Jr.) to be nominated for promotion to the two-star rank. From Alliance, Ohio, he commanded the 3rd Brigade of the 1st Cavalry Division in Vietnam.

HAMLIN, A. C.

Legislator (1881-1912). In 1908 he became the first black to serve in the Oklahoma state legislature and the only black to occupy a seat in that body until 1964. He secured passage of a resolution calling for equal facilities for blacks traveling on trains in Oklahoma.

HAMILTON, CHARLES V.

Scholar and author. Chairman of the political science department of Roosevelt University in Chicago, he co-authored, with Stokely Carmichael, *Black Power: The Politics of Liberation in America* (1967).

HAMMON, BRITON

Writer. In 1760 he published an autobiographical pamphlet titled *A Narrative of the Uncommon Sufferings and Surprising Deliverance of Briton Hammon, A Negro Man.* Of historical rather than literary interest, it foreshadowed a fact of black literary history: autobiographical narratives became the first genre of prose writing of literary importance.

HAMMON, JUPITER

Poet (1717-1787). Born a slave on Long Island, he was probably the first black poet in America. His works include *An Evening Thought: Salvation by Christ with Penitential Cries* (1760), and 'An Address to Negroes in the State of New York' (1787). He dedicated 21 stanzas of his poetry to Phillis Weathley (1778). All of his poetry had religious overtones.

HAMMONS, DAVID

Artist (b. 1943). Born in Illinois and trained in California, he has exhibited his works in California and lectured at the state college in Dominguez Hills. His works capture the black experience in muted tones.

HAMPTON INSTITUTE

In 1867 the American Missionary Association bought a small plantation on the Hampton River for the purpose of establishing a school to train black teachers and leaders. Hampton Institute opened in 1868 with 15 pupils and 2 teachers. Two years later it was chartered by the state of Virginia. Supported by the Freedmen's Bureau and northern philanthropists, it introduced the idea of vocational education for blacks and became a model of its class.

HAMPTON, FRED

Black Panther leader (d. 1969). A federal investigation of his killing led to the conclusion that the Chicago police had used undue force.

HAMPTON, PHILLIP J.

Artist (b. 1922). Now associate professor of art at Southern Illinois University, he has exhibited his works throughout the nation. More than 100 of his paintings and murals are in colleges, public schools, business, and private collections.

HANDY, WILLIAM C.

Musician (1873-1958). Known as 'Father of the Blues,' he was famous as a composer, conductor, and cornetist. He composed 'Mr. Crump' for the political boss of Memphis and caused dancing in the streets of the city when his band played the number, later titled 'Memphis Blues.' In 1913 he formed the Pace and Handy Music Company which in 1914 published his famous 'St. Louis Blues.' In 1928 he presented the 'History of Music,' using black artists to portray the development of musical forms from colonial days to the era of jazz and the blues, at Carnegie Hall. Continuing to compose even after he lost his sight, he completed more than a hundred sacred and secular pieces and his autobiography, *Father of the Blues* (1941).

HANSBERRY, LORRAINE

Playwright (1930-1965). The first negro woman to have a play presented on Broadway, she won the Drama Critics Circle Award for *A Raisin in the Sun,* starring Sidney Poitier. Presented on March 11, 1959, the play continued in its initial run for 530 performances. *To Be Young, Gifted and Black,* her life story told in her own words along with excerpts from her plays, opened off-Broadway in 1968 and was presented in 1972 as an NET Playhouse production, starring Ruby Dee. *The Sign in Sidney Brustein's Window,* focusing on the quandary of a white liberal, had closed after 101 performances on January 12, 1965, the day of the author's death. Her answer to Jean Gênet's *The Blacks* was *Les Blancs,* presented on Broadway in 1970.

HARALSON, JEREMIAH

Public official. He served as U. S. congressman from Alabama, 1875-77.

HARDING, VINCENT

Historian. Born and educated in Harlem, he went on to earn a doctorate in history at the University of Chicago. He has done extensive work in race relations in the South. He has published widely in the field of black history and now heads the department of social science at Spelman College. He also is director of the Institute of the Black World in Atlanta.

HARE, MAUD CUNEY

Musician, lecturer, and writer. She was among the first to write extensively on the musical heritage of the negro. Her main work is *Negro Musicians and Their Music* (1938).

HARE, NATHAN, JR.

Scholar and publisher (b. 1934). Born in Slick, Oklahoma, and educated at Langston University and the University of Chicago, he established one of the first black studies departments, at San Francisco State College, and contributed many articles to black periodicals and scholarly journals. He wrote a book called *The Black Anglo-Saxons* and founded *The Black Scholar,* a journal that seeks to unite black intellectuals and nonintellectuals.

HARLEM GLOBETROTTERS

Since 1927 the name Harlem Globetrotters has been associated with extraordinary basketball skill combined with slapstick comedy routines in a unique spectacle that has become one of the most

199

popular sports shows in the world. Globetrotters teams have traveled millions of miles in a hundred countries and played before more than 60 million spectators. Reese 'Goose' Tatum was the star attraction, 1942-55. Marquis Haynes, billed as 'The World's Greatest Dribbler,' joined him from 1946-52. 'Meadowlark' Lemon and 'Curly' Neal now do most of the clowning and dribbling. In the late 1960s, the Globetrotters' overall record showed 9,200 wins in 9,600 games.

HARLEM HOSPITAL

Opened in 1907, the hospital became an object of controversy as early as 1919, when Dr. Louis T. Wright was appointed as clinical assistant in the out-patient department. Charges of shocking abuses in the way black patients were being treated brought a formal investigation into the affairs of the hospital in 1923. During that same year, the hospital established a training school for black nurses. Three black doctors were added to the hospital's visiting staff in 1926, and by 1930, following a reorganization of the hospital, 19 of the 46 members of the medical board were negroes.

HARLEM IS HEAVEN

First all-black talking movie (1932). Bojangles Robinson had top billing in the film.

HARLEM RENAISSANCE

A period of exceptional creativity by blacks and receptivity by whites, corresponding roughly to the decade of the 1920s and stemming from a fusion of the creative talents of the entrenched intelligentsia of Harlem and those of black writers, artists, singers, dancers, actors, and musicians who flocked there from throughout the nation and as far away as the islands of the West Indies. The luminaries in the artistic awakening were Langston Hughes, Countee Cullen, Claude McKay, Jean Toomer, W. E. B. Du Bois, Alain Locke, Wallace Thurman, and James Weldon Johnson. See Negro Renaissance.

HARLEM RENAISSANCE, NEW

See New Black Renaissance.

HARLESTON, EDWARD

Artist. One of the pioneer black painters of the 20th century, he worked largely in the tradition of older American artists.

HARMON AWARDS

Established by William E. Harmon and administered by the Commission on race relations of the Federal Council of Churches, the first award in the field of fine arts was made in 1926. The awards 'for distinguished achievement among Negroes' originally embraced eight fields but have been most successful in bringing to the attention of the public the outstanding works of a large number of black painters. The Harmon Foundation began to sponsor annual exhibitions in 1928.

HARMON, LEONARD

World War II hero (1916-1942). The USS *Harmon* was named for the naval hero. A mess attendant, he was serving aboard the USS *San Francisco* when he 'deliberately exposed himself to hostile gunfire in order to protect a shipmate and as a result . . . was killed in action.' He was awarded the Navy Cross.

HARPER v. VIRGINIA BOARD OF ELECTIONS

Supreme Court decision (1966) outlawing the poll tax in state elections. The Court held that the poll tax violated the equal protection clause of the Fourteenth Amendment.

HARPER, FRANCES ELLEN WATKINS

Poetess and abolitionist (1825-1911). Miss Watkins, who became Mrs. Harper in 1860, taught school in her native Baltimore, became an underground railroad agent, lectured for the Maine Anti-Slavery Society, and wrote, in addition to pamphlets, poetry dealing mainly with slavery. In both her poetry and prose she expressed 'feelings that are general'—that is, she transcended racial limitations. 'The Two Offers' (in *The Anglo-African Magazine*, 1859) was the first short story published by a negro in America. Her first volume of poetry, *Poems on Miscellaneous Subjects* (1854), sold 10,000 copies during the first five years. Her best novel, *Iola Leroy, the Shadows Uplifted* (1860), was the first novel produced by a black woman.

HARPER, TONI

Entertainer (b. 1937). A child star, she was acclaimed for her performance in *Candy Store Blues* (1947). She made her debut as a recording artist in 1955 and appeared briefly with Count Basie's band in 1959.

HARPERS FERRY

West Virginia town situated on bluffs at the confluence of the Potomac and Shenandoah rivers. It was the site of a federal arsenal attacked on October 16, 1859, by John Brown and his disciplined band of 16 white men and 5 negroes. The attack resulted in the slaughter of 5 proslavery men. The arsenal was retaken, John Brown was hanged, and his campaign to recruit runaways for a liberation army ended. His name lived on, however, as Union soldiers marched across the South singing 'John Brown's Body.' Osborne P. Anderson escaped to serve in the Civil War and write his story. The other four black men who took part in the assault were John A. Copeland, Shields Green, Sherrard Lewis Leary, and Dangerfield Newby.

HARRIS, ABRAM L.

Economist and educator (1899-1963). The most eminent of black academic economists, he taught at Howard University (1927-45) and at the University of Chicago (1946-63). He earned his Ph.D. at Columbia (1931) and co-authored *The Black Worker* (1931). He also wrote many articles, *The Negro as Capitalist* (1936), and *Economics and Social Reform* (1958).

HARRIS, CHARLES F.

Businessman. He manages a major division of Random House.

HARRIS, HENRY

Craftsman. The Clarksdale, Mississippi, slave became an iron molder as a result of his master's decision to send him to an iron foundry in Tuscaloosa, Alabama, to learn the skill.

HARRIS, HOMER

Athlete. The first black captain of a football team in Big 10 competition (Iowa, 1936), he was regarded as the toughest of all.

HARRIS, PATRICIA ROBERTS

Lawyer and diplomat. A graduate of Howard and Georgetown universities, she has several firsts to her credit. In 1966 she was appointed ambassador to Luxembourg. Two years later she was named an alternate delegate to the United Nations. In 1971 she was appointed to the board of directors of International Business Machines and Chase National Bank. In 1971 she was also elected to head the credentials committee at a meeting of the Democratic national committee.

HARRISON, RICHARD B.

Actor (1864-1935). He was acclaimed for his portrayal of 'De Lawd' in Green Pastures. Born of fugitive parents who had made their way to Ontario, he went to Chicago to study dramatics, toured the continent giving dramatic readings, and finally appeared at the Lafayette Theater in New York, in *Pa Williams' Gal.* His masterful acting in *Green Pastures* (the play was presented to full houses throughout the nation 1,659 times and made into a classic movie) won him the Spingarn Medal in 1930.

HASLAM, GERALD

Scholar and teacher (b. 1937). Now teaching at Sonoma State College, he has published many scholarly articles on black literature.

HASTIE, WILLIAM H.

Jurist (b. 1904). He was appointed U. S. district judge in the Virgin Islands in 1937, governor in 1944, and judge of the U. S.

circuit court of appeals in 1949. He was the first black man appointed to the federal bench. He served as civilian aide to the Secretary of war until January 5, 1943. He resigned his position to protest the lack of a positive commitment to recruit negro pilots.

HATCHER, ANDREW

Journalist (b. 1923). He served as associate press secretary in the White House under President John F. Kennedy.

HATCHER, RICHARD G.

Public official. He was elected mayor of Gary, Indiana, in 1967. Since then he has been mentioned as a presidential prospect.

HATHAWAY, ISAAC

Sculptor. He was commissioned to design the Booker T. Washington half-dollar which went on sale on December 16, 1946. He also executed portrait busts of Booker T. Washington and other great black Americans.

HAVERLY'S EUROPEAN MINSTRELS

Famous minstrel troupe that toured Europe in 1880. See Hicks, George B.

HAWKINS, AUGUSTUS

Public official (b. 1907). He is congressman from California and chairman of the House Rules Committee. Born in Shreveport, Louisiana, and educated in Los Angeles, he was active in real estate and youth work before entering state politics. In 1962 he ran for Congress from the 21st district and won by an overwhelming majority.

HAWKINS, EDLER G.

Clergyman. In 1964 he was elected Moderator of the United Presbyterian Church in the U. S. A.

HAWKINS, ERSKINE

Musician (b. 1914). As a band leader he appealed mainly to rhythm and blues audiences. He achieved popularity at the Savoy ballroom in New York City. Among his most famous recordings were 'Tuxedo Junction' and 'After Hours.'

HAYDEN, LEWIS

Abolitionist. A key figure in the Boston vigilance committee in the 1850s, he helped Frederick Jenkins to escape from a U. S. marshal who was preparing to take him from a courtroom to his owner. Hayden put two kegs of dynamite in his cellar and threatened to explode them to keep slavecatchers away.

HAYDEN, PALMER

Artist (b. 1893). He won the Harmon award in the 1920s. His 'Midsummer Night in Harlem' hangs in the Harmon Foundation.

HAYDEN, ROBERT

Poet (b. 1913). He received the Grand Prize at the First World Festival of Negro Arts held in Dakar, Senegal, (1965) for his book of poetry *A Ballad for Remembrance.* He teaches at Fisk and is poetry editor of *World Order,* the Baha'i magazine. He edited *Kaleidoscope: Poems by American Negro Poets* (1967).

HAYES, BOB

Athlete. In the Tokyo Olympics (1964), he won the 100-meter dash and helped his team to win the 400-meter relay. He went on to become the top offensive player for the Dallas Cowboys.

HAYES, ELVIN

Athlete. In 1967-68 he emerged as one of the nation's top college basketball players. The first black to play for the University of Houston, where he smashed every record in the book, he elected to sign with the San Diego Rockets when he joined the NBA.

HAYES, GEORGE EDMUND

Civil rights leader. In 1910 he was one of the co-founders of the National Urban League.

HAYES, ISAAC

Musician (b. 1963). With David Porter he has composed hits like 'Soul Man,' 'Baby,' and 'Black Moses.' At his concerts he plays the organ and sings jazz numbers reflecting the whole experience of the black ghetto.

HAYES, ROLAND

Musician (b. 1887). He was widely acclaimed as a concert singer and succeeded in breaking the color bar in concert halls for other black classical singers. He struggled without success for years to win acceptance in America, then went to England (1920) to study and build his reputation. He sang at a command performance for George V in 1921 and returned in triumph to the United States in 1923 to begin a transcontinental tour under professional management. See MacKinley Helm, *Angel Mo' and Her Son, Roland Hayes* (1942).

HAYNES, GEORGE EDMUND

Sociologist and one of the founders of the Urban League. His pioneering study of the Negro economic conditions is titled The Negro at Work in New York City: a Study in Economic Progress (1912).

HAYNES, H. C.

Businessman. In 1904 he organized the Haynes Razor Strop Company in Chicago to manufacture a strop which he invented. In addition to his mail-order business in the United States, he set up an agency in London.

HAYNES, LEMUEL

Clergyman (1753-1833). A Congregationalist, he was the first black minister to serve regularly as the pastor of white congregations.

HAYNES, MARQUIS

Playing with the Harlem Globetrotters, 1946-52, the diminutive star was billed as 'The World's Greatest Dribbler.' He left the Globetrotters to form his own team, the Fabulous Magicians.

HAYNIE, WILBUR

Artist (b. 1929). Born in Camden, Arkansas. He has received many awards, including one from the Watts Festival in Los Angeles. His works are represented in the collections of the Fine Art Patrons of Newport Harbor in California, the Otis Art Institute, and the Pasadena Art Museum.

HEALY, ELIZA

Nun (1847-c.1917). A sister of three brothers who rose high in Catholicism (James, Patrick, and Sherwood), she became mother superior of the Congregation of Notre Dame. One of her sisters, Josephine, was also a nun.

HEALY, JAMES A.

Catholic bishop (1830-1900). As bishop of Portland, Maine, he was the spiritual leader of a predominantly white diocese comprising Maine and New Hampshire. The eldest child of a white Georgia planter and the mulatto daughter of a prosperous gin owner, he was educated in Quaker schools in New York and New Jersey. With three of his brothers he attended Holy Cross College in Worcester, Massachusetts. He trained for the priesthood in Canada and France. Ordained at Notre Dame Cathedral in Paris in 1855, he returned to Boston and eventually became pastor of St. James Church (1866). In 1875 he became the first black Catholic bishop in America. See Albert S. Foley, *Bishop Healy: Beloved Outcast* (1954).

HEALY, PATRICK FRANCIS

Jesuit theologian (1834-1910). A brother of James A. Healy, he became the first American negro to earn a Ph. D. degree (Louvain, 1865). In 1874 he became president of the oldest Catholic university in America.

HEALY, SHERWOOD

Clergyman (1836-1875). A brother of James A. Healy, he was ordained in Rome (1858) and earned a doctorate in canon law (1860). He served as a priest in Boston, then became professor, vice president, and director of the Catholic seminary at Troy, New York.

HEARD, WILLIAM HENRY

Clergyman and public official (1850-1937). Georgia slave who worked his way through college, became active in state politics, and was appointed minister to Liberia (1895). He was also a bishop in the AME Church. See William H. Heard, From Slavery to the Bishopric in the A. M. E. Church (1924).

HEART OF ATLANTA MOTEL v. UNITED STATES

Supreme Court decision (1964) upholding the constitutionality of the Civil Rights Act of 1964. Only five months after the act was passed, the Court held that 'the action of the Congress in the adoption of the Act . . . is within the power granted it by the Commerce Clause of the Constitution, as interpreted by this Court for 140 years.' On July 1, 1964 white Atlanta restaurant owner Lester Maddox had brandished a pistol in refusing service to three divinity students. Because of a procedural error, the Maddox case was not ready for review as the Supreme Court took up the less celebrated motel case.

HEARTS OF DIXIE

First black motion picture with dialogue (1929). It starred Stepin Fetchit as a shuffling comedian.

HECTOR, EDWARD

Patriot (d. 1834). In charge of the ammunition wagon attached to the regiment fighting at Brandywine Creek in 1777, he refused to abandon his horses to the enemy as the patriots were retreating.

HEIGHT, DOROTHY

Civic leader (b. 1912). She is national president of the NCNW.

HENDERSON, CORNELIUS LANGSTON

Engineer (b. 1887). After studying at Morris Brown College in Atlanta, where his father was president, he began designing and constructing bridges for the Canadian Bridge Company. He has built bridges, tunnels, and factories in many different countries.

HENDERSON, FLETCHER

Musician. About 1919, he formed his first band for Roseland, a Broadway dance hall where he appeared for the next 15 years. He also accompanied Bessie Smith and other blues singers and, with his younger brother Horace, turned out many good scores.

HENDERSON, GEORGE WYLIE

Writer (b. 1904). His works include *Ollie Miss* (1935) and *Jule* (1946).

HENDRIX, JIMi

Musician (1942-1970). A rock superstar, he was born James Marshall in Seattle ,Washington. He became a popular singer and guitarist, formed the Jimi Hendrix Experience in London in 1966, and returned in 1967 to the United States, where he played to overflow audiences. He electrified crowds at the Woodstock Festival in August 1969, shortly before he died as a result of his drug addiction.

HENLEY, BENJAMIN J.

Educator (b. 1911). As acting superintendent of the public school system in Washington, D. C. (1966), he directed one of the largest schools in the nation. Previously he had served as a teacher, principal, and assistant superintendent of schools.

HENRY, HAYWARD

Political theorist. A lecturer in black studies at Harvard and chairman of the black caucus in the Unitarian-Universalist church, he chaired the Congress of African Peoples (1970).

HENRY, JOHN

Folk-hero. See *John Henry*.

HENRY, MILTON R.

Black nationalist leader. Known also by his adopted African name of Brother Gaidi, he became vice president of the Republic of New Africa when it was formed in 1968.

HENRY, RICHARD B.

Black nationalist leader. Also known as Brother Imari, he became minister of information of the Republic of New Africa. Following a split with his brother, Milton R. Henry, he set up headquarters in New Orleans.

HENSON, JOSIAH

Slave and clergyman (1789-1883). He is said to have been the model for Uncle Tom in Harriet Beecher Stowe's novel. He escaped to Canada in 1830, helped to free other slaves, and pastored a Methodist Episcopal Church in Dresden, Ontario. His autobiography, *The Life of Josiah Henson, Formerly a Slave, Now an Inhabitant of Canada, as Narrated by Himself* (1849), was enlarged and retitled in later editions (1858, 1879).

HENSON, MATTHEW ALEXANDER

Explorer (1866-1955). Maryland erected a monument to honor the co-discoverer of the North Pole (1909). A master of survival techniques, he recounted his experiences in *A Negro Explorer at the North Pole* (1912).

HERNDON, A. F.

Businessman (b. 1858). He was active in real estate development, banks, and insurance companies, particularly Atlanta Standard Life Insurance Company.

HERNDON, ANGELO

Activist. In 1932 he was arrested in Atlanta, Georgia, and charged with incitement to insurrection. He was then 19 years of age and was alleged to be a Communist. He was attempting to act in behalf of the unemployed, both black and white. He was sentenced to 18-20 years in prison under an 1861 statute. His autobiography was titled *Let Me Live* (1937).

HERNDON, NORRIS B.

Businessman. The richest black American, he is president of Atlanta Life Insurance Company and has a private fortune of over 18 million dollars.

HEROIC FUGITIVE LITERATURE

A literary school embracing the autobiographies of some 100 runaway slaves. Most of them stressed the sensational, were emotional in tone rather than analytical, and were frequently ghostwritten by white abolitionists. See Slave Narratives.

HEWLETT, A. MOLINEAUX

Educator (d. 1871). He was the first director of physical education at the nation's oldest university. He served as instructor and director of the first Harvard gymnasium, 1859-71.

HICKERSON, JOHN

A disciple of Father Jehoviah. See Divine, Father.

HICKS, GEORGE B.

Minstrel. In 1865 he founded the first successful all-negro minstrel group, the Georgia Minstrels. Reorganized under white management and known as Callender's Original Georgia Minstrels, then as Haverly's European Minstrels, and finally as Callender's Consolidated Minstrels, the troupe became world famous. See Minstrelsy.

HIGGINBOTHAM, A. LEON, JR.

Jurist (b. 1928). Appointed U. S. district judge in Pennsylvania, he was also the first black man to be named to the Federal Trade Commission.

HIGGINBOTHAM, JAY C.

Jazz trombone player. He played and recorded with Luis Russell's band.

HIGHLANDER FOLK SCHOOL

Organized near Monteagle in the Tennessee mountains in 1932, it remained under attack because of its emphasis on integration but was able to survive crises because of its grassroots leadership and the support it received from liberals. One of its projects was teaching and organizing blacks living in the Sea Islands. In 1961 the SCLC joined with the school in a program to train blacks for the civil rights struggle. That year, the state closed the school permanently.

HILL, EDWIN

Musician. The first black to be admitted to the Academy of Fine Arts in Philadelphia (1871), he was a noted composer and violinist.

HILL, LESLIE PINCKNEY

Poet (1990-1960). Born in Lynchburg, Virginia, he graduated from Harvard, taught at Tuskegee Institute, and became principal of the Cheney Training School for Teachers in Pennsylvania. His publications include a volume of verse titled *The Wings of Oppression* and a play titled *Toussaint L'Ouverture—A Dramatic History.*

HILL, TYLER EDWARD

Public official (b. 1883). In 1921 he became director of the West Virginia state bureau of negro welfare and statistics. He had served earlier (1919-21) as publicity director and adjuster for 7 of the state's largest coal enterprises.

HIMES, CHESTER B.

Writer (b. 1909). His works include *If He Hollers Let Him Go* (1945), *Lonely Crusade* (1947), and *Cast the First Stone* (1952). Frustrated by his experiences with editors and publishers,

212

he took refuge in Europe. It was only during the 1960s that he achieved due recognition in his own country with the release of a film version of his *Cotton Comes to Harlem*. Born in Jefferson, Missouri, he began his writing career in the Ohio state penitentiary, where he served time for armed robbery (1929-36). He published the first volume of his *Autobiography* in 1972.

HINTON, WILLIAM AUGUSTUS

Educator and physician (1883-1959). A world-renowned bacteriologist, he developed the Hinton test for syphilis and the Davies-Hinton tests of blood and spinal fluid. Born in Chicago, he studied at Harvard, where he later taught. His book, *Syphilis and Its Treatment* (1936), is a standard reference work.

HIP

A word designating a life style characteristic initially of black youths and later adopted by white students. Rebellious white youth began copying the hip black life style, moved both by their contempt for white middleclass values and their admiration of black acceptance of the earthy, sensual, rebellious elements in man. According to Charles Reich in *The Greening of America* (1970), rebellious white teen-agers 'were copying black language styles' as early as the middle fifties.

HISTORY, BLACK

See Black History.

HOBSON, JULIUS W.

Civil rights leader (b. 1922). Deeply involved in community activities in Washington, D. C., he formed his own, the Association Community Teams, and since the 1950s has led successful campaigns against job and housing discrimination.

HOCUTT, THOMAS

Student. In 1933 the NAACP initiated legal attacks on segregation and discrimination in education by filing suit against the University of North Carolina in behalf of Thomas Hocutt.

213

HODGES, JOHNNY

Jazz musician. In the 1920s he played the saxophone with Duke Ellington's Kentucky Club orchestra.

HODGES, M. HAMILTON

Musician (1959-1928). A baritone with fine natural talent, he traveled here and abroad with the McAdoo Jubilee Singers, then settled in New Zealand, where he was acclaimed for his performances in oratorios and operas.

HOFFMAN, JOHN WESLEY

Scientist. In the late 1800s and early 1900s he proved that color was not a hindrance to intellectual development by becoming an outstanding researcher in the field of agricultural biology and chemistry. Little is known of his personal life. He received his elementary education in Charleston, South Carolina, and his advanced training at Howard, Michigan Agricultural College, Albion College, Harvard, and Cornell. He taught at the leading black colleges and delivered speeches before many learned societies in the United States and Canada. At Tuskegee (1894-96) he conducted a study of the 'Black Belt' of Alabama. He worked directly with farmers, urging them to buy their own land and diversify their crops. He developed the 'Hoffman improved seedling strawberry,' grew tea in Florida, and introduced scientific methods in dairying.

HOGAN, ERNEST

Musician. He was universally known for the one song that he regretted ever having written, 'All Coons Look Alike to Me,' composed in the late 1890s. For years he appeared with the Memphis Students, a jazz group that made its debut at Proctor's 23rd Street Theatre in New York in 1905.

HOLIDAY, BILLIE

Musician and actress (1951-1959). Born in the slums of Baltimore, she moved to New York when she was 13, became a teenage prostitute, finally was able to earn a living as a singer, toured with Count Basie and other bands, played to a packed house at Carnegie Hall a month after she had completed a government-supervised cure for heroin addiction, and in 1957 signed contracts for a film biography of her life. Earlier (1935) she had appeared in the movie *Symphony in Black*.

HOLLAND, JEROME H.

Ambassador, athlete and educator. 'Brud' Holland was the first black to play football for Cornell. In the 1960s he achieved national recognition in educational circles as president of Hampton Institute in Virginia. He now serves as U. S. ambassador to Sweden. In 1972 he was also nominated as the first black member of the governing board of the New York Stock Exchange.

HOLLAND, JUSTIN

Musician (b. 1819). He lived in Norfolk County, Virginia, and in Boston before settling in Cleveland, Ohio, where he gave guitar lessons, studied languages, and wrote several original works. He wrote one book which is still a favorite among students and teachers, *Holland's Comprehensive Method for the Guitar* (1874, rev. 1876).

HOLMAN, M. CARL

Writer and civil rights leader (b. 1919). Born in Minter City, Mississippi, he holds graduate degrees from the University of Chicago and Yale. He has written poetry and prose, plays and commercial scripts. He is vice president of the National Urban Coalition.

HOLMES V. ATLANTA

U. S. Supreme Court decision (1955), based on the Brown ruling of 1954, outlawing segregation on public golf courses in Georgia.

HOLMES, CHARLES
Jazz musician. He played with Luis Russell's band. His alto saxophone inventions are preserved on records.

HOLTZCLAW, WILLIAM H.
Educator (1870-1943). After struggling to prepare for admission to Tuskegee Institute in 1890, he went on to found the Utica Normal and Industrial Institute in Mississippi.

HOME INFIRMARY
Black-operated medical center founded in Clarksville, Tennessee, by Dr. Robert T. Burt.

HONKIE (HONKY, HONKEY)
A disparaging term for a white man.

HOOD, JAMES
Student. On June 11, 1963, he and Vivian Malone successfully integrated the University of Alabama.

HOOD, JAMES W.
Clergyman. He served as president of what was perhaps the first black political convention called after Emancipation. The AMEZ church leader held appointive office under Republican administrations and was assistant superintendent of public instruction in North Carolina.

HOOKS, BENJAMIN
Jurist. In 1972 he was appointed to fill a vacancy on the Federal Communication Commission. Formerly a judge in Memphis, Tennessee, he became the first black man to serve on the FCC.

HOOKS, ROBERT
Stage and television actor. He was given an important role in the direction of the Negro Ensemble Company.

HOPE, JOHN

Educator (1864-1936). His philosophy of education challenged the accommodationist views of Booker T. Washington. A leader in the Niagara Movement, he also served as president of Atlanta Baptist College, Morehouse College, and Atlanta University. See Ridgely Torrence, *The Story of John Hope* (1948).

HORNE, LENA

Entertainer (b. 1917). A popular singer and actress for more than three decades, she has fought for racial dignity from the beginning of her career. Born in Brooklyn, the light-skinned performer launched her career at the Harlem Opera House as a ballet dancer. She danced and sang at the Cotton Club before becoming a vocalist for Noble Sissle's band and for Charlie Barnet's orchestra, scoring a first by being a feature singer for a white band. She was featured in *Cabin in the Sky* and *Stormy Weather* (1943) and in the Broadway musical *Jamaica* (1957-59). A frequent guest on television shows, she co-starred with Harry Belafonte in a memorable special in 1970.

HORNE, MOTHER ROSA ARTIMUS

Cult leader. A former seamstress called by her followers 'Pray for Me Priestess,' she claimed to have raised thousands from the dead. She was said to be a millionaire. She was a rival of Elder Lightfoot Solomon Michaux in the struggle for the spiritual control of Harlem blacks in the 1950s, after Father Divine left the city.

HORSE, JOHN

Famous black chief among the Seminoles.

HORTON, GEORGE MOSES

Poet (1797-1883). He published his first book of verse, *Hope of Liberty*, in 1829. He introduced the humor peculiar to black folk literature in works like 'Jeff Davis in a Tight Place' and 'Creditor to a Proud Debtor.' Born a slave, he gave poignant expression to the predicament of the black man in what was called a democratic society: 'How long have I in bondage lain,/ And languished to be free!/ Alas! and must I still complain,/ Deprived of liberty?'

HOSIER, 'BLACK HARRY'
Methodist preacher. A free Negro, he was a traveling companion of Methodist Bishop Francis Asbury, whom he sometimes replaced in the pulpit.

HOUSTON
Scene of a serious racial disturbance in August 1917. White hostility to black troops of the 24th Regiment provoked violence resulting in the deaths of 17 whites. Subsequently 13 black soldiers were hanged and 41 others sentenced to life imprisonment after conviction for 'murder and mutiny.'

HOUSTON, CHARLES H.
Lawyer (1895-1950). A Phi Beta Kappa graduate of Amherst at nineteen, he earned two doctorates in law, taught at Howard, created a nationally respected law school for the University of Houston, and as the dominant force of the legal arm of the NAACP 'set the pattern for fundamental attacks on barriers to equal justice' that bore fruit in the *Brown v. Board of Education* decision.

HOUSTON, NORMAN O.
Businessman (b. 1893). He was co-founder of the Golden State Mutual Life Insurance Company, which he headed after 1945.

HOWARD UNIVERSITY
Founded in Washington, D. C. by the First Congregational Church, it was opened in 1867 to all races and to members of both sexes. Five years later it had developed 9 departments: normal and preparatory, music, theology, military, industrial, commercial, college, law, and medicine. Supported by the Freedmen's Bureau and philanthropists, the university gradually emerged as

a leading intellectual center, turning out some of the nation's best doctors, lawyers, and scholars. In 1932 the *Journal of Negro Education* was established at Howard by Charles H. Thompson. Under his leadership the results of researches into racial inequalities found their way into print.

HOWARD UNIVERSITY MEDICAL SCHOOL

The medical school of Howard University opened its doors on November 9, 1868 to negro and white students. Its faculty of five included one black physician, Alexander T. Augusta. There were seven black students and one white.

HOWARD, EDWARD C.

Physician. In 1905 he led a group of young physicians who demanded greater opportunities in performing operations in the Frederick Douglass Memorial Hospital in Philadelphia. The dissidents broke away and established Mercy Hospital in 1907.

HOWARD, ELSTON

Athlete. He won the International League's most valuable player award before joining the Yankees and earning the Babe Ruth Award (1958). In 1961 he became the first black player to win the American League most valuable player award.

HOWARD, THEODORE

Physician (b. 1908). Under his supervision the Taborian Hospital in Mound Bayou, Mississippi, became a model medical center. A leader in the struggle for civil rights, he became president of the regional Council of Negro Leadership after white citizens councils in Mississippi tried to thwart the intent of the 1954 Supreme Court ruling.

HUDGINS, WILLIAM R.

Banker. He heads the largest black bank in the United States, New York's Freedom National Bank.

HUDSON, JULIEN

Portrait painter. He lived in New Orleans before the Civil War and painted distinguished Louisianans.

HUGGINS, ERICKA

Black Panther. Her trial in New Haven for crimes arising from the death of suspected informer Alex Rackley ended in a mistrial when the jury reported May 24, 1971, that it was unable to reach a verdict.

HUGHES, BERNICE GAINES

Educator and WAC officer. (b. 1904). Born in Xenia, Ohio, and educated at Ohio State, where she majored in foreign languages, she became the first negro woman to serve as a lieutenant colonel in the U. S. armed forces. She entered the Women's Army Corps as a private in 1942. Upon her retirement in 1958, she resumed her teaching career, becoming associate professor of French and Spanish at Central State University, Wilberforce, Ohio.

HUGHES, LANGSTON

Writer (1902-1967). He wrote of negro life in many poems, plays, short stories, novels, and television scripts. He produced many volumes of poetry, beginning with *The Weary Blues* (1926), for which he received the Writter Bynner prize. He received both Rosenwald and Guggenheim fellowships, the Anisfield-Wolf award (1959), and the Spingarn Medal (1960); wrote a column for the Chicago *Defender* (*Simple Says,* 1940-62); and promoted interracial harmony and understanding through his travels, lectures, and writings. His works include the autobiographical *The Big Sea* (1940), *The Poetry of the Negro* (1949), *Simple Speaks His Mind* (1950), *Famous American Negroes* (1954), *Fight for Freedom* (1962), and *Five Plays* (1963).

HULET, JOHN

Public official. In the 1960s he was elected sheriff in Lowndes County, Alabama.

HUNT, RICHARD

Sculptor (b. 1935). He worked mainly with metals. He uses tubular fittings to imbue inorganic substance with organic qualities, as in his 'Hero Construction.'

HUNTER, KRISTIN

Associated with the New Harlem Renaissance, the novelist has published *Bless the Child* and *The Landlord,* which was made into a successful film.

HURSTON, ZORA NEALE

Novelist and anthropologist (1903-1960). Initiated into the study of anthropology by Franz Boas while she was a student at Barnard College in New York City, she collected much folkloric material. She was the first black writer since Charles Chesnutt to use folkloric materials significantly in fiction. She was the first black writer to publish extensive collections of folklore. Her autobiography is titled *Dust Tracks on a Road* (1942). Her other works include *Jonah's Gourd Vine* (1934), *Their Eyes Were Watching God* (1937), and *Seraph on the Suwannee* (1948).

HYERS SISTERS, THE

Musicians. Anna Madah and Emma Louise Hyers made their debut as singers in 1867 at the Metropolitan Theatre in Sacramento. They later gave concerts in New York, New England, and the West.

HYMAN, JOHN A.

Congressman from North Carolina, 1875-77.

I

IHETU, RICHARD

Boxer (1929-1971). Born in Nigeria and known professionally as Dick Tiger, he won world championships as a light-heavyweight and middleweight.

IKARD, BOSE

Cowboy (1847-1929). Born a slave in Mississippi, he was taken to Texas at the age of 5 and grew up on the frontier. After the Civil War he drove cattle from Texas through New Mexico northward to Fort Summer.

IMARI, BROTHER

See Henry, Richard B.

IMES, ELMER

Physicist (1883-1941). His doctoral dissertation (Michigan, 1918) was published in the *Astrophysical Journal*. His research in physics has been utilized by industry. He did original work in infra-red absorption bands while at Fiske.

IMHOTEP

An organization founded by Dr. W. Montague Cobb and named after the Egyptian physician whose name means 'he who cometh in peace.' Sponsored by the NMA, the NAACP, the NUL, and the Medico-Chirurgical Society of the District of Columbia, the organization sought to end segregation in medicine. The first Imhotep conference was held in Washington in 1957, the second in Chicago (1958), and the third in Washington (1959).

IN DAHOMY

Musical play by Paul Laurence Dunbar and Will Marion Cook. It opened to enthusiastic notices on September 2, 1902, at the Globe Theater in Boston, and ran for 3 years.

INDENTURED SERVANTS

The first negroes to arrive in the English colonies reached Jamestown, Virginia, in 1619. Because they had been baptized, they were regarded as indentured servants rather than as slaves.

INDIAN-NEGRO RELATIONS

A common bond developed between negroes and Indians almost from the beginning of the colonization of the New World. Commenting on a massacre of white settlers, an observer wrote: 'It is significant that in the massacre of 1622 not an African perished at the hands of the Indians.' To discourage Indians from helping runaway slaves most treaties incorporated a clause requiring their help in recovering fugitives. Many blacks, slave and free, chose to live among the Indians, intermarrying with them, adopting their way of life, and rising at times to positions of prominence. James Beckworth, Abraham, John Horse, and Tustennuggee are prime examples. Whole Indian tribes were absorbed by the blacks in some areas of the South. Many black women (including the beautiful Che-cho-ter, wife of Osceola) married Indian braves. Because of the preferential treatment accorded them by the Indians, blacks frequently acted as intermediaries—scouts, interpreters, trappers and traders. The names of George Bush, George Bonga, York, and Jean de Sable stand out. Crispus Attucks, Paul Cuffee, and Salem Poor were part Indian. In the Seminole wars (1817-18 and 1835-45) cooperation between blacks and Indians reached a climax. Some Indian tribes, particularly the Five Civilized Tribes, established a black slavery system of their own. Intermarriage was frequent and demands made on slaves were moderate. A survey of 1,551 blacks in 1926 revealed that one-third of them claimed partial Indian ancestry.

224

INDIAN TERRITORY

Thousands of blacks migrated to Indian Territory in the latter part of the 19th century and became associated with a movement to make Oklahoma an all-black state. Tullahassee, whose records go back to 1850, is the oldest of the 27 all-black towns established in the territory. Boley and Wybark are said to have put up signs barring whites after dark. Langston is now the site of a famous university, first headed by Inman E. Page. At least 24 black newspapers were published in the territory. Edwin P. McCabe's *Langston City Herald* promoted the idea of an all-black state. See Teall, Kaye M. *Black History in Oklahoma* (1971).

INGRAM, REX

Stage, screen, and television star (1896-1969). He earned a medical degree but preferred the life of an actor. During his 50 years in the profession, he appeared in such diverse roles as an African native in *Tarzan* scripts, the emperor in *Emperor Jones,* and God in *The Green Pastures.*

INNIS, ROY

Civil rights leader (b. 1934). An advocate of neoblack nationalism within a community framework, he moved with his family from the Virgin Islands to Harlem when he was 12. He worked briefly in chemistry and research before becoming involved in civil rights causes. He became chairman of the Harlem chapter of CORE in 1965. In 1968 he moved up to the national level and was largely responsible for remaking CORE into a predominantly black organization espousing a program of black liberation. See Congress of Racial Equality.

INSTITUTE FOR COLORED YOUTH

School established in Philadelphia in 1842, under the leadership of Charles L. Reason.

INSTITUTE OF THE BLACK WORLD

Formed in 1969 to bring together a community of black artists, organizers, and scholars for the serious study of the black experience, the institute is centered in Atlanta. An organized network of associates stretches into many parts of the black world. It seeks to develop new strategies for the education of blacks.

INSURANCE AND BANKING

Black executives have for years been active in insurance and banking. Among the many blacks prominent in these fields are A. F. Herndon (Atlanta Life), Truman Gibson and Harry Pace (Supreme Liberty Life), Asa T. Spaulding and C. C. Spaulding (North Carolina Mutual), Jesse Binga (Binga State Bank in Chicago), and Jesse Mitchell (Industrial Bank of Washington, D. C.).

INSURRECTIONS

See Slave Revolts.

INTEGRATION

The central reform issue in American domestic life in the 1960s, integration still loomed large on the American scene in the 1970s. The explanation is to be sought in an impressive array of factors: the awakening of the black conscience, impatience with social and economic conditions that frustrate hopes and promote violence, the persistence of deep-rooted racism, and the emergence of black leadership scornful of gradualist and accommodationist solutions or policies. The great integration decision of 1954 unleashed black demands for action culminating in the Civil Rights Act of 1964, which enabled SNCC, CORE, and the NAACP to move speedily toward the elimination of discrimination in schools, public facilities, and housing. Still, the Kerner Commission concluded in 1968 that 'our nation is moving toward two societies, one black, one white—separate but unequal.' A recent survey indicated that at the end of 1971 more people approved of living in a mixed neighborhood than in 1942, yet fewer actually lived in such a neighborhood.

INTELLIGENCE

See I. Q. Controversy.

226

INTERNATIONAL LABOR DEFENSE
Legal arm of the American Negro Labor Congress, organized in 1925 to defend Communists in the courts. It achieved international notoriety by capitalizing on the Scottsboro Case.

INVISIBLE MAN
Novel written by Ralph Ellison in 1952. It uses symbolism and satire to depict the loneliness of the individual, intensified by his being black.

IOLA
Pen name of Ida B. Wells.

I. Q. CONTROVERY
The racist argument that blacks are intellectually inferior to whites was revived by an article published in the winter issue of the *Harvard Educational Review* in 1969. The Jensen Report suggested that blacks may be marked by a genetic inferiority. Most scientists agreed that until certain conditions can be met in testing for genuine genetic differences between groups, no one can say whether blacks are equal, inferior, or superior to whites. Basing his conclusions on studies of identical twins, another scientist (Richard J. Herrnstein, former chairman of Harvard's psychology department) concluded that rigid stratification along class lines will result from the government's efforts to stabilize environmental factors, leaving heredity as the only variable. Current studies also show that most Americans with low intelligence quotients are white.

IRBY, EDITH MAE
In 1948 she became the first black student to be admitted to a Southern all-white medical school when she enrolled at the University of Arkansas, following a series of legal proceedings instituted by the NAACP.

J

JABBAR, KAREEM ABDUL
See Alcindor, Lew.

JACK, HULAN
Public official (b. 1906). He was the first black president of the borough of Manhattan (1953).

JACK, THOMAS A.
Musician (b. 1884). He was bandmaster for the 10th U. S. Cavalry, maintained studies in New York City and Baltimore, composed *Etude en Noire,* and directed the Baltimore Symphony Orchestra in a concert featuring his composition (1946).

JACKSON FIVE
Musicians. They have appeared in concerts, made recordings (with Motown), and been featured in their own television productions. Joseph Jackson, their father, is also their manager. The five Jackson singers are Michael, the lead singer, age 13; Marlon, 14; Jermaine, 16; Tito, 17; and Jackie, 20.

JACKSON, ALEXANDER
Athlete. A contemporary of Howard Drew, he was an outstanding hurdler at Harvard.

JACKSON, GEORGE
Militant (1941-1971). Charged with the murder of a guard in Soledad Prison, he was shot by another prison guard two days before the opening of his trial. His autobiographical book, *Soledad*

Brother: The Prison Letters of George Jackson (1970), was a best-seller. He also wrote *Blood in My Eye* (published posthumously, 1972). Huey P. Newton called Jackson 'the greatest writer of us all.'

JACKSON, JESSE L.

Civil rights leader (b. 1941). After attending the University of Illinois, North Carolina Agricultural and Technical College, and Chicago Theological Seminary, Jackson came to the attention of Martin Luther King, Jr., joined the SCLC, and became national director of Operation Breadbasket. The boycotts which he organized opened the way to employment and business opportunities for thousands of blacks. He gained national prominence in 1968 as 'city manager' of Resurrection City, the shantytown set up in Washington, D. C., to dramatize the plight of the poor. He resigned his directorship of Operation Breadbasket late in 1971, following a dispute over Black Expo, Inc. Later he announced that he was forming his own civil rights organization on December 25, 1971. The new group, People United to Save Humanity (PUSH), is politically and economically oriented. 'Power . . . must be used . . . to picket, vote, and, if necessary, to engage in civil disobedience,' he said. 'We will be as nonviolent as we can be, and as violent as we must be.' See PUSH.

JACKSON, JIMMIE LEE

Civil rights worker. John Lewis and aides of Martin Luther King, Jr., began a Selma-to-Montgomery march on March 7, 1965, to protest the worker's slaying.

JACKSON, JORDAN C.

Civil rights leader (b. 1848). Born in Fayette County, Kentucky, he became prominent in Republican politics and an alternate delegate to the national Republican convention in 1876. He fought against enactment of the separate-coach law in Kentucky.

JACKSON, JOHN H.

Public official (b. 1850). A graduate of Berea College (1874), he was the first man from Kentucky to be elected delegate-at-large to the 1880 Republican national convention.

JACKSON, JOSEPH A.

Clergyman. Dr. Jackson is president of the five-million member National Baptist Convention.

JACKSON, LEONARD M.

World War II hero. He received the Distinguished Flying Cross and the Air Medal with 7 clusters for destroying 3 German planes.

JACKSON, LEVI

Athlete. In 1948 he became the first black football captain at Yale.

JACKSON, LUTHER PORTER

Historian (1892-1950). As a child in Lexington, Kentucky, he was an avid reader with an inquisitive mind. He became interested in black history as a student at Fisk and was distressed to learn that so little material on the cultural contributions of the negro was readily available. He went on to Chicago University, earned his Ph. D. in history (1937), and spent considerable time researching the history of the negro in Virginia and preparing many scholarly articles on the subject. He was on the editorial staff of the *Journal of Negro History* and the *Negro History Bulletin*.

JACKSON, MAY HOWARD

Sculptor (1877-1931). Trained at the Pennsylvania Academy of Fine Arts in Philadelphia, the city of her birth, she moved her studio to Washington, D. C. after her marriage and based her creative works on racial themes. Her works include portrait busts of Paul Laurence Dunbar, W. E. Du Bois, and Francis Grimké.

JACKSON, MAHALIA

Musician (1911-1972). She was the world's leading gospel singer. Born in New Orleans, she moved to Chicago at the age of sixteen, sang in a church quintet to earn money to open a beauty shop, made her first recording ('God Gonna Separate the Wheat from the Tares,' 1934), and became nationally famous after her second record ('Move on Up a Little Higher,' 1945) sold more than a million copies, becoming the first gospel record to do so. Following her first successful concert in Carnegie Hall (1950), she toured Europe, began a weekly radio program, and appeared frequently on television.

JACKSON, PETER

Athlete. Born in the Virgin Islands, he moved to Australia, where he rose to the top ranks among boxers.

JACKSON, SAMUEL C.

Public official. As general manager of the Community Development Corporation, he directs urban planning involving huge expenditures and providing many jobs for Negroes. He is an assistant secretary in DHEW.

JACKSON, TONY

Early blues pianist, described by his contemporaries as a supreme stylist and a brilliant creator.

JACKSON, WILLIAM J.

Coachman. During the Civil War he served as the personal coachman of Confederate president Jefferson Davis. He was able to impart vital information to Union intelligence services.

JACKSON, WILLIAM TECUMSEH SHERMAN

Athlete. In 1891 the Amherst College football star represented his school at New England track meets.

JAMAICA

Soon after England wrested Jamaica from Spain in 1655, this

English possession became the principal slave market in the New World.

JAMES, DANIEL, JR.

U. S. air force general (b. 1920). Promoted to the rank of brigadier general in 1970, he has received many awards and citations.

JAMES E. SULLIVAN MEMORIAL TROPHY

Awarded annually by the AAU to the 'athlete who by his of her performance, example, and influence as an amateur has done most during the year to advance the cause of sportsmanship,' it has been awarded to Mal Whitfield (1954), Harrison Dillard (1955), Rafer Johnson (1960), and Wilma Rudolph (1961).

JAMES MEREDITH FREEDOM MARCH

Shortly after crossing into Mississippi during his planned march from Memphis, Tennessee, to Jackson, Mississippi in his campaign to encourage Negroes to shed their fears and register to vote, James Meredith was hit by three shotgun blasts. The incident brought leaders of the major civil rights groups to Mississippi to continue his March Against Fear. It also revealed the split between moderates and 'Black Power' activists, marking a turning point in the civil rights movement. The chant of 'Black Power' was heard often as the 'James Meredith Freedom March' continued toward Jackson. The march was dominated by Stokely Carmichael and other leaders of the Student Nonviolent Coordinating Committee. Martin Luther King, Jr., who had always encouraged white persons to take part in the civil rights movement, had little support from the young negroes who shouted 'Black Power.' King later paraphrased his 'I have a dream' speech, saying that the dream had 'turned into a nightmare.' Officials of the NAACP were excluded from the speakers' platform at the Jackson rally following the march. The NAACP leaders had failed to sign a manifesto characterizing the march as an 'indictment and protest of the failure of American society' to fulfill its obligations to Negroes.

233

JAMESTOWN

Landing site of the first negroes to arrive in the English colonies. Captain John Smith reported the event in *The General History of Virginia, New England, and the Summer Isles.* (1624): 'About the last of August, came in a Dutch man-of-war that sold us twenty Negroes.' At least three women were among the twenty who landed in Jamestown, Virginia, in 1619. Having been baptized, they were treated as indentured servants, rather than as slaves, and were distributed among the private settlers by the colonial government.

JAMISON, JUDITH

Dancer. In 1965 she joined Alvin Ailey's American Dance Theater and contributed greatly to its soaring popularity. After becoming a lead dancer, she switched from classical ballet to interpretative American dancing. Ailey created for her the sensational dance *Cry.*

JAMISON, SAMUEL W.

Musician (1855-1930). A brillian pianist, he graduated from the New England Conservatory and taught in Boston.

JARBORO, CATERINA

Musician (b. 1903). The first black woman singer to star in an all-white opera company in the United States, she appeared in the title role of *Aïda* in 1933. Her appearance with the Chicago Opera Company in the Hippodrome in New York City was sensational and necessitated a repeat performance two days later. She earned money for study in Europe by appearing in *Shuffle Along* and *Runnin' Wild,* two musical productions. Born Catherine Yarborough in Wilmington, North Carolina, she received her early education in local Catholic schools. She made her operatic debut as Aïda in Milan (1930).

JAZZ

Developed concomitantly with blues and characterized by syncopated dance rhythms, varied orchestral coloring, and authentic negro melodies, jazz today is heard throughout the world. The 369th Regiment Band is credited with introducing the new music to Europe. See Music and Dance.

JEANES FOUNDATION (ANNA T.)

A fund of one million dollars set up in 1907 to help negroes in 'community, country and rural schools.' Its main concerns are community improvement and industrial education. See Randolph, Virginia E.

JEANES FUND

Popular name of the Rural School Fund established by Quaker Anna T. Jeanes in 1907 with an initial bequest of $1,000,000. In 1937 the Jeanes Fund and the Slater Fund were consolidated to form the Southern Educational Foundation.

JEANNETTE, JOE

Athlete (b. 1881). During his long career, the 195-pound boxer won 74 bouts, lost 6, and fought 56 to a draw.

JEHOVIAH, FATHER

Born Samuel Morris, he claimed Godship and influenced Father Divine.

JENKINS, FREDERICK

Abolitionist. Known as Shadrach, he was the first man arrested in Boston under the Fugitive Slave Law of 1850. Lewis Hayden helped him to escape from the U. S. marshal who was preparing to return Jenkins to his owner.

JENNY COUPLER

See Board, Andrew J.

JENSEN REPORT

Controversial study of the intellectual endowment of blacks. See I. Q. Controversy.

JET

See Johnson Publishing Company.

JIHAD

Publishing house founded in Newark, New Jersey, by LeRoi Jones to spread the message of Spirit House. Since its founding in 1966, it has published Jones' writings under his Muslim name of Imamu Amiri Baraka.

JIM BOY

See Tustennuggee Emarthla.

JIM CROW

Expression popularized by one of the white pioneers in comic representation of the negro, Thomas 'Daddy' Rice. Shuffling across the stage at New York's Bowery Theatre in 1832, wearing old clothes and with his face blackened, Rice imitated the jerky movements and unintelligible utterances of a man he claimed he had once seen, James Crow. He gave America its first international hit song, containing the words 'Wheel about, turn about . . . I jump Jim Crow.' His act was widely copied by other entertainers, and by 1838 Jim Crow had become a synonym for negro. Before another year had ended, an antislavery book had appeared under the title *The History of Jim Crow,* and by 1841 Massachusetts had introduced the Jim Crow railroad car. See Jesse Walter Dees, *Jim Crow* (1951).

JIM CROW CAR

A railroad car set apart for the use of negroes. Massachusetts introduced the term Jim Crow car in 1841, and in 1881 Tennessee initiated the modern segregation movement with a Jim Crow railroad law.

JIM CROW ERA

The civil rights cases of 1883 confirmed the trend toward abandonment of the negro to the whims of state legislature and ushered in what has been termed the Jim Crow Era (1884-1914). Segregation was imposed in state after state, the negro was deprived of civic and political rights, and the concept of Jim Crow embraced all forms of public activity.

JIM CROW LAWS
Statutes requiring segregation of whites and blacks in public accommodations or vehicles.

JOCKEYS
In the last third of the 19th century black jockeys were the mainstays of steeplechase races and flat races, and they had their counterparts in black trainers. In the running of the first Kentucky Derby (1875), 14 of the 15 jockeys were black. Today only a handful of the nation's 1,500 jockeys and 4,000 trainers are black, and none can match the records of their celebrated predecessors. See the names of individual jockeys and trainers: Isaac Murphy, Pike Barnes, William Bird, James Winkfield, etc.

JOEL, LAWRENCE
Hero in Vietnam. 'In the face of death, in the fury of ambush, he risked his life that other men might live,' said President Lyndon B. Johnson in awarding the Congressional Medal of Honor to Specialist Joel. He was the first medical corpsman to win the nation's highest honor in Vietnam.

JOHN A. ANDREW MEMORIAL HOSPITAL
See Tuskegee Institute Hospital and Nurses' Training School.

JOHN BROWN'S RAID
See Harpers Ferry.

JOHN HENRY
'America's greatest ballad,' according to some writers, celebrates a black railroad worker who died during the construction of the Big Bend Tunnel in West Virginia, around 1873. The folk-hero

'drove steel with a twelve-pound sheep-nose hammer . . . and could drive ten hours without missing a stroke. He was the steel-driving champion of the country and his record has never been equaled.'

JOHNS, AL

Musician. He is remembered for a single hit song with a title that became a catch phrase, 'Go 'Way Back and Sit Down,' written in the late 1890s.

JOHNSON PRODUCTS COMPANY

Founded by chemist George E. Johnson, the firm became the first predominantly black-owned corporation to be listed on the American Stock Exchange (1971). It is a leader in the field of black cosmetics.

JOHNSON PUBLISHING COMPANY

Largest black publishing firm in the world. It publishes both magazines and books. Founded by John H. Johnson, who began by publishing *Negro Digest* (1945), a small format magazine extolling black accomplishment, the company now publishes *Ebony, Tan, Jet,* and *Black World. Negro Digest* was discontinued but revived in 1961 and renamed *Black World* in 1970. *Ebony* became the most successful black publication in history, *Tan,* a magazine of interest to women, made its debut in 1950. *Jet,* a weekly news magazine, began in 1951 and by 1970 had the highest weekly paid circulation of any black news medium.

JOHNSON, ANTHONY

Former servant whose 1653 case marked a transition in the treatment of indentured persons. After Johnson became a large landowner in Northampton County, Virginia, he charged that John Casor owed him a lifetime or had to serve him for life. In contesting the charge, Casor pleaded that he had already served Johnson for fifteen years, a term that would have been exceptionally long in the case of a white man.

JOHNSON, BUNK

Musician (b. 1879). He played the coronet in New Orleans with the Eagle Band.

JOHNSON, CAMPBELL C.

Army officer. He served as an executive assistant to Lewis B. Hershey, white administrator of the selective service. By mid-1942, 1,800 negroes served on draft boards.

JOHNSON, CHARLES S.

Sociologist (1893-1956). In 1921 he became executive director of research and investigation for the National Urban League. Two years later he launched the league's official organ, Opportunity. An eminent scholar in the field of negro life and problems, he was the first black president of Fisk University. He co-authored *The Negro in Chicago* (1922), a monumental study of the sociological conditions underlying the 1919 rioting in Chicago. His many other books include *The Negro in American Civilization* (1930), *Shadow of the Plantation* (1934), *Race Relations* (1935), *Growing Up in the Black Belt* (1941), *Patterns of Negro Segregation* (1943), and *Education and the Cultural Crisis* (1951).

JOHNSON, ELIJAH

Missionary. After serving in the War of 1812 and preparing for the ministry, he went to Africa as a missionary and one of a group of one hundred colonists. He represented both the U. S. government and the American Colonization Society.

JOHNSON, EDWARD A.

North Carolina educator, politician, and historian. A pioneer historian, he noted in A School History of the Negro Race in America (1891) that white historians 'studiously left out many of the creditable deeds of the Negro.' In 1917 he became the first black to be elected to the New York state legislature.

239

JOHNSON, FRANK

Musician (d. 1874). He organized a band that toured the United States (1839-41), gave a command performance for Queen Victoria (1841), and returned to continued popularity in America. The Philadelphia-born orchestral conductor was also an accomplished arranger and composer. The Frank Johnson band continued after his death under the leadership of Joseph G. Anderson.

JOHNSON, GEORGE E.

Businessman. He founded Johnson Products Company, specializing in black cosmetics.

JOHNSON, HALL

Musician (1888-1970). Famed for his arrangements of spirituals and other black folk music, he formed (1925) a singing group that made him America's best known black choral director. His choir sang in *Green Pastures* (1930) and in his own show, *Run Little Chillun* (1933). He went to Hollywood in 1935 to work on *Green Pastures* and remained there, arranging and composing for films: *Lost Horizon* (1937), *Way Down South* (1939), *Swanee River* (1941), and *Cabin in the Sky* (1943).

JOHNSON, HAROLD

Athlete. In 1962 he became light heavyweight boxing champion of the world by defeating Doug Jones in Philadelphia.

JOHNSON, HARVEY

Clergyman (1843-1923). As pastor of the Union Baptist Church in Baltimore, he led a successful fight to admit blacks to the Maryland state bar and to first-class passenger service on ships out of Baltimore.

JOHNSON, HENRY

World War I hero (1897-1929). Attacked by a small outpost of several German soldiers, he and Needham Roberts, both privates with the 369th Infantry, were wounded. They succeeded in routing their attackers and received the Croix de Guerre in recognition of their heroism. They were the first Americans to receive the award individually. One of the most acclaimed black heroes of the war, he returned after his discharge to his job as a porter at an Albany, New York, railroad station.

JOHNSON, J. ROSAMOND

Musician (1873-1954). He has written songs of every description but is best remembered as the composer of 'Lift Ev'ry Voice and Sing,' a song used as a national anthem by blacks in schools, churches, and public assemblies. He teamed with Robert Cole in the 1890s to create a string of popular hits, including 'Under the Bamboo Tree.'

JOHNSON, JACK

Athlete (1878-1946). The first black to become world heavyweight boxing champion, he is considered by many historians of boxing to be the greatest boxer of all time. Born in Galveston, he became welterweight champion in 1901, won 57 bouts between 1902 and 1907, and defeated Tommy Burns in Australia to become world heavyweight titleholder on December 25, 1908. He successfully defended his title until April 5, 1915, when he was knocked out by Jess Willard in a controversial 26-round bout in Havana, Cuba. His life style and frequent involvements with white women complicated his career. He was chosen for Boxing's Hall of Fame when it opened in 1954: James Earl Jones was nominated for an Oscar in 1971 for his lead role in *The Great White Hope,* based on the search for a white boxer (Jim Jeffries) to defeat Johnson.

JOHNSON, JAMES

Vice Chairman of the U. S. Civil Service Commission.

JOHNSON, JAMES WELDON

Writer (1871-1938). He wrote poetry, fiction, an autobiography, and miscellaneous prose, and he was a pioneer anthologist and interpreter of black poetry. He was, successively, a teacher, song-writer and composer, diplomat, and activist in the civil rights movement. While in the consular service (first in Venezuela and later in Nicaragua) he published his landmark novel, *The Autobiography of an Ex-Colored Man* (1912). After his return to the United States, he became active in the NAACP, achieved recognition as a poet, and published collections of poetry and spirituals. He was appointed Professor of Creative Literature at Fisk University in 1930. His works include *Fifty Years and Other Poems* (1917), the critical anthology titled *The Book of American Negro Poetry* (1922), *The Book of American Negro Spirituals* (1925), *God's Trombones: Seven Negro Sermons in Verse* (1927), *Black Manhattan* (1930), and his autobiography, *Along This Way* (1933).

JOHNSON, JOHN

Hero. His superior, Comander Nathaniel Shaler, wrote that in a battle at sea in 1812, Johnson was struck by a shot that 'took away all the lower part of his body,' yet exhorted his shipmates to continue the fight.

JOHNSON, JOHN H.

Editor and publisher (b. 1918). He heads the Johnson Publishing Company, whose publications include books, *Ebony, Negro Digest,* and *Jet.* Born in Arkansas City, Arkansas, he moved to Chicago when he was fifteen, majored in journalism and business at the University of Chicago, worked as an assistant to Harry Pace, president of Supreme Liberty Insurance Company, and founded his first Publication, *Negro Digest,* in 1942. He became the nation's leading black publisher and the most successful businessman his race has produced. He is now board chairman of Supreme Liberty Life Insurance Company and owner of a cosmetics company.

JOHNSON, LEW

Minstrel. In the 1860s he formed one of the earliest all-negro minstrel troupes, the Plantation Minstrel Company. See Minstrelsy.

JOHNSON, MALVIN GRAY

Artist (1896-1934). Born in Greensboro, North Carolina and trained at the National Academy of Art, he experimented with many styles but is best remembered for his vivid and original Southern landscapes. His works include 'Convict Labor,' 'Brothers,' and 'Swing Low, Sweet Chariot,' for which he won the Otto Kahn Special Prize at the Harmon show in 1928.

JOHNSON, MORDECAI W.

Clergyman and educator (b. 1890). He became the first black president of Howard University (1926-1960) and established the school as a leading training center for lawyers and doctors. A Baptist minister and graduate of Harvard Divinity School, he served on many commissions and was awarded the Spingarn Medal (1929).

JOHNSON, PETER A.

Surgeon. One of the founders of the NUL and a president of the NMA, he served as surgeon-in-chief of the short-lived McDonough Memorial Hospital in New York City.

JOHNSON, RAFER

Athlete (b. 1934). He had a high scholastic average at UCLA, where he was president of the student body, a basketball star, and the first black to pledge a white fraternity. In 1956 he established a new world record in the Olympic decathlon. In 1968, having turned to sportscasting and become involved in politics, he was at the side of Robert F. Kennedy when the senator was assassinated. Johnson helped to apprehend the assassin.

JOHNSON, SARGENT C.

Sculptor (b. 1888). Born in Boston, he achieved fame as a sculptor in California when his seemingly Egyptian-inspired works were exhibited by the San Francisco Art Association in 1925. He studied at the Boston School of Fine Arts and experimented with wrought metal and other composite materials. His most representative works include American negro types.

243

JOHNSON, WILLIAM

Businessman. In the early 1800s he became wealthy, owning at least three barber shops and keeping a few slaves. A free negro, he traded with white men, lent them money, and gave them advice. He recorded his experiences in a diary that was passed on through his family and later edited by two historians. See William R. Hogan and Edwin A. Davis (eds.), *William Johnson's Natchez: The Ante-Bellum Diary of a Free Negro* (1951).

JOHNSON, WILLIAM D.

Religious educator (b. 1842). In 1884 the general conference of the Methodist Episcopal Church elected him secretary of education. An eloquent speaker, he was invited to address the centennial conference of Methodism at Baltimore, Maryland.

JOHNSON, WILLIAM H.

Contemporary artist. In the middle 1940s he returned to the United States from Scandinavia and adopted a mystical approach to painting negro life. He used black models for 'Jesus and the Three Marys.'

JOHNSTON, JOSHUA

Portraitist (died c. 1825). A highly accomplished craftsman, he practiced his profession in Baltimore from about 1790 until his death. He was probably the first negro in America to become a professional portrait artist.

JONES, ABSALOM

Clergyman (1747-1818). With Richard Allen he founded the AME church. He was the first black minister ordained in America (1794) and the first black Grand Master of Masonary. Manumitted by his master, he was active throughout his life in promoting freedom for other blacks. He was cofounder of the Free Africa Society (1787), founder and pastor of St. Thomas Protestant Episcopal Church (1794), and a leader in caring for the sick when fever worked havoc among the white population of

Philadelphia in 1797. In the War of 1812 he helped to raise a company of militia to defend the city against the British.

JONES, BOOKER T.

Musician. Popular in the 1960s, he helped Bill Withers to launch a highly successful career with 'Ain't no Sunshine.'

JONES, DAVID

Athlete. 'Deacon' Jones of the Los Angeles Rams is one of the best defensive ends in football.

JONES, EUGENE K.

Civic leader (1885-1951). He organized and served as one of the first executive officers of the National Urban League, 1919-41. Born in Richmond, Virginia, he earned a master's degree at Cornell (1908), helped to organize the NUL in 1911, served the U. S. state department as advisor on negro affairs (1933-37), and was appointed a member of the Fair Employment Board of the U. S. Civil Service Commission in 1948.

JONES, HAYES

Athlete. In the 1964 Olympics he won a gold medal in the 110-meter high hurdles. He returned to Detroit, became a public relations official for American Airlines, and chairman of the New Detroit Committee (formed after the riot of 1967). In 1967 he became New York City's first commissioner of recreation.

JONES, J. MCHENRY

Educator (1859). A gifted orator and strong advocate of equal rights for negroes, he was associate editor of the militant newspaper The Charleston Advocate, grand master of the Grand United Order of the Odd Fellows (1902), and the first president of West Virginia Colored Institute, near Charleston, 1898-1909. His speeches were printed, and he also published a book titled *Hearts of Gold.*

JONES, J. RAYMOND

Public official. In 1964 he became the first black man to be named a county leader in New York. He was elected leader of the New York County Democratic Organization (Tammany Hall). He had served previously as a New York City councilman.

JONES, J. W.

Physician. A graduate of Leonard Medical School, he became a successful physician in Winston-Salem, North Carolina, in the early part of the century.

JONES, JAMES EARL

Actor (b. 1931). He won Broadway's most coveted prize, the Antoinette Perry Award, in 1968, for his brilliant portrayal of Jack Jefferson in The Great White Hope.

JONES, JAMES F.

Faith healer (1908-1971). At the height of his fame in the 1950s, he claimed 6 million followers. Born in Birmingham, Alabama, he moved to Detroit in 1938, announced that God had spoken to him, and was known thereafter as Prophet Jones.

JONES, JOHN

Businessman (1816-1879). He moved to Chicago in 1845 in search of full freedom, prospered after establishing the first black tailor shop, and fought successfully for repeal of the Illinois Black Laws (1865). He donated the land for Jones Commercial School of Chicago and was twice elected Cook County commissioner.

JONES, K. C.

Athlete. Drafted in 1957 by the Boston Celtics, he soon carved out a niche for himself as a defensive player, then retired (1967) to become head basketball coach at Brandeis University in Waltham, Massachusetts. He was one of the first blacks to coach at a predominantly white university.

JONES, LEROI

Writer (b. 1934). Everett LeRoi Jones, who now calls himself Imamu Amiri Baraka, began his career as and avant-garde poet in Greenwich Village and became the most powerful exponent of the doctrine of the artist as activist. After graduating from Howard (1953) and earning a master's degree in comparative literature from Columbia University, he became a prominent spokesman for the Beat Generation, co-edited an underground poetry magaizne, lectured at the New School and Columbia, visited Cuba (1960), abandoned Greenwich Village, and became the leading advocate of the Black Revolution. He left his white wife and children in 1965, founded the Black Arts Theatre of Harlem, moved to Newark to set up the Black Community Development with headquarters at his Spirit House, became an orthodox Muslim and a minister of the Kawaida faith, and masterminded the election of Kenneth Gibson as mayor of Newark in 1970. In *Blues People: Negro Music in White America* (1963), he undertook a total revaluation of the cultural matrix of black music. He also had a tremendous impact on the development of a concept of black theater and inspired a new school of black poets who exploited the modes of speech imbedded in the rich black oral tradition. He wrote several volumes of verse but is best known for his controversial plays, including *The Dutchman* (1964), *The Toilet* (1964), *Slave Ship* (1967), and *Arm Yourself, or Harm Yourself* (1967). He has also written many essays and articles, edited several anthologies of poetry, produced an autobiographical novel titled *The System of Dante's Hell* (1965), and published a poetic book with photographs by Fundi (Billy Abernathy), *In Our Terribleness* (1970).

JONES, LOIS MAILOU

Contemporary artist (b. 1905). Well known for her paintings of exotic Haitian scenes, she began teaching design at Howard in 1930. After studying at the Boston Normal Art School and Columbia, she worked as costume and stage designer for the Repertory Theatre in Boston, studied in Paris (1937-38), and executed several outstanding murals.

247

JONES, PROPHET
See Jones, James F.

JONES, RALPH WALDO EMERSON
Educator. In 1936 he founded Grambling College. Dr. Jones has also served as the school's football coach. See Grambling College.

JONES, SAM
Athlete. Drafted by the Boston Celtics in 1957, he made the NBA all-star team eight times before signing to become head basketball coach and athletic director at the Federal City College (1969) in Washington, D. C.

JONES, SCIPIO AFRICANUS
Lawyer. He helped to bring the case of Moore v. Dempsey (1923) before the U. S. Supreme Court.

JONES, SISSERETTA
Musician. In 1892 she appeared in the Jubilee Spectacle at Madison Square Garden. A few months later, she was invited to sing at the White House. Called 'Black Patti' after Adelina Patti, she formed her own company, the Black Patti Troubadours, and toured for many years.

JONES, THEODORE W.
Businessman (b. 1853). His storage warehouse business in Chicago employed 53 workers. He organized the Business Men's League of Cook County and was elected county commissioner in 1894.

JONES, URIAH
Fencing expert. In 1971, at the age of 46, he became the foil champion.

JONES, VIRGINIA LACY
Educator (b. 1912). Born and educated in Cincinnati, she

earned a Ph. D. at the University of Chicago (1945). As catalouger and later director of the Atlanta University school of library service, she has gained valuable experience as a librarian, and she has shared her knowledge and insights with others in two books and many articles.

JOPLIN, SCOTT

Musician. He is credited with creating a distinct piano technique. His ragtime pieces include 'Maple Leaf Rag' (1899) and an opera in ragtime *Treemonisha* (1911).

JORDAN, BARBARA

Public official. Senator Jordan was the first black woman to sit in a southern legislature.

JORDAN, CLARENCE L.

Clergyman (1912-1969). In 1942 he founded a 1,400-acre interracial farm near Americus, Georgia, called the Koinonia Farm. He wrote *Cotton Patch Version of Paul's Epistles.*

JORDAN, JACK

Sculptor. Born in Texas and educated in Oklahoma, he has received more than 30 awards for his creations. He teaches at Southern University in Louisiana.

JORDAN, VERNON, JR.

Civil rights leader. He has served as executive director of the United Negro College Fund and as leader of the National Urban League. The basic issue of the 1970s, according to Jordan, is 'implementation of rights won in the 1960s.'

JOURNAL OF AMERICAN HISTORY, THE

Carefully documented and influential quarterly founded by Carter G. Woodson. It is the official organ of the Association for the Study of Negro Life.

JOURNAL OF THE NATIONAL MEDICAL ASSOCIATION
Founded in 1908 as the official organ of the National Medical Association, it was edited by Charles V. Roman.

JOURNALS
Important journals stressing publication of material relating to negroes include the older *Journal of Negro History, Phylon,* and *Journal of Southern History* as well as new publications such as the *Journal of African History, Comparative Studies in Society and History, Freedomways, Black Scholar, Black World* (formerly the *Negro Digest*), *Essence,* and *Afro-American Studies.* See Press.

JOUSTON, IVAN J.
Businessman. He is president of Golden State Mutual Insurance Company in Los Angeles.

JUBILEES
Term designating negro spirituals. It was made famous by the Fisk Jubilee Singers, who toured the United States and Europe, 1871-78, and raised $150,000 to found Fisk University in Nashville, Tennessee.

JULIAN, HUBERT
Pilot. One of the first blacks to fly a plane, he was known as the Black Eagle. He helped before World War II to train the Ethiopian Air Force.

JULIAN, PERCY
Scientist (b. 1899). The best known black scientist living today, he has achieved international recognition for his work in the development of steroids and for his discovery of new uses for soybeans. His slave grandfather had suffered mutilation of his right hand because of his desire to learn to read, and Julian himself was reprimanded by a Montgomery policeman for climbing a fence to watch white children working in a chemistry laboratory in a white school. He later earned a Ph. D. in organic

chemistry (Vienna, 1931), taught at Howard and De Pauw, directed the Gidden Company's research division, and set up his own Julian Laboratories, Inc., in Franklin Park, Illinois (1954) and Mexico (1955). He has published more than a hundred scientific papers and registered more than fifty patents.

JULIUS ROSENWALD FUND

Incorporated as a nonprofit enterprise in 1917, it was used to build rural schools, support secondary schools and colleges, and provide fellowships for promising students.

JUST, ERNEST E.

Scientist (1884-1940). He is internationally acclaimed for his work in the fertilization and cytoplasm of cells. The first recipient of the coveted Spingarn award (1915), he had already published important papers on his research on egg fertilization. At Dartmouth he was the only magna cum laude graduate in his class (1907). He taught at Howard, earned a Ph. D. in zoology and physiology at the University of Chicago (1916), and became the only black to have a star of distinction beside his name in American Men of Science. He published sixty papers and two books, *Basic Methods for Experiments of Marine Animals* (1939) and *The Biology of the Cell Surface* (1939). He served on the editorial boards of *Biological Bulletin* and *Journal of Morphology*.

K

KANSAS-NEBRASKA ACT

Legislation, passed on May 30, 1854, establishing the territories of Kansas and Nebraska. The act repealed the Missouri Compromise and allowed occupants of the two territories to exercise popular, or squatter, soverignty in determining whether they would enter the Union as slave or free states.

KANSAS COLORED VOLUNTEERS

The First and Second Kansas Colored Volunteers, organized in August 1862 and mustered into the Union army on January 13, 1863, were made up of fugitives from Missouri and free men from the North. They fought against guerrilla forces in Kansas and Missouri, without pay or official recognition at the outset. One of the bloodiest battles in which they were engaged was on on the Osage River in Bates County, Missouri.

KARENGA, MAULANA RON

Teacher and black nationalist leader (b. 1941). Born in Maryland and educated in California, he has done social work, lectured on social urban problems and black culture, and taught Swahili. Concerned with achieving unity among black people, he founded a black nationalist cultural organization in 1965, shortly after the Watts riot. His Los Angeles-based organization, has developed a religio-political nationalism and has chosen Swahili as the Pan-African language most suitable for its purposes.

KARRIEM, ELIJAH

See Muhammad, Elijah.

KAY, ULYSSES
Musician. His symphonic works have been performed by leading orchestras.

KAYE, PHILLIP B.
Writer. His works include Taffy (1950).

KECKLEY, ELIZABETH H.
Ex-slave, seamstress to Mrs. Lincoln, and author of *Behind the Scenes, or Thirty Years a Slave, and Four Years in the White House* (1868).

KELLEY, BEN
Athlete. In 1953 he became the first black player on a predominantly white Texas football team (San Angelo Junior College).

KELLEY, WILLIAM MELVIN
Writer. His novel *A Different Drummer* won him a Rosenthal Foundation award in 1963.

KELLY, LEROY
Athlete. In 1965 he was the NFL's punt-return champion. In 1967 the Cleveland Browns' ball carrier led the NFL in rushing yardage, rushing average, and touchdowns scored.

KELLY, WYNTON
Musician (1932-1971). He played with a number of popular groups in the 1950s and 1960s, including those of Miles Davis and Dizzie Gillespie. He was a blues-oriented jazz pianist.

KELSEY, GEORGE D.
Theologian. Trained at Harvard and Yale, he is professor of Christian ethics at Drew. His definitive work is *Racism and the Christian Understanding of Man* (1965), in which he provides 'a Christian criticism of racism as a faith system.'

254

KEMPER, HARRELD
Musician (b. 1885). An accomplished violinist, he conducted the Atlanta University chorus on a coast-to-coast broadcast in 1946. He studed at Sterns Conservatory in Berlin and taught at Spelman and Morehouse.

KENNEDY, WILLIAM J. JR.
Businessman (b. 1922). He is founder and president of the nation's largest negro life insurance company, North Carolina Mutual Insurance Company.

KENNEY, J. A.
Physician. A graduate of Leonard Medical School, he became secretary of the National Medical Association and the family physician of Booker T. Washington.

KEPPARD, FREDDIE
Musician. In the early 1900s he became the most famous cornet player in New Orleans, working first with the Original Creole Band and later with the Olympia Band.

KERNER COMMISSION
In its 1968 report the commission concluded that 'our nation is moving toward two societies, one black, one white—separate but unequal.'

KERSANDS, BILLY
Comedian. One of the greatest of the early comedians, he performed with the Georgia Minstrels.

KEYES, LEROY
Athlete. In 1967 he was called the most versatile college football player of his time. The Purdue junior ended the season as the highest scorer in college football and everyone's All-American.

KILGORE, THOMAS
Clergyman. In 1969 he became the first black to head the

American Baptist Convention, which has one and one-half million members.

KILLENS, JOHN O.

Writer (b. 1916). His works include the novel *Youngblood,* the screen play *Odds Against Tomorrow,* and the collection of essays *Black Man's Burden.*

KING, B. B.

Musician. A professional singer-guitarist for many years, he made his first big hit with a recording of the scathing social commentary, 'Why I Sing the Blues,' in 1969.

KING, CORETTA S.

Speaker, singer, and civil rights activist. She is the widow of Dr. Martin Luther King, Jr.

KING, MARTIN LUTHER, JR.

(1919-1968) Baptist preacher and civil rights leader. Born in Atlanta Georgia on January 15, 1919, King graduated from Morehouse College in 1948, then attended Crozer Theological Seminary and Boston University, receiving the Ph. D. in 1955. Ordained a minister in 1947 at his father's Ebenezer Baptist Church in Atlanta, he pastored the Dexter Avenue Baptist Church in Montgomery, Alabama, before returning to Atlanta to serve as co-pastor of his father's church. His civil rights leadership began in 1956 with the boycott by Negroes of the Montgomery public transportation system to protest Jim Crow practices. The success of the boycott made King the chief figure in the nonviolent civil rights movement. He was instrumental in securing passage of the civil rights acts of 1964 and 1965. Less successful in his efforts to promote civil rights in Chicago, beginning in 1966, King was challenged by younger, more militant leaders. He retained a huge following among the black population, however, and was active in civil rights causes until his assassination outside a motel in Memphis, where he had gone to lead a march by striking sanitation workers. He was president of the Southern Christian Leadership

Conference and helped to establish the Student Nonviolent Coordinating Committee. He wrote *Stride Toward Freedom* (1958), *Strength to Love* (1963), and *Why We Can't Wait* (1964). In 1964 he was awarded the Nobel Peace Prize. His last major efforts were directed toward organizing the Poor People's Campaign. Following his assassination on April 4, 1968, blacks and whites alike lamented the nation's loss as flags were lowered throughout the land. See L. D. Reddick, *Crusader Without Violence: Biography of Martin Luther King* (1959).

KING, SLATER

Civil rights leader. A prominent businessman ol Albany, Mississippi, he was named vice president of the Albany Movement.

KINGSLOW, HARRY E.

Physician (b. 1882). After a brief career as a pharmacist, he earned his medical degree from Meharry (1915) and became medical examiner for the Masons. He was a member of the West Virginia Medical Society.

KINNEGY, WILLIAM

Civil War spy. He joined a North Carolina unit and, during a scouting assignment, managed to free his wife and four children.

KITT, EARTHA

Entertainer (b. 1928). She enjoys an international reputation as a singer, actress, and night club entertainer.

KNIGHTS AND DAUGHTERS OF TABOR, TWELVE

Radical antislavery group founded in 1844 by Moses Dickson.

KNIGHTS OF LIBERTY

A secret society organized by Moses Dickson. Active in the underground railroad, it may have had 50,000 members before it was disbanded, at the end of the Civil War.

KNOX, CLINTON E.
U. S. foreign service officer (b. 1908). He served as ambassador to Dahomey.

KNOX, WILLIAM J.
Chemist. After earning his doctorate from Massachusetts Institute of Technology, he worked on the Manhattan Project to develop the atomic bomb, 1943-45.

KNOXVILLE MEDICAL COLLEGE
Founded in Knoxville, Tennessee, in 1895, the college had over 45 graduates during its brief history.

KOINONIA FARM
Interracial farm near Americus, Georgia. See Jordan, Clarence L.

KOONTZ, ELIZABETH DUNCAN
Educator (b. 1919). Recently appointed director of the women's bureau of the U. S. department of labor, she had served previously as president of the Department of Classroom Teachers of the National Education Association (1965) and as president of the parent organization, the National Education Association (1968). Educated in the public schools of Salisbury, North Carolina, where for many years she was a special education teacher, Mrs. Koontz was the first negro to be installed as president of the nation's largest association of teachers.

KOREAN CONFLICT
The conflict in Korea speeded up integration in the armed services and gave negro servicemen an opportunity to demonstrate their courage and ability on the battlefield. Mixed units fought side by side. Morale and efficiency were high. Two negroes, Sergeant Cornelius H. Charlton and Private William Thomas, earned the congressional Medal of Honor. Two years after the conflict ended, every all-negro unit in the armed services had been abolished.

KOUNTZ, SAMUEL L.

Medical researcher. Famous as a researcher in human kidney transplantation, he was named 'Outstanding Young Investigator of 1964' by the American College of Cardiology.

KU KLUX ACT

See Civil Rights Act of 1871.

KU KLUX KLAN

Organized in 1865 at Pulaski, Tennessee, as a fun-seeking social group, the Ku Klux Klan soon became an instrument for maintaining white supremacy in the South.

L

LABOR AND LABOR UNIONS

Black manpower was a significant factor in American society from the nation's beginnings. The slavery system set up a standard for labor that affected nonslave labor. Free blacks could hardly compete as equals with white job-seekers. The degraded position of the sailor opened some opportunities for them. It has been estimated that in 1850 one-half of all seamen were black. Negroes also worked as scavengers, cooks, and helpers in other fields. In the post-Civil War period white laborers formed unions that excluded their black counterparts, then were embittered because industrialists used blacks as strike-breakers. In 1902, according to W. E. B. Du Bois, 43 national unions had no black members and 16 of these had direct discriminatory policies; 27 included a few blacks; in all, the AFL counted only 40,000 black workers in its ranks. Recent legislation offers hope of improvement. See Civil Rights Act of 1964; Fair Employment Practices Committee; and Randolph, Philip.

LAFAYETTE, JAMES

See Armistead, James.

LAFTON, THOMY

Philanthropist (1810-1893). He contributed generously to the abolitionist cause and the underground railroad. He willed most of his estate to charitable and educational institutions in New Orleans. In 1893 the Louisiana state legislature voted to honor the philanthropist in memoriam.

LAKE ERIE

Fifty negroes served with Captain Oliver H. Perry when he scored his victory over the British man-o'-war in the battle of Lake Erie (September 10, 1813).

LAMB, GERALD A.

Public official. He was elected state treasurer of Connecticut in 1962.

LAMBERT, LUCIEN

Musician (b. 1828). He achieved recognition in New Orleans as a pianist, teacher, and composer. He studied in Paris, then went to Brazil as chief musician in Dom Pedro's court. His compositions include 'L'Américaine,' 'Le Niagara,' and 'La Juive.' See Lambert, Richard.

LAMBERT, RICHARD

Musician. A member of a talented family of seven in nineteenth-century Louisiana, he was well known as a teacher but better known as the father of two concert pianists, Lucien and Sidney.

LAMBERT, SIDNEY

Musician. The King of Portugal decorated him and named him his court musician. He also taught in Paris and was acclaimed as a concert pianist. His compositions include 'L'Africaine' and 'Transports Joyeux.' See Lambert, Richard.

LANDRY, PIERRE

Public official (b. 1841). An ex-slave, he was elected mayor of Donaldsonville, Louisiana, in 1868, and state senator in 1874.

LANE COLLEGE

Small college in Jackson, Tennessee, founded in 1882 by Bishop Isaac Lane.

LANE SEMINARY

Organized in Cincinnati to produce domestic missionaries to

combat Catholicism in the West, it attracted a brilliant and talented student body. Abolitionist Theodore D. Weld organized a discussion that culminated in a debate on slavery (1834). The debate converted many people throughout the country to the abolitionist cause and impressed upon them its relationship to civil liberties.

LANE, ISAAC

Educator (1834-1937). Born of obscure parentage in western Tennessee and licensed to teach while a slave, he preached, raised cotton, and sold firewood. He was consecrated as a bishop in the Colored Methodist Episcopal Church in 1873. Finally, after many years of poverty and self-denial, he founded Lane College in Jackson, Tennessee (1882). See *Autobiography of Bishop Lane, LL. D., with a Short History of the C. M. E. Church* (1916).

LANE, LUNSFORD

Businessman. Born a slave, he bought his freedom and became a leading tobacco merchant in Raleigh, North Carolina. He was also an effective public speaker and anti-slavery agent.

LANE, WILLARD M.

Physician. A graduate of the medical college of the University of West Tennessee, he became assistant professor of surgery at Howard.

LANEY, LUCY

Educator (1854-1933). She graduated from Atlanta University in 1873, taught in various parts of Georgia, and founded Haines Institute in Georgia (1886).

LANGFORD, SAM

Athlete (b. 1886). The 200-pound boxer, possessed of incredible physical strength, was known as the 'Boston Tar Baby.' He fought more than 250 bouts of record, 1902-23.

LANGSTON, JOHN MERCER

Educator and public official (1829-1897). The offspring of a Virginia slave mother and a plantation master, he was the first negro to be elected U. S. congressman from Virginia (1889). He was also the first black American to win an elective office, as a member of the city council of Brownhelm, Ohio (1855). An active leader in the convention movement before the Civil War, he helped after the war to organize the freedmen in the Negro National Labor Union. President Andrew Johnson in 1868 appointed him inspector general of the Freedmen's Bureau. From 1869 to 1876 he was associated with Howard University in Washington, D. C. President Rutherford B. Hayes appointed him minister to Haiti in 1877. Later he served as president of Virginia Normal and Collegiate Institute at Petersburg, Virginia. Elected to the U. S. Congress as a Republican in 1888, he was not seated until 1890 because the election was contested. He published a collection of addresses, *Freedom and Citizenship* (1883), and his autobiography, *From the Virginia Plantation to the National Capitol* (1894). Langston University, near Guthrie, Oklahoma, is named for him.

LANGSTON, OKLAHOMA

All-negro town, seat of Langston University. See McCabe, Edwin P.

LANIER, RALPH O'HARA

Educator and diplomat (1900-1965). An able college administrator and scholar, he was born in Winston-Salem, North Carolina, and educated at Lincoln University in Pennsylvania, Stanford, and Harvard. He taught and held administrative positions at Tuskegee, Florida A. and M. College in Tallahassee, Sam Houston College in Texas, and Hampton Institute in Virginia. In 1945 he was appointed special assistant in the bureau of services of the United Nations relief and rehabilitation administration. For two years he was U. S. minister to Liberia. After returning to America, he became president of Texas State University in Houston.

264

LARKINS, ELLIS
Musician (b. 1933). A child prodigy, he was playing Mozart at the age of 7 in public performances. He later led his own combos, made recordings, and was much in demand as a composer and arranger. In 1972 he emerged from semi-retirement in Hollywood, where he had been coaching singers for a living, to perform at Gregorys on New York's Upper East Side.

LARSEN, NELLA
Writer. Her works include *Quicksand* (1928) and *Passing* (1929).

LAST POETS, THE
Group of recording artists from New York who presented chorale-like social criticism with a rhythm accompaniment. Inspired by LeRoi Jones, they used modes of speech imbedded in the black oral tradition.

LATIMER, LEWIS H.
Inventor (1848-1928). An associate of Thomas Edison, he invented and patented an electric lamp socket, drafted plans for the first telephone, and supervised the installation of electric lights in New York, Philadelphia, and London. He also wrote the first textbook on the Edison electric system and prepared the drawing accompanying Alexander Graham Bell's application for a patent on the telephone.

LAUTIER, LOUIS R.
Journalist. He was the first black correspondent admitted to the congressional press gallery.

LAW AND ORDER
Popularized during the 1968 political campaign, the expression 'law and order' was interpreted by many as a code word for Negro repression.

LAWLESS, THEODORE K.

Dermatologist (1894). He is internationally known for his research in the treatment of leprosy and syphilis. Born in Thibodaux, Louisiana, and educated at Talladega College in Alabama, the University of Kansas, Columbia, and Northwestern University, he received both the Harmon Award for achievement in medicine (1929) and the NAACP's Spingarn Medal (1954). A clinic in Israel bears the philanthropist's name.

LAWRENCE, JACOB

Artist (b. 1917). One of the outstanding painters of the century, he completed a vast series of paintings of Toussaint L'Ouverture, John Brown, the struggles of the Revolutionary heroes, and Harlem settings.

LAWRENCE, ROBERT

Astronaut (1936-1967). Selected in June 1967 as one of four men to be trained for the first military spacecraft, Major Lawrence had earned a Ph. D. in physical chemistry (1965). He died in an F-104 jet plane as it landed at Edwards Air Force Base on December 8, 1967.

LAWSON, JAMES

Fugitive slave. After escaping from Virginia, he shipped on board a gunboat commanded by Lieutenant Samuel Magaw. He performed heroically as a scout and spy during the Civil War.

LAWSON, JAMES R.

Physicist and educator. In 1968 he became president of Fisk University. A member of the governing board of the Oak Ridge Association Universities, he is a specialist in infrared spectroscopy.

LAWSON, JOHN

Civil War hero. A black landsman serving aboard the Union gunboat *Hartford,* he won the navy's Medal of Honor for meritorious service in the Battle of Mobile Bay, August 5, 1864.

LAWSON, MARJORIE

Public official (b. 1912). She was appointed associate judge of the Washington, D. C. juvenile court in 1962. She has also served as the U. S. representative to UNESCO and to the United Nations Economic and Social Council.

LAWSON, WARNER

Musician. He is dean of music and choral director at Howard University.

LEADERSHIP CONFERENCE ON CIVIL RIGHTS

A group formed to coordinate the lobbying efforts of many civic, labor, and religious organizations. Roy Wilkins serves as its chairman.

LEAGUE FOR THE PROTECTION OF COLORED WOMEN

See National Urban League.

LEARY, LEWIS SHERIDAN

Abolitionist (1835-1859). He was one of John Brown's heroic fighters at Harpers Ferry. Born of free parents in Fayetteville, North Carolina, he answered Brown's call for volunteers. Though he did not tell his family of his plan, he was joined by a cousin, John A. Copeland. See Harpers Ferry.

LEARY, SHERRARD LEWIS

One of John Brown's raiders. See Harpers Ferry.

LEE, CANADA

Actor (1907-1951). In 1941 he appeared in the stage adaptation of Richard Wright's *Native Son.* Other memorable roles: *Anna*

Lucasta (1943), *The Tempest* (1945), and *On Whitman Avenue,* which he also co-produced.

LEE, DON L.

Poet. Four of his works were published by Broadside Press of Detroit: *Think Black, Black Pride, Don't Cry, Scream,* and *We Walk the Way of the New World.* By 1969 he had sold 80,000 copies of his books. He was appointed poet-in-residence at Cornell.

LEIDESDORFF, WILLIAM ALEXANDER

Businessman and diplomat (1810-1848). Born at St. Croix in the Virgin Islands, he sailed for California in 1841, launched the first steamboat to sail on San Francisco Bay, built the city's first hotel, and introduced horse racing to California. He became a Mexican citizen in 1844 and acquired 35,000 acres on the American River. He became the American consul in California and city treasurer of San Francisco, where a street was named in his honor.

LEMON, MEADOWLARK

A star attraction of the Harlem Globetrotters, he is responsible for much of the slapstick comedy practiced by the team.

LEONARD MEDICAL SCHOOL

Established in 1882 with the support of the Baptist Mission Society for Negroes, the Leonard Medical School of Shaw University in Raleigh, North Carolina, numbered among its distinguished graduates L. L. Burwell, J. W. Jones, J. A. Kenney, and L. Martin. Unable to comply with the standards set forth in the Flexner Report (1910), the school closed in 1915.

LES CENELLES

Title of a collaborative anthology of French poetry written by seventeen New Orleans negroes and published in 1845. Victor Séjour was a contributor.

LEVY, JAMES R.
Physician (b. 1861). After graduating from the Chicago College of Physicians and Surgeons (1894), he established a practice in South Carolina. Active in politics, he was Republican chairman for the 6th district of South Carolina.

LEW, BARZILLAI
Patriot (b. 1743). He fought in the French and Indian War as a Pepperell before enlisting in the 27th Massachusetts Regiment. He participated as a soldier and a fifer in the Battle of Bunker Hill and the siege of Boston. He remained in the army until the end of the Revolution, carrying out many dangerous assignments.

LEWIS, EDMONIA
Pioneer woman sculptor (1845-1890). The first black woman in America to be a professional sculptor, she produced neo-classical works which were much in demand. She studied at Oberlin, opened a studio in Boston, earned enough money from sales of copies of the bust of Colonel Robert Gould to move to Europe, and received many commissions from Americans and Europeans until the neo-classical vogue faded in the 1880s and she sank into obscurity. The date of her death is uncertain.

LEWIS, HENRY
Musician. In 1961 he conducted the Los Angeles Philarmonic Orchestra during its regular season. He became director of the Los Angeles Opera Company in 1965. In 1968 he was named musical director of the New Jersey Symphony.

LEWIS, IDA
Journalist. In 1972 she launched a new monthly magazine, *Encore.* In the premiere issue she stated in her dual role as editor and publisher that the aim of the new publication was 'To provoke . . . excite . . . involve: not by sensationalism but by thoroughly researched reportage and analysis.'

269

LEWIS, JAMES

Hero and public official (1832-1914). When the Union troops occupied New Orleans, he abandoned the Confederate ship on which he was serving as a steward, raised two companies of black soldiers, and led the 1st Regiment of the Louisiana National Guard during the battle for Port Hudson. After the war ended, he worked for the Freedmen's Bureau, establishing schools and training centers. Active in Reconstruction politics, he received a number of federal appointments.

LEWIS, JANE

Underground railroad conductor. She lived in New Lebanon, Ohio, and rowed many escaping slaves across the Ohio River.

LEWIS, JOHN

Civil rights leader (b. 1940). Once president of the SNCC, he now serves as executive director of the Voter Education Project. Headquartered in Atlanta, Georgia, the project is active in 11 states. It stresses political action at the local level.

LEWIS, JOHN HENRY

Athlete (b. 1914). Before being defeated by Joe Louis in 1938, he had never been knocked out in 99 fights.

LEWIS, JULIAN

Scientist, physician, and pathologist (b. 1891).

LEWIS, WILLIAM H.

Athlete. A center on the Amherst football teams of the early 1890s, he was the most talked-about star of his day. He later became a line coach at Harvard and wrote one of the first books on football, *How to Play Football*. He was the first black All-American from a major school (1892 and again in 1893) and the first black to coach a major college team.

LIBERATION SCHOOLS

Ghetto schools set up by the Black Panthers to promote political awareness, family unity, and party discipline.

LIBERATION TRAIN

A five-day 'march against repression' organized by the SCLC in May 1970 to dramatize opposition to the climate of oppression associated with student deaths at Jackson State and Kent State colleges. The 110-mile march ended in Atlanta.

LIBERIA

West African republic, founded in 1822 by the American Colonization Society as a colony of freed slaves. It was intended to serve as a new home for American blacks, a place where they could demonstrate their abilities and thus encourage slave-holders to emancipate slaves in greater numbers. Progress in building the new nation was slow since slaveholders were reluctant to part with their property and since some freedmen preferred to remain in America while others reverted to the bush in Africa. Liberia became a republic in 1847, with a government modeled after that of the United States. Some of its operation remained in American hands however, and its resources were systematically exploited by outsiders. Liberia failed to fulfill its founders' dream of serving as a base for the Christianization of Africa and a source of inspiration for both masters and slaves. See Richard West, *Back to Africa; a History of Sierra Leone and Liberia* (1970).

LIBERTY PARTY

Antislavery political party founded in 1840 by white abolitionist James G. Birney, who rejected the nonpolitical stand of William Lloyd Garrison. Birney received enough votes to throw the 1844 presidential election to James K. Polk. In 1848 the Liberty party merged into the Free Soil party. Negroes were active in both parties.

271

LIELE, GEORGE

Clergyman (born c. 1750). Born a slave in Virginia and taken to Georgia by his master before the Revolutionary War, he was converted, baptized, and all allowed to preach on plantations. Later freed to carry on his work as a Baptist minister, he baptized Andrew Bryan and some other blacks who founded the African Baptist Church in Savannah.

LIFT EVERY VOICE AND SING

Written by brothers James Weldon and James Rosamond Johnson, the song is accepted by black Americans as a national anthem because it conveys a sense of birthright and heritage.

LINCOLN, C. ERIC

Theologian. Now professor of sociology and religion at Union Theological Seminary, he is recognized as a specialist in the fields of race relations, sociological research, and theology. Among the first members of the race to be appointed to a major position in a white seminary, he moved into the front ranks of the sociologists of religion by publishing *The Black Muslims of America* (1961), essential to an understanding of the affinity between the Black Muslims and what later became known as the Black Power movement.

LINCOLN HOSPITAL

Founded by Dr. A. M. Moore in Durham, North Carolina with funds supplied by Washington Duke, the medical center is operated by blacks.

LINCOLN UNIVERSITY

Founded in 1854 as Ashmun Institute in Oxford, Pennsylvania, it was the first black college in the United States.

LINKSTERS

Name given to negroes who went into Indian territory to seek land. Often welcomed by the tribes, they were referred to as linksters because of their ability to speak English.

LINTON, HENRI

Artist (b. 1944). A native of Alabama, he teaches at Arkansas A. M. & N. College in Pine Bluff. He has received awards and scholarships from Atlanta and Boston universities. His poignant oil 'Alone' (1968) is in the Negro Collection of Atlanta University.

LIPSCOMB, GENE

Athlete. 'Big Daddy' Lipscomb joined the Baltimore Colts in 1956 and by 1959 was generally considered the top defensive lineman in the NFL.

LISTON, MELBA

Musician (b. 1926). The only outstanding female jazz trombonist, she played with Dizzy Gillespie and Count Basie. In 1959 she played the trombone and acted in the blues opera *Free and Easy*.

LISTON, SONNY

Athlete (1932-1970). He was the world heavyweight boxing champion, 1962-64. He won the championship by knocking out Floyd Patterson in the first round and lost his title to Cassius Clay in the seventh round on a technical knockout.

LITERARY SOCIETIES

At least 45 societies to spread knowldege and promote self-improvement were founded in the North before the Civil War. They provided libraries and reading rooms in many cities.

LITERATURE

See Slave Narratives, Harlem Renaissance, and New Harlem Renaissance.

LITTLE, MALCOLM

See Malcolm X.

LITTLE ROCK CRISIS

Following the 1954 Supreme Court decision outlawing segregation in schools, the Little Rock school board had prepared a comprehensive desegregation plan. Nine negro children were to enter high school on September 3, 1957. Governor Orval Faubus ordered national guard units to surround Central High School to forestall implementation of the plan. Three weeks later President Dwight D. Eisenhower authorized the use of federal troops to insure the admission and protection of the nine children (Executive Order 10730). The door for integrated school systems throughout the nation was opened on September 25, 1957, when six girls and three boys met in the home of Mrs. Daisy Bates and were escorted through the streets to Central High School in Little Rock, Arkansas, by federal troops.

LOCKE, ALAIN L.

Scholar and critic (1886-1954). The first black Rhodes scholar, he was internationally acclaimed as a critic and interpreter of the negro's contribution to American culture. He wrote *Race Contacts and Interracial Relations* (1916), *The Negro and His Music* (1936), *Negro Art: Past and Present* (1936), *The Negro in Art* (1940), and *The Negro in American Culture* (1956), begun under a grant from the Rockefeller Foundation and completed by Margaret Just Butcher (1956). Closely associated with the writers of the Harlem Renaissance, he was a literary critic as well as a philosopher. His book *The New Negro* (1925) is an anthology of Renaissance work.

LOGAN, RAYFORD WHITTINGHAM

Historian (b. 1895). After receiving his Ph. D. from Harvard in 1936, he taught at Virginia Union University, Atlanta University, and Howard University, where he was promoted to department head in 1942. He wrote many scholarly articles, edited the *Journal of Negro History,* and compiled four valuable books: *The Diplomatic Relations of the United States and Haiti, 1876-1891; What the Negro Wants* (1944); *The Senate and the Versailles Mandate System* (1945); and *The African Mandates in World Politics* (1948).

LOGUEN, JERMAIN WESLEY

Clergyman (1813-1872). Born a slave, he escaped to New York, where he became a minister. Noted for his stand against the Fugitive Slave Law of 1850, he censured former slaves who were willing to pay to retain their fredom. The citizens of Syracuse raised money to defend him against a charge of treason (later dropped) and commemorated the incident by holding an annual 'Jerry's Day.' He was elected bishop of the AME Zion Church in 1868. His autobiography is titled *Reverend J. W. Loguen as a Slave and as a Freeman: A Narrative of Real Life* (1868).

LOMAX, LOUIS E.

Writer and commentator (1922-1970). Beginning his career as a writer and radio announcer in New York (1958), he first attracted national attention as a guest on Mike Douglas' television show. In 1961 he received the Ainsfield-Wolf award for his book, *The Reluctant African.*

LONG VIEW, TEXAS

Scene of a riot in 1919. See Red Summer.

LONG, AVON

Actor. He played Sportin' Life in the 1938 production of *Porgy and Bess* and appeared in 1972 in Melvin Van Peebles' *Don't Play Us Cheap.*

LONG, JEFFERSON FRANKLIN

Public official (1836-1900). He educated himself, became a successful tailor, in Macon, and engaged in politics from the beginning of Reconstruction. He was the only negro ever to serve as Congressman from Georgia (1870-71).

LOS ANGELES EAGLE

Oldest negro newspaper in the United States, founded in 1879.

LOS ANGELES ZOOT SUIT RIOT

In June 1943 a riot was touched off in Los Angeles by a rumor that teenage boys wearing zoot suits were attacking servicemen.

LOUIS, JOE

Athlete (b. 1914). Born Joseph Louis Barrow, he won the Golden Gloves light heavyweight title in 1934, fought his first professional fight in 1934, and won the world heavyweight championship by defeating James J. Braddock on June 22, 1937. 'The Brown Bomber' held the title continuously until 1949, when he retired. On June 19, 1936, he was knocked out in the twelfth round of a match with Max Schmeling. Two years later, in a rematch, the most vicious of all championship fights ended after Louis had hit Schmeling 41 times in the first round in the most famous triumph of his career.

LOUISVILLE NATIONAL MEDICAL COLLEGE

Founded in 1888 by Dr. Henry Fitzbutler, the Louisville, Kentucky, school closed in 1911, unable to meet the standards for accreditation set by the Flexner Report.

L'OUVERTURE

See Toussaint L'Ouverture, François Dominique.

LOVE, NAT

Cowboy (born c. 1854). Born a slave in Davidson County, Tennessee, he produced the only book-length autobiography of a black cowboy, *The Life and Adventures of Nat Love, Better Known in the Cattle Country as 'Deadwood Dick'* (1907). He won his title in 1876, in recognition of his ability as a rider and marksman.

LOW RIDER

Los Angeles term for a ghetto youth. It was first used to describe the style of driving perfected by young blacks, who lowered the bodies of their cars so that they could ride close to the ground, slumped in their seats.

LOWERY, J. H.

Physician. A graduate of Flint Medical College of New Orleans, he led a successful civil rights campaign to secure equal accommodations for blacks on Louisiana railroads.

LOWERY, SAMUEL R.

Clergyman (b. 1830). He joined the Church of the Disciples in 1849, began preaching, and became a chaplain in 1863. He served with the 9th Artillery until the end of the Civil War.

LOWNDES COUNTY FREEDOM ORGANIZATION

Independent political party using the black panther as a symbol. It was organized by Stokely Carmichael prior to the elections held in Lowndes County, Alabama, in 1966. Though the movement spread to other counties and inspired the Black Panther movement, none of its candidates were elected. See Black Panther Party.

LUCA, ALEXANDER C.

Musician (1805-1872). He headed a musical family that traveled throughout New England and the Middle West before he migrated to Liberia (1860) and composed that country's national anthem. The family concert company included John W. Luca, bass-baritone and violinist; Simeon G., tenor and violinist; and Cleveland, pianist.

LUCAS, CURTIS

Writer (b. 1914). His works include Third Ward Newark (1946).

LUCAS, SAM

Comedian. One of the greatest of the early comedians, he traveled with the Georgia Minstrels. In the 1870s, he wrote the popular minstrel song, 'Carve Dat Possum.'

LUCY, AUTHERINE

Student. In February 1953 she was admitted to the University of Alabama, following a three-year court battle led by Thurgood Marshall. A series of violent outbursts forced her withdrawal.

LYNCH, JAMES D.

Militant (d. 1872). Born in Baltimore, he had an active role in founding Republican parties and promoting a radical Reconstruction program in South Carolina and Georgia. Moving into Mississippi, the Methodist Episcopal missionary by 1870 had become the most popular black man in the state. Known on account of his oratorical abilities as the Henry Ward Beecher of his race, he served as secretary of state (1870-72) but lost a campaign for nomination for congress from the Vicksburg district. White rivals brought him into court on a charge of adultery, and he never recovered from his defeat.

LYNCH, JOHN ROY

Public official (1847-1939). Son of a slave mother and a white Louisiana planter, he attended night school, worked as a photographer's assistant, began to dabble in politics, and at the age of twenty-four became speaker of the Mississippi House. A personal friend of President U. S. Grant, he was elected U. S. congressman from Mississippi three times. He served with distinction from 1873-77 but had to defend his seat following the disputed election of 1877. In a speech delivered in the House on April 27, 1882, he drew applause when he said: 'The impartial historian will record the fact that the colored people of the South have contended for their rights with a bravery and a gallantry that is worthy of the highest commendation. . . . They have said: You may deprive me for the time being of the opportunity of making an honest living . . . close the school-house door in the face of my children . . . but my manhood, my principles you cannot have.' On April 29, by a Margin of 124 to 84, the House voted to seat him. He continued to serve the Republican party as state chairman of the executive committee (1881-1889) and received federal appointments (1898-1911) as a reward. His published writings include *The Facts of Reconstruction* (1913).

LYNCHING

The act of inflicting punishment by private persons. The word probably derives from the extra-legal methods of trial and punishment used by Charles Lynch (1736-96), a Virginia planter and justice of the peace, against Tories. Southerners frequently resorted to lynching as an instrument of white dominance. Records going back to 1882 show that the reported lynchings often exceeded 100 a year and reached a high of 161 in 1892. Between 1889 and 1918, according to a document compiled by the NAACP (*Thirty Years of Lynching in the United States,* 1919), a total of 3,224 persons were killed by mobs in the United States. Of these, 2,522 were negroes. The NAACP succeeded in bringing about a complete change in public opinion on lynching. Anti-lynching legislation was passed by the U. S. house of representatives in 1922, 1937, and 1940.

LYNK, MILES V.

Physician and educator (b. 1871). Born on a farm near Brownsville, Tennessee, he founded the Medical Department of the University of West Tennessee in 1900. After graduating from Meharry Medical School, he published the first black medical journal in the nation, *The Medical and Surgical Observer* (1892). His autobiography is titled *Sixty Years of Medicine.*

M

MABLEY, JACKIE 'MOMS'
Entertainer. The grandmother of all black comediennes, she has made many television appearances.

MACARTY, EUGENE V.
Musician (b. 1821). Born in New Orleans, he studied in Paris and became an accomplished singer, pianist, and composer of light music. He also acted and took part in public affairs.

MACKEY, JOHN
President of the National Football League Players Association.

MADGET, NAOMI LONG
Poet (b. 1923). The author of three volumes of poetry, she is prominent as one of the Detroit group of poets. In 1965 she became the first recipient of the Mott Fellowship in English.

MAGAZINES
See Press.

MAGEE, SYLVESTER
Born on a North Carolina plantation on May 29, 1841, he held the distinction of being the nation's oldest citizen when he died in Colombus, Mississippi, at the age of 130 on October 15, 1971. He explained his extraordinary longevity by saying: 'It's the good Lord above. . . . He's smiling down on me.'

MAHONEY, CHARLES H.
United Nations delegate (1886-1966). A Michigan attorney,

he served for 5 years as a member of the U. S. delegation to the United Nations. He was a member of several committees and also of the United Nations panel for inquiry and conciliation.

MAHONEY, MARY ELIZABETH

Nurse. She entered the New England Hospital for Women and Children in Boston in 1878, at the age of thirty-three, to begin a sixteen-month course in nursing. On August 1, 1879, she became the first black graduate nurse in America.

MAINE

Battleship that exploded in the Havana harbor and precipitated the Spanish-American War of 1898. Twenty-two negro sailors died as a result of the explosion.

MAJORS, MONROE A.

Nineteenth century physician. A Meharry graduate, he was the

guiding spirit behind the establishment of the Lone Star State Medical Association (1886). He had to leave Texas for the West Coast to avoid being hanged by segregationists. In 1888 he became the first black doctor to pass the medical examinations administered by the California state board.

MAKEBA, MIRIAM

South African jazz singer. She married Black Power militant Stokely Carmichael.

MALARCHER, DAVE

Athlete (b. 1894). As third baseman for the American Giants, he helped his team to dominate the Negro National League in the 1920s.

MALCOLM X

Religious leader and revolutionary (1925-1965). A charismatic leader of the Black Muslims, he was also the foremost spokeman for the downtrodden in the black ghetto, the hero of black revolutionaries, the founder of the Organization for Afro-American Unity (1964), and the author of *The Autobiography of Malcolm X* (1965). Born Malcolm Little in Omaha, Nebraska, he accompanied his father to Garvey rallies after the family moved to Lansing, Michigan. When he was six, his father was bludgeoned and thrown on a streetcar track to be crushed to death. Malcolm drifted into crime, received a ten-year sentence in Boston, in 1946, became a convert to the teachings of Elijah Muhammad, began reading extensively, and recruited other convicts. Released in 1952, he became active in the Detroit temple, became Malcolm X, established a temple in Boston (1954), another in Philadelphia, founded the Muslim newspaper *Muhammad Speaks* (1957), became a popular speaker on college campuses, and was instrumental in increasing the membership of the Nation of Islam to 40,000. On hearing reports that he had been marked for death by the Muslim leadership, he announced his withdrawal from the Nation of Islam (1964), founded the Muslim Mosque Inc., journeyed to Mecca and learned the true Islamic religion, became El Hajj Malik El Shabazz, moderated his anti-white views, founded OAAU, and started to work for black unity and cooperation with other civil rights groups. He was assassinated by Black Muslims as he addressed a rally in New York on February 21, 1965. An anthology of writings by him and about him was edited by John Henrick Clarke and titled *Malcolm X, The Man and His Time.*

MALCOLM X COLLEGE
After Malcolm X died, one of the colleges in Chicago was renamed in his honor. It is administered by Charles G. Hurst, helped by vice presidents Donald C. Scott and Alphonso Hill.

MALCOLM X LIBERATION UNIVERSITY
See Black Studies.

MALCOLM X SOCIETY
Group formed in 1968 by some 200 blacks meeting in Detroit. The group established the Republic of New Africa.

MALONE, VIVIAN

Student. On June 11, 1963, with James Hood she successfully integrated the University of Alabama after the state's governor had 'stood in the schoolhouse door' to prevent their admittance.

MANHATTAN

See Black Manhattan.

MANUEL

A mulatto whose case foreshadowed the coming of slavery in the English colonies. The Virginia Assembly declared in 1644 that Manuel, who had been bought as 'a Slave for Ever' by Thomas Bushrod, was not a slave but must remain with his master for 21 years. Such a long period of indentured servitude was exceptional.

MANUMISSION SOCIETY

See New York Society for Promoting the Manumission of Slaves.

MARABLE, PETE

Musician. In the early 1900s, he led a band aboard the *St. Paul*, a paddle-wheeler out of St. Louis.

MARCH AGAINST FEAR

March organized by James Meredith to encourage 450,000 black Mississippians to register to vote. He and his followers planned to march from Memphis, Tennessee, to Jackson, Mississippi, in June 1966. See Meredith, James.

MARGETSON, EDWARD H.

Musician (b. 1891). He was organist-choirmaster of the Church of the Crucifixion in New York City. His compositions included pieces for chorus, orchestra, violin, piano, and organ.

MAROONS

Fugitive slaves or their free descendants. The earliest independent colonies of runaways dated back to 1542. These Maroons settled in the mountains and forests in the West Indies. Some groups were well organized and posed a threat to colonial authorities. In 1739 Captain Cudjoe succeeded in forcing the governor of Jamaica to sign an agreement guaranteeing the freedom of the Maroons living in Trelawney Town in return for a promise of peaceful conduct. Maroon colonies were also established among the Indians living in Florida.

MARSHALL

A beautifully appointed hotel in New York where actors, musicians, composers, writers, and vaudevillians congregated during the first decade of the 20th century. The first modern jazz band, known as the Memphis Students, was organized there and performed on a New York stage in the spring of 1905.

MARSHALL, PAULE

Writer (b. 1929). An accomplished writer of the newer generation, she was born in Brooklyn of West Indian parents. Her first novel, *Brown Girl,* was published in 1959. A Phi Beta Kappa, she has also published a collection of four stories, *Soul Clap Hands and Sing* (1961), and a critically acclaimed novel *The Chosen Place, the Timeless People* (1969).

MARSHALL, PETER MURRAY

Physician. He became president of the New York County medical society in 1954, the first black doctor to head a unit of the American Medical Association.

MARSHALL, THURGOOD

U. S. Supreme Court justice (b. 1908). He served for many years (1938-61) as NAACP counsel before he became the nation's first black Supreme Court justice in 1967. Born in Baltimore, Maryland, the foremost civil rights lawyer in America graduated from Lincoln University in Pennsylvania and from the Howard University School of Law in Washington, D. C., where he ranked first in the class of 1933. He engaged in private practice for a brief period before joining the Legal Defense Fund in New York in 1936. He became the most famous Negro attorney in America as head of the Legal Defense and Education Fund of the National Association for the Advancement of Colored People. Between 1938 and 1962, he won 29 of 32 cases which he argued before the Supreme Court. One of these was the 1954 decision banning segregation in schools. His first signal victory had come in 1936, when the University of Maryland Law School, which had denied him entrance several years earlier, was ordered to admit its first Negro student. He became the first Negro associate justice of the U. S. Supreme Court on October 2, 1967, following Senate confirmation of his nomination on August 30 by a vote of 69 to 11. Justice Hugo L. Black, once a member of the Ku Klux Klan, administered the oath to Marshall, the great-grandson of a slave.

MARTIN, D. L.

Physician. He was the first secretary of the National Medical Association (1895).

MARTIN, L.

Radiologist. A graduate of Leonard Medical School, he practiced in Philadelphia in the first half of the twentieth century.

MARTIN, MACEO C.

Businessman (b. 1897). He became president of the National Bankers Association.

MARTIN, ROBERTA

Musician. In the early 1900s, she composed such gospel songs as 'Didn't It Rain?'

MARTIN, SELLA

Antislavery orator. In 1867 he addressed the Paris Antislavery Conference, presenting the plight of freedmen in America. He was one of the most eloquent spokesmen of his time. In 1870 he represented the National Labor Union at the World's Labor Conference in Paris. He was selected as a delegate because of his knowledge of the French language and labor problems.

MARYLAND COLONIAL ASSEMBLY

In 1664 the Maryland Colonial Assembly imposed the status of slavery on negroes. Both houses of the General Assembly decreed (*Assembly Proceedings,* September, 1664, Liber WH & L, pp. 28-29, Maryland Archives, I, pp. 533-34) 'that all Negroes or other slaves already within the province, and all Negroes and other slaves to be hereafter imported into the province, shall serve *durante vita* . . . (and) that all the issues of English or other freeborn women that have already married Negroes shall serve the masters of their parents till they be thirty years of age and no longer.'

MASON, BIDDY

Practical nurse (1818-1891). She came to California as a slave. She worked hard to acquire property in the area incorporated by the city of Los Angeles. She retained her vast holdings until values rose, then began selling and reaping a substantial profit in each transaction.

MASON, JOHN

Conductor on the underground railroad. In one 19-month period he brought 265 slaves to the home of William Mitchell. Captured   and sold back into slavery, he managed to escape. During his lifetime he succeeded in helping some 1,300 slaves to make their way to freedom.

MASONIC ORDER

Founded in 1787 by Prince Hall, the Masonic order for negroes helped to inspire and uplift its members.

MASSACHUSETTS ANTI-SLAVERY SOCIETY

Abolitionist association formed in 1834 to succeed the New England Anti-Slavery Society. James G. Barbadoes and Joshua Easton were named to its board of counselors.

MATSON, OLLIE

Athlete. After winning a silver medal in the 1952 Olympic track competition, he signed with the Chicago Cardinals and became one of the top runners in the NFL.

MATTHEWS, SAUL

Patriot. Born a slave·in Virginia, he served as a soldier and spy in the Revolution, earning his freedom for 'many essential services' rendered to the commonwealth of Virginia (1792).

MATTHEWS, VICTORIA E.

Settlement worker (1861-1898). In 1897 she opened a social center in New York City for children 3-15 years of age, offering them domestic training along with training in the fundamental skills. She founded White Rose Home for young women who migrated to New York looking for work.

MATZELIGER, JAN E.

Inventor (1852-1887). His patent for a machine to attach soles to shoes was bought by the Boston United Shoe Machinery Company in 1883.

MAYFIELD, JULIAN

Actor and writer. He published three novels *(The Hit, The Long Night,* and *The Grand Parade)* before relocating in Africa during the 1960s.

MAYNOR, DOROTHY

Musician (b. 1910). She is internationally acclaimed as a leading soprano and an interpreter of German Lieder.

MAYOR AND CITY COUNCIL OF BALTIMORE V. DAWSON

U. S. supreme court decision (1955) declaring segregation invalid on public beaches. The ruling was an extension of the Brown decision of 1954.

MAYORS

In 1970 there were 48 black city mayors in America. Among them: Douglas F. Dollarhide (Compton, California), George L. Livingston, (Richmond, California), Herbert White (Pittsburg, California), Richard Hatcher (Gary, Indiana), Luska Twyman (Glasgow, Kentucky), Robert Blackwell (Highland Park, Michigan), John H. Burton (Ypsilanti, Michigan), Henry G. Marsh (Saginaw, Michigan), Floyd J. McCree (Flint, Michigan), Charles Evers (Fayette, Mississippi), Earl Lucas (Mound Bayou, Mississippi), Howard N. Lee (Chapel Hill, North Carolina), Matthew G. Carter (Montclair, New Jersey), Kenneth Gibson (Newark, New Jersey), William S. Hart (East Orange, New Jersey), Hilliard T. Moore (Lawnside, New Jersey), James T. Henry (Zenia, Ohio), Carl Stokes (Cleveland, Ohio), Penn Ziegler (Lincoln Heights, Ohio), and Walter Washington (Washington, D. C.).

MAYS, BENJAMIN E.

Clergyman and educator (b. 1895). He served as president of Morehouse College from 1940 until his recent retirement. A graduate of the University of Chicago and one of the nation's great orators, he desired always to be looked upon first as a human being and only incidentally as a negro. He began his career as a teacher of mathematics at Morehouse in 1921 and was the mentor of a generation of students who included Martin Luther King Jr. His autobiography is titled *Born to Rebel* (1971). Recently he set a precedent by becoming the first black president of the Atlanta school board.

MAYS, WILLIE

Athlete (b. 1931). One of baseball's greatest stars, he is the only player to have batted 600 home runs *and* scored 3,000 hits. His skill as a centerfielder helped to make him the most exciting all-around player and highest paid player for many years. After he helped the Giants to win the World Series in 1954, he was named the Most Valuable Player in the National League. He

received the same designation a second time in 1965. His autobiography is titled *Born to Play Ball* (1955).

McCABE, EDWIN P.

Public official (born c. 1850). He was appointed clerk in the
county treasurer's office in Chicago in 1872. He was elected state
auditor in Kansas in 1882. In 1889 he came to Oklahoma after
the Republican party refused to let him run for a second term
as Kansas state auditor. He helped found Langston City, calling
it 'the only distinctively negro city in America,' published the
Langston City Herald, and joined the movement to promote black
immigration to Oklahoma Territory. An interview with President
Harrison (1890) gave rise to rumors that he would be named
territorial governor. He did serve for several years as deputy
territorial auditor.

McCLINTOCK, ERNIE

Director of the Afro-American Studio for Acting and Speech
in Harlem.

McCONE COMMISSION

Formed in 1965 to investigate the Watts riot, the commission
found that charges of police brutality were unfounded and
urged massive efforts to prevent recurrence.

McCOO, MARY HOLOWAY

Physician. She is a specialist in anesthesiology at University
Hospital in Los Angeles.

McCOY, ELIJAH

Inventor (1884-1928). His name is immortalized in the expression 'the real McCoy.' Inventions for oiling railroad cars were
suspect unless they had his mark on them. Between 1872-1920
he was granted more than fifty-seven patents on lubricating
appliances and inventions relating to telegraphy and electricity.

McCRUMMELL, JAMES

Abolitionist. In 1833 he took part in the formation of the American Anti-Slavery Society at Philadelphia. One of three blacks present at the organizational meeting, he presided at one of the sessions. He also took part in the first meeting of the Pennsylvania Anti-Slavery Society, at Harrisburg, in January 1837.

McDANIEL, HATTIE

Actress (1898-1952). Often referred to as 'the colored Sophie Tucker' while she was on tour in 1924-25, she was labeled 'Mammy' by Hollywood and given stereotyped roles in films like *Gone with the Wind, The Little Colonel,* and *I'm No Angel.* Born in Wichita, Kansas, and educated in Denver, Colorado, she first sang on the radio at the age of 17. In 1939 she won an Oscar for her 'Mammy' role in *Gone with the Wind.*

McDONOUGH, DAVID K.

Nineteenth-century medical practitioner. His master, to prove that the innate mental capacity of a negro is not circumscribed, sent McDonough to Lafayette College and to New York, where he attended lectures at the College of Physicians and Surgeons. He received a license to practice and an appointment at the New York Eye and Ear Infirmary, where he was a consultant to many white physicians. The first private black hospital in New York City was named for him.

McDONOUGH MEMORIAL HOSPITAL

Named after David K. McDonough the New York City institution was the first voluntarily to open its doors to doctors, nurses, and patients of every race and creed. Dr. Peter A. Johnson was its first surgeon-in-chief (1898).

McFERRIN, ROBERT

Musician. At the Metropolitan he has sung in *Pagliacci, Faust, Il Trovatore,* and *Rigoletto.*

McGEE, HENRY W.

Postmaster. He heads the largest post office building in the world. The Chicago postmaster began as a substitute mail carrier in 1929 and now directs the activities of 28,000 employees.

McGRAWVILLE CENTRAL COLLEGE

School employing black professors before the Civil War. Charles L. Reason, William G. Allen, and George B. Vashon for a time held the professorship of belles letters at the New York college.

McHENRY, JERRY

Runaway slave. Members of the Liberty party helped to resist re-enslavement after he had lived as a free man in Syracuse, New York.

McKAY, CLAUDE

Writer (1889-1948). A leading poet of the Harlem school of the Black Renaissance of the 1920s, he published an exceptional collection of sonnets and lyrics, *Harlem Shadows* (1922), which typified the movement. The Jamaican poet came to the United States in 1912, entered Tuskegee Institute, transferred to Kansas State University, moved to Harlem, and began publishing in magazines. He went to England in 1919, published *Spring in New Hampshire and Other Poems* (1920), and returned to New York to become associate editor of *The Liberator* and *The Masses*. *Harlem Shadows* contained 'If We Must Die,' a poem quoted by Winston Churchill in his appeal to the U. S. Congress to join the struggle against Nazism: 'Like men we'll face the murderous, cowardly pack, Pressed to the wall, dying, but fighting back.' His other works include poems in Jamaican dialect *(Constab Ballads,* 1912); a trilogy of novels exploiting the conflict between primitive purity and the decadence of overly civilized intellectuals —*Home to Harlem* (1928), *Banjo* (1929), and *Banana Bottom* (1930); a collection of short stories, *Gingertown* (1932); and his autobiography, *A Long Way From Home* (1937).

292

McKINNEY, A. W.

Clergyman and teacher (b. 1853). After joining the Methodist Episcopal Church in 1872, he divided his time between teaching and studying. He graduated from Central Tennessee College in 1884. Two years later he was elected president of the Central Alabama Academy.

McKISSICK, FLOYD B.

Lawyer and civil rights leader (b. 1922). The first black to receive a law degree from the University of North Carolina (1955), he replaced James Farmer as National Director of CORE (1966) and promptly steered the organization toward a more aggressive policy in the achievement of full equality and freedom. After 3 years he resigned his position and returned to his native state to create F. B. McKissick Enterprises and promote black economic development. In January 1969 he launched a major program, the creation of Soul City in Warren County, North Carolina. Frequently controversial, he has long advocated an end to U. S. involvement in Vietnam. See Soul City.

McKNIGHT, ALBERT

Clergyman. Father McKnight is executive director of the Southern Cooperative Development Fund.

McLAURIN, G. W.

See McLaurin v. Oklahoma State Regents.

McLAURIN v. OKLAHOMA STATE REGENTS

U. S. Supreme Court decision (1950) ordering Oklahoma to desist from subjecting G. W. McLaurin to special requirements that segregated him from other students.

McLEAN, JACKIE

Musician (b. 1931). A teen-age prodigy, he was born and educated in New York City. He has been a member of various jazz vanguards of the last two decades and is known for the distinctive tones of his alto saxophone. See A. B. Spellman, *Black Music* (1966).

McLENDON, JOHNNY
Basketball coach. He coached the Cleveland Pipers during the 1961-62 season.

McPHERSON, JAMES ALAN
Writer. A protégé of Ralph Ellison, he was welcomed as a major talent by critics who reviewed his book of short stories, *Hue and Cry* (1969).

McRAE, CARMEN
Musician (b. 1922). A unique song stylist she is best known as a night club performances. She won *Down Beat's* critics poll as New Star of 1954.

McVEY, SAM
Athlete (b. 1885). The 205-pound boxer won 47 fights, defeating both Sam Langford and Joe Jeannette.

MEDAL OF HONOR
See Congressional Medal of Honor.

MEDICAL AND SURGICAL OBSERVER, THE
First black medical journal, founded in 1892 by Dr. Miles V. Lynk.

MEDICINE
Slaves were familiar with the medicinal value of several minerals, plants, and herb concoctions, with birth by Caesarian section, and with 'buying the smallpox,' that is, using serum from mildly infected patients to produce immunity to the dread disease.

MEHARRY MEDICAL COLLEGE
Established solely for the education of negro doctors, Meharry Medical College in Nashville, Tennessee, was part of Central

294

Tennessee College, chartered in 1866 and supported by the Freedmen's Aid Society. The medical school opened in 1876 and became the mecca for many southern blacks interested in a medical education. Between 1877 and 1890 the school graduated 102 students.

MEMPHIS STUDENTS

The first modern jazz band ever heard on a New York stage, it was organized at The Marshall and made its debut at Proctor's 23rd Street Theatre early in 1905. Its members, neither students nor residents of Memphis, included Will Dixon, Jim Europe, Ida Forsyne, Abbie Mitchell, and Ernest Hogan, the famous comedian. The Memphis Students introduced both the dancing conductor (Will Dixon danced out the rhythm all through a number) and the trick trap-drummer as features of the jazz band.

MEMPHIS-TO-JACKSON MARCH

See James Meredith Freedom March.

MENARD, JOHN WILLIS

Public official (1838-1893). The first Reconstruction politician to be elected U. S. congressman (1868), he was awarded his full salary but never seated. The committee on elections ruled that it was too early to admit a negro to the U. S. congress. He was appointed inspector of customs of the port of New Orleans. Born of French Creole parents living in Illinois, he had moved to New Orleans after the Civil War to work for the Republican party's Reconstruction policies.

MERCY HOSPITAL

See Frederick Douglass Memorial Hospital.

MEREDITH, JAMES

Civil rights leader (b. 1933). He began the battle for equal educational opportunities in Mississippi by applying for admission to the University of Mississippi the day after President John F. Kennedy was sworn into office. In October 1961 he began attending classes under the protection of U. S. marshals, following a nationally televised address by the President demanding compliance with a federal order to admit Meredith as a student. He graduated (1963), studied law at Columbia University, wrote a book about his experiences (Three Years in Mississippi), and visited and studied in Africa. In 1966 he returned to the South to lead a March Against Fear, beginning in Memphis, Tennessee, and ending in Jackson, Mississippi. He set out with his followers on June 5, 1966, encouraging blacks living in towns along the way to register to vote. Wounded on the second day by a white segregationist, he was replaced as leader by Dr. Martin Luther King, Jr. He rejoined the march and entered Jackson with Dr. King, confident that 'One day, right here in Mississippi, justice will become a reality, that this will be an oasis of freedom for all men.'

MERIDIAN MASSACRE

In 1871, 30 black men were killed in a massacre in Meridian, Mississippi.

MERIWETHER, LOUISE

Writer. Associated with the New Harlem Renaissance, she was acclaimed for her interpretation of the recent past of blacks in *Daddy Was a Number Runner.*

MERRICK, JOHN

Businessman (1859-1919). He founded the North Carolina Mutual Life Insurance Company. Starting as a bricklayer, he became a barber and operated five shops in Raleigh. White tobacco industry magnate J. B. Duke encouraged him to invest his profits in various business enterprises.

MESSENGER, THE

Paper published by Chandler Owen and A. Philip Randolph. Owen and Randolph set up a small employment bureau and were commissioned to publish *The Hotel Messenger* for a new union of black headwaiters. After the union ceased to support them, they continued to publish *The Messenger,* making it one of the most outspoken papers in New York City. Originally subtitled 'The Only Radical Negro Magazine in America,' it later became 'The Official Organ of the Brotherhood of Sleeping Car Porters.' The editors were jailed in World War I for urging black men to resist the draft.

METCALFE, RALPH
Athlete (b. 1910). He earned a place on the U. S. Olympic track team in 1932 and again in 1936 but failed to win an individual sprint title.

METOYER, MARIE
See Slaveowners.

MICHAUX, ELDER LIGHTFOOT SOLOMON
Cult leader. His disciples call him 'Happy Am I Prophet.' Reputed to be a millionaire, he had considerable political influence and a large popular appeal. He has held mass baptisms in the Griffith Stadium in Washington. A former fish peddler, he contested with Mother Rosa Artimus Horne for control of the black Harlem masses after Father Divine moved to Philadelphia.

MICHAUX, LEWIS
Bookseller. Born at the turn of the century, he owns the oldest black bookshop in America, the National Memorial Bookstore in New York.

MICHEAU, OSCAR
Writer (b. 1884). His works include *The Conquest* (1930), *The Forged Note* (1915), and *The Case of Mrs. Wingate* (1945).

MIGRATION OF NEGROES
See Population.

MILES, LIZZIE
Blues singer (1897-1963). Born in New Orleans, where she

died on March 17, 1963, she sang with the great bands of the jazz era.

MILBURN, RICHARD

Musician. In 1855 the whistling, guitar-playing Philadelphia barber saw in print his beloved tune, 'Listen to the Mocking Bird,' after it had been set down by Septimus Winner. As originally published, the song is described as a 'sentimental Ethiopian ballad' with the 'melody by Richard Milburn—written and arranged by Alice Hawthorne,' the name of his mother. Milburn published some of his other compositions under his mother's name. Later editions have erroneously omitted his name from the song.

MILLER, AARON

Artist. Devoting himself entirely to painting church murals, he produces works reminiscent of those of Piero della Francesca.

MILLER, DORIE

World War II hero (1919-1943). A messman on the battle-ship *West Virginia,* Miller became the first hero of World War II in the first few minutes of the conflict at Pearl Harbor. He rushed to the deck of his ship when the alarm sounded, carried his dying captain to a safer place, took over a machine gun, and brought down four Japanese dive bombers. Awarded the Navy Cross for his 'distinguished devotion to duty, extraordinary courage and disregard for his own personal safety during the attack on Pearl Harbor,' he was later killed in action in the South Pacific. He was awarded the Medal of Honor posthumously. His heroism drew attention to the 'messmen only' policy of the Navy. On April 7, 1942, Secretary Frank Knox announced that negro volunteers could perform general services and not be restricted to service as mess attendants.

MILLER, JAMES

Musician (b. 1907). He earned his master's degree at Carnegie Institute of Technology and became the first black music teacher in the public schools of Pittsburgh, Pennsylvania. He arranged and published spirituals. He also served as organist at the Pittsburgh Bethesda Church.

MILLER, KELLY

Educator (1863-1939). A mathematician by profession, he became dean of the college of arts and sciences at Howard University and authored the famous polemic of World War I, *The Disgrace of Democracy.* He also wrote *Race Adjustment* (1908), *Out of the House of Bondage* (1917), and *The Everlasting Stain* (1924). He helped to edit *Crisis,* became the first black academician to write a weekly column for the black press, and helped to found Sanhedrin.

MILLER, LOREN

Jurist (b. 1903). He is a judge on the Los Angeles municipal court.

MILLER, THOMAS E.

Public official (b. 1849). He was South Carolina's representative to the 51st Congress (1889-91). Previously, he had passed the bar (1875) and set up a practice in Beaufort. In 1895 he was chosen a member of the state constitutional convention. Defending the accomplishments of Reconstructionists, he told the convention that black legislators had placed the state 'upon the road to prosperity.'

MILLIKEN'S BEND, LOUISIANA

A small town twenty miles from Vicksburg defended by 1,250 negro and 160 white Union soldiers who in June 1863 engaged in the longest bayonet fight of the Civil War. The soldiers suffered heavy losses but never flinched under their ordeal.

MILLS, FLORENCE

Entertainer (1895-1927). A leading Broadway star in the 1920s, she captivated audiences with her songs, dances, and acting. Stardom came with her appearance in *Shuffle Along* (1921). The next year she starred in *Plantation Revue,* later enlarged and presented in London as *From Dover to Dixie* (1923) and on Broadway as *Dixie to Broadway* (1924-25). Another revue, *Blackbirds,* was built around her and presented not only in Harlem's Alhambra Theater but also in Paris and London. Unspoiled by success, she was described by many of her admirers as the most lovable person they had ever known.

MILTON, L. D.

Banker. He is president of the Citizens Trust Company in Atlanta.

MINER ACADEMY

A school for negro girls opened in Washington, D. C., in 1851. See Miner, Myrtilla.

MINER, MYRTILLA

Educator. In 1851 she founded the Miner Academy in Washington, D. C. Her experiences are related in *The School for Colored Girls in Washington, D. C.* (1854). Her biography, *Myrtilla Miner, a Memoir,* by Ellen O'Connor, was published in 1885.

MING, WILLIAM ROBERT

Lawyer (b. 1911). In 1957 he was elected chairman of the American Veterans Committee. Earlier he had been co-counsel of the Chicago civil liberties union (1947-53).

MINNY

Pilot in the navy of Virginia. He died during the Revolutionary War while trying to board an enemy supply ship.

MINSTRELSY

Originating on the slave plantations of the South, minstrelsy incorporated antics, capers, eccentric dancing, jokes, and songs accompanied by the banjo and the beating of bleached sheep ribs. It was introduced to the American stage by white actors, who impersonated negroes in 'blackface' acts around 1830. White Dan Rice copied an act from a black stable hand named Jim Crow

300

and introduced it successfully at the Bowery Theatre in New York, November 12, 1832. The following year he introduced Thomas Jefferson, age 4, as a co-minstrel singing the same 'Jim Crow.' The Plantation Minstrel Company and the Georgia Minstrels were early black teams. The second age of minstrelsy (1875-95) brought in the jig, the clog, the double shuffle, the pigeon wing, the minstrel ballad, and the coon song. The age of caricature was marked by burlesque and buffoonery which left the stereotype of the negro as 'an irresponsible, happy-go-lucky, wide-grinning, loud-laughing, shuffling, banjo-picking, dancing sort of being' permanently imbedded in the minds of millions. See Alain Locke, *The Negro and His Music* (1936).

MIRROR OF LIBERTY

First negro magazine, published by David Ruggles in New York City in 1838.

MISSISSIPPI PLAN, THE

The means by which conservatives won the state elections in Mississippi in 1875. Staged riots, political assassinations, and intimidation were used effectively in Mississippi and later in South Carolina and Louisiana to overthrow Reconstruction governments.

MISSISSIPPI SUMMER PROJECT

Organized in 1964 to encourage voter registration among black people in Mississippi, the project suffered an initial setback when 3 of its activists were killed by a mob of racists. The project workers hoped to bring about changes through voter registration and education in 'freedom schools.'

MISSOURI COMPROMISE OF 1820

Legislation regulating the extension of slavery into the Louisiana Purchase. Slavery was prohibited in Maine, Kansas, and Nebraska but allowed in Missouri. In 1854 the Kansas-Nebraska Bill repealed the Missouri Compromise and unleashed antislavery pronouncements that culminated in the formation of the Republican Party.

MITCHELL, ABBIE

Musician (1884-1960). A dramatic soprano, she sang for many years in vaudeville and musical comedies but never realized her dream of singing in opera. She was born in New York City and educated in Baltimore and Paris. Having gained stage presence by performing in musical comedies produced by her husband, Will Marion Cook, she made several concert tours and was accorded high praise by the critics. She had the leading role in the Lafayette Players' productions of *Madame X, In Abraham's Bosom,* and *Help Wanted.* She taught at Tuskegee. Mercer Cook, her son, was U. S. ambassador to Senegal.

MITCHELL, ARTHUR

Dancer. One of the stars of the New York City Ballet, he founded his own Dance Theater of Harlem in 1969.

MITCHELL, ARTHUR

Public official (b. 1886). He was the first black Democratic congressman (1934). He defeated Republican congressman Oscar DePriest, who in 1928 had become the first black sent to the U. S. congress from a northern state (Illinois).

MITCHELL, CLARENCE, II

Director of the Washington bureau of the NAACP.

MITCHELL, CHARLES L.

Public official. One of the first two blacks to serve in a state legislature, he was elected to the Massachusetts house of representatives in 1866.

MITCHELL, LOFTEN

Playwright. His plays include *A Land Beyond the River, Ballad of the Winter Soldiers,* and *Star of the Morning.* He also authored

Black Drama: The Story of the American Negro in the Theatre (1967).

MITCHELL, PARREN J.
U. S. representative from Maryland.

MITCHELL, WILLIAM
Missionary. His Canadian home received many slaves who traveled to freedom along the underground railroad.

MOLYNEUX, TOM
Athlete (1784-1818). The first American black to fight in a major championship bout (England, 1810), Molyneux is said to have earned his freedom by his pugilistic feats. In a disputed decision, he was declared the loser after the 40th round.

MONMOUTH, BATTLE OF
Some 700 black soldiers are estimated to have fought in the battle of Monmouth, New Jersey, on June 28, 1778.

MONROE, EARL
Athlete. In 1967-68 he was the NBA rookie-of-the-year. 'Earl the Pearl' excites fans as few other players can. He dominates the floor game and plays with a flair.

MONTGOMERY, BENJAMIN T.
Planter. After the Civil War. he bought the Jefferson Davis plantation at Davis Bend, Mississippi. He lived in splendor at the mansion of the former president of the Confederacy.

MONTGOMERY BOYCOTT
Ministers and civic leaders of Montgomery, Alabama, called a boycott on December 5, 1955, the day set for the trial of Mrs. Rosa Parks, who had refused to give up her seat on a bus to a white man. Martin Luther King, Jr. and Ralph Albernathy figured prominently in events leading to a decision to continue the boycott until bus operators promised to seat passengers on a first-come,

first-served basis and to treat all passengers courteously, and until black bus operators were employed on predominantly black routes. The boycott continued for 382 days, until word was received that the U. S. supreme court had affirmed a lower court ruling declaring Alabama's segregation laws unconstitutional.

MONTGOMERY IMPROVEMENT ASSOCIATION

Forerunner of the Southern Christian Leadership Conference, It was organized in December 1955 to deal with the crisis arising from a decision of civic and church leaders in Montgomery, Alabama, to call a boycott on December 5, the day set for trial of Mrs. Rosa Parks, a seamstress who had refused to relinquish her seat on a bus to a white man. Martin Luther King Jr. was named president of the MIA. He presented the group's demands to city officials. The demands were refused, but King continued the struggle to achieve integration through nonviolent direct mass action. His success made him the leader of the nonviolent protest movement.

MOORE v. DEMPSEY

Supreme Court decision (1923) emphasizing the Court's responsibility to insure fair trials and its role as the protector of constitutional rights. Mob violence triggered by whites resentful of the organizational activities of negro sharecroppers in Phillips County, Arkansas, in 1919, resulted in the deaths of more than two hundred persons. In the court trial that followed, negro witnesses were intimidated, negroes were excluded from the jury, and the defense counsel called no witnesses. The proceedings lasted less than an hour, the jury deliberations not more than five minutes. Twelve negroes were sentenced to death, 67 to long prison terms. Justice Oliver Wendell Holmes delivered the opinion stating that 'if the case is that the whole proceeding is a mask—that counsel, jury and judge were swept to the fatal end by an irresistible wave of public passion, and that the State Courts failed to correct the wrong, neither perfection in the machinery for correction nor the possibility that the trial court and counsel saw no other way of avoiding an immediate outbreak of the mob can prevent this Court from securing to the petitioners their constitutional rights.'

MOORE, ARCHIE

Athlete, actor, and author. In 1952 he won the light heavyweight boxing championship. In 1959 he scored his 127th knockout, setting a new boxing record, and was named fighter of the year (at the age of 42, or 45, or 49, depending on which of his statements is to be accepted as true). Before he retired from boxing, the indomitable raconteur had already begun a new career in motion pictures.

MOORE, DAVEY

Athlete (1933-1963). He won the featherweight boxing championship in 1960 but died as a result of injuries suffered in a title bout with Sugar Ramos in 1963.

MOORE, FRED

Soldier. He was the first black soldier to guard the Tomb of the Unknown Soldier. He was assigned to sentry duty at Arlington National Cemetery in March 1961.

MOORE, LENNY

Athlete. In 1956 he came to the Baltimore Colts as a first draft choice. He helped his team to win its first conference championship in 1958, another in 1959, and still another in 1964.

MOORE, O'NEAL

Deputy sheriff of Washington Parish, Louisiana. One of the first of his race to hold such a post, he was slain while on duty on June 2, 1965, in the racially troubled town of Varnado.

MOOREHEAD, SCIPIO

Artist. Thought to have been the first formally trained black artist in colonial America, he is known to have produced two paintings, one based on the legend of Damon and Pythias and the other titled 'Aurora.'

MORGAN V. VIRGINIA

U. S. Supreme Court decision, handed down in 1946, affirming the right of an individual in interstate commerce to complete his journey without subjecting himself to state segregation laws.

MORGAN, GARRETT A.

Inventor (1875-1963). His inventions include the first automatic stop signal and a smoke inhalator. Born in Paris, Tennessee, he moved to Cleveland, Ohio (1895), where he developed his first invention, a belt fastener for sewing machines. In 1914 he won a gold medal at the Second International Exposition of Sanitation and Safety for his invention of a breathing helmet and smoke protector. In 1916 the device enabled him and three other men to save the lives of more than twenty men trapped 228 feet below Lake Erie, five miles from shore. His inhalator was converted into a gas mask in World War I. The rights to the stop signal which he invented in 1923 were sold to General Electric for $40,000.

MORRIS, ELIAS C.

Clergyman (1855-1922). Born in northern Georgia and trained as a shoemaker, he pastored the Centennial Baptist Church in Helena, Arkansas, 1879-1922, established the first religious paper for blacks in the state, founded Arkansas Baptist College (1884), and organized the National Baptist Convention of the United States (1895), over which he presided until his death.

MOORISH SCIENCE TEMPLE MOVEMENT

Black nationalist movement founded in Newark, New Jersey, in 1913 by Timothy Drew, also known as Noble Drew Ali.

MORRIS, SAMUEL

See Jehoviah, Father.

MORROW, FREDERIC E.

Public official (b. 1909). An administrative aide to President Dwight D. Eisenhower, he recounted his experience in *Black Man in the White House.*

MORROW, JOHN

Public official. He was appointed U. S. ambassador to Guinea.

MORTON, JELLY ROLL

Musician (c. 1885-1941). Also known as Ferdinand Joseph Le Menthe, he had a key role in the origin of jazz. He sang, played the piano, arranged, composed, and directed one of the best blues bands in New Orleans. Among his players were Fletcher Henderson, Charlie Creath, Fate Marable, and Bennie Moten. Some of his best performances are preserved in *The King of New Orleans Jazz* (RCA Victor). See Martin Williams, *Jelly Roll Morton* (1962).

MOSELEY, JAMES ORVILLE B.

Musician (b. 1909). He performed with the 313th Army Air Field Band in Tuskegee, Alabama, and composed the Field Post song. He also composed 80 other musical pieces, including a string quartet, a symphony, and the Morehouse College Hymn.

MOSELY, JIMMIE

Artist (b. 1927). The first student to graduate from Texas Southern University with a bachelor of fine arts degree (1952), he has taught art at Lincoln, Texas Southern, and Maryland universities and now directs art education at Maryland State College. One of his watercolors, 'Waiting to Vote' (1968), captured the spirit of his era.

MOSES, ROBERT

Civil rights leader. In 1964 he announced that his Mississippi Freedom Project would challenge Mississippi's political structure on many fronts. His statement of November 24 proved to be a significant step in the civil rights struggle. Moses was field secretary for the SNCC.

MOSELL, MARY ELLA

Missionary (1853-1886). Born of free parents, she accompanied her husband to Haiti in 1879. She mastered the native dialect and brought many Haitian women into the work of the AME church and mission school.

MOSELL, NATHAN FRANCIS

Physician (1856-1946). Remembered mainly as the founder of Philadelphia's Frederick Douglass Memorial Hospital (now the Mercy-Douglass Hospital), the Canada-born physician was the first black admitted to the nation's oldest medical school, the University of Pennsylvania, and the first black admitted to the Philadelphia Medical Society.

MOST VALUABLE PLAYER

The most coveted award in baseball has been won by National League players Jackie Robinson, Willie Mays, Don Newcombe, Hank Aaron, Ernie Banks, and Maury Wills, and by Elston Howard in the American League.

MOTHER HORNE

See Horne, Mother Rosa Artimus.

MOTLEY, ARCHIBALD J.

Artist (b. 1891). After studying at the Chicago Art Institute, the Louisiana-born painter became the first black to hold a one-man show in New York City (1928). His protrait, 'A Mulatress,' won the Frank G. Logan medal. He also received the Harmon award, gold medal, and prize.

MOTLEY, CONSTANCE BAKER

Public official (b. 1921). Elected to the state senate in 1964, she became president of the Borough of Manhattan in 1965 and was appointed judge of the Federal circuit court of the southern district of New York in 1966. She became the highest paid negro woman in municipal government and the first negro woman federal judge.

MOTLEY, WILLARD

Writer (1912-1965). His novels include *Knock on Any Door* and *We Fished All Night*.

MOTON, ROBERT RUSSA

Educator and public official (1867-1940). After succeeding Booker T. Washington as president of Tuskegee Institute (1915), he went on an official mission to France to 'do morale work among colored troops.' At one time he also headed a committee to aid Liberia. He received both the Harmon Award (1930) and the Spingarn Medal (1932). He published an unpopular autobiography, *Finding a Way Out* (1920), and *What the Negro Thinks* (1924). As president of Tuskegee Institute in 1923, he conferred with President Warren Harding and persuaded him to give black physicians and nurses an opportunity to qualify for service in the Tuskegee Veterans Hospital through special civil service examinations.

MOTOWN

Company founded by Berry Gordy, Jr. to produce records. Its main product was a catchy popular kind of music dubbed 'the Motown sound.' The music caught on immediately and made stars of many black artists: Smokey Robinson and the Miracles, The Supremes, Temptations, Marvin Gaye, Stevie Wonder, and the Jackson Five. By 1966 the company had grown into a multi-million dollar firm and was the nation's leading producer of single records.

MUHAMMAD ALI

Former world heavyweight boxing champion. Born Cassius Clay in Louisville, Kentucky on January 17, 1942, he fought more than 100 bouts before winning the light heavyweight title at the Olympics in Rome in 1960. As a professional boxer, reputed to be the fastest hard-hitting heavyweight in boxing history, he won the world championship by defeating Sonny Liston in 1964. His title was vacated in 1967 by boxing authorities after he was indicted for refusing induction into the Army. Having adopted his Muslim name of Muhammad Ali and affirmed his acceptance of the pacifist principles of the Nation of Islam, he had repeatedly stated his refusal to support the armed forces. Following his indictment, a Texas jury found him guilty of refusing induction (he had refused to take the symbolic step forward after appearing for induction). He was given the maximum penalty of a five-year prison term and a fine of $10,000. He appealed the conviction and eventually (1971) had it reversed by the U. S. Supreme Court. His attempt to recapture the heavyweight crown in 1971 failed, however, when Joe Frazier, the world champion recognized by the World Boxing Association, successfully defended his title.

MUHAMMAD, ELIJAH

Cult leader (b. 1897). The self-styled messenger of Allah and leader of the Nation of Islam, he heads the nation's largest militant, disciplined, black separatist cult. Born Elijah Poole, in Sandersville, Georgia, he underwent a religious conversion and assumed the name by which he is internationally known today. In the early 1930s, as a follower of Wali Farad, founder of the Nation of Islam, he began to formulate and preach the Black Muslim doctrine. After choosing a Muslim name (Elijah Karriem) to replace the name forced on him by 'white devil' slave masters, he founded Temple Number One in Detroit. Farad appointed him Supreme Minister and renamed him Elijah Muhammad. In 1932 Muhammad founded Temple Number Two in Chicago and laid the groundwork for Temple Number Three in Milwaukee. After a sacrificial killing led to Farad's imprisonment, Muhammad risked jail by trying to protect him from persecution by police. Before he disappeared mysteriously in 1934, Farad formed the Fruit of Islam, a protective, militaristic group. Muhammad then declared that Farad had been Allah in disguise and that Muhammad had learned from Farad secrets imparted to no one else. Muhammad claimed to be 'The Messenger of Allah to the Lost-Found Nation of Islam in the Wilderness of North America.' Arrested in 1934 for sending his children to the unaccredited University of Islam rather than to Detroit's public schools, he moved to Chicago. Living a fugitive's existence from 1935 to 1942, he still managed to found Temple Number Four in Washington, D. C., and to read books bolstering Farad's teachings. Convicted of encouraging draft resistance, he spent more than three years in jail (1942-46). By the time of his release, membership in his cult had fallen from 8,000 to 1,000. Under the dynamic leadership of Malcolm X, and with the help of publicity generated by the mass media, such as Mike Wallace's television documentary 'The Hate That Hate Produced' (1959), membership probably reached 100,000 by the end of 1960. One of Muhammad's sons, Wallace, is minister of the Philadelphia temple and his heir apparent; another, Herbert, is public relations director; and Elijah, Jr., is second in command of Fruit of Islam.

MUHAMMAD, FARAD W. D.
See Farad, Wali.

MULZAC, HUGH NATHANIEL
Sea captain (1886-1971). The first black to command a ship in the American merchant marine, he passed his examinations in 1920 but refused to accept an assignment as captain until 1942, when he was granted the right to man the *Booker T. Washington* with the best crewmen available, regardless of race. His ship saw antiaircraft action on several occasions.

MURPHY, CARL
Journalist (b. 1889). He is president and editor of the *Afro-American.*

MURPHY, ISAAC
Jockey (1861-1896). The first jockey to win the Kentucky Derby three times, he is considered by many veteran horsemen to be the greatest of all time. Born in Fayette County, Kentucky and christened Isaac Murphy Burns, he first won the Kentucky Derby in 1884, on Buchanan; then in 1890, on Riley, and in 1891, on Kingman.

MURPHY, JOHN HENRY
Publisher (1840-1922). Born a slave in Baltimore, he worked

at many menial trades before he learned the printing trade at the age of 50 and launched the Baltimore *Afro-American* newspaper. Setting the type himself and delivering the first issues, he built the *Afro-American* into one of the largest and most reliable black newspapers in America, run by black employees using modern equipment.

MURRAY, ALBERT LEE

Writer (b. 1916). He studied at Tuskegee, became an air force major, and worked for Harper's magazine. His published works include *The Omni-Americans,* in which he criticized white sociologist Daniel Patrick Moynihan's study of the negro family, and *South to a Very Old Place* (1971), described by Time magazine as 'a highly syncopated memoir of youth and a celebration of U. S. Negro culture.'

MURRAY, GEORGE W.

Public official (1853-1926). The only black member of the 53rd Congress (1893-95), the South Carolina representative advocated an increase in the circulation of silver and voted against the repeal of federal election laws.

MURRAY, PETER M.

Physician. Appointed to Harlem Hospital in 1929, he became a member of the hospital's surgical division the next year, following a reorganization order issued by the New York City hospital commissioner. The Lousiana-born surgeon received his M. D. from Howard in 1914, was medical inspector in the public schools of the District of Columbia, and had a private practice as a surgeon and gynecologist in Harlem. He insisted on the highest standards in medicine and believed that 'proper professional training should come through physicians of all races working together.'

MUSIC AND DANCE

H. E. Krehbiel analyzed 527 negro spirituals and traced their essential 'intervallic, rhythmical and structural elements' to their African prototypes. Rhythmic tunes eased the monotony, anxiety, and drudgery of work. Blues and jazz creations have imbued much modern music with African elements. Ancestral ritual dance patterns fused with European secular dances to produce notable results, such as the tango, beguine, samba, rhumba, conga, and habanera in Latin America, and the juba and fox trot in North America. Many of the songs heard on Southern plantations lent themselves to two interpretations. The popular 'protest' songs equated spiritual fredom with physical freedom ('I got a right— we all got a right,/ I got a right to the tree of life); Pharaoh with the white master ('Tell ole Pharoah/ To let my people Go'); and Canaan with the North ('I am bound for the land of Canaan'). See Miles Mark Fisher, *Negro Slave Songs in the United States.*

MUSIC, CONCERT

There are more than 100 established black composers of concert music. A few of the more prominent ones are William Grant Still, Ulysses Kay, Howard Swanson, William Dawson, Olly Wilson, T. J. Anderson, Frederick Tillis, and Hale Smith.

MUSIC, FOLK

Most black folk music consists of songs, either sacred or secular. Sacred songs are called slave songs, jubilees, sorrow songs, plantation songs, or mellows. Secular songs are classified according to the social functions with which they are associated: lullabies, dance songs, work songs, love songs, game songs, ballads, blues, and folk minstrels. Spirituals constitute a specific body of musical literature. The best guide to black folk music is Harold Courlander's *Negro Folk Music, U. S. A.* (1963). See Slave Songs, Jubilees, Blues, Minstrelsy, Spirituals, Sorrow Songs.

MUSLIMS

See Black Muslims.

MUSLIM MOSQUE, INC.

Founded by Malcolm X on March 12, 1964, the Muslim Mosque was intended to supplant the Nation of Islam. Malcolm X turned against Elijah Muhammad after he learned that the founder of the Nation of Islam had ordered his assassination.

MUSLIMS

See Black Muslims.

MYERS, ISAAC

Labor leader (1835-1891). Born of free parents in Baltimore and apprenticed to a ship caulker, he soon became the supervisor of caulking work done on some of the largest ships, then raised money to build a shipyard employing 300 negroes. He tried to educate negroes so that they could have their own local unions, published a weekly newspaper (*Colored Citizen*, 1882), sponsored a home for aged ministers, and organized the Maryland Colored State Industrial Association (1888). His first call for a meeting on the first Monday in December 1869 in Washington, D. C., to discuss the condition of black workers, was answered by 156 delegates.

MYERS, STEPHEN

Key figure in the Albany Vigilance Committee.

N

NAACP

See National Association for the Advancement of Colored People.

NAACP V. ALABAMA EX REL FLOWERS

Supreme Court decision (1964) striking down an order of the Alabama courts barring the NAACP from conducting its activities in the state.

NAACP V. ALABAMA EX REL PATTERSON

Supreme Court decision (1958) unanimously reversing an order of the Alabama courts to submit NAACP membership lists or be barred from conducting its activities in the state.

NAACP V. BUTTON

Supreme Court decision (1963) reversing an order of the Virginia courts barring the NAACP from conducting its activities in the state. The NAACP had been included in the statute against 'improper solicitation of any legal or professional business.' In a split decision the Court held 'that the activities of the NAACP, its affiliates and legal staff . . . are modes of expression protected by the First and Fourteenth Amendments.'

NABRIT, JAMES M., JR.

Lawyer (b. 1900). He taught the first formal course in civil rights law, served for 24 years on the Howard University law school faculty, and was named president of the university in 1960. He also served in the United Nations.

NABRIT, SAMUEL

Scientist (b. 1905). The first black scientist to serve on the Atomic Energy Commission, he has taught at Atlanta University and at Texas Southern University, where he also served as president. He earned his Ph. D. at Brown.

NACW

See National Association of Colored Women.

NAIROBI COLLEGE

See Black Studies.

NANM

See National Association of Negro Musicians.

NANTON, JOE

Jazz musician. In the 1920s he played the trumpet with Duke Ellington's Kentucky Club orchestra.

NAPIER, JAMES C.

Lawyer (b. 1848). Active in Republican politics, he served for 16 years on the Tennessee state committee. He was revenue agent for the federal district that included Kentucky, Tennessee, Alabama, and Louisiana.

NASH, CHARLES E.

Public official (1844-1913). He served in the 44th Congress (1875-77) as U. S. representative from Louisiana. Later he became postmaster of Washington, Louisiana.

NAT TURNER, THE CONFESSIONS OF

A historical work by white novelist William Styron. Published in 1968, it won the Pulitzer Prize for fiction and generated considerable controversy. The book purports to explore the experience of Nat Turner, the slave who organized a rebellion that inspired the killing of 61 whites around Southampton County, Virginia, in 1831. Black critics accused Styron of perpetuating misunderstanding and racist myths. James Baldwin credited him with fusing 'two points of view, the master's and the slave's' and beginning 'the common history—ours.'

NATION OF ISLAM
See Black Muslims.

NATIONAL ADVISORY COMMISSION ON CIVIL DISORDERS
In March 1968 the National Advisory Commission on Civil Disorders, headed by Mayor John Lindsay of New York City and Governor Otto Kerner of Illinois, issued its 1,485-page report. The commission noted that the United States 'is moving toward two societies, one black, one white—separate but unequal.' It pinpointed the causes of a trend toward polarization that would destroy democratic values: racism, manifested in bars against employing negroes institutionalized racism in employment, housing, and education. It advocated specific remedies: creation of two million jobs, an end to de facto school segregation, an on-the-job training program, open housing legislation and six million housing units for low and middle-income families.

NATIONAL ASSOCIATION FOR THE
ADVANCEMENT OF COLORED PEOPLE
A call for the 'renewal of the struggle for civil and political liberty' was issued on January 12, 1909, the centennial of Abraham Lincoln's birth, by Oswald Garrison Villard, the grandson of white abolitionist William Lloyd Garrison. The four negro signers were W. E. B. Du Bois, Ida Wells Barnett, Francis J. Grimke, and Alexander Walters. Two subsequent meetings in New York led to the formation of the NAACP, whose basic aim was to make negroes 'physically free from peonage, mentally free from ignorance, politically free from disfranchisement, and socially free from insult.' Control of the association was vested in an interracial board of directors. Du Bois, the only negro on the first board, served as director of publications and research. In 1910 he began publishing *Crisis*, the official organ of the association. Soon the monthly journal launched an attack on the Wilson administration

317

of President Woodrow Wilson, who failed to convince negroes that they could count on him for 'absolute fair dealing.' The NAACP led the fight against discriminatory policies within the federal government and thereby promoted a sense of racial solidarity. Roy Wilkins, who became its chief executive in 1955, on his 70th birthday (August 30, 1971) restated his belief in making changes through legal channels. His strategy for the 1970s includes improving relations with police, bettering the lives of servicemen, effective use of selective buying power, and electing to public office 'black people and friends of black people.' At its 62nd annual convention in 1971 the NAACP reaffirmed its historic commitment to the 'elimination of racial segregation in all forms.' The association now has 400,000 dues-paying members in 1700 chapters in all 50 states. See Langston Hughes, *Fight for Freedom: The Story of the NAACP* (1962), and Charles Flint Kellog, *A History of the National Association for the Advancement of Colored People, Volume I 1909-1920* (1967).

NATIONAL ASSOCIATION OF COLORED GRADUATE NURSES

Founded by Martha Franklin in 1908, with 26 charter members the association worked toward raising professional nursing standards. In 1951 the board of directors dissolved the organization, agreeing unanimously that it should be integrated into the American Nurses Association.

NATIONAL ASSOCIATION OF COLORED WOMEN

Organized in Washington, D. C., in 1896, it was headed by Mary Church Terrell.

NATIONAL ASSOCIATION OF NEGRO MUSICIANS

Organized in 1919 by Carl Diton to encourage the development of musical talent through scholarships for needy students, to promote professionalism through workshops and conferences, and to serve as a showcase for black music and musicians, the NANM gave Marian Anderson her first scholarship.

NATIONAL BAPTIST CONVENTION OF THE UNITED STATES

Formed from three separate organizations (American National Convention, Foreign Mission Convention, and National Education Convention), the National Baptist Convention of the United States was organized by Elias C. Morris in 1895.

NATIONAL BUSINESS LEAGUE

On August 23, 1900, in Boston, 400 delegates from 34 states met to organize a league to strengthen black businesses by sharing ideas and information, and to inspire and educate the masses.

NATIONAL CONFERENCE FOR NEW POLITICS

Held in Chicago August 31-September 4, 1967, the National Conference for New Politics drew civil rights moderates Floyd McKissick and Martin Luther King, Jr. Comedian Dick Gregory also attended the conference.

NATIONAL COUNCIL OF NEGRO WOMEN

Founded on December 5, 1935, in New York City, its membership is comprised of over a million women. Mary McLeod Bethune founded the organization, which is concerned primarily with the economic, social, and educational welfare of blacks.

NATIONAL DEFENSE ADVISORY COMMISSION

The NDAC recommended in 1940 that contractors in the new war industries adopt equal employment practices. The following year this recommendation was officially reaffirmed in Executive Order 8802.

NATIONAL DEFENSE TRAINING ACT

Designed to provide industrial training for defense industries, the NDTA, passed in 1940, contained an antibias clause. Significant numbers of negroes were not trained for defense work, however, until President Franklin D. Roosevelt, faced with the threat of a national march on Washington, issued Executive Order 8802.

NATIONAL ECONOMIC GROWTH AND RECONSTRUCTION ORGANIZATION

A self-help organization founded in New York in 1964. Financed by bonds, some of which were sold for as little as $25.00, NEGRO had over $3,000,000 in assests after only three years of operation.

NATIONAL FEDERATION OF AFRO AMERICAN WOMEN

Association formed in 1895, with Mrs. Booker T. Washington as president. Responding to an invitation issued by Josephine Ruffin, representatives from over 20 women's clubs met to organize the federation. It soon had affiliates in 16 states. It merged with the Colored Women's League of Washington to become the National Association of Colored Women, with Mary Church Terrell as the first president. In 1971, with its name changed to the National Association of Colored Women's Clubs, it had a membership of 120,000.

NATIONAL LABOR CONVENTION OF COLORED MEN

Established in Washington in 1869, the union was dominated by civil rights advocates and remained outside the mainstream of organized labor. It had died out by 1874.

NATIONAL LEAGUE ON URBAN CONDITIONS AMONG NEGROES

Interracial group later known as the National Urban League. It evolved from a New York conference called in 1910 by Mrs. Ruth Standish Baldwin, a wealthy white woman. Local branches, numbering 51 by 1925, helped workers to train for suitable jobs or find gainful employment. The league publishes a monthly magazine, *Opportunity.*

NATIONAL LIBERTY CONGRESS

Anti-lynching organization. On July 29, 1918, the National Liberty Congress of Colored Americans petitioned Congress to make lynching a federal crime.

NATIONAL MEDICAL ASSOCIATION

Founded by twelve doctors present at a meeting in the First Congregational Church in Atlanta, Georgia, in October 1895, the NMA had fewer than 50 members in 1904, over 500 in 1912, and 5,500 in 1970. R. F. Boyd was elected the first president; D. H. Williams, vice president; D. L. Martin, secretary; D. N. C. Scott, treasurer; and H. R. Butler, chairman of the executive board. The meeting was called to order by Professor I. Garland Penn, commissioner of the negro division of the Cotton States and International Exposition.

NATIONAL MEDICAL SOCIETY OF THE DISTRICT OF COLUMBIA

Founded in 1870 in protest against the Jim Crow practices of the existing medical society, it was the antecedent of the Medico-Chirurgical Society.

NATIONAL NEGRO BASEBALL LEAGUE

The first successful black baseball league in history, it was formed February 13, 1920, through the efforts of Rube Foster.

NATIONAL NEGRO BUSINESS LEAGUE

Organization founded in 1900 by Booker T. Washington to make the negro a force in the business world. The 'black man's Chamber of Commerce' brought together men who could encourage and inspire each other. By 1915 it had some 600 state and local branches.

NATIONAL NEGRO CONFERENCE

Meeting in New York on May 31, 1909, black and white leaders launched the NAACP. Among the participants were John Dewey and W. E. B. Du Bois. Their speeches are recorded in *Proceedings of the National Negro Conference:* 1909, reprinted by Arno Press.

NATIONAL NEGRO LABOR UNION

Established in Washington in 1869, the organization was dominated by civil rights advocates and remained outside the mainstream of organized labor. Although the union urged whites to 'aid in the protection and conservation of their and our interest,' it failed to draw support and ceased to exist by 1874.

NATIONAL NEWS BULLETIN

Official organ of the National Association of Colored Graduate Nurses.

NATIONAL URBAN LEAGUE

Organized in 1911 as the National League on Urban Conditions Among Negroes, it owed its formation to the merger of three early social agencies: the League for the Protection of Colored Women, headed by a white social worker, Mrs. William H. Baldwin, Jr.; the Committee on Urban Conditions Among Negroes, formed in 1910 by George Edmund Haynes, a young graduate student in social work at Columbia University; and the Committe for Improving the Industrial Conditions of Negroes in New York. Interracial from its inception, the league had an executive board of 15 members. The president traditionally was white, the executive secretary black. The league is somewhat parallel in purpose and growth to the NAACP. Booker T. Washington joined the group of sponsors of the league, which established headquarters in New York and organized a number of branches. Eugene Kinkle Jones became executive secretary in 1914, and sociologist Charles S. Johnson became director of research and investigation in 1921. Concerned primarily with the improvement of conditions of blacks in cities, the league became increasingly interested in promoting employment opportunities. In 1923 Johnson founded the league's magazine, *Opportunity, A Journal of Negro Life,* which had as its slogan 'Not Alms, but Opportunity.'

NATIVE GUARDS

The first black combat troops mustered for service in the Civil War. See Corps d'Afrique.

NATIVE SON

Landmark novel by Richard Wright. Published in 1940 and alternately praised and cursed by the critics ('one of the finest novels ever written by an American,' 'a disgrace to Negroes because it labels them killers,' 'an American version of Crime and Punishment,' 'sheer Communist propaganda'), it was the first novel by a black selected for the Book-of-the-Month Club or publication in the Modern Library collection. Set in Chicago, it develops the theme of a brutalized ghetto black created by a society that robs of him of his manhood. Society's victim, Bigger Thompson, is a violent and degraded black who accidentally smothers the drunken daughter of his employer. A play based on the novel opened at the St. James Theatre in 1941 and ran for 114 performances. Canada Lee played the role of Bigger Thomas in the play, directed by Orson Wells.

NCNW
See National Council of Negro Women.

NEAL, GASTON
Black power advocate (b. 1934). He has acted, written poetry, and promoted black power concepts in the East, and particularly as cultural director of the New School of Afro-American Thought in Washington, D. C.

NEGRITUDE
A word adopted from French and used to designate pride in and love for the African cultural heritage.

NEGRO
Word derived from the Spanish *negro,* meaning black. In 1878 Ferdinand Lee Barnett demanded through his newspaper *(The Conservator)* that the word no longer be spelled with a small *n.* He maintained that 'This breach of orthography is the white man's mark of disrespect.'

NEGRO DIGEST
See Johnson Publishing Company.

NEGRO ENSEMBLE COMPANY
New York repertory group. It was founded in 1967 by Robert Hooks and Douglas Turner Ward to train and encourage new

negro actors, playwrights, and backstage personnel. Its recent productions include *Ceremonies in Dark Old Men,* a realistic portrait of Harlem life by Lonne Elder, III; *God Is a (Guess What?),* a satirical play by Ray McIver; and *Man Better Man,* a Trinidadian musical by Errol Hill.

NEGRO FORT
Fort built on the Appalachicola River by the British during the War of 1812. In 1816, after it had been occupied by runaway slaves who were assumed to pose a threat to free residents of Florida, a U. S. gunboat killed or wounded most of the occupants of the fort.

NEGRO HISTORY WEEK
An annual week-long observance of the contributions of black Americans, initiated by the Association for the Study of Negro Life and History, under the direction of Carter G. Woodson, in 1926.

NEGRO IN THE AMERICAN REBELLION, THE
Book by William Wells Brown. *The Negro in the American Rebellion: His Heroism and His Fidelity,* originally published in 1867, was the first attempt to write a history of black involvement in the Revolutionary War, the War of 1812, and the Civil War.

NEGRO-INDIAN RELATIONS
See Indian-Negro Relations.

NEGRO NATIONAL LEAGUE
Baseball league formed in 1920 by the leading black clubs in the Midwest. Meeting in Kansas City, the managers of 8 teams agreed to support the league.

NEGRO RENAISSANCE
A creative outpouring in art, music, and literature in the 1920s, giving expression to the discontent of the Negro and his recogni-

tion of 'a renewed race-spirit,' in the words of Alain Locke, which 'consciously and proudly sets itself apart.' Abandoning the use of dialect, writers of the twenties displayed considerable talent and craftsmanship in developing Negro themes in a highly personal way. The three foremost poets of the movement were Claude McKay, Langston Hughes, and Countee Cullen. Novelists included Jessie Faucet, Jean Toomer, and Rudolph Fisher. Dramatists like Willis Richardson, together with white dramatists of the stature of Eugene O'Neill and Paul Green, gave Charles Gilpin, Paul Robeson, and other black actors a chance to perform in serious plays. Though they still faced an uphill fight in the field of serious music, in popular music and dance Negroes enjoyed a new surge of popularity. Jazz, which Robert Goffin, the Belgian musicologist, later (1945) called 'the great art of democracy,' became the musical idiom of the twenties. Such innovations in the dance as the Charleston and the Black Bottom, combined with other dance patterns introduced by Negroes before the twenties, caused James Weldon Johnson to conclude that the Negro influence 'on the art of dancing in this country has been almost absolute.' See Alain Locke, ed., *The New Negro: An Interpretation* (1925). and Hugh M. Gloster, *Negro Voices in American Fiction* (1948).

NEGRO SLAVE SONGS IN THE UNITED STATES

Important study by Miles Mark Fisher, published in 1953. Dr. Fisher started with the use made of songs in Africa and interpreted negro spirituals in that light.

NEGRO WORLD

Weekly newspaper published by Marcus Garvey to spread the doctrine of the UNIA. During its brief history (1918-33) it reached a circulation of 200,000.

NELL, WILLIAM COOPER

Abolitionist (1816-1874). A native of Boston, he spoke and wrote in defense of the anti-slavery cause. He collected and preserved valuable data on early personalities engaged in the movement, in his *Services of Colored Americans in the Wars of 1776 and 1812* (1852) and *Colored Patriots of the American Revolution* (1856). He was the first black man to hold an appointment as a postal clerk (Boston, 1861).

NELSON, LOUIS 'BIG EYE'

Musician. In the early 1900s, he played the clarinet in the New Orleans Olympia Band.

NEW BLACK RENAISSANCE

A ferment of creativity of unprecedented proportions in literature, music, and the graphic and dramatic arts, initiated during the era of challenge and reassessment ushered in by the U. S. supreme court decision of 1954, and bolstered by the emergence of new talent. The name was suggested by Arna Bontemps as early as 1961. The focus of public attention on the civil rights movement and the black revolution generated by the movement created a ready market for the creations of the new artists. Growing from a power base within the black sub-society and constituting a vital element in a situation of intense social upheaval, the new renaissance (in some views the only true renaissance of black culture) stressed the functional aspects of art. Epitomizing the concept that art has a place in the betterment of man was the formation of the Organization for Black American Culture, which sponsored a mural in the heart of a Chicago ghetto. Black music became the dominant music of contemporary life throughout the world. New forms emerged in the dramatic arts as little theaters acquired an educational and unifying purpose within black communities. Charles White and Jacob Lawrence were finally recognized as supreme interpreters of the black experience in art, and they were joined by many younger artists. More books on black themes were published in the 15 years following the Montgomery Boycott of 1955-56 than during any period since blacks reached this continent. Among the most prominent names of those associated with the new renaissance are the following: James Baldwin, Gwendolyn Brooks, Lorraine Hansberry, Margaret Walker (called 'the mother of young black poets'), John A. Williams, John O. Killens, Paule Marshall, Ronald Fair, Don L. Lee, Ossie Davis, Charles Gordone, Lonne Elder, Marian Anderson, Dean Dixon, Alvin Ailey, Arthur Mitchell, Miles Davis, LeRoi Jones, Ray Charles, and James Brown.

NEW CANAAN ACADEMY
New Hampshire secondary school. It was destroyed by townspeople in 1831 after it had admitted several negro youths.

NEW ENGLAND ANTI-SLAVERY SOCIETY
Abolitionist association formed in 1832 and later supplanted by the Massachusetts Anti-Slavery Society (1834). Though no negroes were among the twelve founders of the association, one-fourth of the signers of its constitution were black and Samuel Snowden was a member of its board of counselors.

NEW HARLEM RENAISSANCE
See New Black Renaissance.

NEW LADY
Magazine for upper-class women, launched in 1969 with financial help from the Ford Foundation.

NEW LAFAYETTE THEATER
Founded in 1968, it was supported by grants from the Ford and Rockefeller foundations as well as by state and private contributions. Located in the heart of Harlem, it had Ed Bullins as writer-in-residence.

NEW ORLEANS
Louisiana city, site of race rioting in 1900. Some 30 negro homes and one school were burned, July 24-27.

NEW ORLEANS, BATTLE OF
Two negro regiments helped General Andrew Jackson to defeat the British in the closing stages of the War of 1812. After the

decisive victory on January 8, 1815, Jackson praised the two regiments for 'their courage and perseverance.'

NEW ORLEANS TRIBUNE

Founded in 1864, it was the first black daily newspaper. It was printed in English and French.

NEW ROCHELLE

In 1961 a federal district judge ruled that segregation in the New Rochelle schools was unconstitutional, giving New York the distinction of becoming the first northern state to have one of its schools desegregated by court order.

NEW YORK ANTI-SLAVERY SOCIETY

Abolitionist association formed in Peterboro, New York, in 1835. David Ruggle was among the 400 delegates in attendance.

NEW YORK RENAISSANCE BIG 5

Founded in 1923, it was one of the first organized professional basketball teams. In 1939, the Rens won the first professional world championship basketball tournament. The team was organized by Robert J. Douglas. The first team included Hilton Slocum, Frank Forbes, Leon Monde, Hy Monte, Zack Anderson, and Harold Mayers. Slocum was the team captain until he left the club in 1932.

NEW YORK SOCIETY FOR PROMOTING
THE MANUMISSION OF SLAVES

Organized in New York in 1885, with white antislavery leader John Jay as president, it opened the African Free School in 1887.

NEWARK RIOT

In Newark, New Jersey, police arrested a Negro cabdriver on July 12, 1967, for assaulting an officer. False rumors that the cabdriver had been beaten enraged the black community and brought on a confrontation with three thousand National Guardsmen. The riot continued for six days and resulted in the death of 26 persons, the arrest of 1,200, and damage of more than $15,000,000.

NEWBERRY, DANGERFIELD
One of John Brown's raiders. See Harpers Ferry.

NEWHOUSE, RICHARD
Public official. In the 1960s he served as state senator in Illinois and organized a national meeting of black state legislators.

NEWSPAPERS
See Press.

NEWTON, HUEY
Black Panther leader (b. 1942). With Bobby Seale he founded the Black Panther Party in Oakland, California, in 1966. The youngest of seven children born to a laborer and part-time Baptist preacher in Grove, Louisiana, Newton moved to California when he was 2. He met Seale while both were students at Merritt College in Oakland, became active in the Afro-American club, was inspired by the teachings of the late Malcolm X, and worked with Seale to found a new party based on a ten-point program, including black power ('power to the people'). Founded in October 1966, the Black Panther Party provided free breakfasts, along with indoctrination, to ghetto children, called for replacing capitalism with black socialism, and raised funds by conducting rallies and selling the Panther newspaper. The young militants were frequently involved in clashes with the police, and Defense Minister Newton was charged with murder of an Oakland police-man in 1967. His conviction was appealed and a new trial ordered in 1970. The proceedings ended in a mistrial in 1971. The most revered leaders of the Black Revolution, Newton and Seale have won wide admiration among young blacks living in the ghettoes. Rejecting racism, he maintains that 'the only culture worth holding on to is revolutionary culture.' He was nominated for a U. S. congressional seat by the radical Peace and Freedom Party. He wrote To Die for the People (1972).

NIAGARA MOVEMENT

Founded in the summer of 1905 by W. E. B. Du Bois at Niagara Falls, Canada, the Niagara Movement was opposed by Booker T. Washington and faded away before five years had passed. Twenty-nine members of the Talented Tenth attending the Niagara meeting drew up a manifesto calling for the abolition of discrimination, acceptance of the principle of human brotherhood, and freedom of the press and speech. Subsequent meetings were held in places with historic freedom ties, such as Harpers Ferry and Faneuil Hall in Boston. State chapters of the movement scored minor successes, but its numbers remained small, its grandiose hopes unrealized. It helped to lay the foundation for the NAACP.

NICHOLS, HERBIE

Musician (b. 1919). Born in Manhattan, he grew up in Harlem, played in a small combo in high school, and joined the Royal Baron orchestra in 1937. His original style as a pianist and composer had an impact on his successors but never enabled him to live even modestly from his earnings. He considered African music the key to jazz. He continued studying traditional and newer forms of music until death brought an end to his career, while he was still in his mid-forties. See A. B. Spellman, *Black Music* (1966).

NICKERSON, WILLIAM, JR.

Businessman (1879-1945). He was founder and first president of the Golden State Mutural Life Insurance Company.

92nd DIVISION

Negro combat division praised by General John J. Pershing as being 'one of the best in the A. E. F.' Seven weeks after landing in France in June, 1918, it moved to the front and remained there, under enemy fire most of the time, until the end of the war. Its artillery brigade was noted for its accuracy, and its 367th infantry regiment forced the Germans to retreat in the drive on Metz.

93rd DIVISION
Black combat division unit organized during World War I. It never existed as a division, except on paper. Its four infantry regiments were split up and assigned separately to the French command. It had no field-grade black officers. Its 369th Infantry Regiment was the first American unit to face enemy fire in France, in the Champagne sector. The 370th was involved in the Oise-Aisne offensive. The 371st and 372nd fought on the Meuse-Argonne front. Troops in all four regiments fought bravely and well, earning numerous individual citations. Its 371st Infantry drew praise from Marshal Henri Pétain; the 370th won 22 American Distinguished Service Crosses and 68 French decorations; the 369th won the Croix de Guerre.

NINO, PEDRO ALONSO
A black crewman on Colombus' ship.

9TH CAVALRY REGIMENT
Composed of 12 companies of black volunteers who had enlisted for a period of 5 years, the all-negro unit was organized in February 1867 and ordered to duty in Texas in March. There for years the regiment struggled to maintain stability along strife-ridden frontiers. The commanding general said: 'Everything that men could do they did. . . . Their duties were performed with zeal and intelligence and they are worthy of all consideration.' See Buffalo Soldiers.

NIX, ROBERT N. C.
Public official (b. 1905). Elected U. S. congressman from the 2nd district of Pennsylvania in 1958 (to fill the unexpired term of Earl Chudoff), he has won re-election to each subsequent Congress and holds membership on the foreign affairs, post office, and civil service committees. Born in Orangeburg, South Carolina, he studied in New York City and Pennsylvania, practiced law, and was executive committeeman of the 8th division of 44th ward in Philadelphia for 26 years. In 1958 he was a delegate to the Democratic national convention in Chicago.

331

NOBLE, JEANNE L.

Educator (b. 1926). Born in Palm Beach, Florida, she studied at Howard and Columbia, where she earned her doctorate. She was dean of women at Langston University in Oklahoma, professor at Albany State College in Georgia, the University of Vermont, and Tuskegee, and guidance counselor at the City College of New York before she joined the Center for Human Relation Studies at New York University. She received the Pi Lambda Theta Research award in 1965 for her book *The Negro Woman's College Education.*

NOONE, JIMMY

Musician. In 1917 he joined the Original Creole Band, replacing George Baquet as the clarinetist.

NORRIS v. ALABAMA

Supreme Court decision (1935) setting forth the principle that the exclusion of negroes from jury lists violated the equal protection clause of the Fourteenth Amendment. See Scottsboro Cases.

NORTH STAR

Newspaper launched in 1847 by Frederick Douglass, supported by contributions from English abolitionists and named after the guide used by slaves in their journey to freedom. The newspaper's name was changed in 1850 to *Frederick Douglass' Paper.* Founded as an antislavery publication, it gradually became a political organ.

NORTHRUP, SOLOMON

The son of an emancipated slave, he was kidnapped in 1841, at the age of 32, and transported to New Orleans. Separated for 12 years from his family, who lived in upstate New York, he finally managed to get word of his enslavement to friends who finally secured his freedom. He told of his life on a Louisiana plantation in his autobiography, *The Narrative of Solomon Northrup* (a 'told to' account, 1857).

NORTHWEST ORDINANCE

Enacted by the Congress under the Articles of Confederation, the Northwest Ordinance of 1787 incorporated Thomas Jefferson's suggestion to outlaw slavery in the territory northwest of the Ohio River even though it allowed the capture and return of fugitive slaves.

NOYES ACADEMY

Integrated school opened in Canaan, New Hampshire, in 1835. The school was destroyed by angry white villagers.

NUL

See National Urban League.

O

OAAU

See Organization for Afro-American Unity.

OBAC ARTISTS WORKSHOP

Sponsored by the Organization for Black American Culture, the Chicago workshop sponsored creation of a mural to illustrate the modern black artist's concept of his role in the black community. Called 'The Wall of Respect,' the mural depicted blacks whose contributions to society are significant.

OBERLIN COLLEGE

Founded in 1833, it became a coeducational college in 1934 when it received the seceded students of Lane Seminary. It was a center of abolitionism and a station on the underground railroad. Its leaders were involved in a notable incident provoked by their role in the forcible removal and transportation to Canada of a fugitive in 1858. After John Price, a fugitive slave, was seized by slave-catchers in 1858, he was rescued by Oberlin College students and a professor, who helped him to reach Canada safely. Many reformers and persons of distinction graduated from the college.

ODD FELLOWS

Established in 1843 under a dispensation from the English lodge, the Grand United Order of Odd Fellows, like the Masonic order, had affiliates in cities throughout the north and helped to uplift and inspire negroes.

O'FAKE, PETER P.

Musician. In 1848 he conducted the Newark Theater orchestra. He also organized a small orchestra and turned out some popular dance compositions.

OGDEN, PETER

Civic leader. In 1843 he helped to organize one of the major black fraternal groups, the Grand United Order of Odd Fellows.

O'HARA, JAMES

Public official. Self-educated, he was elected congressman from North Carolina, 1883-87.

OKLAHOMA

Negroes who came to Indian territory in search of land often settled among friendly tribes, who referred to them as 'linksters.' Twenty negroes visited the White House to urge President William Henry Harrison to appoint a negro as secretary of the Oklahoma Territory. All-negro towns were founded at Langston (1891), Boley (1904), and elsewhere in Oklahoma. Negroes living in such small towns were the most enthusiastic supporters of Alfred Charles Sam's proposal in 1914 to transport negroes to Africa. See Indian Territory.

OLIVER, JOSEPH 'KING'

Jazz musician (1885-1938). In the early twenties, his Creole Jazz Band played in New Orleans. He was famous as the 'talking trumpet' player.

OLUGEBEFOLA, ADEMOLA

Artist (b. 1941). One of the pioneers of the contemporary black art movement, he was born in the Virgin Islands. He is a popular lecturer on traditional African art forms and their contemporary manifestation. Concerned with the issues that confront humanity, he is completing a series of paintings, sculpture, and woodcuts which he calls 'Burden of Injustice.'

O'NEAL, FREDERICK

Actor. In 1964 he became the first black president of Actor's Equity.

ONEIDA INSTITUTE

Training center in upper New York State. Several distinguished negroes, including Martin R. Delany, received training there.

O'NEIL, JOHN

Athlete (b. 1911). In 1962 he became the first black to coach a major league ball team, the Chicago Cubs. One of the greatest first basemen in baseball history, he played with the Memphis Red Sox (1937-48) and the Kansas City Monarchs (1948-55) before signing as a Cub scout.

OPEN CITY CAMPAIGN

In 1966 the Southern Christian Leadership Conference announced that it would initiate a series of marches through white Chicago neighborhoods. The 'Open City' campaign dramatized the need for open housing legislation to rid the nation of the slums which, in the words of Martin Luther King, Jr., are 'chiefly responsible for the Northern urban race problem.' The demonstrations, marked by heckling and jeering on the part of angry white residents, ended on August 26 when Chicago officials agreed on a program to end de facto segregation in the city.

OPEN OCCUPANCY

Policy of freeing sales and rentals from racial restrictions and integrating housing. President John F. Kennedy promoted the policy by an executive order issued in November 1962. By February 1963 eighteen states had adopted open occupancy laws.

OPERATION BOOTSTRAP

A self-help project founded in Los Angeles in 1965. Black businessmen provided funds for the undertaking, which sought to provide the hard-core unemployed with marketable skills.

OPERATION BREADBASKET

Designed to promote economic development among Negroes, 'Operation Breadbasket' was conceived by the Southern Christian Leadership Conference. See Jackson, Jesse.

OPPORTUNITIES INDUSTRIALIZATION CENTERS

Established largely through the efforts of Leon Sullivan, the centers train black workers and help them to find employment. By early 1971, some 20,000 blacks in 90 centers in the United States, Nigeria, and Ghana had found jobs through the centers.

OPPORTUNITY

Official organ of the National Urban League. Launched by sociologist Charles S. Johnson in 1923, the magazine, subtitled 'A Journal of Negro Life,' had as its slogan 'Not Alms, but Opportunity.'

OREO

Name used by blacks to describe another black who tries to win acceptance by whites.

ORGANIZATION FOR AFRICAN UNITY

Group founded by Malcolm X on June 28, 1964, to work for black unity. The secular organization was intended to promote cooperation with other civil rights group.

ORGANIZATION FOR BLACK AMERICAN CULTURE

In 1967 a group of Chicago artists formed OBAC for the purpose of using their creative tools to meet the needs of the black community. They sponsored a mural on the side of a building in the heart of the city's black ghetto. Called 'The Wall of Respect,' it depicted black accomplishment through the images of those who had achieved most in black terms: Marcus Garvey as a black nationalist; Malcolm X as a religious activist; Muhammad Ali in sports; Charlie Parker, Ornette Coleman, John Coltrane, and Nina Simone in music; Lerone Bennett, Jr. in history; W. E. B. Du Bois and LeRoi Jones as social thinkers and writers; and Gwendolyn Brooks, John O. Killens, and James Baldwin as prime movers in the field of literature. Its purpose was to enlighten, motivate, and reassure ghetto dwellers.

ORGENA

A Muslim morality play (the word is *a negro* spelled backward) in which the white man is found guilty of being the greatest robber, deceiver, and trouble-maker on earth.

ORIGINAL CREOLE BAND

Organized by string bass player Bill Johnson, the jazz band became the first important group to leave New Orleans. The group started on a series of Vaudeville tours in 1911. Johnson's brother Dink was the drummer; Norwood Williams played the guitar, Jimmie Palao the violin, Eddie Venson the trombone, and George Baquet the clarinet.

OTTLEY, ROI

Writer (1906-1960). As a journalist and essayist, he stressed 'respectable achievement.' His works include *New World A-Coming* (1943), *Black Odyssey* (1948), *No Green Pastures* (1952), and *Lonely Warrior: Life of Robert S. Abbott* (1955).

OVERTON, ANTHONY

Businessman (1864-1936). He published a newspaper, manufactured cosmetics, founded Victory Mutual Life Insurance Company, headed the first black national bank in America (Douglass National Bank of Chicago), and received the Spingarn Award (1929).

OWENS, JESSE

Athlete (b. 1913). The foremost sprinter and broad jumper of his day, he was the star of the Olympic games held in Germany in 1936. He received the Associated Press citation as the outstanding track athlete of the first half of the twentieth century (1937), worked to combat juvenile delinquency through sports, and went to India in 1955 as a good-will ambassador.

P

PACHECO, LOUIS

Interpreter (born c. 1798). In 1835 he was hired from his owner, Mrs. Antonio Pacheco, to serve as an interpreter and guide for soldiers who were to force the Seminoles out of Florida. He informed his friends of the plan, with the result that most of the soldiers were killed by Seminoles and Maroons.

PAGE, INMAN E.

Educator (d. 1935). Born a slave on a Virginia plantation, he served as president of 4 universities, including Langston University in Oklahoma, 1898-1915.

PAIGE, LEROY

Athlete. One of the greatest pitchers in baseball history, 'Satchel' began his career in the 1920s and signed his last contract (with the Atlanta Braves) in 1968. In 1952 Casey Stengel chose him as a pitcher for his American League all-star team. In 1971 he was belatedly admitted to the Hall of Fame.

PAIGE, MYLES A.

Jurist (b. 1898). Born in Alabama, he served as city magistrate of New York City, beginning in 1936, and as judge of the New York state family court, 1962-66.

PAIRING

A means of accomplishing school desegregation by assigning pupils from a predominantly black school to a predominantly white school, and vice versa. See Green v. New Kent County, Virginia.

PALAO, JIMMIE

Musician. He played the violin with the New Orleans Original Creole Band in the early 1900s.

PAN-AFRICAN CONGRESSES

W. E. B. Du Bois, over the protest of the American government, was allowed by the French to hold a Pan-African Congress at the Grand Hotel in Paris, in February 1919. The first congress attracted 57 delegates and had limited results. The second one convened between August 29 and September 6, 1921, in London, Brussels, and Paris, attracting 113 accredited delegates from 26 groups and receiving press coverage throughout Europe. A third congress met in London, Paris, and Lisbon in 1923, and a fourth was held in New York in 1927 'just to keep the idea alive.'

PARIS PEACE CONFERENCE

William Monroe Trotter was denied a passport when he tried to attend the Paris Peace Conference in 1919 to place the negro question before the statesman who had vowed to 'make the world safe for democracy.' Denied his passport, he signed aboard a steamer as a second cook and appeared before the conference as a delegate of the National Equal Rights League and secretary of the Race Petitioners to the Peace Conference. See Trotter, William Monroe.

PARKE, CHARLES STEWART

Scientist. Chairman of the biology department at Howard during the 1930s, he discovered and described 39 species of plants and wrote some 60 papers.

PARKER, CHARLIE

Jazz musician. In the late 1940s he was one of the initiators of 'cool' jazz.

PARKER, JIM

Athlete. In 1957 the two-time All-American player from Ohio State was the first draft choice of the Baltimore Colts. The all-pro tackle and guard helped his team to win NFL championships in 1958 and 1959.

PARKS, GORDON

Photographer, movie director, and author (b. 1912). A free-lance photographer with *Life* magazine since 1949, he is also a writer, composer, and the first black to direct movies for a major studio. In 1961 the American Society of Magazine Photographers named him 'Magazine Photographer of the Year.' The youngest of fifteen children born to a poor farm family living in Fort Scott, Kansas, he moved to St. Paul, Minnesota, after his mother died. The 16-year-old lad had to drop out of high school but continued to read in public libraries in his spare time. He wrote many songs, painted, and tried his hand at sculpture and semi-pro basketball. While working as a railroad porter in the late 1930s he became interested in photography, moved to Chicago, and won a Rosenwald fellowship by exhibiting ghetto photographs in September 1941. He wrote two autobiographical works, *The Learning Tree* (1963), covering his childhood, and *A Choice of Weapons* (1966), based on his migration northward and experiences through the mid-forties. He signed a contract in 1968 to direct four movies, including an adaptation of *The Learning Tree*, for which he also wrote the musical score, and *Shaft* (1971). He composed a piano concerto which was first performed in Vienna in 1953 and three piano sonatas, first performed in Philadelphia in 1955.

PARKS, ROSA

Seamstress (b. 1909). The college-educated church worker initiated a chain of events that culminated in the U. S. Supreme Court decision outlawing segregation on public buses. On December 1, 1955, Mrs. Parks boarded a bus in Montgomery, Alabama, took a seat in a section reserved for whites, and refused to move. Her arrest entailed a boycott of the bus line and the formation of the Montgomery Improvement Association, headed by Martin Luther King, Jr. The Supreme Court decision reversing Plessy v. Ferguson was handed down in December 1956.

PARROT, RUSSELL

Abolitionist. A prominent public speaker, he was assistant to Absalom Jones, pastor of St. Thomas Episcopal Church in Philadelphia. He participated in the 1817 all-colored assembly in Philadelphia to discuss colonization.

PARSONS, JAMES B.

Jurist (b. 1911). He was the first appointed black judge of a U. S. district court in the continental United States. In 1961 he was appointed judge of the U. S. district court for the northern district of Illinois.

PATRIOTS, BLACK

See Black Patriots.

PATTERSON, FLOYD

Athlete. In 1956 he became the youngest man ever to hold the world heavyweight boxing title by defeating Archie Moore in five rounds.

PATTERSON, FREDERICK D.

President of Tuskegee Institute (b. 1901).

PATTERSON, LINDSAY

Writer. He has written both fiction and non-fiction. He compiled and edited *The Negro in Music and Art* (1967).

PATTERSON, MARY JANE

First negro woman to attain the distinction of becoming a college graduate. She obtained her degree from Oberlin College in 1862.

PATTERSON, WILLIAM

Lawyer (b. 1892). He has had a prominent role for many years as a civil rights advocate.

PAUL, WILLIAM

One of Denmark Vesey's lieutenants. His attempt to recruit a slave led to the suppression of a plot to capture the town of Charleston, South Carolina, in 1822.

PAYNE, CHRISTOPHER

Clergyman and diplomat (1848-1925). He was born in Virginia, where he taught school, pastored churches, and was admitted to the bar. Active in politics, he went to the Virgin Islands (then the Danish West Indies) as consul general in 1903 and remained there after 1917, when the islands were purchased from Denmark. Thereafter he practiced law and served initially as assistant prosecuting attorney and subsequently as judge advocate of the islands.

PAYNE, DANIEL A.

AME bishop and educator (1811-1893). A pillar of the African Methodist Episcopal Church, he worked to improve the education of AME ministers, contracted for his denomination to purchase Wilberforce University, and became its first black president (1863-76). Licensed to preach (1837) and ordained a Lutheran minister (1839), he joined the mother church of the AME denomination, Philadelphia's Bethel (1841), and held his first pastorate at Israel AME church in Washington, D. C. (1844). He described his many years of service to the cause of interracial harmony in *Recollections of Seventy Years* (1883). His other writings include *The History of the A. M. E. Church from 1816 to 1856* (1891).

PAYTON, PHILLIP

Businessman (b. 1876). As founder and president of the Afro-American Realty Company, in 1908 he controlled property in New York City valued at $630,000. His company acquired property in Harlem to prevent white relators from forcing out black tenants.

PEACE AND FREEDOM PARTY

The radical group formed a controversial coalition with the

345

Black Panther party in December 1967, supporting the candidacy of Huey Newton for Congress, Eldridge Cleaver, for president, and Jerry Rubin (white leader of the Yippies, or Youth International Party) for vice president.

PEACOCK, EULACE

Athlete. A standout in the sprints, jumps and pentathlon, he might have rivaled Jesse Owens in the Olympics except for an injured tendon.

PEAKE, MARY S.

Teacher (1823-1862). A free negro, she established the first school for contraband blacks, the Red Cottage School in Hampton, Virginia. She helped the American Missionary Association to set up other schools at Norfolk and Newport News. Her activities are described in a book by Lewis C. J. Lockwood, *Mary S. Peake, the Colored Teacher at Fortress Monroe* (1864).

PEASE, JOACHIM

Civil War hero. He won the navy's Medal of Honor for his outstanding performance as 'loader of the No. 1 gun' on the *Kearsarge* in the historic duel between that gunboat and the *Alabama,* off the coast of France.

PECULIAR INSTITUTION, THE

Euphemism for the slave system. Also the title of a book by Kenneth M. Stampp (1956) describing slavery as a bestial regime that violated every fundamental of the dignity of man.

PEDEE RIVER

The mouth of the Pedee River in what is now South Carolina was the scene of America's first slave revolt. Lucas Vasquez de Ayllon founded a town there in the summer of 1526. The settlement consisted of 500 Spanish colonists and 100 slaves. Toward the end of the year the slaves revolted, killed several of the Spaniards, and escaped to live among the Indians.

PEEBLES, MELVIN VAN

See Van Peebles, Melvin.

PELHAM, BENJAMIN AND ROBERT

Publisher. In 1883 the two brothers founded the Detroit *Plaindealer* and made it a leading negro newspaper which they used effectively for the next 11 years to gain political influence on the national level. Ben Pelham was appointed to local offices and finally became chief accountant of the Wayne County board of supervisors. Robert went on to the nation's capital, to a post in the Interior Department.

PENN, I. GARLAND

As commissioner of the negro division of the Cotton States and International Exposition in Atlanta, Georgia, in 1895, he had a major role in the founding of the National Medical Association. Penn called the meeting to order with twelve doctors present in October 1895 and announced that the purpose of the meeting was to organize a national association of black physicians, dentists, and pharmacists. See National Medical Association.

PENNINGTON, JAMES W. C.

Clergyman and scholar (1809-1870). He received the Doctor of Divinity degree from the University of Heidelberg, was active in anti-slavery causes, presiding over the 1853 Rochester convention attended by 140 delegates from eight states, and wrote the early history of the negro as well as his autobiography, titled *The Fugitive Blacksmith; Or, Events in the History of James W. C. Pennington, Formerly a Slave in the State of Maryland, United States* (3rd ed., 1850). His scholarly work, *A Text Book of the Origin and History of the Colored People* (1841), was the first black history book written by a black man.

PENNSYLVANIA ANTI-SLAVERY SOCIETY

Abolitionist association formed in Harrisburg in January 1837. Seven blacks participated: James Forten, Robert Purvis, James

McCrummell, John C. Bowers, Charles W. Gardner, John Peck, Stephen Smith.

PENNSYLVANIA AUGUSTINE SOCIETY
Association founded in 1818 by negroes to promote education among 'people of colour.'

PEOPLE UNITED TO SAVE HUMANITY (PUSH)
Organization founded on December 25, 1971, to 'unite people, provide action, urgency, and pushing.' PUSH founder Jesse Jackson, former head of Operation Breadbasket, announced that he would lean heavily on politicians to expand black economic opportunity. He explained that PUSH would be a 'rainbow coalition' of people, white and black, and that all would 'push for a greater share of economic and political power for all poor people in America in the spirit of Dr. Martin Luther King, Jr.'

PERIODICALS
See Press.

PERKINS, BILL
In the last third of the 19th century, he trained and handled some of the nation's leading thoroughbreds.

PERKINS, MARION
Sculptor (1908-1961). His first works were carved from bars of soap. Trained at the South Side Community Art Center in Chicago, he became an outstanding sculptor and teacher. His 'Man of Sorrow' won the Art Institute of Chicago purchase prize in 1951.

PERKINSON, COLERIDGE-TAYLOR
Modern composer. His works include the *Concerto for Viola and Orchestra,* performed at Philarmonic Hall under the auspices of the NAMN.

PERRY, JOE

Athlete (b. 1927). The greatest ground-gainer in NFL history, he was the first black signed by the San Francisco 49ers in 1948.

PERRY, JOHN S.

Physician. A graduate of the medical college of the University of West Tennessee, he became president of the Medico-Chirurgical Society of the District of Columbia.

PERRY, JULIA

Contemporary composer. Her *Stabat Mater*, for contralto soloist and string orchestra, drew favorable comments after it was performed in New York by Clarion Concerts. She has also made choral arrangements of spirituals.

PERRY SANITARIUM

Founded in 1910 by Dr. John E. Perry, the Kansas City, Missouri, sanitarium served black patients from a wide area.

PETERSBURG

Virginia port near the site of one of the bloodiest encounters of the Civil War. Union sappers dug a tunnel beneath a strong point in the Confederate defenses and exploded a mine at dawn. Later the 4th Division, composed entirely of black infantrymen, was ordered to break the Confederate lines. Hundreds died in the futile undertaking.

PETERSON V. GREENVILLE

Supreme Court decision setting aside sit-in convictions based on criminal trespass laws.

PETERSON, LOUIS

Writer (b. 1921). He grew up in a white middle-class neighborhood in Hartford, Connecticut, and graduated from Morehouse College and New York University. *Take a Giant Step* was produced on Broadway in 1953. Since then he has written television scripts and screenplays for movies, including *The Confessions of Nat Turner.*

PETION, ALEXANDRE SABES

Haitian leader (d. 1818). After Dessalines was assassinated (1806), Pétion led the mulatto faction that established the republic of Haiti.

PETIT, JOSEPH

Musician. A leading valve trombone player in New Orleans in the early 1900s, he was also the manager of the Olympia Band.

PETRY, ANN LANE

Writer (b. 1911). A practicing pharmacist, she worked for the *Amsterdam News* and the *People's Voice* before publishing one of her short stories in *Crisis* in 1943. 'Like a Winding Sheet' was named the best American short story for 1946. Her other works include the highly praised novel *The Street* (1946), *Country Place* (1947), and *Harriet Tubman: Conductor on the Underground Railroad* (1955).

PETTIFORD, W. R.

Banker (b. 1847). Born in Granville County, North Carolina, he founded the Alabama Penny Saving Bank in 1890 and served as its president, 1899-1905.

PEYTON, THOMAS R.

Physician. Born in Brooklyn, he was the only black in a class of one hundred at Long Island College of Medicine in the early 1920s. After practicing in Jamaica, Long Island, he specialized in proctology, studying in Paris and London. He has published original papers on proctology. His autobiography is titled *Quest for Dignity* (1950).

PHILHARMONIC SOCIETY OF NEW YORK CITY

Organized in 1876, the musical group was conducted by P. H. Loveridge.

PHILLIPS, CHANNING

Civil rights leader. In 1968 he was nominated for President during the Democratic national convention.

PICHON, WALTER 'FATS'

Jazz pianist (1907-1967). He began his career at the age of 14. For many years he played on riverboats, a master of the calliope as well as the piano. From about 1940 through 1958 he played regularly at the Absinthe House in New Orleans.

PICKENS, WILLIAM

Educator and scholar (b. 1881). Born to migrant South Carolina sharecroppers, he managed to learn enough in the Little Rock, Arkansas, schools to enter Talladega College in Alabama. After earning his first B. A. degree there, he moved on to Yale for a second one. The recipient of three honorary degrees, he taught at Talladega (1904-14) and Wiley College before becoming dean at Morgan College in Baltimore, Maryland. In addition to many scholarly articles, he has authored several books, including *Abraham Lincoln, Man and Statesman* (1909), *Frederick Douglass and the Spirit of Freedom* (1912), *The New Negro* (1916), and an autobiography, *Bursting Bonds,* 1923.

PICKETT, BILL

Cowboy (1862-1932). Credited with originating the art of bulldogging or steer wrestling, he worked at one of the largest and most famous ranches in the West, the 101 Ranch in Ponca City, Oklahoma.

PICOU, ALPHONSE

Musician. He played clarinet with the Olympia Band in New Orleans and composed many classics, including 'Alligator Hop.'

PINCHBACK, PICKNEY BENTON STEWART

Politician and lawyer (1837-1921). He was educated in the public schools of Cincinnati, Ohio, enlisted in the Union army in 1862, became inspector of customs at New Orleans in 1867, and

351

had a leading role in Republican politics. A delegate to the Louisiana Reconstruction Convention in 1867, he became a state senator in 1868, a lieutenant governor in 1871, and acting governor in 1872. He won election to the U. S. Senate in 1873 but was never seated. He was appointed surveyor of customs in New Orleans in 1882. Four years later he was admitted to the bar.

PINKARD, MACEO
Popular composer. He is best known as the composer of 'Sweet Georgia Brown.'

PIPPIN, HORACE
Painter (1888-1946). Critics regard him as an outstanding primitive painter.

PLANTER
Rebel gunboat captured by her black crew on May 13, 1862. The New York *Herald* reported the event (May 18, 1862): 'Nine colored men, comprising the pilot, engineers, and crew . . . took the vessel under their exclusive control, passed the batteries and forts in Charleston Harbor, hoisted the white flag, ran out to the blockading squadron. . . .' The leader of the group was Robert Small. Other members of the crew were William Morrison, A. Gradine, and John Smalls.

PLATT, IDA
Lawyer. In 1894 she became the first black woman lawyer in Chicago. She was a graduate of the Chicago College of Law.

PLAYER, WILLA BEATRICE
Educator (b. 1909). After joining the faculty of Bennett College in North Carolina (1930), she taught French and Latin, then filled various administrative positions prior to her appointment as president of the college in 1955.

PLEASANTS, MARY E.

Abolitionist (d. 1904). Bought and freed by a Georgia planter, she married Alexander Smith, who left her a large sum of money and asked her to use it for the abolition of slavery. She is supposed to have accumulated a fortune by investing her money in San Francisco and to have used it to finance John Brown's raid on Harpers Ferry. 'Mammy' Pleasants is often identified as the mother of civil rights in California.

PLESSY v. FERGUSON

U. S. Supreme Court decision of 1896 upholding a Louisiana law that required separate railroad accommodations for whites and negroes. The majority held that laws were 'powerless to eradicate racial instincts or to abolish distinctions based on physical differences.' Justice John Marshall Harlan, in a dissenting opinion, held that the 'Constitution is color-blind, and neither knows nor tolerates classes among citizens.'

PLYMOUTH HOSPITAL

Boston hospital for blacks established in 1908 by Dr. C. N. Garland.

POAG, GEORGE C.

The first black to enter Olympic competition, he placed third in both the 200-meter and 400-meter hurdles (1904).

POINDEXTER, HILDRUS A.

Medical scholar. He has contributed to medical journals and carried out health assignments in the United States and foreign countries.

POITIER, SIDNEY

Actor (b. 1927). He was the first black recipient of an 'Oscar,' awarded to him for his performance in *Lilies of the Field* in 1963. His first important role was in the Broadway play *Lysistrata*. He was praised for his roles in *A Raisin in the Sun* (1959), *The Defiant Ones* (1959), *No Way Out, Blackboard Jungle,* and *A*

Man Is Ten Feet Tall. He received the Silver Bear Award at the Berlin Film Festival, the New York Film Critics Award, and the Sylvania TV Award.

POLL TAX

Instituted by Mississippi in 1890 to disenfranchise blacks, the poll tax was outlawed for all elections by a U. S. supreme court decision handed down in 1966.

POLLARD, FRITZ

Athlete. During the infancy of professional football, he became the first black to coach a major team (Akron Indians, American Professional Football League, 1919). As a Brown University student, he had been the first black to play in the Rose Bowl (1916).

POMARE, ELEO

Dancer. Associated with the New Harlem Renaissance, he interprets the black experience in dance.

POMPEY

Spy during the American Revolution. He learned the enemy password, led a group of soldiers through enemy lines, and made it possible for Anthony Wayne to capture the vital British outpost at Stony Point, New York.

POOLE, CECIL F.

Public official (b. 1907). The first black U. S. attorney, he held the title of assistant district attorney in San Francisco.

POOLE, ELIJAH

See Muhammad, Elijah.

POOR PEOPLE'S CAMPAIGN

A peaceful movement organized in 1968 by Martin Luther King Jr., to bring pressure on Congress to enact legislation to reduce poverty. Ralph Abernathy became head of SCLC and directed the campaign after King was assassinated. The first nine caravans of the poor arrived in Washington on May 11 and began to build Resurrection City. The campaign reached its climactic moment on May 19, when speakers at the Solidarity Day demonstration lamented the assassinations of King and Kennedy, called the Vietnam war racist and immoral, and warned that there might never be another peaceful demonstration.

POOR, SALEM

Colonial soldier. He fought at Bunker Hill, where his exceptional conduct prompted 14 officers to petition the Massachusetts legislature in his behalf, and later at Valley Forge and White Plains.

POPULATION

In 1790 the total population of the United States was about 4 million, including 757,000 negroes, most of whom lived in the South. In 1860, the black population had risen to 4.4 million. All but 10 percent were slaves, and 90 percent of the black population was concentrated in the South. There was an exodus northward during and after the Civil War, another in the late 1870s, and there were others following both world wars. By 1960 the negro population had increased to 19 million, with 7.5 million blacks living outside the South and 14 million living in cities. By 1970 it had risen to 22.3 million, about equally distributed between the North and the South. A third of all blacks were living in 15 cities; half of them were living in the nation's 50 largest cities. Negroes made up 11 percent of the total population in 1970. See Social and Economic Status of Negroes in the United States, 1970.

PORT HUDSON

Confederate fortification bravely but unsuccessfully attacked by five Louisiana colored regiments in the spring of 1863. The New York *Times* editorialized (June 30, 1863): 'No body of troops . . . have fought better in the war.'

PORT ROYAL EXPERIMENT

An early attempt to educate ex-slaves under Yankee missionary auspices. Details of the operation of the pioneering project of acculturation and education on the South Carolina Sea Islands are given in Charlotte Forten's *Life on the Sea Islands* (1864). See Willie Lee Rose, *Rehearsal for Reconstruction: The Port Royal Experiment* (1964).

PORTER, DAVID

Musician. Working with Isaac Hayes, who cannot read music, he has arranged hits like 'Hold On, I'm Coming' and 'Black Moses.'

PORTER, HENRY

One of the conspirators in the Southampton County, Virginia, insurrection of 1831. See Turner, Nat.

PORTER, JAMES A.

Artist and writer. He teaches art at Howard and is the author of *Modern Negro Art* (1943).

POWELL v. ALABAMA

Supreme Court decision (1932) affirming the constitutional right to counsel. Asserting that where the accused in a capital case was unable to secure counsel or to present his own defense, the trial court had to assign appropriate counsel, the court held that the failure to do so was a violation of due process of law. Thus the court applied the principle of the right 'to have the assistance of counsel' (Sixth Amendment) to a state case, along with the principle of the right guaranteed by the due process clause of the Fourteenth Amendment. See Scottsboro Cases.

POWELL, ADAM CLAYTON, JR.

Congressman (b. 1908). As Harlem's representative (1945-1970) and chairman of the House Committee on Education and Labor during the 1960s, he exercised more power than any other black congressman in U. S. history. Born in New Haven and educated in New York City, where his father pastored the largest black church in America, he became a powerful crusader for Harlem's black masses, a spellbinding orator, and a brilliant legislator before his tragic flaws brought an end to his highly successful political career.

His parliamentary skill enabled him to secure passage of the major antipoverty and aid to education bills of the Kennedy and Johnson administrations. His arrogant stand against racism alienated powerful Democrats and caused the party to try unsuccessfully to purge him in 1958, but it made him a great hero to many blacks who rallied to his cause, renominating and reelecting him by an overwhelming majority. Excluded from his seat on the grounds that he had misused funds, he won reelection in a special election in 1967 and in the regular election of 1968. Stripped of his seniority in 1969, he lost the Democratic primary in June 1970 to Charles B. Rangel, who was later elected congressman. Powell became pastor of the Abyssinian Baptist Church (1937), the first black ever to serve on the City Council in New York (1941), and founder and editor of the militant *The People's Voice* (1942).

POWELL, ADAM CLAYTON, SR.

Clergyman (1865-1953). He founded America's largest black congregation, the Abyssinian Baptist Church of New York City. He wrote many pamphlets on civil rights and religion. His books include an autobiography *(Against the Tide,* 1938), *Saints in Caesar's Household* (1939), and *Picketing Hell* (1942).

POWELL, C. P.

Publisher of the *New Amsterdam News.*

POWELL, WILLIAM FRANK

Educator and diplomat (1844-1921). After graduating from the Collegiate Institute of New York City, he taught in private and public schools, where he experimented with practice teaching (having normal school students participate in a classroom situation). In 1897 he was appointed minister to Haiti.

POYAS, PETER

One of Denmark Vesey's co-conspirators. A slave of extra-ordinary ability, he was selected as the leader's lieutenant. See Vesey, Denmark.

PRATTIS, PERCIVAL L.

Journalist (b. 1895). He worked for the Chicago *Defender,* the *Amsterdam News,* and the Pittsburgh *Courier.* His assignments took him to Europe and the Middle East.

PRAYER PILGRIMAGE

In 1957, on the third anniversary of the U. S. supreme court decision outlawing segregation in public schools (May 17), a crowd of 15,000 from more than 30 states assembled at the Lincoln Memorial in Washington, D. C., to dramatize the need to enforce the decision.

PREJEAN, CHARLES

Leader in the cooperative movement. He is executive director of the Federation of Southern Cooperatives.

PREJUDICE, ORIGIN OF

In the English colonies, the legal definition of slavery, incorporating the twin features of lifelong servitude and inheritance of status, was a formality that came later. In contrast, under the Latin, Spanish and Portuguese system, permeated by religious concern for the Negro as a person, slaves who achieved their freedom were no longer victims of discrimination.

In a recent article, 'Slavery and the Genesis of American Race Prejudice' *(Comparative Studies in Society and History,* II, October 1959), Carl Degler insists that prejudice against blacks was already established in Bermuda, Barbados, and New Providence, and that the American colonists simply accepted the attitudes of their compatriots. It would seem, he writes, 'that instead of slavery being the root of the discrimination visited upon the Negro in America,' it complemented colonial discrimination 'against the outsider.'

358

PRESIDENT'S COMMITTEE ON CIVIL RIGHTS

President Harry S. Truman's Executive Order 9808, issued in December 1946, empowered the PCCR to investigate and report on the status of civil rights. Though the proposals submitted the following year were rejected by Congress, they reflected the goals sought by interracial reformers of the time and during the twenty years that followed. The comprehensive and far-reaching recommendations of the committee were titled *To Secure these Rights.*

PRESS

The development of the black press has been an important element in the struggle for full equality in the national life and culture. *Freedom's Journal* (1827-30) was the first publication to champion militant abolitionism. In 1837 Samuel E. Cornish, who had been its co-editor, became editor of another New York City newspaper, *The Weekly Advocate.* Several such periodicals were started in the 1840s and 1950s, including Frederick Douglass' *North Star* (1847). Renamed *Frederick Douglass' Paper* in 1850, it continued until 1864. Some 30 newspapers were launched by blacks before 1863, but only a few lasted more than a year or two. The only one which survives from this period is the *Christian Recorder* (1852). Among those read by free negroes were the *Colored American* (New York, 1837), the *Elevator* (Albany, 1842), *Genius of Freedom* (New York, 1842), the *Ram's Horn* (New York, 1847), and the *Alienated American* (Cleveland, 1852). From Emancipation to the close of the century, negro newspapers were only moderately more successful, even though some 50 were launched. These included the *California Eagle* (Los Angeles, 1870), the *Savannah Tribune* (Georgia, 1875), *The Conservator* (Chicago, 1878), *The Planet* (Richmond, Virginia, 1884), the *New York Age* (1885), and the *Cleveland Gazette* (1883), the Philadelphia *Tribune* (1884), and the Baltimore *Afro-American* (1892). Then came the Norfolk *Journal and Guide* (1900), the Chicago *Defender* (1905), the *Amsterdam News* (1909), and the Pittsburgh *Courier* (1910). By the beginning of the 1960s, 400 black periodicals were being published across the nation. Scholarly black journals include the *Journal of Negro*

Education, Journal of Negro History, Negro College Quarterly, Negro History Bulletin, Phylon, Afro-American Studies, and the *Quarterly Review of Higher Education Among Negroes.* Action journals dealing mainly with the social, political, and economic welfare of blacks include *Crisis, Opportunity, Negro Digest, Negro Quarterly, Encore,* and *Racial Digest.* Successful pictorial magazines include *Brown American, Color, Criterion, Ebony,* and *Our World.* Newspapers owned and published by blacks came into their own as an important channel of mass communication early in the 20th century. Organized militancy found expression in the Boston *Guardian* (1901), but it was the Chicago *Defender* that set the pattern for other militant organs. The earliest survey of the black press in the U. S., beginning with the pre-Civil War era, is I. Garland Penn's *The Afro-American Press and Its Editors* (1891). In *Black Bourgeoisie* (1957) E. Franklin Frazier maintained that the negro press, one of the most successful of all black business enterprises, created and perpetuated a world of make-believe for middle-class society.

PRICE, JOHN

Fugitive slave rescued by students and a professor of Oberlin College, Ohio, after his seizure by slave-catchers in 1858.

PRICE, LEONTYNE

Operatic soprano (b. 1927). One of the great sopranos in the history of opera, she became the reigning prima donna of the Metropolitan Opera Company. Born Mary Leontyne Price in Laurel, Mississippi, she attended Wilberforce University and Juilliard School of Music. She performed as Saint Cecilia in an all-black Broadway revival of Virgil Thompson's *Four Saints in Three Acts* (1952), as Bess in a revival of *Porgy and Bess* (1952-54), made her Town Hall concert debut (1954), appeared with American and European operatic companies, and scored a great triumph in her first appearance with the Metropolitan Opera, as Countess Leonora in Verdi's Il Trovatore, on January 27, 1961. She married concert baritone William Warfield in 1952.

PRIGG V. PENNSYLVANIA

An 1842 decision of the U. S. supreme court upholding the constitutionality of the Fugitive Slave Act of 1793 but stipulating that state officials did not have to help return fugitives.

PRILLERMAN, BYRD

Educator (b. 1859). One of the founders of West Virginia State College (1891), which he later headed (1909), he helped to organize the West Virginia Teachers' Association and became a member of the National Education Association (1891).

PRIMUS, PEARL

Anthropologist and dancer (b. 1921).

PROCTOR, SAMUEL D.

Public official (b. 1921). He served as director of the Peace Corps in Nigeria (1961), as associate director of the Peace Corps (1962), and as regional director of the Office of Economic Opportunity (1964-65).

PROJECT C

Name given to the plan formulated by Martin Luther King, Jr. and his aides, Wyatt Walker and Fred Shuttlesworth, to promote civil rights causes in Birmingham, Alabama, in the late summer of 1962. 'C' stood for confrontation. 'Commandments for the Volunteers' defined the behavior of participants. The Birmingham Manifesto explained the SCLC's demands: fair hiring practices, desegregation of public facilities, and the establishment of a biracial committee to settle grievances. Early in 1963 the SCLC movement forces went into action. Thousands of demonstrators were jailed before white leaders agreed, on May 10, to meet the demands of the black leaders. The next night segregationists caused widescale rioting that had repercussions throughout the nation. President John F. Kennedy made an inspired speech that King called 'the most earnest, human and profound appeal for understanding that any president has uttered since the first days of the Republic.' Subsequently Kennedy submitted to Congress the most far-reaching legislation on civil rights since Reconstruction.

PROPHET CHERRY
Cult leader. See Church of God.

PROPHET JONES
See Jones, James F.

PROSSER, GABRIEL
Militant (1775-1800). He plotted a revolt of several thousand slaves on August 30, 1800. His plan was betrayed and the Richmond, Virginia, uprising was never accomplished.

PROVIDENT HOSPITAL
Chicago hospital founded by Daniel Hale Williams, who performed the world's first successful heart surgery there on July 9, 1893. It was the first American hospital operated by blacks. It inspired blacks to establish similar hospitals in many other cities.

PUBLIC OFFICIALS
In 1970, according to the Voter Education Project of Atlanta, 665 blacks held elective office in the South, and 1500, including 48 mayors, held office in the nation. See Mayors.

PUNCH, JOHN
One of three Jamestown, Virginia, servants caught in flight. The two white servants were forced to serve an additional four years, but Punch had to 'serve his master or his assigns for the time of his natural Life here or elsewhere.' The 1640 case foreshadowed the coming of slavery.

PURIFOY
Athlete (b. 1924). In 1945, while a student at Tuskegee, she won the national AAU 80-meter hurdle championship.

PURLIE VICTORIUS

Play by Ossie Davis, later filmed under the title *Gone are the Days*. In a series of satirical portraits the play parodies the racial situation. Davis describes it as 'the adventures of Negro manhood in search of itself in a world for white folks only.' The support of black audiences caused him to turn from integrationism to the view that black people can avoid 'artistic prostitution' and 'begin to take a truly independent position within the confines of American culture.'

PURVIS, ROBERT

Abolitionist (1810-1898). One of the founders of the American Anti-Slavery Society in Pennsylvania, he was the only black abolitionist with money. He used both his pen and his purse to support many worthy causes, but he opposed attempts to encourage emigration to Africa.

PUSH

See People United to Save Humanity.

Q

QUAKERS

Besides spearheading the abolitionist movement and being involved in humanitarian and antislavery work from the earliest years of slavery in America, they established schools for negroes and by 1808 had instituted a system of individualized instruction on a familial basis, designed to prepare slaves for manumission.

QUARLES, BENJAMIN

Historian (b. 1904). After receiving his doctorate from the University of Wisconsin in 1940, he taught history and served as dean of instruction at Dillard University, was appointed professor at Morgan State College, and produced a number of scholarly works: *Frederick Douglass,* (1948), *The Negro in the Civil War* (1952), *The Negro in the American Revolution* (1961), and *Lincoln and the Negro* (1962). He is a contributing editor to *Phylon* and an associate editor of the *Journal of Negro History.*

QUINLAND, WILLIAM S.

Appointed professor of pathology at Meharry in 1922, he taught there and headed the department for a quarter of a century. Born in the British West Indies, he graduated from Meharry, then studied bacteriology and pathology at Harvard under the first Rosenwald medical scholarship.

QUOCK WALKER CASE

Legal case heard in Massachusetts in 1783 involving the punishment of a slave. See Commonwealth v. Jennison.

R

RABBIT FOOT MINSTRELS
See Rainey, Gertrude.

RACE RELATIONS INFORMATION CENTER
Data-gathering center established by a grant from the Ford Foundation and headquartered in Nashville, Tennessee.

RACE RIOTS
Emancipation ushered in the first massive outbreaks of violence against blacks. The killing of blacks particularly those who had helped the Union forces, occurred throughout the South as an aftermath of the Civil War. Exceptionally brutal were massive attacks on blacks in Memphis and New Orleans in 1866, and the Meridian, Mississippi, massacre of 1871. Urbanization at the beginning of the 20th century was a factor in racial violence in Springfield, Ohio (1904 and again in 1906), Atlanta and Brownsville (1906), and Springfield, Illinois (1908). Mob violence erupted in East St. Louis, Illinois, and in Houston, Texas, in 1917. During the 'Red Summer' (1919) riots occurred in 25 cities, North and South, and assumed monstrous forms in Longview, Texas, Washington, D. C., and Chicago. In 1921 racial strife engulfed Tulsa, Oklahoma. During World War II black troops were trained in small groups at separate locations to avoid explosive confrontations between black servicemen and white civilians. In 1943 riots occurred in Detroit, Los Angeles, and Beaumont, Texas. On a smaller scale, there was rioting in New York and in several southern cities. In 1965 the worst rioting

since 1917 destroyed Watts, the black ghetto section of Los Angeles and brought comfort only to the Black Power activists who accept Marcus Garvey's thesis that riots 'work to our advantage by teaching the Negro that he must build a civilization of his own or forever remain the white man's victim.' In 1967 rioting in Newark, Detroit, and other cities was partially responsible for the ascendancy of a 'white backlash' calling for a slow-down in integration and the exercise of civil rights.

RACKLEY, ALEX

Black Panther (d. 1969). Two other Panthers, Bobby G. Seale and Ericka Huggins, were charged with crimes arising from his death. At the New Haven trial, which ended in a mistrial, the state charged that Rackley had been killed because the party leadership considered him an informer.

RAIMOND, JULIEN

Haitian journalist. During the American Revolution, he offered to provide a brigade of mulattoes for the Continental Army.

RAINEY, GERTRUDE

Pioneer blues singer (1886-1939). 'Ma' Rainey's Rabbit Foot Minstrels performed at tent shows and carnivals that barnstormed the southern states. She began recording in 1923. Her most famous protegée was Bessie Smith.

RAINEY, JOSEPH H.

Public official (1832-1887). A delegate to the state constitutional convention in 1868 and to the state senate in 1870, he was the first black U. S. congressman from South Carolina, 1871-79.

RAISIN IN THE SUN, A

Play by Lorraine Hansberry. The first Broadway play by a negro woman starred Sidney Poitier (and later Ossie Davis) and focused on the dreams of ghetto dwellers. The play received the Drama Critics Circle award for 1958-59.

RANDALL, DUDLEY

Writer (b. 1914). Prominent in the Detroit circle of poets, he won Tompkins Awards in 1962 and 1966. He worked with other poets in the Boone House cultural center in Detroit, and in 1965 founded the Broadside Press to publish single poems suitable for framing. In 1966, in Moscow, he read his own translations of Russian poetry into English. He was responsible for bringing to public attention poets like Etheridge Knight, James Emanuel, Keorapetse Kgositsile, Sanchez, and Giovanni.

RANDOLPH, ASA PHILIP

Labor leader (b. 1889). One of the most revered leaders in the civil rights movement, he is founding president of the Brotherhood of Sleeping Car Porters, the first black union chartered by a major labor federation. Born in Crescent City, Florida, where his father was a minister, he attended Cookman Institute in Jacksonville, then migrated to New York City. He worked at various jobs while taking evening courses at City College. With Chandler Owen, he founded *The Messenger*. Until 1925 he considered himself primarily an editor and writer. That year he began to organize Pullman workers. In August 1925 he organized the Brotherhood of Sleeping Car Porters and made The Messenger its official organ. A radical and a socialist but never a Communist, he was jailed briefly in 1918 for refusing to serve in World War I, and he advocated nonviolent protest demonstrations as early as 1940. He was one of the organizers of the 1941 March on Washington that persuaded President Franklin D. Roosevelt to end job discrimination in the defense industry and set up the FEPC. He became a vice president of the AFL-CIO in 1957. He retired as president of the Brotherhood in 1968 to devote his time to the A. Philip Randolph Institute.

RANDOLPH, VIRGINIA E.

Teacher. Working with a negro shcool in Henrico County, Virginia, at the turn of the century, she became the forerunner of legions of teachers using Jeanes Foundation funds to improve rural schools, promote community welfare, and involve pupils in applying in their everyday environment what they learned from books.

RANGEL, CHARLES B.

Public official. In 1970 he took his seat as U. S. congressman from New York.

RANGER, JOSEPH

Patriot. A freeborn black from Northumberland, he enlisted in the Virginia navy in 1776 and served with distinction until 1787, when Virginia disposed of its last vessel.

RANSIER, ALONZO J.

Public official. Self-educated, he served as chairman of the South Carolina Republican executive committee and lieutenant governor before winning election as U. S. congressman.

RAPIER, JAMES THOMAS

Public official (1840-1883). Educated and admitted to the bar in Canada, he returned to the South after the Civil War as a newspaper correspondent, then bought land and became a wealthy Alabama cotton planter. He attended the constitutional convention of 1867, tried unsuccessfully to become secretary of state (1870), won election as a Republican representative to the 43rd Congress.

RAY, CHARLES

Abolitionist (1807-1886). A minister, he is best known for his work as publisher of The Colored American and president of the New York Society for the Promotion of Education Among Colored Children.

RAY, CHARLOTTE E.

Lawyer. The first black woman lawyer as well as the first American woman to graduate from a university law school (Howard, February 27, 1872), she was admitted to the bar on April 23, 1872.

RAYNER, JOHN B.

Populist (1850-1918). The son of a North Carolina plantation owner and a slave woman, he taught and preached before becoming involved in politics. He moved to Texas and became active in the populist movement, serving without pay as a member of the state executive committee and a regular lecturer. His name appeared often in The Southern Mercury, 1894-96. In 1898 he helped to organize a black military unit. After World War I broke out, he urged government officials to enlist black servicemen. His last years were devoted to writing his philosophy of the role of the negro in society.

REASON, CHARLES L.

Poet, scholar, and educator (1818-1898). Some critics consider his long poem 'Freedom' the best poem written by a negro before the Civil War. His reputation for scholarship won him an appointment at Central College, in McGrawville, New York, in 1844. He was also responsible for establishing the Institute for Colored Youth in Philadelphia.

REASON, PATRICK

Artist. He was a portrait painter and engraver of the 1850s.

RECONSTRUCTION

Period in American history roughly spanning the decade 1867-77 when the first real attempt was made to establish an interracial democracy. Though the history of this period has been a matter of extreme controversy, it now seems clear that the political reorganization of the secessionist state governments accomplished through the Reconstruction Acts of March 2 and March 23, 1867, with the subsequent election of black legislators in every Southern state, represented an attempt on a scale never before envisioned to accomplish a social and economic revolution. In an unprecedented racial experiment, former slaves were enfranchised and given their civil rights as the national purpose was restated through legislative acts and constitutional amendments. Before federal troops were withdrawn from the South following the disputed presidential election of 1876, black men had been lifted to a position of real political power, having served as legislators at every level of government, as lieutenant governors, and as cabinet officers. Until recently most white historians treated Reconstruction as 'a soul-sickening spectacle' of graft, inefficiency, and military inefficiency. Students of William A. Dunning of Columbia University wrote many basic works on reconstruction in the Southern states. According to the Dunning interpretation, which prevailed until the 1960s, the South was repentant and willing to treat freedmen decently; Andrew Johnson was an unselfish champion of constitutional principles and a faithful advocate of Lincoln's reconstruction plan; vindictive, self-seeking radical Republicans were responsible for enacting a program of doubtful constitutionality giving uneducated freedmen political power, allowing Carpetbaggers and Scalawags to bring the South to ruin, and inciting suffering whites to resort to violence and intimidation in order to overthrow corrupt regimes. Woodrow Wilson, the champion of democracy throughout the world, went so far as to refer to blacks of the Reconstruction era as 'a host of dusky children untimely put out of school.' In recent years historians, rejecting the Channing interpretation and electing instead to follow the course charted by W. E. B. Du Bois and other black scholars, have tried to offset white-oriented distortions by preparing a series of remarkable studies. See Eric McKitrick, *Andrew Johnson and Reconstruction* (1960); John Hope Franklin, *Reconstruction after the Civil War* (1961); Kenneth Stampp, *The Era of Reconstruction, 1865-1887* (1965); Rembert Patrick, *The Reconstruction of the Nation* (1967); Lerone Bennett Jr., *Black Power U. S. A.: The Human Side of Reconstruction, 1867-1877* (1967); and Rayford W. Logan, *The Betrayal of the Negro* (1968).

RECONSTRUCTION ACTS

Passed by a Republican-controlled Congress dominated by the radical wing, and by a vote that immunized the veto power of President Andrew Johnson, the Reconstruction Acts of March 2, and March 23, 1867, divided the South (except Tennessee) into five military districts, each commanded by a major general whose instructions were to prepare his province for readmission to the Union. The March 2 act gave former slaves the right to take part in the reconstructed governments of the southern states.

RECONSTRUCTION CONGRESS
During the Reconstruction period, 22 negro congressmen held office. Two of these, Hiram R. Revels and Blanche K. Bruce, served as U. S. Senators from Mississippi. South Carolina sent eight negroes to Washington, North Carolina four, Alabama three, and Florida, Georgia, Louisiana, Mississippi, and Virginia one apiece. Thirteen of them were ex-slaves, five were college graduates, and five others had some college training. Negro congressmen generally were moderate in their demands and judicious in their conduct as legislators. See Congressmen, Black; consult John Hope Franklin, *Reconstruction After the Civil War* (1961).

RED COTTAGE SCHOOL
First school for contraband blacks, established by Mary Smith Peake in Hampton, Virginia, in September 1961.

RED RECORD
The first serious statistical treatment of lynching, it was written in 1895 by Ida B. Wells.

RED SUMMER
Name given by James Weldon Johnson, then serving as an NAACP field secretary, to the summer of 1919, when race riots occurred throughout the nation, in cities as large as Washington and Chicago and as small as Elaine, Arkansas, and Longview, Texas. In June the U. S. Provost Guard had to be called in to restore order in the nation's capital. That same month whites burned the negro section of Longview. Rioting caused by the drowning of 17-year-old Eugene Williams, who had entered a part of Lake Michigan used by whites, resulted in appalling casualties in Chicago: 23 blacks and 15 whites were dead; 537 persons were injured; more than 1,000 families were left homeless.

373

In Elaine farmers attempting to organize a union in order to get better prices for their cotton were confronted by a deputy sheriff and a posse. In the aftermath to the killing of the deputy, more than 100 blacks were killed or injured, 79 were brought to trial, and 12 were sentenced to die. The NAACP succeeded in reversing the conviction of the 12 men, and by 1925 had won the freedom of the last of the imprisoned 67.

REDDICK, L. D.

Historian (b. 1910). At the twenty-first annual meeting of the ASNLH, held at Petersburg, Virginia, October 24, 1936, he delivered an address on 'A New Interpretation for Negro History.' He called attention to the need for research into the origins of slavery and slave uprising, and he asked his colleagues to draw up a new 'catalog of the determinative influences affecting Negro life and re-examine the social philosophy implicit throughout the work.' He is the author of *Crusader Without Violence: Biography of Martin Luther King* (1959).

REDDING, J. SAUNDERS

Educator and writer (b. 1906). A social critic of negro life in America, he held several appointments before settling at Hampton Institute in 1943 as professor of creative literature. His books include *To Make a Poet Black* (1939), *No Day of Triumph* (1942), *Stranger and Alone* (1950), and *The Lonesome Road* (1958). *Stranger and Alone* is a critique of social life among American blacks. Redding exposes conditions in negro colleges and develops the theme that education trains the negro for failure by aiming at keeping him submissive.

REDDING, OTIS

Musician (1941-1967). 'Sitting on the Dock of the Bay' was one of the singer's most popular recordings. Other hits were 'Pain in My Heart' and 'Try a Little Tenderness.'

REED, ADOLPH L., JR.

Black nationalist. Born in New York City, he is Field Representative for the Foundation for Community Development in Fayetteville, North Carolina. At the age of 24, he was awarded first prize in a Black Scholar contest for his essay 'Pan-Africanism —Ideology for Liberation.'

REED, CHARLES LENOX
Lawyer and public official (1866-1938). After serving a single term in the Massachusetts state legislature, he was appointed deputy collector of internal revenue (1898). He held other appointive offices and was active in community affairs.

REED, ISHMAEL
Writer. A poet associated with the New Harlem Renaissance, he is also the author of a novel, *The Free-Lance Pallbearers*.

REEVES, BASS
Lawman (d. 1910). Though illiterate, he served for many years as a U. S. deputy marshall in Indian Territory, acquiring a reputation second to none in the territory.

REFORMER, THE
Newspaper established by Washington Browne. See Grand United Order of True Reformers.

REID, IRA DE A.
Sociologist (b. 1901). He published the most serious study of the influence of West Indian blacks on American blacks *(The Negro Immigrant,* 1939).

REMOND, CHARLES LENOX
Abolitionist and orator (1810-1873). Born in Salem, Massachusetts, of free parents, he was the first black man to appear as a regular lecturer for the Anti-Slavery Society. He went to England in 1840 as a delegate to the World Anti-Slavery Convention. Two years later he spoke before the legislative committee of the Massachusetts house of representatives against segregation in

375

traveling accommodations. He was reputed to be most effective orator until Frederick Douglass surpassed him.

RENS
See New York Renaissance Big 5.

REPUBLIC OF NEW AFRICA
Political entity established by followers of Malcolm X. Delegates to the organizational meeting signed a declaration of independence stating that the black people of America were 'forever free and independent of the jurisdiction of the United States' and picked exiled Robert F. Williams as president, Milton R. Henry as vice president, and Richard B. Henry as minister of information. The republic was to be established on lands in the United States heavily populated by blacks. After Williams resigned his office, the separatist movement was headed by Imari Abubakari Obadele I (formerly known as Richard Henry). The Detroit-born movement tried unsuccessfully to establish a national capital near Jackson, Mississippi, as the first step in the conquest of Mississippi, Alabama, Georgia, Louisiana, and South Carolina.

RESURRECTION CITY
A number of temporary plywood shacks erected near Lincoln Memorial in Washington, D. C. in May 1968, to shelter the poor who were trying to persuade Congress to enact legislation to reduce poverty. See Poor People's Campaign.

REVELS, HIRAM R.
Educator and public official (1822-1901). He was born free in Fayetteville County, North Carolina and educated at the Quaker seminary in Union County, then at Knox College in Galesburg, Illinois. He became a minister in the AME church, a teacher, and a Freedmen's Bureau worker in Mississippi. He was elected to the state senate in 1869 and appointed the first black U. S. senator in 1870, filling the term vacated by Jefferson Davis. Afterwards he served as president of Alcorn College.

REVOLUTIONARY WAR
See American Revolution.

REYNOLDS, JOHN P.
Nineteenth-century medical practitioner. A member of the eclectic school that traced its origin back to the colonial period and stressed native remedies, he established a thriving practice in Zanesville, Ohio, and later in Vincennes, Indiana.

RHODE ISLAND REGIMENT
During the American Revolution some 350 free negroes and slaves made up the major part of a Rhode Island regiment that saw action at Fort Mercer, inflicting many casualties on their Hessian opponents. The slaves had been promised their freedom from masters who were paid for their services.

RHODES, TODD W.
Musician (b. 1900). His first band, organized in 1922, became the most popular black band of the mid-1920s. Another band which he formed in 1947 became popular in rhythm and blues circles.

RHUMBA
A dance of Afro-Spanish origin. Cuban negroes first performed it as a rural dance suggesting simple farm chores.

RHYTHM AND BLUES (ROCK AND ROLL)
With simple tunes, short phrases, and a simple but compelling rhythm featuring a heavily accented afterbeat, the music that captured the imagination of the nation's youth in the 1950s had existed in the 1920s as 'race music.' It has brought celebrity to many individuals and groups, including: LaVern Baker, The Supreme, The Ronettes, The Chiffons, The Marvelettes, The Drifters, The Temptations, The Four Tops, and The Contours.

RICHARD, CYPRIAN
See Slave owners.

377

RICHARD, FANNIE M.

Educator (1840-1923). The first black public school teacher in Detroit, she rendered 47 years of service to the profession. She worked courageously to bring about the integration of the public schools of Detroit, was active in community affairs, and served as the first president of the Phillis Wheatley Home for Aged Women.

RICHARDSON, SCOVEL

Jurist. Beginning in government service in 1940 as senior attorney in the Office of Price Administration, he became the presiding judge of the Third Division of the U. S. Customs Court in 1966.

RICHMOND, BILL

Athlete (1763-1829). Taken as a boy to England, he was the first black American to make a name for himself in boxing. He won 12 of 14 major bouts.

RIDDLE, JOHN T., JR.

Artist (b. 1933). He has lectured on the relation of art to great social protest movements of the past. He is noted for his strong yet sensitive portrayal of the black experience.

RILES, WILSON C.

Educator. As head of California's secondary education system, he became the highest ranking black educational administrator in the United States.

RILLIEUX, NORBERT

Machinist, engineer, and inventor (1806-1894). Born a slave in Louisiana he was educated in France. In 1846 he devised a vacuum cup which revolutionized the process of refining sugar. New Orleans rejected the method which he designed for handling sewage, but the nation's largest sugar manufacturers have placed a bronze tablet honoring him in the state museum of Louisiana.

RIVERS, FRANCIS E.

Civil rights leader and jurist (b. 1893). A Phi Beta Kappa graduate (Yale, 1915), he tried unsuccessfully to find employment with banking and insurance firms in New York City. He won a scholarship to Columbia University law school, was admitted to the bar (1922), served as Manhattan district attorney (1937-43) and as a justice of the city courts (1943-63), and won the right of membership in the American Bar Association. After Judge Rivers retired from the bench in 1963, he became president and chief policymaker of the NAACP legal defense and education fund (1965). He had previously served as vice president of this fund, which is the legal arm of the civil rights movement. Born in Kansas City, Kansas, he set two firsts in New York City: he was the first black man to be admitted to the bar association and the first to serve as a court justice.

ROBERTS v. BOSTON

The Massachusetts Supreme Court held in Roberts v. Boston (1849), despite an eloquent plea from Charles Sumner and a provision of the state constitution that 'all men, without distinction of color or race, are equal before the law,' that school segregation was neither illegal nor unreasonable. In 1855, however, the legislature ended school segregation throughout the state.

ROBERTS, BENJAMIN

In 1849 he filed the first integration suit on behalf of his daughter. The Massachusetts supreme court ruled against him, establishing the separate but equal precedent.

ROBERTS, E. P.

Physician. He was one of the first black doctors to serve in the clinics of the health department of New York City.

ROBERTS, FILMORE

Soldier. Detailed to carry the mail to Fort Gibson while serving with the Tenth Cavalry Regiment on the Great Plains in the winter of 1967-68, he died in a vain attempt to ford the Canadian River with his mail pouch.

ROBERTS, JOSEPH JENKINS

Statesman (1809-1876). Born in Virginia, he became the first president of Liberia in 1847.

ROBERTS, NEEDHAM

Winner of the Croix de Guerre. See Johnson, Henry.

ROBERTSON, OSCAR

Athlete. After compiling a record unequaled in basketball history at the University of Cincinnati (scoring a total of 2,987 points in three seasons and averaging 33.8 points per game), he signed with the Cincinnati Royals and soon achieved the reputation of being one of the greatest all-around players of all time.

ROBESON, PAUL

Actor (b. 1898). Excelling as an actor, singer, and athlete, Robeson is also a Phi Beta Kappa, a lawyer, and a leader in civil rights struggles. He made the All-American Football Team of 1918, received a law degree from Columbia University in 1923, played the leading role in Emperor Jones in London in 1925, sang in Florenz Ziegfield's production of Show Boat in 1928, performed as Othello in London in 1930 and in America in 1934 and 1943, starred in The Hairy Ape in London in 1931, and played the leading role in the film production of Emperor Jones in 1933. He lived in Russia from the late forties through the mid-sixties. Though he sustained financial losses, experienced ostracism, and suffered political persecution, he refused to compromise his beliefs and continued to speak out against oppression. In his book *Here I Stand* (1958) he outlined a program of action for negroes.

ROBINSON, BERNARD W.

First black commissioned in the U. S. navy (1942). The Harvard medical student was made an ensign in the U. S. naval reserve.

380

ROBINSON, BILL 'BOJANGLES'

Entertainer (1878-1949). The nation's first great tap dancer and inventor of the stair tap dance (moving up and down steps in a rhythmic pattern) delighted millions who witnessed his spectacular performances in Broadway musicals and in Hollywood movies. He was born Luther Robinson in Richmond, Virginia, but changed his name to Bill and later was nicknamed Bojangles as a vaudeville headliner at the Palace Theater in New York. He danced onto the legitimate stage in 1928, appearing in Liberty Theater's production of *Blackbirds*. During the 1930s he made 14 pictures for major studios, co-starring in some of them with Shirley Temple. In 1943 he starred in *Stormy Weather*.

ROBINSON, BILLY

Writer and activist in the black liberation movement. Born in the Chicago ghetto in 1935, he has spent much of his life in prison, following early addiction to drugs and alcohol.

ROBINSON, EDDIE

As head football coach at Grambling College, he has interested many young men in professional football careers. See Grambling College.

ROBINSON, FRANK

Athlete. In 1966 he led the Baltimore Orioles to a pennant and a World Series victory, becoming the first man since 1956 to win the triple crown (batting, runs-batted-in, and home runs) and the first man ever to win the Most Valuable Player award in both the National League and the American League.

ROBINSON, HILYARD R.

Architect and educator. He taught at Howard University, where he was chairman of the architecture department, and held important appointments during President Franklin D. Roosevelt's administration. He specialized in slum clearance and public housing projects.

ROBINSON, JACKIE

Athlete (1919-1972). Born Roosevelt Robinson on a Georgia sharecropper's farm, he was elected to the baseball Hall of Fame in 1962. The first black player to enter major league baseball in modern times, he was hired by Branch Rickey, white owner of the Brooklyn Dodgers, on April 18, 1946. Chosen to 'break the color barrier,' he accepted the challenge courageously, won the Rookie of the Year award, and two years later was named the National League's Most Valuable Player. Still, his greatest achievement was in focusing public attention on the black athlete. His experiences are recorded in *Baseball Has Done It* (1964) and *I never Had It Made* (1972).

ROBINSON, JAMES

Patriot (1753-1868). He received a gold medal from Lafayette for military valor in the battle of Yorktown but not the freedom promised him by his master before the latter's death. Sold on the New Orleans slave market, he answered General Andrew Jackson's call for volunteers to defend the city against the British in the War of 1812, then returned to the life of a plantation slave until Emancipation, when he moved to Detroit.

ROBINSON, SPOTTSWOOD W., III

Jurist (b. 1916). He was the first black district judge in the District of Columbia.

ROBINSON, SUGAR RAY

Athlete (b. 1920). Born Walker Smith in Detroit, he was called by many the greatest boxer who ever lived. In 1949 he won the middleweight championship of the world.

ROBINSON, ZUE

Musician. A leading and influential slide trombone player, he performed with the New Orleans Olympia Band.

ROCHESTER

See Anderson, Eddie.

ROCK AND ROLL
See Rhythm and Blues.

ROCK MUSIC
According to Charles Reich *(The Greening of America,* 1970), rock music has become for American youth 'the chief means by which inner feelings are communicated. It combines elements from various sources, including the blues. Reich maintains that a spontaneous transformation occurred in the mix-sixties as white rock groups began experimenting with the blues, combining elements from this art form and jazz with elements from Indian ragas, country music, and even more diverse sources.

ROCK, JOHN S.
Lawyer. He was the first black man admitted to practice before the U. S. Supreme Court (February 1, 1865). A native of Salem, New Jersey, he practiced both dentistry and medicine before his health forced him to give up his practice and study law. One of the best educated blacks of his day, he was fluent in both French and German.

RODGERS, DANIEL
California pioneer. He traveled to California as a slave, bought his freedom, and settled with his family in the area of Watsonville. His descendants were active in the San Francisco area.

RODGERS, MOSES
Pioneer and mining engineer (d. 1890). Born a slave in Missouri, he arrived in California at the peak of the gold rush and soon acquired a reputation as a metallurgist and mining expert. He established his family in Stockton, where he successfully drilled for gas.

ROGERS, CHARLES C.
Hero. Lt. Col. Rogers was the highest ranking officer to win the congressional Medal of Honor in Vietnam. He was cited for heroism as commander of an artillery battery in 1968. Later

he attended the Army War College, then requested assignment
to Germany in the hope that he could help ease tensions felt
by many black soldiers in Europe.

ROGUES, CHARLES
See Slave owners.

ROLLA
One of the conspirators in the plot to capture Charleston, South
Carolina, in 1812. He was presumably to have led a band charged
with killing Governor Bennett Mills. See Vesey, Denmark.

ROLLINS, BERNARD HASSEL
Artist. A talented young West Coast artist and designer, he
was born and educated in New York City. He is art director for
Soul Illustrated, an associate of Progressive Black Associates, and
art director for *Black History in Calendar Form.*

ROLLINS, CHARLEMAE
Writer (b. 1897). She worked as a librarian but also found
time to lecture and write. Her books include They Showed the
Way (1964) and Famous American Negro Poets (1965).

ROLLINS, F. W.
Businessman (b. 1849). He operated a painting business in
Chicago, made shrewd investments, and left a $100,000 estate
to his sons.

ROMAN, CHARLES V.
Physician. Born in Pennsylvania, he was reared in Canada but
spent most of his life in the South. A graduate of Meharry
Medical School (1890), he practiced in Dallas, Texas, headed the
department of ophthalmology and otolaryngology at Meharry, and
edited the *Journal of the National Medical Association* (1909).

ROSE, ARNOLD M.
Sociologist (1918-1968). Born in Chicago, he taught sociology

at the University of Minnesota. His books include *The Negro in America* (1948) and *The Negro's Morale: Group Identification and Protest* (1949).

ROSENWALD FUND

Beginning in 1911, Julius Rosenwald offered to help provide school buildings in the rural South. By 1932 he had contributed over $4,000,000 to the construction of such schools. A fund bearing his name was established in 1928. Its sole purpose is to promote negro education.

ROSS, ARAMINTA

See Tubman, Harriet.

ROWAN, CARL T.

Public official and journalist (b. 1925). The only journalist to win three successive Sigma Delta Chi awards for reporting, he was also the first black to serve on the National Security Council. One of five children born to a poor family in Ravenscroft, Tennessee, he attended college in Nashville, became a communications officer in the Navy, and earned a master's degree in journalism at the University of Minnesota while writing for the Minneapolis *Spokesman* and the St. Paul *Recorder*. He became a general assignment reporter for the Minneapolis *Tribune,* toured the South to write a series of articles later expanded into *South of Freedom* (1952), traveled to India as an international exchange lecturer for the state department and recorded his observations in *The Pitiful and the Proud* (1956), and returned to the South to gather material for *Go South to Sorrow* (1957). He won the 1954 Sigma Delta Chi award for reporting on school segregation cases, the 1955 award for his articles on India, and the 1956 award for coverage of affairs in Southeast Asia. He was deputy assistant secretary of state for public affairs, 1961-63, ambassador to Finland, 1963-64, and head of the United States Information Agency (1964-65). His column appears in the Chicago Daily News and is nationally syndicated.

385

RUCKER, HENRY A.

Public official. In 1883 he became a clerk for the Internal Revenue Service in Georgia. In 1897 he was appointed revenue collector for the district of Georgia.

RUDOLPH, WILMA

Athlete (b. 1940). Known as the world's fastest woman runner, she won three Olympic gold medals in 1960.

RUFFIN, GEORGE LEWIS

Jurist (1834-1886). A graduate of the Harvard law school (1869), he held elected offices before being named judge of the district court of Charleston, Massachusetts.

RUFFIN, JOSEPHINE ST. PIERRE

Civic leader (1842-1924). In 1893 she organized the Women's Era Club of Boston. She called the first convention of the National Federation of Colored Women's Clubs and founded *Women's Era,* a monthly publication that endured for 10 years.

RUGGLES, DAVID

Medical practitioner (1810-1849). Known as the 'water-cure doctor,' he operated a successful hydrotherapeutic center in Northampton, 1846-49. An active abolitionist, he was editor and publisher of *The Mirror of Liberty* (New York, 1838). His quarterly was the nation's first black magazine. One of the first black men to escape slavery, he was reported to have helped more than six hundred others to escape from the southern states. In addition to his work with the underground railroad, he was active in the struggle for the social and political elevation of free negroes. He also owned a bookstore.

RUGGLES, DAVID

Dedicated reformer and secretary of the New York Vigilance Committee.

386

RUNAWAY SLAVES

Some slaves escaped into the wilderness and intermarried with Indians. Others banded together in gangs, in cities, on waterfronts, and in isolated areas. In New York City, for example, members of one notorious gang called themselves the Geneva Club; others were known as the Free Masons, the Smith Fly Boys, and the Long Bridge Boys. They represented a cross section of the entire slave population but shared the common tie of revulsion for a life of bondage.

RURAL SCHOOL FUND

Established by Anna T. Jeanes, a white Quaker philanthropist by a deed of trust drawn on April 22, 1907, the fund was to be expended to help the 'rural schools of the Southern U. S. Community.'

RUSHING, JIMMY

Blues singer (d. 1972). His highpitched voice and physique inspired the sobriquet and song 'Mr. Five by Five.' He recorded 'Harvard Blues' and other classics with Count Basie's band in the 1930s. He died at the age of 68.

RUSSELL, BILL

Athlete (b. 1934). A star basketball player and coach, he set many precedents during his 13-year career with the Boston Celtics. The greatest defensive player of all time, he revolutionized basketball style while leading his team to eight straight world championships. The blocked shot was the trademark of the only 5-time winner of the Podoloff Cup. In 1966 he became the first black to manage a major professional U. S. team. One of the first two blacks ever named to the NBA All-Star team (the other was Elgin Baylor), Louisiana-born William Felton Russell, a lifelong opponent of discrimination, retired in 1969 to devote more time to his rubber plantations in Liberia.

RUSSELL, HARVEY

Businessman (b. 1918). As vice president of the Pepsi-Cola

Corporation, he became the first black to hold such a position in a major international corporation. He was born in Louisville and educated at Kentucky State College in Frankfort, then at Indiana University. He went to work for Pepsi-Cola in 1950, following a successful career in sales with Graham Associates and the Rosa-Meta Cosmetics Company.

RUSSELL, LUIS

Musician. He led a band in New York in the 1920s. In 1929 he played at the Saratoga Club in Harlem. Playing with him were Henry Allen, Jay C. Higginbotham, and Charles Holmes.

RUSSELL, LOUIS B.

World's longest-living heart transplant recipient. The Terre Haute, Indiana, native received his new heart from the Medical College in Richmond Virginia. He teaches industrial arts at an Indianapolis junior high school.

RUSSELL, TOM

One of the conspirators in the plot to capture Charleston, South Carolina, in 1812. A mechanic, he made weapons for the conspirators. See Vesey, Denmark.

RUSSWORM, JOHN B.

Publisher and abolitionist (1799-1851). He was the first black college graduate (Bowdoin, 1826), co-editor of the first black newspaper in the United States *(Freedom's Journal* March, 1827), and the first superintendent of schools in Liberia. He also edited a paper titled *The Rights of All* (1828). He was born in Jamaica of a white American father.

RUSTIN, BAYARD

Civil rights leader (b. 1910). Born in Westchester, Pennsylvania, he completed his education at the City College of New York before beginning his long career of civil rights activity as a youth organizer for the 1941 March on Washington. Now executive secretary of the A. Philip Randolph Institute, dedicated

388

to the achievement of a better life for all oppressed and forgotten Americans, he is vitally concerned about racial injustice. He was jailed as a conscientious objector in World War II, jailed again for his participation in the first Freedom Ride in 1947, became field secretary of CORE, was an adviser to Martin Luther King, Jr., 1955-60, helped to organize the 1963 March on Washington, and was named executive secretary of the War Resisters' League. He rejects violence in favor of political action and social reform, with all Americans working toward a common goal.

S

SABLE, JEAN BAPTISTE POINTE DU
See De Sable, Jean.

SADAT-SINGH, WILMETH
Athlete. Reared in Harlem and adopted by a Hindu, he played football for Syracuse, 1937-38, then led his school to 14 straight victories in basketball, 1938-39.

SADDLER, SANDY
Athlete. He won the featherweight boxing title in 1949 by defeating Willie Pep, but lost it to Pep three months later. Recovering the title 18 months later, he reigned as undisputed king of the featherweights until his retirement in 1957.

ST. JOHN THE VINE
See Hickerson, John.

ST. CYR, JOHN A.
Musician (b. 1890). Best known for his recordings with Jelly Roll Martin in 1926, Johnny St. Cyr won the Record Changer All-Time All-Star poll in 1951 for banjo performances.

ST. LOUIS WOMAN
Play by Arna Bontemps and Countee Cullen (1946). Performed at the Martin Beck Theatre in New York City, with Ruby Hill playing the leading role, it was a hit.

ST. THOMAS PROTESTANT EPISCOPAL CHURCH
Organized with the help of Benjamin Rush, the first Protestant episcopal church for Negroes was received into the Anglican communion after it had been organized by Absalom Jones, its first pastor, in 1794.

SALEM, PETER
Revolutionary War hero (c. 1750-1816). He fought on the first day of the War for American Independence, was a hero at the Battle of Bunker Hill, and continued to serve in Massachusetts regiments throughout the Revolution. Born a slave in Framingham, he took his name from the birthplace of his master. A member of the Framingham Minute Men Company at the outbreak of the Revolution on April 19, 1775, he marched with his company to Concord and fought there. Later, on June 17, as the patriots were about to be defeated near Bunker Hill, Salem stepped forward and killed Major John Pitcairn, who had ordered them to surrender. By serving his country, Salem won his freedom.

SALVATION BY CHRIST WITH PENITENTIAL CRIES
Poem by Jupiter Hammon. It was probably the first published work by an American negro (1760).

SAMBA
A dance of Afro-Spanish origin. It derives from the quizomba, the wedding dance of Angola.

SAMMS, ADOLPHUS
Inventor. A sergeant in the U. S. army, he developed an 'air frame center support' making greater payloads possible by stripping rockets of unnecessary dead weight. He also has four patents on other aspects of rocketry.

SAMPSON
Pilot in the service of the British navy during the Revolution. He was highly regarded by his officers, who ordered him to a safe place below deck when they attacked Charleston in 1776.

SAMPSON, EDITH SPURLOCK

Jurist (b. 1901). In private practice, she specialized in criminal law and domestic relations. She served as probation officer in Chicago (1930-40), was appointed as alternate delegate to the United Nations in 1950, and became an associate judge of the Cook County circuit court in 1964. She was the first negro woman to be elected judge of a municipal court.

SAMPSON, JAMES DRAWBORN

Educator (b. 1801). Freed by his white father and established as a carpenter in Wilmington, North Carolina, he taught his apprentices to read and write even though he was violating the law by doing so. He married a free woman and established a school for their ten children and other negroes. One of his sons became a teacher at Wilberforce University, another became a prominent minister, his daughter Franconia numbered among her pupils Asa Spaulding and Arthur Moore, and his daughter Susie taught in the public schools of Washington, D. C. Sampson accumulated a fortune through his carpentry business.

SANDERSON, J. B.

California pioneer. He advocated schools for black youths in Oakland, Sacramento, San Francisco, and Stockton.

SAN JUAN HILL

Battle in which four negro units participated with distinction. See Black Regulars.

SANFORD, JOHN

Entertainer. See Foxx, Redd.

SAUNDERS, DORIS

Editor of a publishing company (b. 1921).

SAUNDERS, PRINCE

Statesman and diplomat (c. 1784-1839). A freeborn black, he was educated in Vermont. He taught in Connecticut and Mas-

393

sachusetts, joined the African Lodge of Masons, helped to found the Boston Belles Lettres Society, and helped to organize a school system in Haiti. He served the Haitian King Henri I (Christophe) as his special envoy to England. He is credited with writing Haiti's criminal code.

SAUNDERS, RAYMOND

Artist (b. 1934). His awards include the coveted Prix de Rome. His works appear in the collections of the Whitney Museum of American Art, the Pennsylvania Academy of Fine Arts, and the Addison Gallery of American Art in Andover, Massachusetts.

SAVAGE, AUGUSTA

Sculptor (1900-1962). She became interested in negro types and in 1939 was commissioned to produce a sculptural group symbolizing the negro's contribution to music. She sculptured many prominent Americans. One of her most successful works is 'The Negro Urchin.'

SAVOY, WILLARD

Writer (b. 1916). He is the author of Alien Land (1949).

SAYERS, GALE

Athlete (b. 1943). He set a new record in professional football, scoring a total of twenty-two touchdowns in one season, and he tied the all-time record by scoring six touchdowns in one game. He played as a halfback for the Chicago Bears.

SCARBOROUGH, WILLIAM S.

Educator and linguist (1852-1926). The first black classical scholar, he became president of Wilberforce University in 1908. Proficient in Latin, Greek, Hebrew, Sanskrit, and the Slavic languages, he was an AME minister, an able administrator, and a gifted lecturer. He wrote a Greek textbook and published Birds of Aristophanes.

394

SCHOOL DESEGREGATION CASES
See Brown v. Board of Education.

SCHUYLER, GEORGE
Writer (b. 1895). His works include *Black No More* (1931) and *Slaves Today* (1931). He was the editor of the *Pittsburgh Courier*. His daughter was the famous child prodigy, Philippa Schuyler.

SCHUYLER, PHILIPPA
Musician (1932-1967). A child prodigy, she had written two hundred musical pieces by the time she was fourteen. Fluent in French, Spanish, and Italian, she gave piano concerts throughout the world. Prior to her death in a plane crash in 1967, she had appeared as guest soloist with the major symphony orchestras.

SCLC
See Southern Christian Leadership Conference.

SCOBEL, JOHN
Civil War spy. The former slave of a Scotsman, he was well educated and resourceful. He assumed various disguises in order to carry out assignments at Dumfries, Fredericksburg, Leesburg, Manassas, and Centerville.

SCOTT, CHARLOTTE
In 1865 she contributed the first 5 dollars to be used to erect a monument to Abraham Lincoln. The monument proposed by the ex-slave now rests on a pedestal in Lincoln Park in the nation's capital and is called Emancipation. It was dedicated in 1876.

SCOTT, D. N. C.
Physician. The Montgomery, Alabama, physician was the first treasurer of the National Medical Association (1895).

SCOTT, DRED
Slave. His petition for freedom resulted in a controversial

U. S. supreme court ruling. He had been sold to Dr. John Emerson in 1835, taken from Missouri to free parts of the Louisiana Territory, and returned to his home state, where slavery was legal. He sued for his freedom but lost. Mrs. Emerson's second husband, abolitionist congressman Calvin C. Chaffee, managed to bring Scott's case to the attention of the federal courts by selling him to F. A. Sanford of New York and claiming that the litigants were 'citizens of different states.'

SCOTT, EMMET J.

Public official. In 1917 he was appointed confidential adviser to the U. S. secretary of war, representing black citizens in the nation's military efforts. He wrote the *Official History of the American Negro in the World War* (1919). He was also a confidential secretary to Booker T. Washington, a member of an American commission to Liberia, and director of the Tuskegee news bureau.

SCOTT, HUGH J.

Educator. Recently he became superintendent of schools in Washington, D. C.

SCOTT, NATHAN

Theologian. An enlightened critic of literature as well as theology, he moved into a concern for a 'theology of culture,' producing his most important work, *Modern Literature and the Religious Frontier* (1957). He was appointed chairman of the theology and literature department of the University of Chicago divinity school.

SCOTT, WILLIAM E.

Artist (1884-1964). He specialized in portraits but also won praise for his landscapes. One of his best oils, 'The Lord Will Provide,' is in the Harmon Foundation.

SCOTTSBORO CASES

Two sensational trials held in Scottsboro, Alabama, in 1932

and 1935. Nine negro youths accused of raping two white girls on a freight train went on trial in 1931. Eight were convicted and sentenced to death. The Alabama Supreme Court set aside one of the eight convictions. The case involving the remaining seven went to the U. S. supreme court. In Powell v. Alabama (1932) the Court ruled that they had been denied their constitutional right to counsel and ordered a new trial. In Norris v. Alabama (1935) the court ruled that the equal protection clause of the Fourteenth Amendment had been violated since negroes had been systematically excluded from the jury. Beclouding the whole issue was the propaganda campaign waged by the International Labor Defense, the legal arm of the American Negro Labor Congress. Communist agitators portrayed the youths as victims of racial injustice in a capitalistic society. Subsequently charges against five of the nine were dropped. Of the four who were retried and convicted in 1936 and 1937, three were later paroled. The fourth escaped but later died in a Michigan prison. Many historians agree that the only crime committed by the Scottsboro boys was that of being born black since more than reasonable doubt clouded the accusations made against them, and since one of their accusers was an admitted prostitute. See Haywood Patterson and Earl Conrad, *Scottsboro Boy* (1950).

SCRUGGS, RAMON

Businessman. A pioneering black corporate executive, he served for eight years as customer relations manager for Michigan Bell Telephone Company before becoming public relations manager for the parent company.

SEALE, BOBBY

Black Panther leader (b. 1937). Co-founder of the Panthers, he has become a hero to many ghetto blacks by fearlessly defying the forces that have long intimidated them. Born in Dallas, Texas, he moved to California at the age of 7, met Huey Newton at Merritt College in Oakland, and joined with him to found the Black Panther Party in October 1966. Party chairman Seale replaced Eldridge Cleaver as a speaker during the Chicago Democratic nominating convention of 1968 and was later tried, along with seven white radicals, for conspiracy to provoke disruptive demonstrations. He was given a four-year sentence for contempt of court and ordered to stand trial separately. He was also one of 13 Panthers charged in Connecticut with murdering Alex Rackley, an informer. The New Haven trial ended in a mistrial on May 24, 1971, when the jury was unable to reach a verdict. While in prison he wrote *Seize the Time*.

SEJOUR, VICTOR

Poet and dramatist (1817-1874). The New Orleans writer contributed to the collaborative anthology *Les Cenelles* (1845) but achieved his greatest fame in France, where 21 of his plays were produced. His father was French, his mother a quadroon.

SELIKA, MADAME MARIE

Taking her stage name from Meyerbeer's opera *L'Africaine*, Mrs. Sampson Williams created a furor in the 1880s with her marvelous coloratura voice. She gave successful concerts in Europe and America before settling down to teaching voice at the Martin-Smith school in Harlem.

SELMA

Alabama town that made headlines in 1965 as Ralph Bunche and Martin Luther King, Jr., led civil rights marchers from Selma to Montgomery to focus attention on racial discrimination and persuade Negro voters to register. The deaths of Jimmie Lee Jackson (February 26), the Reverend James Reeb (March 11), and Mrs. Viola Gregg Liuzzo (March 25) brought demands for new legislation against discrimination, culminating in the enactment of the Voting Rights Act of 1965.

SEMINOLE WAR

Conflicts (1817-18 and 1835-42) triggered by the capture and enslavement of Che-Cho-Ter (Morning Dew), black wife of Seminole chief Osceola.

SENGSTAKE, JOHN H.

Publisher (b. 1912). A nephew of Robert S. Abbott, he converted the semi-weekly Chicago *Defender* into a daily newspaper (1956).

SEPARATE BUT EQUAL

Doctrine that stood from 1896 to 1954 as the main legal obstacle to civil rights for negroes. See Plessy v. Ferguson.

SESSIONS, LUCY

Educator (d. 1910). A graduate of Oberlin College (1850), she was the first black woman in America to earn a college degree. During Reconstruction she taught school in the South. She died in Los Angeles.

SETTLE, JOSIAH T.

Public official (b. 1850). After receiving a degree from Howard law school and being admitted to practice before the U. S. supreme court, he returned to Mississippi and entered politics. He served as district attorney in the 12th judicial district, attended national political conventions, and won election in 1883 to the Mississippi legislature, as an independent candidate. After 1885 he developed a successful law practices in Memphis, Tennessee.

SHADRACH

See Jenkins, Frederick.

SHAFT

A major success in 1971, the film was directed by Gordon Parks. It dealt intimately and positively with the black experience.

SHARIFF, RAYMOND

Commander of the protective, militaristic group, the Fruit of Islam, formed by Wali Farad before his disappearance.

SHAW, LESLIE

Postmaster. As head of the Los Angeles post office, he is in charge of the third largest post office building in the world. He began his career as a janitor.

SHELLEY V. KRAEMER

Supreme Court decision (1948) affirming that the 'coercive power of government' may not be used to enforce a private agreement to maintain segregated housing patterns. The court held 'that in granting judicial enforcement of . . . restrictive agreements . . . , the States have denied petitioners the equal protection of the laws and that, therefore, the action of the state courts cannot stand.'

SHORT, BOBBY

Entertainer. Born in Danville, Illinois, he has been called the last of Manhattan's supersophisticated cafe troubadours. His autobiography is titled *Black and White Baby* (1971).

SHUFFLE ALONG

Written, composed, and directed by blacks, *Shuffle Along* (1921) made entertainment history and launched the Harlem Renaissance. Produced by composers Noble Sissle and Eubie Blake and the writing-comedian team of Flournoy Miller and Aubrey Lyles, the show provided both Florence Mills, who sang such hit songs as 'I'm Just Wild About Harry,' and Josephine Baker, who appeared in the chorus, with an opportunity to display their talents before huge audiences. The show ran a year at New York's 63rd Street Theater and for two more years on tour.

SHUTTLESWORTH, FRED L.

Civil rights leader. He has served as president of the Alabama Christian Movement and secretary of SCLC.

SICKNESS AND BURIAL SOCIETIES

Poor, landless blacks organized socities to meet the crises of life. These benevolent societies flourished after Emancipation, inspired by the spirit of Christian charity and bearing names such as 'Love and Charity,' 'Sons and Daughters of Esther,' and 'Brothers and Sister of Love.'

SIERRA LEONE

Settled in the late 18th century by liberated but destitute slaves from England, the territory became a base for enforcing abolition after Great Britain abolished the slave trade in 1807. In 1795, seven years after native chiefs had ceded the land to Captain John Taylor, a group of negroes in Providence, Rhode Island, unsuccessfully petitioned Zachary Macauley, acting governor, for permission to settle there. In 1815 Paul Cuffe transported 38 fellow negroes to Sierra Leone at his own expense. See Richard West, *Back to Africa; a History of Sierra Leone and Liberia* (1970).

SIFFORD, CHARLIE

Athlete. In 1952, at the age of 28, he began playing the professional golf tour. In 1957 he won his first major tournament (Long Beach Open). He was the first black golfer to have profited financially by endorsing particular brands of golfing equipment.

SIKI, BATTLING

Athlete (d. 1925). Described as a 'Senegalese Negro,' he became the first black to win the world's light heavyweight boxing title by knocking out Georges Carpentier in Paris on September 24, 1922.

SILL, WILLIAM

Key figure in the Philadelphia Vigilance Committee. His father gained his freedom by self-purchase, his mother by flight.

SILVERA, FRANK

Actor (b. 1914).

401

SIMMONS, SAMUEL J.

Assistant secretary of the U. S. Department of Housing and Urban Development.

SIMMS, WILLIE

Jockey (b. 1870). The first black jockey to win international acclaim, he rode five winners in six months at Sheepshead Bay in New York (1893) and again at Jerome Park (1894). He won the Kentucky Derby twice (on Ben Brush in 1896 and on Plaudit in 1898).

SIMONE, NINA

Musician. In the 1960s she injected heavy social messages into her original songs. A nightclub chanteuse, she wrote protest songs like 'Mississippi Goddam!, 'Four Women,' and 'To be Young, Gifted and Black,' inspired by her friend Lorraine Hansberry. The autobiography of the high priestess of soul, titled *Still Out in the Wind*, was scheduled for publication in 1973.

SIMPSON, GEORGINIA ROSA

In 1921 she became the first black American woman to receive a Ph. D. in the United States.

SIMPSON, O. J.

Athlete. Born Orenthal James Simpson and nicknamed 'Orange Juice,' the Southern California All-American halfback led the nation in rushing in 1967. The following year he won the Heisman trophy.

SIMPSON, WILLIAM H.

Artist (1830-1872). A popular portrait painter working in Boston, he showed unusual talent in painting children and family groups.

SINCLAIR, WILLIAM A.

Writer. An ex-slave from South Carolina, author of *The After-*

math of Slavery: A Study of the Condition and Environment of the American Negro (1905).

SINGLETON, BENJAMIN

Colonizationist (1809-1892). 'Pap' Singleton took the lead in promoting mass migrations of blacks from the South in the 1870s. He formed the Tennessee Real Estate and Homestead Association in 1869 and by 1880 had helped seven thousand negroes to leave the deep South. He and other negroes incorporated the Singleton Colony of Morris and Lyon Counties, Kansas, in 1879. It was one of many centers populated by refugees.

SIPUEL, ADA LOIS

Law students. In 1945 Miss Sipuel (now Mrs. Fisher) was denied admission to Oklahoma University law school. She won her battle before the state supreme court (Sipuel v. Board of Regents of University of Oklahoma, 1948), and opened the doors for other blacks throughout the land. Helping her were NAACP attorney Amos T. Hall, state NAACP president H. W. Williamson, and Thurgood Marshall.

SIPUL v. BOARD OF REGENTS

U. S. supreme court decision (1948) ordering the state of Oklahoma to provide Ada Louise Sipuel with a legal education.

SISSLE, NOBLE

Jazz band leader (b. 1889). A pioneer in the development of jazz, he wrote (with Eubie Blake) 'I'm Just Wild about Harry' for the musical show *Shuffle Along* (1921).

SISSON, TACK

Patriot. During the American Revolution, he executed commando raids and was one of the abductors of Major General Prescott, commander of British forces in Rhode Island (1177).

SIT-INS

Negroes had protested segregation since Reconstruction days

by occupying white sections of theaters and streetcars, but it was not until February 1, 1960, that the modern sit-in movement began. On that day four students kept their seats at a segregated lunch counter in Greensboro, North Carolina, after they were refused service. The counter was closed down, but the four students returned the next day. Soon CORE field workers arrived and conducted workshops devoted to the techniques of nonviolent protest. Students were taught not to laugh, curse, strike back, or display anger but to bear insult and pain with equanimity. The sit-in movement captured the imagination of southern negroes and stirred the conscience of the nation. Young whites and blacks joined the movement by the thousands during the next two years, enduring punishment and abuse as one eating place after another abandoned the practice of segregation. Their songs of freedom and love, particularly their theme song, 'We Shall Overcome,' were heard throughout the land.

SKINNER, ELLIOT P.

Public official. He was appointed ambassador to Upper Volta.

SLATER FUND

In 1882 John F. Slater set up a $1,000,000 fund for the 'uplifting of the lately emancipated population of the Southern states, and their posterity, by conferring upon them the blessings of Christian education.' The first president of the fund was Rutherford B. Hayes. The fund provided normal and industrial training for blacks in county training schools and in colleges throughout the South. It encouraged the construction of 5,295 new buildings, and established 384 county training schools in 13 southern states, 1914-30.

SLATER, FRED W.

Athlete and jurist (1899-1966). A native of Illinois, he was elected to the Chicago Municipal Court in 1948 and to the Superior Court in 1960. He became a Circuit Court judge in 1964. Earlier in his career, 'Duke' was the first negro player to be named (in 1954) to the National Football League's Hall of Fame.

SLAUGHTER HOUSE CASES

The U. S. supreme court ruling in The Butchers' Benevolent Association of New Orleans v. the Crescent City Live-Stock Landing and Slaughter-House Company, etc. (1873), affirming the judgments of the Louisiana supreme court. The cases did not involve negroes; at issue was the constitutionality of a butchering monopoly granted by the state legislature to one slaughterhouse syndicate in New Orleans. But the court, in a five to four decision, took the position that butchers protesting the monopoly were not protected by the Fourteenth Amendment, designed solely to protect negroes from discrimination based on color. The court interpreted the privileges and immunities clause to mean that the amendment protected only the privileges of national citizenship, and had no power to enforce equality in matters incident to state citizenship, such as discrimination in education. The court held that 'our statesmen have still believed that the existence of the States with powers for domestic and local government, including the regulation of civil rights, the rights of person and of property, was essential to the perfect working of our complex form of government.' The decision became a significant barrier to civil rights enforcement.

SLAVE

Though 20 negroes were sold in Jamestown, Virginia, in 1619, the word 'slave' was not used in Virginia to designate negroes until 1662.

SLAVE CODES

Legal codes adopted by various local and state bodies to maintain the slave system. Though not uniform, they followed a familiar pattern, particularly in defining who was slave and who was free, making slaves subject to punishments for violations of the code, and denying slaves any civil or legal rights. The status of a mulatto mother usually determined the status of her children.

405

SLAVE NARRATIVES

During the early 1800s the American Anti-Slavery Society took down the narratives of thousands of ex-slaves, as did other abolitionist groups. Thus an extensive body of literature developed and became a strong force in the battle to sway public opinion against slavery. Interest in slave narratives declined after the Civil War and was not revived until the Federal Writers' Project undertook in the 1930s to preserve oral accounts of the experiences of ex-slaves, storing them at the Archive of Folksong at the Library of Congress. See Julius Lester, *To Be a Slave* (1968).

SLAVE REVOLTS

As many as 20 million slaves may have been sent to the New World during the slave era. Half of them may have died before reaching American shores, victims of mistreatment, starvation, suicide, or death at the hands of their enslavers. At least 50 slave revolts occurred at sea. At least 200 uprisings took place between 1626 (at the mouth of the Pedee river in what is now South Carolina) and 1864 in at least four of the southern states, most of them led by slaves (Denmark Vesey, leader of the plot to capture Charleston in 1922, was a notable exception). In 1741 poor whites were alleged to have joined with negroes in an abortive plot to seize New York City. Though there was no proof of their guilt, 18 negroes were hanged, 13 were burned alive, and 70 were banished; 4 white persons were hanged. In 1800 Gabriel Prosser organized thousands of slaves for an attack on Richmond, Virginia. A revolt led by Charles Deslandes in southern Louisiana was suppressed in 1811. The largest slave revolt, organized by Nat Turner in Southampton County, Virginia, resulted in the deaths of some 60 white persons in 1831. A slave revolt occurred aboard the *Creole* in 1841. The next year slaves in the Cherokee and Creek Nations were involved in an uprising centered in Webbers Falls in Oklahoma Territory. Individual attempts to defeat the system of slavery were more numerous and produced visible results. Murder, arson, and poison were favorite weapons. Flight was such a common practice that physicians gave

it the name 'monomania' and considered it to be a disease
indigenous to negroes. See Herbert Aptheker, *American Slave
Revolts* (1943), and John Hope Franklin, *From Slavery to Freedom* (1956).

SLAVE SONGS

Name used by the compilers of the first collection of spirituals
to designate the sacred folk music in their collection. See William
Francis Allen, Charles Pinkard Ware, and Lucy McKim Garrison
(eds.), Slave Songs of the United States (1867).

SLAVE TRADE

The slave trade that lasted about two centuries (1650-1850)
and extended the frontiers of Europe across the Atlantic on the
basis of African manpower resulted in the transplantation of a
third of the people of African descent to alien shores. Recent
research indicates that a high level of culture in Africa and the
stamina and efficiency of Negro slaves resulted in the importation
of as many as 100,000 captives in a single year. The institution
of slavery had existed since classical antiquity, when the Slavs
were the underlings. It continued through the Middle Ages, based
mainly on religion rather than race: Christians enslaved Muslims
and vice versa. The Hispanic conquerers and settlers soon discovered that of the three groups of potential workers, Europeans
forced under various circumstances to perform services, enslaved
Indians, and negroes, the latter had a better survival rate and
were more efficient workers. Africa, which had already perfected
its own systems of domestic slavery, was capable of providing
great numbers of workers for export. African commercial organization made it possible for traders to exchange captives for
foreign goods. The industrial revolution increased the demand
for labor but at the same time brought increasing concern over
the inhumanity of the slave trade. The Catholic Church condemned the slave trade on the grounds that free persons were
illegally sold into slavery and that the search for human beings
to be sold at a profit entailed rapine, cruelty, and war. Condem-
nations came from Pius II (October 7, 1462), Paul III (May

407

29, 1537), Urban VII (April 2, 1639), Benedict XIV (December 20, 1741), and Gregory XVI (December 3, 1839). The Church urged negroes to attend religious services and participate in the sacraments. Between 14 and 20 million Africans may have been involved in transatlantic slave trade, and an equal number may have died during slave hunts. See Oliver Ransford, *The Slave Trade* (1971).

SLAVE SYSTEMS

In *Slave and Citizen* (1946), Frank Tannenbaum identified three slave systems in the Western Hemisphere: one with no effective tradition, no slave law, and little religious influence; one with a slave law and a belief in the sanctity of the person; and the intermediate system of the French, combining elements from both extremes. The Dutch, Danish, British, and Colonial American practiced the first system, the harshest from the viewpoint of the negro. The Spanish and Portuguese went to the other extreme, encouraging church attendance and incorporating many provisions favoring manumission.

SLAVEOWNERS

Some blacks owned slaves, usually their relatives or friends who could not be freed because of legal restrictions, but sometimes for profit. Cyprian Richard owned an estate in Louisiana with 91 slaves; Charles Rogues had 47 and Marie Metoyer 58.

SLAVERY, LEGAL BASIS

Sir William Blackstone's *Commentaries on the Law of England* had a decisive influence on American jurisprudence. Blackstone set forth the legal principles that a slave became free as soon as he touched English soil, that slavery contracts were invalid, and that English common law did not automatically extend to the English colonies. Thus his writings were used to support the doctrine that slavery could be legally maintained in the colonies even though the institution violated English tradition and practice.

SLEET, MONETA, JR.

Photographer. Her feature photography for *Ebony* earned her a Pulitzer Prize in 1969.

SLEW, JENNY

In 1766 a woman slave, Jenny Slew, used the courts to win her freedom from her master, John Whipple of Ipswich, Massachusetts. Her successful legal struggle encouraged other slaves to sue for their freedom. The court also awarded her 'the sum of four pounds' in damages.

SMALLS, ROBERT

Hero and public official (1839-1915). Of limited education, he became a pilot, sailed an armed Confederate gunboat, *The Planter,* out of Charleston and turned it over as a prize of war to the Union Navy on May 13, 1862. Born a slave, he became a captain in the Union Navy and a congressman from South Carolina for three terms (1875-87), a longer period than any other black legislator. See Dorothy Sterling, *Captain of the Planter: The Story of Robert Smalls* (1958).

SMITH v. ALLRIGHT

U. S. Supreme Court decision handed down in 1944. In it the Court decreed that in a primary election a political party could not exclude a voter because of race.

SMITH, AMANDA

Missionary (1837-1915). Beginning her work in 1860 in New York, she traveled to England, India, and West Africa, where she remained for 8 years.

SMITH, B. S.

Lawyer (b. 1862). He earned his law degree at the University of Michigan in 1866. The next year he began practicing in Kansas City, Kansas. After serving 4 years as an alderman, he returned to his law practice.

SMITH, BESSIE

Blues singer (1900-1937). Beginning her career under the tutelage of Ma Rainey, she started her recording career in 1923 and went on to write her own tunes and lyrics, including 'Backwater Blues.' One of the first blues and jazz singers to win national acceptance, she set the pattern for many who came after her. See Paul Oliver, *Bessie Smith* (1961).

SMITH, CHARLES EDWARD

Writer. He authored the first serious study of jazz (The Symposium, 1930), wrote the script for the first new network jazz program, and was co-editor (with Frederic Ramsey) of *Jazzmen* (1939).

SMITH, HALE

Musician. His *Music for Harp and Orchestra* was commissioned and played by the Symphony of the New World. His *Contours* was premiered by the Louisville Orchestra and later performed by the Cleveland Orchestra and the Cincinnati Orchestra.

SMITH, JAMES MCCUNE

Scholar, physician, and abolitionist (1813-1865). A graduate of the University of Glasgow, he distinguished himself as a scientist, orator, and writer on abolition. He was also the proprietor of several drug stores in New York City. In 1844 he refuted the 1850 census returns on the mental health of free blacks, purporting to show a high rate of mental illness.

SMITH, JAMES W.

West Point cadet. In 1870 he became the first black to enter West Point.

SMITH, MAMIE

Musician. She was the first singer to record blues. Her recording of 'Crazy Blues' in 1921 created a rush to put the voices of blues singers on record.

SMITH, OTIS M.
Public official (b. 1922). He became Michigan state auditor general in 1962.

SMITH, STEPHEN
Businessman. A free negro, he became a successful lumber merchant in Columbia, Pennsylvania.

SMITH, TOMMIE
Athlete. At the Olympic games held in Mexico City in 1968, he attracted international attention by raising his first in a black power salute, protesting against racism in America.

SMITH, WALKER
See Robinson, Sugar Ray.

SMITH, WILLIAM GARDNER
Writer (b. 1926). His books include *Last of the Conquerors* (1948) and *Anger at Innocence* (1950).

SMYTHE, HUGH
Public official (b. 1913). In 1965 he was appointed ambassador to Syria, becoming the tenth black in the nation's history to fill an ambassadorial post. After that country broke diplomatic relations with the United States, he served as ambassador to Malta, 1967-70.

SMYTHE, JOHN H.
Artist and lawyer (1844-1908). He served as U. S. minister to Liberia.

SNAER, SAMUEL
Musician (born c. 1834). He taught piano and violin in New Orleans, and he composed orchestral pieces as well as dances.

SOCIAL AND ECONOMIC STATUS OF NEGROES IN THE UNITED STATES, 1970, THE

A study conducted jointly by the Bureau of Labor Statistics and the U. S. Census Bureau. The study revealed that black Americans made important gains in employment, incomes, housing, and education between 1960 and 1970 but remained behind whites in most social and economic areas. Among the findings: incomes rose by 102%, yet the median income of the nonwhite family was $2,602 under that of the white family; illiteracy was cut in half, most adults were high school graduates, and 40% more were college graduates (6.1% versuss 4.3% in 1960); employment in professional and technical jobs increased 131% and unemployment dropped from 10.2% to 8.2% but remained almost double that of whites in 1970; home ownership increased from 38% to 42% and dwelling units without at least one plumbing facility dropped from 41% to 17% (versus 12% to 5% for whites); families headed by a female rose from 21.8% to 28.3% as families in homes occupied by both husband and wife decreased from 74.7% to 68.1% (versus a stable figure of 88.7% for white families). The study concludes that Negroes made record gains during the decade; although they trailed whites in most categories, 'the differences . . . continued to narrow even during the 1970 economic downturn, rather than becoming wider as might have been expected.'

SOCIETY FOR THE PROPAGATION OF THE GOSPEL

Toward the end of the 17th century the society raised funds to establish schools for slaves and Indians in Charleston, Savannah, and other parts of Georgia.

SOJOURNER TRUTH

See Truth, Sojourner.

SOLEDAD BROTHER

Book published by George Jackson. Titled in full *Soledad Brother: The Prison Letters of George Jackson* (1970), it was hailed as the most important work of its kind since the *Autobiography of Malcolm X*.

SOLIDARITY DAY

On May 19, 1968, the Poor People's Campaign reached its climax as speakers at the Solidarity Day demonstration at the Lincoln Memorial in Washington warned that this day might witness the last peaceful demonstration of the blacks.

SOMERSET v. STEWART

The most important decision on slavery ever handed down by a court in England. By his 1772 decision (Lofft. 1, 98 Eng. Rep. 499, 20 How. St. Tr. 1) Lord Chief Justice William Murray Mansfield freed all Negro slaves in Great Britain and ended the practice of selling human beings in the British Isles. He held that 'the state of slavery is of such a nature that it is incapable of being introduced on any reasons, moral or political . . . so odious, that nothing can be suffered to support it.'

SONS OF THE AFRICAN SOCIETY

A self-help group formed in Boston in 1798 by members pleged to conduct themselves 'as true and faithful Citizens of the Commonwealth in which we live.'

SORROW SONGS

Term used by W. E. B. Du Bois to designate negro spirituals. See 'The Sorrow Songs' in his book *The Souls of Black Folk* (1903).

SOUL

Elusive but omnipresent term used to denote the feeling a person has for his roots, his heritage, his black authenticity and essence. Clarence Major describes it in his *Dictionary of Afro-American Slang* (1970) as 'the sensitivity and emotional essence that derives from the blues.' Soul is reflected in art, music, literature, and life styles. Artists and writers explore the black experience in its myriad forms; soul music is popular music (James

Brown, a rhythm and blues singer, was recently named Number One Soul Brother); and soul, with its stress on what is natural and human, is linked to a life style of 'staying loose,' studying black history and identifying with black negroes, eating certain foods, and adopting African-inspired hair styles and fashions.

SOUL BROTHER

Term used to express the common bond shared by black men.

SOUL CITY

Term used first to designate Harlem. Now Soul City describes a major program initiated in January 1969 by Floyd McKissick to build a city in which blacks and whites will live and work together as equals. McKissick's proposed experiment in integrated living, to be conducted in Warren County, North Carolina, is an attempt to reverse the effects of industrialism which has concentrated unskilled blacks in urban ghettoes.

SOUL FOOD

Term designating black Southern-style cooking. Chief items include blackplate, chitlins, cornbread, cow pea soup, crakling bread, dumplings, and ham-bone soup.

SOUL SISTER

Term used by one black girl or woman to designate another black member of her sex.

SOULS OF BLACK FOLK, THE

A classic essay by W. E. B. Du Bois. Described by one critic as 'a monument to the black man's struggle in this country,' it reveals the 'strange meaning of being black.' Published in 1903, it reversed the tendency of Negroes to consider themselves and their past with shame, pleaded for mutual understanding between whites and blacks, and called upon Negroes, by merging their African and American experiences, to create a better and truer image of themselves. According to James Weldon Johnson, the book had a greater impact on Negroes 'than any other single book . . . since Uncle Tom's Cabin.'

SOUTH CAROLINA VOLUNTEERS

Organized in May 1862, they were probably the first black soldiers to be recruited, trained, and mustered by the Union army. They served without pay for three months, then all except one company were disbanded. That company, led by Sergeant C. T. Trowbridge, saw action on St. Simon's Island off the coast of Georgia, where they were assigned to flush out guerrilla forces. The disbanded members of the regiment formed the nucleus of the official First South Carolina Volunteers. See Brown, John.

SOUTHAMPTON SLAVE REVOLT

See Turner, Nat.

SOUTHERN CHRISTIAN LEADERSHIP CONFERENCE

Founded in January 1957 by 60 black leaders to promote 'full citizenship rights and total integration of the Negro into American life,' the 'nonsectarian coordinating agency' of organizations and individuals operates under a philosophy of nonviolent direct mass action. It was founded as a logical extension of the Montgomery Improvement Association and is now headquartered in Atlanta. It has a full-time staff of more than 60 and an annual budget of one million dollars. Under the leadership of Martin Luther King, Jr. it became one of the foremost civil right organizations. After King was assassinated, Ralph Abernathy took over the leadership.

SOUTHERN COOPERATIVE DEVELOPMENT FUND

Association set up to provide loans for cooperatives seeking to expand or improve their operation.

SOUTHERN EDUCATION BOARD

Organized in 1901 to create public opinion favoring public schools, the board influenced the shaping of educational institutions in the South. Segregated systems at all levels, with the

Hampton-Tuskegee pattern serving as the model at the most advanced level, had come into existence throughout the South by 1930.

SOUTHERN EDUCATIONAL FOUNDATION
Philanthropic organization resulting from the consolidation in 1937 of the Slater Fund and the Jeanes Fund.

SPANISH AMERICAN WAR
Colonel Charles Young, the third West Point graduate, and the highest ranking black officer at the outbreak of World War I, was an outstanding hero of the Spanish American War. Black volunteers from Alabama, Illinois, Kansas, Ohio, and Virginia took part in the war. See Black Regulars.

SPAULDING, ASA T.
Businessman (b. 1902). He is president of the North Carolina Mutual Life Insurance Company, a trustee of the National Urban League, and a director of the W. T. Grant Company.

SPAULDING, CHARLES C.
Businessman (1874-1952). He developed and served as president of the North Carolina Mutual Life Insurance Company. His nephew, Asa T. Spaulding, succeeded him.

SPAULDING, JANE M.
Public official (d. 1965). She represented the U. S. Council of Women at the 1951 conference of the International Council of Women in Athens, Greece. In 1953 she was appointed to DHEW when it was established.

SPELLMAN, MITCHELL
Physician. An internationally renowned heart surgeon, he has pioneered in repairing the inner walls of the heart. He has also been active in promoting better hospital privileges for black doctors.

SPINGARN AWARD

A gold medal presented annually by the NAACP 'to the man or woman of African descent and American citizenship, who shall have made the highest achievement during the previous year or years in any honorable field of endeavor.' The first award was made in 1915 to Ernest E. Just.

SPIRIT HOUSE

Founded in 1966 by LeRoi Jones in an attempt to bring drama, poetry, and music to the mases of Newark, the city of his birth, Spirit House became the moving force behind his Black Revolution. Active in promoting voter registration, exerting political persuasion, and fostering civic pride, the House has attracted the most militant new black artists: poets like Yusef Iman and Ed Spriggs; musicians like Pharaoh Saunders and Sun Ra; and some of the earlier Black Arts Theatre members like Charles Patterson and Clarence Reed as well as newcomers Ben Caldwell and Ed Bullins.

SPIRITUALS

A body of folk literature produced by slaves and sung in a certain way. They defy notation, but they use the pentatonic scale and notes alien to the conventional major and minor sequences, including the flatted third and seventh. They incorporate influences which are African, European, Christian, Jewish, and secular. They are choral and communal expressions of a racial experience, frequently using Old Testament sources to illustrate their plight. In a stricter sense, contemporary performing artists may treat Spirituals as a body of literature constituting a new art form, similar to the German Lieder.

SPORTS

Segregation in American sports ended in 1946 when managers of professional baseball and football teams decided to add blacks to their teams, but blacks had been active in most sports long before Jackie Robinson made his courageous decision to 'break the color barrier' (his words) and set an example for other athletes. In sports to a larger degree than elsewhere, perhaps, the American dream of freedom and equality is now being realized. See Baseball, Boxing, Football, Basketball, Tennis, and Track and Field.

SPOTTSWOOD, STEPHEN

Clergyman. A bishop in the AMEZ church, he is chairman of the board of directors of the NAACP.

SPRINGFIELD

Illinois city, scene of a race riot in 1908. Troops were called out to deal with the rioting, August 14-19. The turmoil led to the founding of the NAACP.

STADLER, JOSEPH

Athlete. In 1904 he competed in the Olympic standing broad jump competition, but failed to place.

STANCE, EMANUEL

Army hero. Sgt. Stance had several successful encounters with Indian warriors. On May 20, 1870, he left Fort McKavett on a scouting expedition. His bravery and skill in repulsing Indians who repeatedly attacked him and his 10 troopers won him the Congressional Medal of Honor. He served with the Ninth Cavalry Regiment.

STARLIN, MARK

Patriot. A runaway slave, he became the only black naval captain in the history of Virginia. During the American Revolution, he made daring raids on British vessels in Hampton Roads.

STAUPERS, MABEL K.

Nurse. In 1934 she became executive secretary of the NACGN National Association of Colored Graduate Nurses and initiated an all-out campaign to provide more job opportunities for black nurses.

STEAL AWAY

Spiritual, supposed to have been sung at meetings to signal the departure of one or more slaves on the journey northward over the underground railroad.

STEPHENS, SANDY

Athlete. He was the first black quarterback to lead his team in a Rose Bowl game (Minnesota, 1961 and 1962).

STEWARD, MARIA W.

Abolitionist. In 1833 she spoke at the African Masonic Hall in Boston. Deeply religious, she was the first American woman to leave extant texts of her public speeches. Condemning the American Colonization Society, she maintained that she would rather die by the bayonet than be driven to a strange land.

STEWARD, SUSAN McKINNEY

Physician (1848-1918). After graduating from New York Medical College in 1870, she practiced in Brooklyn for more than 20 years. She was a member of Kings County Homeopathic Society and a founder of the Women's Royal Union of New York and Brooklyn.

STEWARD, REX

Musician. He played the trumpet with Duke Ellington's Kentucky Club orchestra.

STEWARD, T. McCANTS

Lawyer (b. 1854). After graduating from the University of South Carolina (1875), he gained an outstanding reputation. A skillful, articulate, and eloquent speaker, he was admitted to practice before the general term of the New York state supreme court in 1886.

STILL, JAMES

Medical practitioner (b. 1812). Called by his contemporaries 'black doctor' and 'doctor of the pines,' he was born in New

Jersey. His two brothers, William and Peter, became prominent abolitionists. Self-taught, he practiced successfully for thirty years. His autobiography is titled *Early Recollections and Life of Dr. James Still* (1877).

STILL, WILLIAM

Underground railroad director (1821-1902). He was secretary of the Philadelphia 'station' of the underground railroad. He compiled the only surviving complete record of such a station, *The Underground Rail Road: a Record of Facts, Authentic Narratives, Letters, etc., Narrating the Hardships, Hair-Breadth escapes and Death Struggles of the Slaves in their Efforts for Freedom, as Related by Themselves and Others, or Witnessed by the Author* (1872).

STILL, WILLIAM GRANT

Musician (b. 1895). America's greatest black composer and conductor. The first of his race to lead a symphony orchestra (the Los Angeles Philarmonic), he has composed a number of symphonies, ballets, suites, and other works based on Afro-American themes. His works include a symphonic poem, *Darker America* (1924); the *Afro-American Symphony,* generally regarded as his greatest work; and the operas *Troubled Island* (1937), *Costaso* (1949), and *Highway No. 1, U. S. A.* (1963).

STOKES, CARL

Public official (b. 1927). As mayor of Cleveland, in 1967 he became the first black ever elected mayor of one of the nation's ten largest cities. The younger son of a Cleveland laundry worker and cleaning woman, he dropped out of high school to work in a foundry but returned after serving in the Army to earn his diploma (1947) and begin college training that finally prepared him to pass the Ohio bar and begin practicing law. He became the first black Democrat ever elected to the Ohio legislature (1962), lost by a hair in his first campaign for mayor (1965), but was easily elected to the office in 1967 and again in 1969.

STOKES, LOUIS

Public official (b. 1925). Elected U. S. congressman from Cleveland, Ohio, in 1968, he is a member of the Black Caucus. He is Carl Stoke's older brother.

STOKES, MAURICE

Athlete (1934-1970). His basketball career ended in 1958 when he received a blow that damaged the motor-control center of his brain, leaving him immobile and speechless. Two years earlier he had been named rookie-of-the-year. With the help and encouragement of many friends, he learned to speak again.

STONE, FRED

Musician. His 'My Ragtime Baby' is one of the earliest ragtime tunes.

STONO

Cato led a slave revolt that started on a plantation near Stono, South Carolina, in 1739. See Cato.

STOUT, JUANITA K.

Jurist (b. 1919). She was the first negro woman appointed to serve as a judge in Pennsylvania.

STRAKER, HILDA G.

Internationally acclaimed dermatologist.

STRANGE FRUIT

An international best seller written by Lillian Smith, an early champion of civil rights. Published in 1944, the controversial book dealt with racism.

STRAUDER V. WEST VIRGINIA

Supreme Court decision (1880) declaring a state law barring negroes from jury service unconstitutional in as much as it violated the equal protection clause of the Fourteenth Amendment.

STRAYHORN, WILLIAM THOMAS

Jazz composer (1915-1967). He was a lyric writer, pianist, and arranger for his close associate, Duke Ellington, who made 'Take the "A" Train' the theme number of the Ellington band. Billy Strayhorn's last major composition, written in collaboration with Ellington and released on records in 1967, was *Far East Suite.*

STRODE, WOODY

Actor. He had the starring role in *Black Jesus,* a film based on the life of Patrice Lumumba.

STUBBS, F. D.

Surgeon. The Philadelphia physician was elected to membership in the American College of Surgeons in the mid-1940s, becoming the second black member of the association. The first was Dr. Louis T. Wright (1934).

STUCKEY, STERLING

Civil rights leader (b. 1932). He is chairman of the Amistad Society and has long been active in the freedom schools in the South.

SUBSTITUTION SYSTEM

During the American Revolution some states allowed the substitution of slaves for white draft eligibles who wanted to avoid conscription.

SULLIVAN MEMORIAL TROPHY

See James E. Sullivan Memorial Trophy.

SULLIVAN, LEON HOWARD

Clergyman and educator (b. 1922). He founded the Philadelphia Opportunities Industrialization Center and is chairman of its board of directors. The recipient of many honors and awards, he is also pastor of the Zion Baptist Church.

SUPREMES, THE

Musicians. In 1965 they sang at Philharmonic Hall in Lincoln Center, New York City, to a capacity crowd. The top-rated group presented its first television special in 1968.

SUTHERN, ORRIN C.

Musician. In 1946 he became the first black organist to perform on the CBS network. Earlier, as a student at Western Reserve University, he had the unique distinction of performing in a recital before the American Guild of Organists at Youngstown, Ohio.

SUTTON, PERCY E.

Public official. Manhattan Borough President Sutton, of New York, has been mentioned as a presidential prospect.

SWANN V. CHARLOTTE-MECKLENBURG COUNTY, N. C.

In April 1971 the Supreme Court ruled in the case of Swann v. Charlotte-Mecklenburg County, N. C., that local school authorities may 'be required to employ bus transportation as one tool of desegregation,' but that busing may not be appropriate 'when the time or distance of travel is so great as to risk either the health of the children or significantly impinge on the educational process.'

SWANSON, HOWARD

Musician. His *Short Symphony* won a New York Critics Circle award for the best new orchestral work during the 1950-51 seaʳᶜn.

SWFATT v. PAINTER

U. S. Supreme Court decision (1950) ruling that a negro applicant for admission to the University of Texas Law School be admitted to that school even though the Texas State University for Negroes had hastily established a separate law school. Chief Justice Vinson wrote that the applicant was entitled to 'legal education equivalent to that offered by the State to students of other races.'

SWEET, OSSIAN H.
Physician. After studying in Vienna and conducting research under the direction of Madame Curie, he returned to the United States in 1925 and bought a house in a white neighborhood in Detroit. After one of the white demonstrators besieging the house was killed by a burst of gunfire, Dr. Sweet and the other occupants were arrested. Clarence Darrow and Arthur Garfield Hayes, engaged by the NAACP to defend them, won their acquittal.

SYDENHAM HOSPITAL
Reorganized along interracial lines in 1943, the 50-year-old Harlem hospital added 23 black members to its staff. One of these, Dr. Peter M. Murray, became the first black physician to serve on the executive board of a Grade-A voluntary hospital.

T

TALBERT, MARY BURNETT

Civil rights worker (1886-1923). After receiving her Ph. D. from the University of Buffalo, she became active in promoting humanitarian and civil rights causes. She sold Liberty Bonds, served in France as a Red Cross nurse, and became president of the Colored National Association of Women's Clubs (1916-20), vice-president and director of the NAACP, and chairman of the anti-lynching committee set up to promote passage of the Dyer Anti-Lynching Bill. She lectured throughout the nation and Europe on race relations and women's rights.

TABOR, TWELVE KNIGHTS AND DAUGHTERS OF

Antislavery group established in 1844 by Moses Dickson. See Temple and Tabernacle of the Knights and Daughters of Tabor.

TALENTED TENTH

Expression used by W. E. B. Du Bois to designate negro college graduates. Du Bois expected them to provide leadership for the masses. Twenty-nine members of the elitist group met in 1905 at Niagara Falls, Canada, and drew up the manifesto that helped to lay the foundations for the NAACP. See Niagara Movement.

TALLADEGA COLLEGE

Established in Alabama by the American Missionary Association in 1865, the liberal arts college today draws almost half of its predominantly black student body from other states.

TAN

Magazine for women, published since 1950 by the Johnson Publishing Company.

TANGO

A ballroom dance derived from an African rhythmic pattern.

TANNER, HENRY O.

Artist (1859-1937). An outstanding artist, he is best known for his Biblical paintings. The eldest of seven children of Pittsburgh AME minister Benjamin Tucker Tanner, he moved with his family to Philadelphia, studied at the Pennsylvania Academy of the Fine Arts (1884-88), moved to Atlanta, where he opened a photographic studio and taught drawing, then lived in poverty in Paris until he painted his best known work, 'The Resurrection of Lazarus,' which inspired philanthropist Lewis Wanamaker to become his patron (1897). He set up a studio in an artist's colony outside Paris, at Trépied. He made several trips to the Holy Land and to the United States. Leading museums bought his paintings. He won a gold medal at the San Francisco exposition of 1915 and the French Legion of Honor. He prospered and settled into semi-retirement at his country home in Normandy. Alone among the early artists of the twentieth century to enjoy truly international fame, he was made a member of the French Legion of Honor.

TARRANT, CAESAR

Patriot (d. 1796). A valiant seaman, he served in the Virginia navy for over four years, until the *Patriot* which he piloted was captured on the eve of the battle at Yorktown. Emancipated for his services (1786), he acquired property and became a man of considerable influence.

TATUM, ART

Musician (1910-1956). His unique technique inspired a new school of jazz piano soloists.

TATUM, REESE

Basketball player (1821-1967). Born in Calion, Arkansas, 'Goose' Tatum played with the Harlem Globetrotters from 1942 to 1954, when he organized the Harlem Road Kings. He was known affectionately as the 'Clown Prince of Basketball.'

TAYLOR, A. A.

Historian. He wrote three important studies on Reconstruction. A Harvard Ph. D., he was named dean of Fisk University.

TAYLOR, CECIL

Musician. Born and educated in Long Island, he studied music at the New England Conservatory. He maintained, however, that he learned more music from Duke Ellington than from his teachers at the conservatory. 'Music to me was in a way holding on to Negro culture,' he said. One of the most important new jazz musicians of the 1960s, he displays overwhelming flights of power at the keyboard. Called a Bartók in reverse, he has been able to incorporate classical elements into his own distinctive kind of blues. See A. B. Spellman, *Black Music* (1966).

TAYLOR, CHARLES H. J.

Lawyer (b. 1858). Admitted to the bar in 1878, he served as city attorney of Kansas City, Missouri, and as recorder of deeds in the District of Columbia (1894).

TAYLOR, MRS. E. D. CANNADY

Civil rights leader (b. 1889). Before her retirement from public life, she had won the admiration and respect of the citizens of the Northwest for her untiring and unselfish efforts to promote better race relations. Born and educated in Texas, then Portland Oregon (Bachelor of Law, 1922), she was constantly in demand as a speaker before civic and religious groups. She was owner and associate editor of Oregon's only black newspaper *(The Advocate)*, hostess at the 4th Pan-African Congress (New York City, 1927), founder of the Fellowship for Better Interracial Relations, and Northwest director of the NAACP.

TAYLOR, GEORGE EDWIN

Politician (b. 1857). In 1904 he was the presidential candidate of the National Liberty Party. Earlier he had served as an Iowa delegate to the Republican national convention (1892) and had led the anti-Harrison faction at the convention.

TAYLOR, HOBART, JR.

Public official (b. 1920). He was named executive vice chairman of the Equal Emploment and Opportunity Committee.

TAYLOR, JOSEPH B.

Athlete. Intercollegiate champion in the 440-yard dash in 1904, 1907, and 1908, the University of Pennsylvania athlete was an Olympic team member in 1908. He helped his team to win the 1600-meter relay.

TAYLOR, MAJOR

Athlete (b. 1878). The fastest bicycle rider the world had ever known, he won three national sprint championships (1898, 1899, and 1900) before invading Europe to defeat all of its champions before huge crowds. One of the most glorified black athletes in history, he received a public tribute from President Theodore Roosevelt.

TAYLOR, PRESTON

Businessman (b. 1849). He succeeded in winning a contract to build two sections of the railway from Mt. Sterling to Richmond, Virginia. He employed 150 men and completed the project in 14 months.

TAYLOR, SUSIE KING

Teacher and nurse. A slave who managed to 'get herself some schooling,' she worked as a nurse with Clara Barton and as a teacher of troops in the first Negro regiment during the Civil War. Her autobiography is titled *Reminiscenses of My Life in Camp with the 33d United States Colored Troops Late 1st S. C. Volunteers* (1902).

428

TEER, BARBARA ANN
Actress. She won the Vernon Rice award as best actress for her role in *Home Movies,* a 1965 off-Broadway production. She was director of the National Black Theater Workshop in Harlem.

TEMPLE AND TABERNACLE OF THE
KNIGHTS AND DAUGHTERS OF TABOR
Secret society formed in 1871 by Moses Dickson. Its aim was 'to help to spread the Christian religion and education.' Founded in Independence, Missouri, it claimed to have nearly 200,000 members by the end of the century. Members were urged to 'acquire real estate, avoid intemperance, and cultivate true manhood.'

TEMPLE, LEWIS
Inventor (d. 1854). He perfected the Temple Toggle Harpoon.

TENNIS
Color bars until recently prevented black athletes from competing in this predominantly white sport. Notable exceptions: Arthur Ashe and Althea Gibson.

TENT CITY
See Fayette County.

10TH CAVALRY REGIMENT
Composed of black volunteers who had enlisted for a 5-year term, the all-negro unit was assigned to the Great Plains in August 1867, marking the beginning of over two decades of service under trying conditions. Called Moacs, Brunettes, Niggers, and Africans by all manner of people, they received a fitting sobriquet from the Indians, to whom they were Buffalo Soldiers. They facilitated the peaceful settlement of the Great Plains. See Buffalo Soldiers.

TERRELL, MARY CHURCH
Civil rights leader (1863-1964). Born in Memphis and educated at Oberlin College, she went as a delegate to the International

Council of Women in Berlin and addressed the organization in French and German as well as her native language. A life-long leader in the fight against discrimination, she was once president of the National Association of Colored Women. Her auto-biography is titled A Colored Woman in a White World (1940).

TERRY, JESSE A.
Businessman. He developed the Terry Manufacturing Company into a million-dollary business in six years and was honored by the city of Roanoke, Alabama, for his feat.

TERRY, LUCY
Poet. In 1746 she qualified for the honor of being the first black poet of American by writing a verse account of an Indian raid, 'Bars Fight.'

TERRY, SONNY
Musician (b. 1911). A country blues artist, he has toured here and abroad with Brownie McGee.

TEXAS FARMERS' COLORED ASSOCIATION
In 1890 the association proposed the idea of a separate state for negroes. Oklahoma Territory was chosen as the location, and the all-black town of Langston was established in line with this idea in 1891.

THARPE, SISTER ROSETTA
Gospel singer. In the early 1900s she was a popular church singer. Later she joined Cab Calloway.

THIERRY, CAMILLE
Ante-bellum poet of New Orleans (1814-1875).

THIRD STREAM MUSIC
Name given to the blending of classical and jazz traditions. John Lewis and J. J. Johnson are now associated with Third

Stream music, which goes back to Jelly Roll Morton, James P. Johnson, and Willie Smith.

13TH AMENDMENT
Approved by Congress on January 31, 1865, and proclaimed in force on December 18, 1865, the 13th Amendment abolished slavery throughout the United States, 'or any place subject to their jurisdiction.'

THOMAS, BIGGER
See Native Son.

THOMAS, JOHN
Athlete. One of the greatest high jumpers in the world, he set a new world record during the trials for the 1960 U. S. Olympic meet but failed to equal the mark in Russia.

THOMAS, WILL
Writer (b. 1905). His works include God Is for White Folks (1947).

THOMAS, WILLIAM
Private in the U. S. Army. He received the Congressional Medal of Honor, posthumously, for heroism in the Korean conflict.

THOMPSON, BOB
Contemporary artist. The most original black painter since Hale Woodruff, his style is primitive but evidences technical perfection.

THOMPSON, ERA BELL
Journalist, author, and magazine editor.

THOMPSON, FRANK
Athlete. In 1885 he organized the Cuban Giants, the first black baseball team, in Long Island, New York. Thompson, a head-waiter, formed his team from a group of black waiters at the Argyle Hotel.

THOMPSON, GEORGE

Officer in the U. S. navy. One of the first two black officers selected to attend the U. S. Naval War College (1963), Lt. Commander Thompson later served as captain of the USS *Finch*. See Gravely, Samuel L.

THOMPSON, SOLOMON H.

Physician. In 1899 he was co-founder, with Dr. Solomon H. Thompson, of Douglass Hospital in Kansas City, Kansas.

THOMS, ADAH B.

Nurse. She headed the National Association of Graduate Nurses for seven years. During World War I she fought successfully for acceptance of black nurses in the American Red Cross and the Army Nurse Corps.

THORNE, GEORGE D.

Surgeon. A member of the surgical staffs at Lincoln Hospital and at Sydenham, he was denied an application for membership in the American College of Surgeons. Mounting pressures generated by his case forced the association to admit other black surgeons.

THREE-FIFTHS CLAUSE

Article I, Section 2 or the U. S. constitution uses the expression 'three-fifths of all other Persons' in stipulating how taxes and representatives are to be apportioned. Thus the negro was considered a person, giving reformers grounds for asserting that they could not be treated as property.

369TH INFANTRY REGIMENT

The first group of black combat soldiers to arrive in Europe (December 1917). Cited for bravery 11 times, the regiment was awarded the Croix de Guerre by the French government. The regimental band, conducted by James Reese Europe and Noble Sissle, is credited with the introduction of American jazz abroad. The regiment had its day of glory on February 17, 1919, when it paraded up Fifth Avenue in New York City, with Sergeant Henry Johnson, one of the most acclaimed black heroes of the war, riding in a car carrying a bouquet of flowers.

370TH REGIMENT
See 93rd Division.

371ST INFANTRY
Formed in 1917 when 14 black recruits began training for combat, the unit served under French officers during World War I. The 371st received praise from its commanders and was awarded the army citation.

THURMAN, HOWARD
Religious philosopher (b. 1900). One of the great mystics of all time, he has traveled and lectured throughout the United States and in foreign countries. His mysticism is practical, urging men toward involvement and engagement in the real world where social and ethical issues are at stake. *Jesus and the Disinherited* (1949) stresses the affinity between the circumstances of Jesus and all disinherited people. *The Luminous Darkness* (1965) is concerned with what segregation does to the human spirit.

THURMAN, WALLACE
Writer (1902-1934). Co-author of the Broadway play *Harlem* (1929), he also wrote two novels, *The Blacker the Berry* (1929) and *Infants of the Spring* (1932).

THURMOND, NATE
Athlete. One of the best all-round centers in the NBA, he began his career with the San Francisco Warriors in 1966.

TIBBS, ROY WILFRED
Musician (1888-1944). He was the first person to earn the master of music degree from the Oberlin conservatory (1919). A member of the American Guild of Organists, he also studied

in Paris and Vienna. He appeared as organ soloist with the National Symphony Orchestra.

TIGER, DICK
See Ihetu, Richard.

TILL, EMMETT
Mississippi youth whose kidnapping and death stirred the conscience of the nation. The fourteen-year-old boy was abducted in 1955. An all-white jury acquitted the two white men who were charged with the crime.

TILLMAN, WILLIAM
Civil War hero. In June 1861 the rebel privateer *Jefferson Davis* captured the schooner *S. J. Waring* and placed it in the hands of a captain, mate, and four seamen. Tillman, the steward and cook of the schooner, killed the captain and mate, took command of the vessel, and brought it to New York, where he was hailed as a hero. 'To this colored man,' said the New York *Tribune*, 'was the nation indebted for the first vindication of its honor at sea.'

TINDLEY, C. A.
Musician. Between 1901 and 1906 he wrote many gospel songs. In 1921, in Chicago, his 'I Do, Don't You?' was sung by A. W. Nix and lifted participants in the National Baptist Convention out of their chairs. It may have been the first of the gospel songs.

TITUS
Agent for privateers. He made a good income acting as a business agent for privateers in Salem, Massachusetts, during the Revolution.

TO SECURE THESE RIGHTS
Comprehensive statement on civil rights. See President's Committee on Civil Rights.

TOBIAS, CHANNING H.

Civil rights leader (1882-1961). Long active in the YMCA, he became chairman of the board of directors of the NAACP, a member of the advisory committee on selective service during World War II, and a member of President Harry S. Truman's Committee on Civil Rights (1946).

TOLAN, EDDIE

Athlete (d. 1967). In August 1932 he became the first black athlete to win a gold medal while also setting a new world record (in the Los Angeles Olympic 100-meter dash). He also starred at the 1936 Berlin Olympic games.

TOLSON, MELVIN B.

Writer (1898-1966). Though hailed by major critics and poets as a great writer, he lived in obscurity until he published his last volume of verse, *Harlem Gallery* (1965). Born in Moberly, Missouri, he taught for several decades at Langston University in Oklahoma, directed the Dust Bowl Theater, and wrote several plays. His first volume of verse, *Rendezvous with America,* was published in 1944. After he had written a poem for the Liberian Centennial and produced his *Libretto for the Republic of Liberia,* he was named Poet Laureate of Liberia.

TOLTON, AUGUSTUS

Clergyman (1834-1897). The first black American priest to be ordained at Rome (1886), he was assigned to St. Joseph's Catholic Church for Negroes in Quincy, Illinois, and later to St. Monica's Church for Negroes in Chicago. He was born in Missouri and taken by his mother, a fugitive slave, to Quincy, where he grew up in the Catholic faith.

TOM, GEORGIA

See Dorsey, Thomas A.

TOOMER, JEAN

Writer (1894-1967). The most promising voice of the Negro

Renaissance, he died in obscurity even though he had lifted the modernist mode of the 1920s to new levels of artistic achievement. Born in Washington, D. C., he went to Georgia in 1922 and worked for a while as a school principal. It was from his experiences in the deep South that he created the stories and poems in *Cane* (1923). His later works—fiction, aphorisms, poems, nonfiction—were rejected by publishers. He was educated in France.

TOPPIN, EDGAR A.

Educator and scholar. Born in Harlem, he received a Ph. D. in history from Northwestern, joined the faculty of Virginia State College, and published a comprehensive account of black accomplishments, *A Biographical History of Blacks in America Since 1528* (1969).

TORRES, JOHN

Contemporary artist. He had a one-man show in New York in 1963, joined the MacDowell Colony in 1964, and by 1966 was producing drawings, stone carvings, and poems at a fantastic pace.

TOUSSAINT L'OUVERTURE, FRANCOIS DOMINIQUE

Haitian patriot and martyr (c. 1744-1803). A self-educated slave, he did more than any other man in history to quicken the hopes of American slaves for freedom through resistance. Gaining control of more than 100,000 slaves who in the revolution of 1791 had killed their masters and embarked on a three-week rampage, burning and destroying property, he shaped them into a disciplined army, took full advantage of the rivalry between France, Spain, and Britain, and through a combination of military genius and shrewd diplomacy forced the withdrawal of all foreign troops. His feats encouraged slaves to plan similar uprising in Virginia, South Carolina, and elsewhere in the United States. See Herbert Aptheker, *American Slave Revolts* (1943).

TOWNSEND, A. M.

Physician. In 1910 he headed the NMA commission on pellagra.

He is credited with recognizing the first case of pellagra in Nashville Tennessee.

TOWNSEND, WILLARD

Labor leader (1895-1957). He organized the redcap workers into the United Transport Service Employees Union, an affiliate of the CIO. He automatically became a member of the executive board and the first black vice president in organized labor. Previously, he had been a chiropodist, a first lieutenant in the Ohio National Guard, a redcap, and a teacher. His handbook, Trade Union Practices and Problems (1952) was translated into Japanese. After he addressed the Japanese Diet, a monument was erected in his honor.

TRACK AND FIELD

Blacks have been pre-eminent in track and field sports for more than half a century and have practically monopolized Olympic honors. Among the greatest: Howard P. Drew, Rafer Johnson, Milt Campbell, Ralph Boston, John Thomas, Hayes Jones, Otis Davis, Bob Hayes, Wilma Rudolph, Wyomia Tyus.

TRADE UNION CORPORATION

Group chartered in North Carolina in 1899 to engage in business transactions.

TRAVERS, BOB

Athlete (b. 1831). He fought a 57-round bout with Gypsy heavyweight Jem Mace and lost on a foul.

TRAVIS, DEMPSEY J.

Banker. A Chicago real estate broker, he launched his Sivart Mortgage Company with only $7,500 in capital. By 1970 he was servicing nearly 60 million dollars in mortgages. He founded the all-black United Mortgage Bankers of America In 1962.

TRAVIS, HARK

One of the conspirators in the Southampton County, Virginia, insurrection of 1831. See Turner, Nat.

TROTTER, JAMES MONROE

Musical publisher. In 1878 he published *Music and Some Highly Musical People,* containing biographical sketches of black musicians and composers and an appendix reproducing the scores of 13 negro compositions.

TROTTER, WILLIAM MONROE

Civil rights leader and journalist (1872-1934). A Harvard graduate, he launched his career in Boston as a realtor. In 1901 he founded the militant newspaper, the *Guardian,* to wage a campaign against discrimination and 'denial of citizenship rights because of color.' In 1905 he joined W. E. B. Du Bois in organizing the Niagara movement. He challenged President Theodore Roosevelt over an incident in Brownsville, Texas, in 1906; demonstrated against *The Clansman* in 1910 and *Birth of a Nation* in 1915; and worked his way across the Atlantic in 1919 to appear at the Paris Peace Conference as a delegate of the National Equal Rights League. Like DuBois, he opposed Booker T. Washington Rights League. Like Du Bois, he opposed Booker T. Washington and had a high regard for liberal arts colleges and their graduates. On November 6, 1913, he headed a delegation that delivered to President Woodrow Wilson a petition bearing 20,000 signatures in protest against federal Jim Crow policies.

TRUE REFORMERS

See Grand United Order of True Reformers.

TRUE REFORMERS BANK

Chartered in 1888, the bank operated in Richmond, Virginia, and had more than 14 million dollars in assets after 16 years.

TRUTH, SOJOURNER

Abolitionist (c. 1797-1883). Convinced that she was the chosen instrument of God, she toured the nation, denouncing slavery and injustice and advocating integrity and the recolonization of freedmen in the undeveloped West. Brilliant though illiterate, she was born Isabella, slave of a Dutch family in Ulster County, New

York, and sold eventually to a New Paltz landowner who fathered five children by her but gave her an elderly slave husband for the sake of appearances. Drawn in 1829 to a cultist commune that later collapsed, she labored for several employers, had a second revelation, and left New York City in 1843 to carry God's message to America. She adopted the name Sojourner Truth and became a familiar figure at revivals. William Lloyd Garrison, Harriet Beecher Stowe, and Abraham Lincoln were among those who fell under her spell. She stressed cleanliness and hard work, helped to end Jim Crowism on Washington streetcars, and tried to arouse public support for her solution to the race problem. Her career is detailed in her autobiography, *Narrative of Sojourner Truth; a Bondswoman of Olden Time, Emancipated by the New York Legislature in the Early Part of the Present Century; with a History of Her Labors and Correspondence Drawn from her "Book of Life"* (1878).

TUBMAN, HARRIET

Underground railroad conductor (c. 1821-1913). One of the bravest women who ever lived, she led some 300 slaves out of bondage, served the Union army as a nurse and spy, and set up a home in Auburn for indigent blacks. Born Araminta Ross on Maryland's Eastern Shore, she was married by her master to a free negro, John Tubman, who benefited by her labors. She fled to Philadelphia (1849) but returned later to her home to lead others to freedom. She made nineteen trips without losing a single passenger and became the most famous conductor on the underground railroad. She would have joined John Brown at Harpers Ferry except for a cataleptic seizure caused by an old injury. 'Black Moses' married Nelson Davis, a Civil War veteran, in 1869. After he died in 1890, she used her meager pension to operate a home for elderly, indigent blacks. See Sarah Bradford, *Harriet Tubman, the Moses of Her People* (1866), and Dorothy Sterling, *Freedom Train: The Story of Harriet Tubman* (1954).

TUCKER, STERLING

Civil rights leader (b. 1923). A graduate of the University of

Akron, Ohio, he is executive director of the Washington, D. C., Urban League and consultant to the National Urban League. He served as vice-chairman and organizer of the March on Washington (1963).

TUCKER, WILLIAM
He was the first black child born in America (1624).

TULSA RIOT
On May 31, 1921, a riot occurred in Tulsa, Oklahoma, following rumors that a lynching was about to take place. 'Little Africa,' the black section of the city, comprising 30 blocks, was burned and 85 people died before the state militia could bring the rioting to an end.

TUNNEL, ELIJAH B.
Clergyman and military hero. The Baltimore clergyman enlisted as a cabin cook on the Winslow, a torpedo boat, in the Spanish-American War. He left the galley to participate in the action from the deck and was killed by an exploding shell.

TURNER, BENJAMIN STERLING
Public official (b. 1825). He was born a slave in Halifax, North Carolina, moved to Alabama, prospered in business, and entered Reconstruction politics. Unanimously nominated by the Republican party for his congressional seat, he served one term (1871-73) as representative of the 1st district of Selma, Alabama.

TURNER, CHARLES HENRY
Scientist (1867-1923). His studies on animal behavior were significant contributions to the scientific world. He was known in zoological circles for his studies of ants. 'Psychological Notes on the Gallery Spider' was published in the *Journal of Comparative Neurology* (1892).

TURNER, DARWIN T.
Scholar and teacher (b. 1931). A Phi Beta Kappa at 15, the

Cincinnati-born scholar has published many articles, fiction, and a volume of poetry. He is dean of the graduate school at North Carolina A. and T. State University in Greensboro.

TURNER, HENRY MacNEAL

Clergyman and legislator (1833-1915). The first black chaplain in the U. S. Army, a leader of the Reconstructed Negro Church, a bishop, and the recipient of an honorary degree from the University of Pennsylvania, he was an eloquent spokesman for his people. In a speech delivered on September 3, 1868, The Bibb County senator charged that the white legislators had acted unconstitutionally in declaring black legislators ineligible to the take their seats. 'We are willing to let the dead past bury its dead,' he said; 'but we ask you now for our RIGHTS.' Congress refused to readmit Georgia until Turner was given his senate seat. He had learned law, after escaping from his master, by working in an office in Abbeville, South Carolina, and he had gained valuable experience by serving as a member of the Georgia Constitutional Convention (1867-68). Following his period of service as a state legislator (1868-70), he served in the publication division of the AME church. Elevated to the bishopric in 1880, he built up the largest negro conference in the world. Always active in civil rights, he urged Negroes to move to Africa, there they could realize their manhood and their human rights. See Edwin S. Redkey (ed.), *Respect Black: The Writings and Speeches of Henry McNeal Turner* (1971).

TURNER, JAMES MILTON

Educator and diplomat (1840-1915). Purchased by his father and given his freedom at the age of 4, he enrolled in the preparatory department of Oberlin College, served as a Union officer's valet during the Civil War, and returned to Missouri to become one of the state's first black teachers. He advocated equal educational opportunities for negroes and succeeded in raising funds to establish Lincoln University in Missouri. In 1871 he was appointed consul general at Monrovia, Liberia.

441

TURNER, LORENZO

Scholar (b. 1895). He is an expert on language and literature.

TURNER, NAT

Negro slave, preacher, and instigator of the 'Southampton Insurrection' (1800-1831). Born in Southampton County, Virginia, in 1800, he was executed at Jerusalem, Virginia, on November 11, 1831. In 1828 he declared that a voice from heaven had told him 'the last shall be first.' The solar eclipse of February 1831 and subsequent natural phenomena were taken as the signal for Negroes to rise up and slay their oppressors. With seven companions Turner murdered his master and five other members of the family while they were still in their beds. The next day, joined by 45 other slaves, the band massacred 13 men, 18 women, and 24 children. Advocates of slavery attributed the insurrection to the abolitionists; they succeeded in bringing about the enactment of stricter slave codes and impeding the liberation movement. William Styron used a document dictated by Turner while awaiting execution in writing *The Confessions of Nat Turner* (1968). See Henry Irving Tragle, *The Southampton Slave Revolt of 1831: A Compilation of Source Materials* (1971).

TURNER, THOMAS WYATT

Scientist. Chairman of the biology department at Hampton Institute, he studied the effect of mineral nutrients upon seed plants, examined the physiological effects of phosphorus and nitrogen on plants, and experimental with cotton breeding.

TURPIN, THOMAS MILLION

Called by W. C. Handy 'the real father of jazz,' the St. Louis pianist played classics as easily as ragtime. He wrote 'Harlem Rag' in 1896.

TUSKEGEE INSTITUTE

An outstanding educational institution founded in 1881 by Booker T. Washington and committed to promoting vocational competency along with humanistic learning. Its full name was

442

Tuskegee Normal and Industrial Institute. It has attracted some outstanding students who have become leaders in their communities and in the nation. Half of its students now come from outside Alabama, and 92 percent of them are black.

TUSKEGEE INSTITUTE HOSPITAL AND NURSES' TRAINING SCHOOL

Founded in 1892 primarily to serve students and faculty, the center expanded, paritcularly after Dr. John A. Kenney became the administrator in 1902, to serve townspeople and neighboring communities. The main building, named the John A. Andrew Memorial Hospital (1912), houses clinics where doctors and nurses have received invaluable training and patients by the thousands have received treatment.

TUSKEGEE VETERANS HOSPITAL

Constructed on land owned by Tuskegee Institute and dedicated on Lincoln's birthday in 1923, the publicly supported, all-negro veterans hospital was to be supervised by a white physician. Vigorous efforts on the part of the NAACP and the NMA caused President Warren Harding to agree to staff the hospital with negro doctors and nurses. Dr. Joseph H. Ward was named medical officer-in-chief in July 1924.

TUSTENNUGGEE EMARTHLA

Leading Creek chief of partial black ancestry. He was also known as Jim Boy.

TWELVE KNIGHTS AND DAUGHTERS OF TABOR

Radical antislavery group organized in Cincinnati in 1844 by the Reverend Moses Dickson.

24TH AMENDMENT

Constitutional amendment eliminating the poll tax in federal elections. The amendment was adopted on February 5, 1964.

24TH INFANTRY

One of four black regiments continuing service after demobilization following the Civil War. Its recruits served in the Western territories, garrisoning outposts and lending themselves to national expansion. See Black Regulars.

25TH INFANTRY

One of four regiments serving in the Western territories after the Civil War. Like the 25th, it was composed of volunteers who lent their energies to the stabilization of national control along the frontier. See Black Regulars.

TWENTY-NIGGER LAW

An act of the Confederate congress (April 1862) exempting from conscription men who were required to oversee 20 or more slaves.

TWIGGS, LEO F.

Artist. In 1969 he was named an Outstanding Young Man of America for his success in teaching art to disadvantaged children. He teaches art at South Carolina State College. His paintings have been exhibited in many colleges and are in the collections of Atlanta University, South Carolina State College, and the Charlotte Model Cities Program.

TYLER, MANSFIELD

Public official (1829-1904). As an ordained minister, he helped to organize the Alabama Colored Baptist State Convention and was influential in establishing Selma University. Advocating free public schools and civil rights legislation, he served as a member of the Alabama house of representatives (1870-72).

TYLER, RALPH W.

War correspondent. Appointed to report news of interest to negroes in World War I, he was the only negro accredited by the Committee on Information.

444

TYUS, WYOMIA

Athlete (b. 1945). In 1965 she won the national 100-yard title. In 1968 she was a member of the U. S. Olympic team which set a world record for the 400-meter relay in Mexico City.

U

UGGAMS, LESLIE

Television star (b. 1943). After appearing on the *Mitch Miller Sing-Along* show, she had her own short-lived variety program in 1969, then achieved fame as a singer.

UNCLE REMUS

The pretended narrator of stories collected by white writer Joel Chandler Harris. He is an old darky well versed in folklore. The stories deal mainly with animals, particularly 'Brer Rabbit.' See Folk Story.

UNDERGROUND RAILROAD

A system of receiving, concealing, and forwarding fugitives, based on a loosely knit network of stations established at points separated by not more than a day's journey. Conductors guided slaves, mostly by night, over routes between stations, which often were the homes of abolitionists. By the time of the Civil War, the system existed in every free state and had delivered about 75,000 slaves to freedom in the North and in Canada. The initial contact generally was made with the slave by a field agent posing as a peddler, map maker, or census taker. Harriet Tubman conducted more than 300 negroes to freedom. Northern blacks prominent in the operation of the underground railroad included Robert Purvis, William Still, David Ruggles, Frederick Douglass, J. W. Loguen, Martin Delany, and Lewis Hayden. See Henrietta Buckmaster, *Let My People Go; the Story of the Underground Railroad* (1941); and Gara, Larry, *The Liberty Line: The Legend of the Underground Railroad* (1961).

UNIA

See United Negro Improvement Association.

UNION LEAGUE CLUBS

Political clubs organized and financed by the Republican party. Formed in the North during the Civil War, they moved South early in 1867 and controlled the Negro vote. They survive today as social organization in New York, Philadelphia, and Washington. Renamed the Loyal League, the movement developed a strong organization and operated as a secret society. Its password was the four L's—Lincoln, Liberty, Loyal, League. It was strongly supported by former slaves who sensed that they could achieve their freedom through political action.

UNITARY SCHOOLS

The U. S. supreme court ruled unanimously on October 29, 1969, that segregation must end 'at once' and that school districts must operate only 'unitary schools.'

UNITED BLACK ARTISTS

A group of more than 250 artists, writers, and intellectuals. Subscribing to the doctrine of artist as activist, they have been outspoken in their defense of LeRoi Jones and other black leaders.

UNITED HOUSE OF PRAYER FOR ALL PEOPLE

See Grace, Bishop Charles Emmanuel.

UNITED MORTGAGE BANKERS OF AMERICA

Association formed by Dempsey J. Travis in 1962.

UNITED NATIONS

Negroes were strong supporters of the United Nations, which they felt might bring an end to racism, colonialism, and economic injustices. The first article of the 'Universal Declaration of Human Rights' declares that 'All human beings are born free and equal in dignity and rights.' In 1946 Ralph J. Bunche became chief of the Division of Trusteeship. In 1947 the NAACP presented to the Office of Social Affairs a lengthy document detailing infringements on the human rights of negroes in the United States.

UNITED NEGRO COLLEGE FUND
Chartered in New York in 1944, the fund represented the first attempt in the history of private colleges to establish a cooperative fund-raising association.

UNITED NEGRO IMPROVEMENT ASSOCIATION
Movement founded in Jamaica in 1914 by Marcus Garvey. Its aim was to unite and advance blacks everywhere under the slogan 'One God! One Aim! One Destiny! A Harlem branch was established in 1917, and branches in London and Paris were set up after Garvey's deportation. The Harlem branch served as world headquarters until 1935, when London became the new headquarters. See Garvey, Marcus.

UNITED STATES v. CRUIKSHANK
Supreme Court decision (1876) establishing the principle that the Fourteenth Amendment protects citizens against encroachment of their rights by the states, not by individuals. The Court also held that a person who violated the civil rights of another person was guilty of a crime only when national citizenship was involved, and that Constitution forbade the Congress to infringe on civil rights but did not grant such right.

UNIVERSITY OF ISLAM
Detroit institution established by Wali Farrad to give elementary and secondary level instruction to blacks.

UNTHANK, THOMAS C.
Physician. In 1899 he was co-founder, with Dr. Solomon H. Thompson, of Douglass Hospital in Kansas City, Kansas.

UP FROM SLAVERY
Autobiography or Booker T. Washington, published in 1900. The most successful autobiography by a post-Reconstruction black,

it inspired many blacks to follow in his footsteps and certain potential leaders, including Marcus Garvey, to adopt other courses of action.

UP TIGHT!
A powerful all-negro film (1968) dealing with dissent in the ghetto.

URBAN LEAGUE
See National Urban League.

US
A black militant movement headed by Harold Karenga.

U. S. COMMISSION ON CIVIL RIGHTS
See Commission on Civil Rights, U. S.

V

VAN PEEBLES, MELVIN

Writer. As an expatriate in France he published four novels and directed *The Story of a Three Day Pass,* an award-winning film. He returned to the U. S. to write, produce, and direct films and plays. *Watermelon Man* (1970), in which a white man turns black, was based on one of his stories. His sensational *Sweet Sweetback's Baadassss Song* grossed millions of dollars and enabled him to stage *Ain't Supposed to Die a Natural Death* and *Don't Play Us Cheap* in 1972. He produced, directed, and wrote the music and lyrics for *Don't Play Us Cheap.* The play featured Joe Armstead, Esther Rolle, and Avon Long.

VANN, ROBERT L.

Public official (1887-1940). A lawyer, he transformed the Pittsburg Courier from a two-page news sheet into a national newspaper. He supported President Franklin D. Roosevelt's New Deal and was appointed assistant U. S. attorney general in the late thirties, then minister to Liberia.

VARICK, JAMES

Clergyman (b. 1750). Born in New York about 1750, he became first bishop of the AMEZ church in 1821.

VASHON, GEORGE B.

Educator (1822-1878). A lawyer with a degree from Oberlin and a poet, he was one of three black members of the faculty of abolitionist Central College in McGrawville, New York.

451

VASHON, SUSAN PAUL

Civic worker (1838-1912). She raised thousands of dollars for the care of sick and wounded soldiers during the Civil War. In addition to directing sanitary relief bazaars in Pittsburgh, Pennsylvania, she helped to provide housing for the homeless after the war ended.

VASSA, GUSTAVUS

Abolitionist (1745-1801). Sold into bondage during the American Revolution, he worked as a seaman. In his autobiography, *The Interesting Narrative of the Life of Oloudah Equiano, or Gustavus Vassa* (1813), he treated slavery in the United States as part of the global problem of oppression.

VAUGHN, ROYCE H.

Artist (b. 1930). He is project director of the Arts and Business Experiences (ABLE) and has produced two documentary films, *The Street* and *The Afro-American Thing,* which explores the resources of black artistic talent.

VEAN, JOHN 'RATTY'

Musician. In the early 1900s, he was a drummer with the Olympia Band in New Orleans.

VENABLE, ABRAHAM S.

Now director of urban affairs for General Motors Corporation, he has written a book on black economic development.

VENSON, EDDIE

Musician. He played the trombone with the Original Creole Band in the early 1900s.

VERMONT

The first state to abolish slavery (1777).

VESEY, DENMARK

Conspirator (1767-1822). A freeman, he plotted an uprising

involving thousands of blacks in Charleston, S. C. The May 1822 conspiracy was betrayed, and Vesey was hanged, along with 37 of his co-conspirators. A strong-willed, well-read and prosperous member of Charleston's free black community and master carpenter, the charismatic plotter is said to have held intense religious convictions. He and most of his lieutenants were leaders in the African Church of Charleston. One of his followers testified that Vessey used the Bible to prove that slavery should not exist. (Another, Gullah Jack, was supposed to have the power to make the conspirators invulnerable.) The plot failed when William Paul, one of Vesey's lieutenants, tried to recruit a slave who promptly reported the event to his master. According to slaves who testified at Vesey's trial, the date of the uprisnig had been set for July 14, 1822. Weapons were said to have been assembled and stored, and a detailed plan for attacking the city from surrounding plantations was said to have been drawn up. Evidence is inconclusive, however, since no lists of conspirators or caches of arms were ever found. See Robert S. Starobin, *Denmark Vesey: The Slave Conspiracy of 1822* (1971).

VIGILANCE COMMITTERS

Antislavery groups formed to help slaves gain their freedom. Frequently dominated by blacks, they raised money to help fugitives. David Ruggles became secretary of the New York Vigilance Committee in 1835. Robert Purvis headed the first vigilance committee of Philadelphia and was succeeded by William Still. Other key figures included Lewis Hayden in Boston, Stephen Myers in Albany, and William Still in Philadelphia. They worked closely with the underground railroad, and they also helped escaped slaves to find homes and jobs in their new locations.

VOTING RIGHTS

Only Georgia and South Carolina denied the ballot to free negroes at the beginning of the American Revolution. In every state prior to 1810 all free men possessing the requisite amount of property were allowed to vote. Maryland prohibited voting by blacks in 1810, and no southern state was allowing blacks to vote at the beginning of the Civil War. For a very brief period after that conflict blacks, protected by federal law and bayonets, were granted the elective franchise. Then in the 1890s they were again relegated to a political limbo from which they did not emerge until the 1960s.

VOTING RIGHTS ACT OF 1965

Following a civil rights march from Selma to Montgomery, Alabama, organized by Martin Luther King, Jr., to assist in the voter registration campaign, Congress passed the Voting Rights Act of 1965. Signed by President Johnson on August 6, the measure provided for federal examiners to monitor elections in six southern states and Alaska, directed the attorney general to challenge the legality of the poll tax, and stipulated that illiterate citizens, provided they were otherwise qualified, must be registered as voters. The U. S. supreme court unanimously upheld its constitutionality on March 8 and swept aside the pool tax on March 25.

W

WADDY, JOSEPH C.

Jurist (b. 1911). He was admitted to the bar in the District of Columbia in 1939 and appointed to the domestic relations court in 1962.

WAINWRIGHT, CHESTER D.

Physician (b. 1884). After graduating from Howard (1904), he began his medical practice in Charleston, West Virginia. He was medical examiner for the Standard Life Insurance Company and a member of the West Virginia Medical Society.

WALCOTT, JERSEY JOE

Athlete (b. 1914). Born Arnold Raymond Cream in Merchantville, New Jersey, he beat Ezzard Charles in 1951 to become the heavyweight boxing champion of the world.

WALCOTT, JOE

Athlete (1872-1935). The original Joe Walcott (not to be confused with 'Jersey Joe,' whose real name was Arnold Cream), was the first black to hold the welterweight boxing title, 1901-04. He was elected to the boxing Hall of Fame in 1955.

WALDEN COLLEGE

Founded by the Methodist Episcopal Church at Nashville, Tennessee, in 1865, the college for freedmen later became Meharry Medical College.

WALKER, MADAME C. J.

Business executive (1868-1919). A financial genius, she invented and manufactured cosmetics for blacks. She founded the oldest business specializing in cosmetics, particularly hair preparations, for blacks. One of the first American women to become a millionaire through her own efforts, she was also the most successful black manufacturer in the nation. Sarah Breedlove was born in Delta, Louisiana, orphaned at 6, married at 14 to C. J. Walker, and widowed at 20. She invented a hair conditioner in 1905, started to build a factory in 1910, and introduced sales techniques later copied by other businesses—salesmen's clubs, conventions, prizes, etc.

WALKER, DAVID

Abolitionist (1785-1830). Born free, he called upon other negroes to struggle against slavery in his famous *Appeal* (1829). The first edition of his book was titled *Walker's Appeal, with a Preamble to the Coloured Citizens of the World, but in Particular and Very Expressly to Those of the United States of America.* Despite efforts to suppress it, his *Appeal* became one of the most widely circulated books of the time. His son Edwin was one of the first two blacks elected to a state legislature.

WALKER, EDWIN G.

Public official. He was one of the first two blacks elected to a state legislature (Massachusetts House of Representatives, 1866).

WALKER, HARRY

Student. In 1971 he became the first black student ever to hold the highest student office at a predominantly white university in the Deep South, the University of South Carolina.

WALKER, JAMES E.

Military officer. As commander of the District of Columbia National Guard, he was responsible for the defense of the nation's capital after March 25, 1917. His unit had served on the Mexican border in 1916.

WALKER, MAGGIE L.

Business executive (1867-1934). An energetic civic worker, she was also active in insurance and banking. She expanded the Order of St. Luke into a solid insurance enterprise, a bank, and a newspaper (the St. Luke Herald).

WALKER, MARGARET

Writer and educator (b. 1915). Her poetry, stressing negritude, has appeared in *Crisis, Phylon,* and *Creative Writing.* A Houghton Mifflin literary fellowship (1966) enabled her to complete her first novel, *Jubilee.* She is known as 'the mother of the young black poets' and credited with a major role in the New Black Renaissance.

WALKER, MOSES FLEETWOOD

Athlete (1857-1924). He became the first black player in the major leagues when his Toledo team joined the American association. He began his career as catcher on the Oberlin varsity team.

WALKER, QUOCK

Slave. In 1783 the Massachussetts supreme court found that the slave's master was guilty of assault and battery against him. See Commonwealth v. Jennison.

WALKER, RACHEL

Musician. She sang before the crowned heads of Europe before she returned to the United States in 1914 to sing in concerts and musical festivals.

WALKER, WELDAY

Athlete. In 1884 he played with Toledo in the old American Association. His brother, Moses Fleetwood Walker, was the first major league baseball player.

WALKER, WILLIAM

Civil War soldier. Sgt. Walker was court-martialed and shot after he led his company to their white captain's tent to demonstrate for equal pay.

WALKER, WYATT T.

Civil rights leader (b. 1929). Prominent in SCLC, he is also the editor of *Negro Heritage.*

WALL OF RESPECT

See Organization for Black American Culture.

WALLER, THOMAS 'FATS'

Musician (b. 1904). He toured Europe, played the piano and organ, made recordings, appeared in movies, and finally teamed up with Andy Razaf to write 'Honeysuckle Rose' and 'Keeping Out of Mischief.'

WALLS, JOSIAH T.

Public official (1842-1905). Born of poor Virginia parents, he moved to Florida after the Civil War, became a delegate to the state constitutional convention (1868), a member of the state house of representatives, a state senator, and U. S. congressman from Florida (1871). He served in the 42nd Congress, but lost his contested seat in the 43rd and retired to his farm near Tallahassee.

WALTERS, ALEXANDER

Bishop of the African Methodist Episcopal Zion church. He was a moving spirit behind the first Pan-African Conference, held in London in 1900. He was also one of the four negroes who signed the 1909 proclamation that led to the formation of the NAACP. As founder of the National Colored Democratic League, he supported Woodrow Wilson in the latter's presidential campaign.

WAR OF 1812

Captain Oliver H. Perry had the support of fifty negroes when he won the battle of Lake Erie. Andrew Jackson used two battalions of free negroes to break the hold of the British on New Orleans.

WARS

The important history of the role of blacks in American wars is contained in works such as these: Joseph T. Wilson, *The Black Phalanx: a History of the Negro Soldiers of the United States in the Wars of 1775-1812, 1861-65* (1890); William C. Nell, *The Colored Patriots of the American Revolution* (1855); George W. Williams, *History of the Negro Race in America from 1619 to 1880; Under Fire with the Tenth U. S. Cavalry* (1899) by Herschel V. Cashin and others (about the Spanish-American War); Luis F. Emilio, *History of the Fifty-Fourth Regiment of Massachusetts Volunteer Infantry, 1863-1865* (1891); *Scott's Official History of the American Negro in the World War* (1919) by Emmett J. Scott; T. G. Steward, *The Colored Regulars in the United States Army with a Sketch of the History of the Colored American, and an Account of His Services in the Wars of the Country, from the Period of the Revolutionary War to 1899* (1904); Dudley Taylor Cornish, *The Sable Arm: Negro Troops in the Union Army, 1861-1865* (1966); John D. Silvera, *The Negro in World War II* (1947); Benjamin Quarles, *The Negro in the Civil War* (1961); and Ulysses Lee, *The Employment of Negro Troops* (1966). See separate entries for the American Revolution, War of 1812, Civil War, Spanish American War, World War I, World War II, and the Korean Conflict.

WARBURG, EUGENE

Sculptor (c. 1816-1921). He worked in New Orleans.

WARD, CLARA

Gospel singer. With the Ward Singers, she took her gospel into night clubs.

WARD, DOUGLAS TURNER

Writer. His satirical play *Day of Absence* (1965) featured blacks in white-face. *Happy Ending* won the Drama Disk-Vernon Rice award for 1966. He has also acted and directed the Negro Ensemble Company.

WARD, JOSEPH H.

Physician. In July 1924, he was appointed medical officer-in-chief of the Tuskegee Veterans Hospital. Previously he had been a successful practitioner in Indianapolis and had held the rank of lieutenant colonel in the medical corps during World War I.

WARD, SAMUEL RINGGOLD

Clergyman (1817-1866). The leading black abolitionist before Frederick Douglass. He lectured against slavery in the U. S., England, and Canada. See his *Autobiography of a Fugitive Negro* (1855).

WARFIELD, WILLIAM

Entertainer (b. 1920). Acclaimed as a baritone concert singer, he has also distinguished himself as an actor.

WARFIELD, WILLIAM ALONZA

Surgeon. A graduate of Howard Medical School (1894), he became surgeon-in-chief at Freedmen's Hospital in Washington in 1901.

WASHINGTON CROSSING THE DELAWARE

Emanuel Leutze's famous painting, showing two negroes, Oliver Cromwell and Prince Whipple, manning the oars of Washington's boat.

WASHINGTON, BOOKER TALIAFERRO

Educator, lecturer, and greatest American exponent of vocational education (c. 1858-1915). As founder and principal of Tuskegee Institute, he advocated the mastering of trades and character development. Andrew Carnegie's admiration for 'the foremost of living men' caused him to contribute $600,000 to Tuskegee. Largely through Washington's influence, white schools stressing industrial education were modeled on negro schools like Tuskegee and Hampton. He minimized negro grievances, stressed better understanding between the races, and focused attention on the need for a helping hand from whites as negroes practiced self-reliance and self-improvement. He founded the National Negro Business League in 1900. No other negro ever wielded such influence in the area of political patronage Presidents William McKinley, William Howard Taft, and Theodore Roosevelt held him in high esteem and sought his advice. In 1895 he set forth his accommodationist views in a speech delivered at the Cotton States Exposition in Atlanta. His widely publicized speech was welcomed by whites, and the Atlanta Compromise, as the philosophy outlined in it was called, prevailed for a generation. *Working with the Hands* (1904) contains his most explicit statement on the value of industrial education and its role in elevating black people. His autobiography is titled *Up from Slavery* (1901). The first two of 15 projected volumes of *The Booker T. Washington Papers*, edited by Louis R. Harlan, are scheduled for publication by the University of Illinois Press late in 1972. Voume 1, *The Autobiographical Writings*, contains *Up From Slavery, The Story of My Life and Work*, and six other autobiographical writings. Volume 2, *1860-89* contains over 400 letters, speeches, articles, and other writings. His birthplace, near Roanoke, Virginia, is a national monument.

WASHINGTON, GEORGE

Pioneer (1817-1905). The Virginia-born son of a white mother and a slave father, he accompanied a white family to Ohio and later to Missouri, where he set himself up as a sawmill owner and tailor. He moved on to the state of Washington to escape discriminatory laws, bought land, and founded Centralia by offering free lots and moving services to people willing to settle on his land along the Northern Pacific Railroad.

461

WASHINGTON, JOSEPH R., JR.

Theologian. A native of Iowa, he was educated at the University of Wisconsin, Andover Newton Theological School, and Boston University. His first major book, *Black Religion* (1964), develops the idea that the socio-economic forces excluding blacks from full participation in society also exclude him from full participation in the Christian faith. His second work, *The Politics of God* (1967), concludes that white religion is bankrupt and advocates a militant, separatist policy.

WASHINGTON, KENNY

Athlete. In 1939 he led UCLA to the greatest triumphs in its history. Named to the All-American team for 1939 by every opponent he faced, in 1946 he became one of the first black professional football players (Los Angeles Rams, 1946-48).

WASHINGTON, MADISON

Fugitive slave who arrived in Canada in 1840, worked for several months, then returned to Virginia to buy his wife's freedom. Captured and sold to a slave-trader, he was placed on board the *Creole* for shipment with one hundred and thirty-four other slaves, one of them his wife, to New Orleans. Washington led a revolt at sea and succeeded in winning his own freedom and that of his comrades.

WASHINGTON, WALTER E.

Public official. In 1967 President Lyndon Johnson appointed him mayor of Washington, D. C.

WATERS, ETHEL

Actress and singer (b. 1900). After many years of groping, she finally joined the revival team of Billy Graham and found for herself what she was able to convey miraculously to others—peace, happiness, and love. She was born in Chester, Pennsylvania, to an unwed 12-year-old who had been raped by a youth named Waters. Unwanted and unloved, she made her way from squalor to stardom. She sang in saloons, theaters, and clubs;

toured with a road show, made recordings, and formed her own group. She appeared on Broadway for the first time in a musical, *Africana* (1927), sang in Daryl Zanuck's film *On With the Show*, and starred in Lew Leslie's *Blackbirds of 1930*. She married her first husband at age 13, her second after a succession of unhappy love affairs. She introduced 'Stormy Weather' at the Cotton Club in Harlem in 1932. She was acclaimed for her singing in *Rhapsody in Black* (1931), *As Thousands Cheer* (1933), and *At Home Abroad* (1935-36), and for her dramatic talents in *Mamba's Daughters* (1939). Millions remember her rendition of 'Stormy Weather' in the film version of *Cabin in the Sky* (1943). Then it seemed that she was finished as an entertainer. *Pinky* (1949) and *The Member of the Wedding* (1950) interrupted her enforced idleness, as did the filming of *The Member of the Wedding* (1953). Then her career faltered again, until she joined Billy Graham during the 1960s. Her autobiography is titled *His Eye Is on the Sparrow* (1951).

WATSON v. MEMPHIS

U. S. Supreme Court decision (1963) ordering immediate integration of the Memphis recreational facilities.

WATSON, GEORGE

World War II hero. A private in the quartermaster corps, he was the first black man to win the Distinguished Service Cross in World War II.

WATSON, IVORY

Musician (1909-1969). The original tenor of the Ink Spots, he sang with various groups until his retirement in 1969. He was known to his friends as Deek Watson.

WATSON, JAMES L.

Jurist (b. 1922). Formerly a member of the New York state senate, he was appointed to the U. S. customs court in 1966.

WATTS RIOTS

Riots erupted in the Watts section of Los Angeles in 1965. The six-day rampage of some 10,000 Negroes who took to the streets, looting and burning in the worst race riot since the one that occurred in East St. Louis, Illinois, in 1917, resulted in 35 deaths, 1,032 injuries, 3,952 arrests, and 200,000,000 in property damage. The rioting began on August 11, following the arrest of Marquette Frye, a 21-year-old Negro charged with reckless driving.

WATTS, ANDRE

Musician (b. 1946). A gifted pianist, he performed at the age of 9 with the Philadelphia Orchestra. Later he was widely acclaimed for his performances with the New York Philarmonic Orchestra.

WEARS, ISAIAH T.

Abolitionist (1822-1900). Born in Baltimore, the prominent abolitionist became a leader in the black community of Philadelphia after the Civil War.

WEAVER, GEORGE

Public official (b. 1912). He was named director of the AFL-CIO and asssitant secretary of the U. S. department of labor.

WEAVER, ROBERT C.

Public official (b. 1907). Named Secretary of Housing and Urban Development on January 13, 1966, the Harvard Ph. D. (1934) became the first black to serve in the cabinet of a President. He entered President Franklin D. Roosevelt's 'Black Cabinet' as a race relations officer in the Department of the Interior (1933-37). He then served as special assistant to the administrator of the U. S. housing authority, held administrative positions relating to employment of minorities, held housing posts, taught, and became chairman of the board of NAACP. His writings include *Negro Labor: A National Problem* (1946), *The Negro Ghetto* (1948), *The Urban Complex* (1964), and *Dilemmas of Urban America* (1965).

WEBB, CHICK
Musician (1902-1939). Born William Webb, he became a powerful drummer with magnificent control of the cymbals and bass drums. In 1926 he formed his own band, which gained in popularity after the discovery of Ella Fitzgerald.

WEBBERS FALLS
Oklahoma settlement, scene of a slave uprising in 1842. Conflicting reports suggest that black leaders among the Seminoles led 200-600 slaves who had imprisoned their masters toward Mexico. Mounted soldiers, reinforced by infantry and artillery units from Fort Towson, killed or captured the renegades.

WEEKLY ADVOCATE
Negro newspaper which began publication in New York in 1837.

WELD, THEODORE DWIGHT
White abolitionist. See American Slavery as It Is.

WELLS, IDA B.
Journalist and anti-lynching crusader (1869-1931). A crusading newspaper editor who dared to tell the truth about lynching while living in the South, she battled for justice all her life. Orphaned at 14, the Mississippi girl managed to support four younger children while continuing her education. She taught in Memphis, wrote for the black weekly *Living Word,* became editor and co-owner of the weekly *Free Speech,* fled to New York after her exposure of the lynching of three blacks caused a mob to threaten her life, worked for the New York *Age,* and issued publications documenting lynching, including *Southern Horrors* (1892) and *A Red Record* (1894). She lectured in the United States and abroad, settled in Chicago, and founded the first Chicago club for black women, the Ida B. Wells Club. She married Ferdinand L. Barnett in 1895 but continued publishing her anti-lynching articles in the Chicago Defender and in leading magazines. She headed the Anti-lynching Speakers Bureau of the Afro-American

Council, founded the Negro Fellowship League (1908), and signed the document that led to the formation of the NAACP (1909). She became the first black adult probation officer in Chicago (1913) and vice president of Chicago's Equal Rights League (1915).

WELLS, JAMES L.
Contemporary artist. Known as the dean of negro woodblock printers, he teaches graphic arts at Howard.

WESLEY, CHARLES HARRIS
Historian and educator (b. 1891). An ordained minister in the AME church, he pastored three congregations while serving as chairman of the department of history and dean of the college of liberal arts and the graduate school at Howard University. Later he served as president of Wilberforce University, president of Central State University, and executive director of the Association for the Study of Negro Life and History. His scholarly works include Negro Labor in the United States: 1850-1925. He co-authored The Negro in Our History, Negro Makers of History, and The Story of the Negro Retold.

WESLEY, RICHARD
Dramatist. In 1972 the 26-year-old writer had two plays on the stage: *The Black Terror,* at the New York Shakespeare Festival Public Theater; and *Gettin' It Together,* at the Public Theater's Annex. He studied with Ed Bullins.

WEST INDIES
Most of the 800,000 negroes in Spanish America at the end of the eighteenth century were concentrated in the West Indies. Over half of them were in Cuba and Puerto Rico.

WEST TENNESSEE, MEDICAL DEPARTMENT OF THE UNIVERSITY OF
During its brief existence (1900-23), the medical department of the University of West Tennessee graduated 266 students.

Founded in Memphis by Dr. Miles V. Lynk, a prominent black physician, it had to close because of its limited financial resources. Its graduates included Willard M. Lane and John S. Perry.

WEST, DOROTHY
Writer (b. 1905). She wrote The Living Is Easy (1948).

WEST, NARCISSA
Nurse (b. 1867). After completing her training at Spelman Seminary (1892), she worked as a trained nurse in Atlanta, Georgia, where her services were continually in demand. She was esteemed by physicians and patients alike.

WESTERFIELD, SAMUEL Z.
Economist (b. 1919). He served as dean of the Atlanta University school of business administration before being appointed associate director of the debit analysis staff of the U. S. treasury department (1961) and deputy assistant secretary of state for economic affairs (1963).

WESTONE, ANTHONY
Businessman. In the early 1800s he was head of a famous millwright business in Charleston.

WHARTON, CLIFTON R., JR.
Economist (b. 1927). The first black to become president of a major university, he was also the first of his race to serve on the board of one of the ten largest corporations in America. The eldest of the four children of an eminent career diplomat, Clifton R. Wharton, Sr., he attended Boston Latin High School, Harvard, Johns Hopkins (M. A., 1948), where he became the first black ever admitted to the international studies division, and the University of Chicago (Ph. D., 1958), where he was the first black to receive a doctorate in economics. In 1969 he became president of Michigan State University and a director of the Equitable Life Assurance Society. His publications include Subsistence Agriculture and Economic Development (1970).

WHARTON, CLIFTON R., SR.

Career diplomat (b. 1899). As ambassador to Norway (1961-64), he was the first black to be appointed America's ambassador to a white nation. Born in Baltimore, he received a master's degree in law from Boston University, passed the career examination in 1925, became vice consul in Monrovia, Liberia (1925) then advanced to consul general in Lisbon, Portugal (1950), and in Marseilles, France (1953). He was appointed U. S. minister to Romania in 1958, the first black career diplomat to become the nation's highest representative in a foreign country.

WHEATLAND, MARCUS F.

Physician. The Newport, Rhode Island, practitioner headed the tuberculosis commission appointed in 1910 by the NMA.

WHEATLEY, PHYLLIS

Poetess (c. 1753-1784). Bought as a slave by Boston merchant John Wheatley after she arrived from Africa in 1760, she learned to write and produced beautiful poetry. A volume of verse published in 1773 attracted attention on both sides of the Atlantic. It was titled *Poems on Various Subjects, Religious and Moral.* Her letters were edited by Charles Deane *(Letters of Phyllis Wheatley,* 1864).

WHEELER, JOHN H.

Businessman. He is president of the Farmers and Mechanics Bank of Durham, North Carolina.

WHIPPLE, PRINCE

Patriot. Sold into slavery at Baltimore, Maryland, at the age of 12, he earned his freedom by serving in the Revolution. He crossed the Delaware with Washington (Christmas, 1776).

WHIPPER, WILLIAM

Abolitionist (1805-1885). He was a founder of the American Moral Reform Society and editor of the National Reformer.

WHITE, CHARLES

Artist (b. 1918). His mural, 'Five Great American Negroes' (1941) is in the Museum of Modern Art in New York City. His graphic art and paintings have won him recognition as one of the foremost contemporary artists. He is on the executive board of the Black Academy of Arts and Letters. His illustrations have appeared in many books, and his work as been the subject of many publications. A talented craftsman, he uses his brush to protest social injustice. He is interested in painting murals of negro history, but he achieves universality by affirming man's triumph over adversity. The social realism of his heroic drawings and the compassion, dignity, and power of his portraits make him the most admired or all contemporary black artists. Eighty-eight works are reproduced in *Images of Dignity: The Drawings of Charles White* (1967).

WHITE, CLARENCE CAMERON

Musician (1880-1960). He achieved recognition as a violinist and composer. He graduated from the Conservatory at Oberlin, taught at the Washington Conservatory of Music, and was director of music at West Virginia State College (1924). He received the David Bispham Medal for his opera *Ouanga,* based on the life of Dessalines, the Haitian liberator. He also made arrangements of spirituals and composed the violin suite 'From the Cotton Fields'.

WHITE, CLARENCE R.

Mathematician (1907-1969). An outstanding teacher and inventor, he had a pioneering role in the space program. With an impressive background in mathematics and astronomy, he became a member of the team of scientists who beamed the first radar signal to the moon.

WHITE, GEORGE H.

Public official (1852-1918). Born in Tarboro, North Carolina, he was the last negro to serve in Congress until the election of

469

Oscar DePriest in 1928. In a moving speech delivered in January 1901, he said: '. . . I want to submit a brief recipe for the solution of the so-called American negro problem. He asks no special favors, but simply demands that he be given the same chance for existence, for earning a livelihood, for raising himself in the scales of manhood and womanhood that are accorded to kindred nationalities.' A member of the last post-Reconstruction congress, he served as U. S. representative from North Carolina, 1897-1901. He was active later as a lawyer and banker in Philadelphia. Still later, he established an all-black community in New Jersey.

WHITE, JOSH

Musician (1908-1969). A folk singer, he became nationally famous with the release of his first album, *Chain Gang*. His best known songs include 'John Henry' and 'Hard-Time Blues.' He also appeared in plays and on the concert stage.

WHITE, WALTER F.

Civil rights leader (1893-1955). Born in Atlanta, fair-skinned and blue-eyed, he worked as assistant secretary of the NAACP (1918-1931) and thereafter as executive secretary (1931-1955). He directed its campaigns for antilynching legislation, voting rights, an end to job discrimination, and for desegregation in the armed forces and in education. His books include *Fire in the Flint* (1924), *Rope and Faggot: A Biography of Judge Lynch* (1929), *A Rising Wind* (1945), the autobiography titled *A Man Called White* (1948), and the posthumously published *How Far the Promised Land?*

WHITE, WILLIAM

Contemporary artist. An abstract expressionist trained at Howard, he sold his painting 'African Metamorphosis' to the Nigerian government.

WHITFIELD, MAL

Athlete. In 1948 he set a new Olympic record in the 800-meter race. In 1952 he matched his own feat and again won the race in 1 minute, 49.2 seconds.

WHITTICO, MATTHEW T.
Editor (b. 1866). In 1904 he founded the *McDowell Times* in Keystone, West Virginia. Active in politics, he was a member of the state Republican executive committee.

WILBERFORCE UNIVERSITY
Founded by the Methodist Episcopal Church near Xenia, Ohio, in 1855, it is the second oldest black college in America. It was run by whites, even though its student body was black, until purchased by the AME church in 1863. Its first black president was Bishop Daniel A. Payne (1863-76).

WILCOX, PRESTON
Educator. He is a leader in the black studies movement.

WILKINS, ERNEST
Musician (b. 1922). He arranged for Tommy Dorsey's band and made a major contribution to the success of Count Basie's band, which he joined in 1951.

WILKINS, J. ERNEST, JR.
Scholar (b. 1923). A Phi Beta Kappa, he received a Ph. D. in mathematics from the University of Chicago at the age of nineteen.

WILKINS, J. ERNEST SR.
Public official (1894-1959). President Dwight D. Eisenhower appointed him assistant secretary of labor in 1954.

WILKINS, ROY
Civil rights leader (b. 1901). A leading figure in the NAACP for more than four decades, he served under Walter White (1931-55) before succeeding him as executive secretary on April 11, 1955. Born in St. Louis, Missouri, he earned a degree from the University of Minnesota in 1923, edited the Kansas City *Call,* and

attracted national attention by waging a vigorous campaign against the reelection of a segregationist senator. While continuing as White's assistant, he edited *Crisis* (1934-49), traveled widely speaking for the NAACP, and wrote many articles on racial issues. In 1943 he represented the NAACP in the Philadelphia transit strike negotiations resulting in the promotion of eight blacks to motormen, a job previously reserved for whites. It was under his leadership that the NAACP adopted at its fifty-fourth annual convention in Chicago (1963) a resolution urging local chapters to promote 'picketing, sit-ins, mass action protests' and selective-buying campaigns. Along with White and W. E. B. Du Bois, he was a consultant to the American delegation at the San Francisco conference (1945) that led to the foundation of the United Nations. Intense lobbying by the NAACP under his leadership helped to bring about passage of the civil rights acts of 1957, 1960, 1964, and 1965. Approaching his seventieth birthday, he reaffirmed his belief that minority groups can 'achieve equality by using the tools within the system—voting, legislation, court action.' He has earned the title of 'Mr. Civil Rights.' President Lyndon B. Johnson conferred upon him the Medal of Freedom.

WILLIAMS, BERT

Entertainer (1878-1922). He was one of the first black men to achieve recognition as a stage personality. Some knowledgeable persons, including W. C. Fields, considered him the greatest comedian America has ever produced. Born Egbert Austin Williams in Antigua, British West Indies, he reached California at the age of 7. He teamed with George Nash Walker in vaudeville routines, first in San Francisco, then in New York City, where they made theatrical history by opening their new show, *In Dahomey,* on Broadway at the New York Theatre (1902). An accomplished musician and a cultivated intelligent man, he played convincingly the role of a drawling, dim-witted buffoon.

WILLIAMS, CAMILLA

Musician. In 1946 she portrayed Cio-Cio in Madama Butterfly.

She appeared regularly thereafter with the New York City Center Opera Company.

WILLIAMS, CLARENCE
Musician. His many blues compositions include 'Baby, Won't You Please Come Home?'

WILLIAMS, COOTIE
Jazz trumpeter. He played with Duke Ellington's Kentucky Club orchestra in the 1920s.

WILLIAMS, DANIEL HALE
Pioneer heart surgeon (1856-1931). On July 9, 1893, he performed the world's first successful operation on the heart at Provident Hospital in Chicago, a hospital founded by him. He opened the chest of James Cornish, a laborer who had been stabbed in a brawl, and sewed the pericardial sac. His daring operation was the first step toward the spectacular heart operations accomplished more than half a century later by other surgeons using more modern facilities and techniques. He was founder and first vice president of the National Medical Association, the only black invited to become a charter member of the American College of Surgeons, and the author of many important articles.

WILLIAMS, FRANKLIN
Public official. He was named ambassador to Ghana.

WILLIAMS, GEORGE WASHINGTON
Historian (1849-1891). The greatest black historian of the 19th century, he is often called the 'black Bancroft.' The first black graduate of Newton Theological Seminary (1874), he compiled a massive reference of primary source documents, his two-volume *History of the Negro Race in America* (1888). His other writings include a history of the black governments of Sierra Leone and Liberia, and the *History of the Negro Troops in the War of the Rebellion* (1877).

WILLIAMS, HENRY F.
Musician (b. 1813). Able to play many instruments, the Boston-born composer published many compositions, including an anthem.

WILLIAMS, IKE
He became undisputed lightweight boxing champion in 1947 by defeating Bob Montgomery.

WILLIAMS, JIM
Civil War scout. He joined an Illinois regiment and led it to his master's Louisiana plantation, where it routed a Confederate unit.

WILLIAMS, JOHN A.
Writer. His novels include *Night Song* (1962) and *The Man Who Cried I Am* (1967).

WILLIAMS, MARY LOU
Musician. Known as the greatest female in the field of jazz, she composed, plays the piano, and sings. Her jazz Mass was choreographed and presented in 1971 as a new ballet by Alvin Ailey.

WILLIAMS, NELSON
One of the conspirators in the Southampton County, Virginia, insurrection of 1831. See Turner, Nat.

WILLIAMS, PAUL R.
Architect (b. 1894). The most successful black architect in the field, he has designed and built many homes and commercial buildings on the West Coast. Born in Los Angeles and orphaned at 3, he worked his way through the University of Southern California and became a certified architect in 1915. In addition to designing more than 3,000 houses ranging in value from $10,000 to $600,000 (including homes for Cary Grant, Frank Sinatra, and CBS board chairman William Paley), he has served

as associate architect for the $50,000,000 Los Angeles International Airport. He has published two books, *Small Homes of Tomorrow* and *New Homes for Today*.

WILLIAMS, PETER, JR.
Clergyman. He was the first black to be ordained a priest in the Protestant Episcopal Church.

WILLIAMS, PETER, SR.
Church leader. He joined with other blacks to establish the Zion Church in New York City, forerunner of the African Methodist Episcopal Zion Church.

WILLIAMS, ROBERT
Black nationalist leader. He was named president of the New Republic of Africa when it was formed in 1968. He had spent several years abroad to escape legal prosecution. He resigned his office and asked to be repatriated in 1969, saying that America represented 'the best chance ever' for achieving racial equality.

WILLIAMS, MRS. SAMPSON
See Selika, Madame Marie.

WILLIAMS, SPENCER
Musician (1890-1965). He wrote some of the early jazz classics: 'Basin Street Blues,' 'I Ain't Got Nobody,' and 'I Found a New Baby.' He was born in New Orleans and died in New York.

WILLIS, BILL
Athlete. In 1946 he signed a contract with the Cleveland Browns. The former guard became the first black listed in the *Encyclopedia of Sports* as a member of the official all-time, all-pro football team.

WILLS, HARRY
Athlete (b. 1892). The master boxer of his day, he defeated

Sam Langford, Sam McVey, and Joe Jeannette, and he was credited with 31 knockouts.

WILLS, MAURY

Athlete. In 1962 he broke Ty Cobb's record by stealing 104 bases in one season.

WILMINGTON RIOT

Aimed at disenfranchising voters in North Carolina, the Wilmington Riot resulted in the deaths of 8 negroes on November 10, 1898. The incident was fictionalized by Charles W. Chesnutt in *The Marrow of Tradition* (1905).

WILMOT PROVISO

An amendment to a bill authorizing the President to negotiate a border settlement with Mexico. It stipulated that the territory acquired from Mexico be closed to slavery. Though passed by the House, the bill was purposely ignored by the Senate. The Wilmot Proviso of 1846 intensified feelings and further divided North and South.

WILSON, A. B.

Artist. He rose to prominence during the latter part of the 19th century.

WILSON, DEMOND

Entertainer. Early in 1972 he appeared on television in a situation comedy series, *Sanford and Son,* built around the theme of the generation gap. See Foxx, Redd.

WILSON, FLIP

Entertainer (b. 1933). Reared in a dismal succession of foster homes in the Jersey City ghetto, he became a serious student of comedy while serving in the U. S. air force. Starting in a small Greenwich Village club in 1963, he finally had a chance to appear before a nation-wide audience on *The Tonight Show.* Soon he was invited to appear on several television shows, in television specials (1968 and 1969), and in his own weekly variety show, the top-rated *Flip Wilson Show*.

WILSON, J. FINLEY
Fraternal leader. He was Grand Exalted Ruler of the black Elks, 1921-52.

WILSON, JOHN
Artist (b. 1922). Currently teaching at Boston University, he has his works exhibited widely. Several of his paintings are owned by the Boston Public Library, the Museum of Modern Art, and the Bezalel Museum in Jerusalem. He has also illustrated three books.

WILSON, OLLIE
Musician. A classical composer, he found a long-denied audience for his works in the late 1960s.

WILSON, NANCY
Musician (b. 1937). Beginning her career as a vocalist with a band, she became one of the nation's top jazz singers, appearing on television as well as on the stage and in nightclubs.

WINKFIELD, JIMMY
Athlete. At the turn of the century he became the second man to win the Kentucky Derby twice in a row, riding His Eminence to victory in 1901 and Alan-a-Dale in 1902.

WINTERS, LAWRENCE
Musician (1916-1965). When he appeared as Rigoletto with the New York Opera Company in 1951, he became the first black singer to perform a leading operatic role. He was the leading baritone of the Hamburg, Germany, state opera company from 1961 until his death.

WITHERS, BILL
Singer. In 1972, at the age of 33, he achieved national fame

as a blues-rock composer and singer. His album titled *Still Bill* gently explored his black personal experience.

WOOD, ROBERT H.

Public official. He was elected mayor of Natchez, Mississippi, in 1870.

WOOD, THOMAS A.

Businessman. In 1970 he became a member of the board of directors of Chase Manhattan Bank. He is an expert in the field of computer technology.

WOODRUFF, HALE

Artist (b. 1900). He studied under French modernist painters and mastered the techniques of abstract formal painting. He won his place among the acknowledged masters, however, by painting the scenes and people of his native Georgia. His two panels of negro communities in a WPA project series, 'Shantytown' and 'Mudhill Row,' were compelling witnesses in a racial plea for slum clearance.

WOODS, GRANVILLE T.

Inventor (1856-1910). He perfected several industrial appliances and instruments used in telegraphy and telephone operations. His induction telegraph system (1887) greatly increased safety of rail traffic by making possible communication between moving trains and station operators. Born in Columbus, Ohio, he settled in Cincinnati and took out his first patent, for a steam boiler furnace, in 1884. The versatile electro-mechanical genius took out more than fifty patents during his lifetime.

WOODSON, CARTER G.

Father of negro history (1875-1950). The first scientifically trained black historian, he founded the principal organizations and journals, systematically collected and organized the basic source materials, and wrote a lengthy series of books to fill the long-neglected gap in the history of mankind and make black history a respected discipline. He studied at Harvard (Ph. D., 1912) and the Sorbonne, taught in public schools, became a professor and dean of the college of liberal arts at Howard University and West Virginia State College, and retired in 1922 to devote his energies to research and writing. Among the first to realize that negroes had made a unique contribution to American history and culture, he devoted his energies to correcting misconceptions about American blacks and their African ancestors. He organized the Association for the Study of Negro Life and History in 1915. The following year the association was incorporated and published the first issue of the Journal of Negro History. In 1921 Woodson organized the Associated Publishers to promote the sale of books about negroes. In 1926 Associated Publishers initiated the observance of National Negro History Week. He founded the Negro History Bulletin in 1930 to disseminate information for school children and the general public. His books include *The Education of the Negro Prior to 1861* (1915), *A Century of Negro Migration* (1918), *The History of the Negro Church* (1922), *The Negro in Our History* (1922), *The Mis-Education of the Negro* (1933), *The African Background Outlined* (1936), and *African Heroes and Heroines* (1939). His popular textbook, *The Negro in Our History,* was adapted for elementary grades under the title *Negro Makers of History* (1928) and for secondary schools as *The Story of the Negro Retold* (1935).

WOODWARD, BEULAH

Artist (1895-1955). An accomplished painter and sculptress, she was known for her African types and masks.

WOODWARD, SIDNEY

Musician (1889-1924). A talented tenor, he gave concerts in Europe, taught voice at Clark University and in New York City, and gave a concert in Carnegie Hall in 1924.

WORK, JOHN WESLEY JR.

Musician. In 1946 his festival chorus *The Singers* was performed by the Michigan State Chorus and the Detroit Symphony. His composition won first prize in a competition sponsored by the Fellowship of American Composers.

WORK, JOHN WESLEY SR.
Musician (1873-1925). At Harvard he prepared to teach Latin, but he is best remembered as a collector and interpreter of negro spirituals and as director of the Fisk Jubilee Singers. He and his brother Frederick published *Folk Songs of the American Negro* (1907). He published some original musical songs and wrote *The Folk Song of the American Negro* (1915). In 1923 he became president of Roger Williams College in Nashville.

WORK, MONROE NATHAN
Scholar and publisher (1866-1945). After earning his M. A. degree at the University of Chicago, he taught at Georgia State Industrial College, then became director of the research department at Tuskegee Institute, 1908-38. In 1928 he received the Harmon award for 'scholarly research and educational publicity through periodic publication of the Negro Yearbook and the compilation of a Bibliography of the Negro.' His biennial publication of the Negro Yearbook supplied factual materials for schools and libraries. His other achievement was the first of its kind, for the *Bibliography* presented information about black publications in all parts of the world from ancient times to 1928.

WORLD WAR I
Ten thousand blacks were in the regular army and an equal number in the National Guard at the beginnnig of World War I. More than two million black men (2,290,529) registered for service with the U. S. army between June 5, 1917, and September 12, 1918. About 42,000 of the two hundred thousand negroes who went to France served as combat troops. One negro regiment, the 15th of New York, remained under fire for 91 days. Henry Johnson and Needham Roberts, who destroyed a German raiding party of 20 men, were the first American soldiers decorated in World War I. They received the Croix de Guerre. Altogether,

480

194 officers and men received decorations. Still, the war brought dissatisfaction to many blacks. At the outset, the government refused to provide training for black officers. Colonel Charles Young was retired from service on grounds of health. Pressure by the NAACP resulted in the establishment of segregated officer training camps. The Buffalo Soldiers Units of the Black Regulars were not assigned to combat duty. The 92nd and 93rd divisions did see action, however, and the 369th Regiment received an enthusiastic welcome in New York upon its return. During the war 500,000 blacks moved northward for better-paying jobs. Race riots erupted as early as 1917 (East St. Louis) and culminated in a strife-marked Red Summer in 1919. The democracy that blacks had fought for in Europe seemed even more elusive at home after President Wilson introduced segregation into federal facilities in Washington, D. C. See Emmett J. Scott, *Official History of the American Negro in the World War* (1919).

WORLD WAR II
Industrial training programs and employment in war-related industries brightened the negro worker's outlook after 1939. Though segregation was maintained in the armed services as a whole, mixed officer candidate schools for army officers were highly successful. Initially, the two guiding principles of the War Department were that the number of negroes serving in the armed forces would correspond to their proportion of the total population and that whites and blacks would be grouped in separate units. At first the Navy confined negroes and Filipinos to the Steward's Branch, following a 'messmen only' policy. The policy was abandoned on June 1, 1942. In April 1944 negroes shattered precedent when they became commissioned officers. On February 27, 1946, the Navy lifted 'all restrictions governing the types of assignments for which naval personnel are eligible.' The civilian Merchant Marine, integrated from the outset, named 14 Liberty ships after outstanding negroes, 4 after negro colleges, and 4 after heroic seamen. The all-negro 92nd Division, though it sustained reverses in the Italian campaign in February 1945, received 12,096 decorations and citations. Forty-three pilots

481

graduated from a flying school set up at Tuskegee Institute on July 19, 1941. They formed the nucleus of the 99th Pursuit Squadron. Of the three million negro men who registered for service in World War II, 701,678 served in the Army, 165,000 in the Navy, 5,000 in the Coast Guard, and 17,000 in the Marine Corps. Four thousand negro women were WAVES or WACS. Half a million blacks served overseas. Benjamin O. Davis, Sr., became the first black general. His son, Lt. Colonel Benjamin O. Davis, Jr., served in a negro air combat unit. Some 2,500 black soldiers were engaged in the Battle of the Bulge (December 1944). World War II heroes included Dorie Miller and Leonard Roy Harmon. Thirteen Liberty ships were named in honor of negroes. Protest over segregation in the armed forces were counterbalanced by economic successes on the home front. Robert C. Weaver reported that between 1942 and 1945 negroes 'secured more jobs at better wages . . . than ever before.' There was widespread hope that the end of the war would bring a better life to all. Negro leaders meeting at Durham, North Carolina, in 1944, voiced the feelings of many Americans: 'We have the courage and the faith to believe that it is possible to evolve in the South a way of life . . . that will free us all . . . from want, and from throttling fears.' See Ulysses Lee, *United States Army in World War II: The Employment of Negro Troops* (1966); Lee Nichols, *Breakthrough on the Color Front* (1954).

WORMLEY, JAMES

Businessman (1820-1884). After serving as a steward on naval vessels and at the Metropolitan Club, he became proprietor of the Wormley Hotel in Washington and earned a national reputation as a caterer. It was in his hotel that the disputed presidential election of 1876-77 was settled, after Rutherford B. Hayes promised to withdraw federal troops from the South.

WRIGHT, ALONZO

Businessman. Arriving in Cleveland with six cents, he formed a chain of gas stations and became a millionaire.

WRIGHT, BENJAMIN H.

Businessman (b. 1923). He served as a U. S. state department official in Liberia before becoming market development manager of Clairol, Inc. (1963) and president of the New York chapter of the National Association of Market Developers, Inc.

WRIGHT, CHARLES

Writer. Associated with the New Harlem Renaissance, he has written *The Wig* and *The Messenger*.

WRIGHT, JANE COOKE

Physician (b. 1919). A noted surgeon and researcher in cancer chemotheraphy, she became the first black associate dean of New York Medical College (1967). In 1968 she received the Myrtle Wreath Award.

WRIGHT, JONATHAN J.

State supreme court justice (1840-1885). He practiced law in Pennsylvania after studying at the University of Pennsylvania. After the Civil War, he moved to South Carolina, where he served as associate justice of the state supreme court for nearly six years.

WRIGHT, LOUIS T.

Surgeon and civil rights leader. The first black physician to be appointed to a municipal hospital in New York City (Harlem Hospital, 1919), he made significant contributions to medicine. A graduate of Harvard Medical School (1915), the 24-year-old practitioner returned to Georgia, donned a uniform and went to France after World War I broke out, and served Harlem Hospital with distinction for more than thirty years. He challenged traditional theories of the treatment skull fractures, devised instruments for the treatment of fractures of the knee joint and vertebrae, perfected an interdermal smallpox vaccination, supervised the first tests on aureomycin, and conducted cancer research.

WRIGHT, MARIAN ELIZABETH

Lawyer. The first black woman lawyer in Mississippi and one of six black lawyers in the state in 1966, she graduated from Yale Law School.

WRIGHT, NATHAN, JR.

Educator and activist. He succeeded Adam Clayton Powell, Jr., as chairman of the planning committee for the 1967 Black Power Conference. He has earned five degrees, participated as a Freedom Rider, worked as a field secretary for CORE, and played a major role in making the concept of Black Power understandable to the public. He is professor of urban affairs and chairman of the Afro-American studies department at the State University of New York at Albany. His writings include *Black Power* and *Urban Unrest*.

WRIGHT, RICHARD

Writer (1908-1960). Born in poverty in Natchez, Mississippi, he sought to escape ignorance and poverty by moving to Chicago. He became a member of the Federal Writers' Project (1935), moved with the project to New York (1937), and won a Guggenheim Fellowship (1939). His works include *Uncle Tom's Children* (1938), which established his reputation and won him a $500 prize; *Native Son* (1940), his most famous fictional work, which became the first creation by a black writer selected for the Book-of-the-Month Club or for publication in the Modern Library series; and his autobiography, *Black Boy* (1945). The story of his disillusionment with communism is told in *The God That Failed*.

WRIGHT, RICHARD ROBERT, JR.

Clergyman (b. 1878). A leading AME bishop and editor, he was co-founder and later president of the Philadelphia bank founded by his father.

WRIGHT, RICHARD ROBERT, SR.

Educator and businessman (1855-1945). After graduating from

Atlanta University, he worked to eradicate illiteracy among Georgia freedmen, founded and devoted most of his life to Savannah State College (1891-1921), and moved on to Chicago to found the highly successful Citizens and Southern Bank and Trust Company.

WRIGHT, STEPHEN J.
Educator (b. 1910). He was named president of Fisk University.

WRIGHT, THEODORE SEDGEWICK
Abolitionist (1797-1847). The first black to receive a degree from Princeton's theological seminary, (1828), he assumed a role of leadership in the free colored convention movement, using his pulpit to challenge pro-slavery Presbyterians who supported the colonization movement. He urged blacks to remain in America and fight for their rights, and he was one of the most active underground railroad conductors.

X

X, MALCOLM

See Malcolm X.

XENIA

Site of Wilberforce University. A convention of Ohio negroes met there in 1865 and adopted a set of resolutions stressing the need for insuring the rights of ex-slaves. An Equal Rights League was founded by the 56 delegates from 29 cities and villages of Ohio.

Y

YAZOO CITY
Mississippi town where a score of negroes were killed on September 1, 1875, during a period of racial strife.

YERBY, ALONZO SMYTHE
Physician and educator (b. 1921). He became field medical officer for the International Refugee Organization in Germany (1948), deputy chief of medical affairs in the office of the U. S. High Commissioner for Germany (1949), associate medical director of the Health Insurance Plan of Greater New York (1950), executive director of medical services for New York City (1960), and assistant professor at the Columbia University School of Public Health and Administrative Medicine (1960-66). Since 1966 he has been head of the department and professor of health services administration at Harvard University School of Public Health.

YERBY, FRANK
Writer (b. 1916). After receiving his M. A. from Fisk University (1938), he taught in Florida and Louisiana. With the successful publication of The Foxes of Harrow (1946) and its filming, he ended his teaching career and settled down to the writing of popular historical fiction. His other works include *The Vixens* (1947), *The Golden Hawk* (1949), *Pride's Castle* (1949), *A Woman Called Fancy* (1951), and *The Saracen Blade* (1952).

YMCA
See Young Men's Christian Association.

489

YORK

Slave who accompanied Lewis and Clark on the Oregon Trail, serving as their unofficial ambassador and guide. Because the Indians were more impressed by his magnificent physique and ability to regale them with his singing, dancing, and fiddling than by the merchandise which the party had brought along for purposes of barter, he became the expedition's passport to the Pacific. Awarded his freedom for his extraordinary services, he remained in the Oregon Territory and became the prosperous owner of a fleet of freight wagons.

YOUNG MEN'S CHRISTIAN ASSOCIATION

The first negro YMCA was organized in Washington, D. C., by Anthony Bower, on May 31, 1853.

YOUNG, CHARLES

Military officer (1864-1922). At the outbreak of World War I, the nation's third black West Point graduate (1889) was the highest ranking black officer. He held the rank of lieutenant colonel and had served as a major in the Spanish-American War. The only black West Pointer in the military at the beginning of the war, he was forced to retire on July 30, 1917, because his rank and seniority qualified him to lead a regiment and command white officers.

YOUNG, CLAUDE

In 1946 he helped to lead Illinois to the Big 10 championship. Following a brilliant career with the Baltimore Colts, he was appointed special assistant to the NFL commissioner. In 1968 he was voted into the football Hall of Fame.

YOUNG, LESTER

Musician (1901-1959). One of the initiators of cool or modern jazz in the late 1940s, he composed original works for Count Basie's band. A vital influence on tenor saxophone playing, he was elected to *Down Beat Magazine's* Hall of Fame in 1959.

YOUNG, ROBERT A.

Abolitionist. In 1829 he published his *Ethiopian Manifesto, Issued in Defence of the Blackman's Rights, in the Scale of Universal Freedom.* He prophesied that a messiah with the strength to free his people would arise and act.

YOUNG, WHITNEY MOORE, JR.

Civil rights leader (1921-1971). Born in Lincoln Ridge, Kentucky, he studied under a private tutor, then at Lincoln Institute, a high school administered by his father. He earned a bachelor's degree at segregated Kentucky State College (1941) and a master's degree in social work at the University of Minnesota (1947). He worked with Urban Leagues in St. Paul and Omaha, served as dean of the Atlanta University school of social work (1954-61), and became executive director of the National Urban League (1961). Under his dynamic leadership, the league responded to the challenge of black uprisings and calls for militancy in the 1960s by expanding its professional interracial staff to more than 500 and its local chapters to almost 70. A prominent lecturer and writer, he proposed a 'domestic Marshall Plan' to overcome the effects of long years of deprivation suffered by blacks. His book, *To Be Equal,* was published in 1964. He served on many commissions and was an effective link between corporate power and the black masses. Death came while he was making a final attempt to bridge the gap of ignorance and misunderstanding by attending an African-American conference in Lagos, Nigeria.

YOUTH MARCH

On January 25, 1958, approximately 10,000 youths of all races participated in the Youth March for Integrated Schools in Washington, D. C.

Z

ZONING

One means of accomplishing school desegregation. In Green v. New Kent County, Virginia, the Supreme Court suggested zoning and pairing as possible methods of eliminating discrimination. Zoning means redefining school-attendance zones so as to bring white and black pupils into the same school.

ZUBER, PAUL B.

Civil rights leader (b. 1927). A lawyer, he has been active in de facto segregation cases.

493